Prophet in the Marketplace

Prophet in the Marketplace

THOREAU'S DEVELOPMENT AS A PROFESSIONAL WRITER

Steven Fink

OHIO STATE UNIVERSITY PRESS

COLUMBUS

Published in 1992 by Princeton University Press.
Paperback edition published in 1999 by the Ohio State University Press.

Library of Congress Cataloging-in-Publication Data
Fink, Steven, 1952–
Prophet in the marketplace : Thoreau's development as a professional writer / Steven Fink.
p. cm.
Includes bibliographical references and index.
ISBN 0-8142-5040-8 (pbk. : alk. paper)
1. Thoreau, Henry David, 1817–1862—Criticism and interpretation.
2. Authorship—Economic aspects—United States—History—19th century.
3. Authors and readers—United States—History—19th century.
4. Thoreau, Henry David, 1817–1862— Authorship. I. Title.
PS3054.F48 1999
818'.309—dc21 99-24878
CIP

Printed in the United States.

The paper used in this publication meets the minimum requirements of the American National Standard for Information Sciences—Permanence of Paper for Printed Library Materials. ANSI Z39.48–1992.

9 8 7 6 5 4 3 2 1

For my Parents,
Daniel and Carroll Fink

With love and gratitude

CONTENTS

ACKNOWLEDGMENTS

I AM DEEPLY GRATEFUL for the support and encouragement I received during the writing of this book. Throughout the entire life of this project, Martha Banta has been a mentor, colleague, and invaluable friend. I have depended upon her shrewd intelligence, her rigorous intellectual standards, her humane and gentle manner, and her unflagging support; the publication of this book changes none of that. I am indebted to Lawrence Buell for his extraordinarily attentive and perceptive commentary on my manuscript during its later stages and for his support of this project. I would like to thank my colleagues in the English Department and the College of Humanities at The Ohio State University for all the warm and generous support they have given me ever since I joined the faculty. My thanks also to Hillary Foote for her great help in typing the manuscript; to Lauren Lepow, Manuscript Editor at Princeton University Press, for her careful and friendly editing; and to Robert Brown, Literature Editor at Princeton University Press, for his indulgent patience and support.

Earlier versions of some parts of this study appeared in the *Bucknell Review* (1983) and the *New England Quarterly* (1986); I thank the editors for permission to include that material here.

I could never adequately thank my wife, Nancy Kaufmann, or my daughters, Sarah and Jessica, for all their encouragement, concern, and enduring patience with me during the writing of this book. This has seemed at times to be a family project, and upon its completion I fully share my sense of accomplishment with them. Finally, I want to acknowledge another debt I can never repay, to my parents, Daniel and Carroll Fink, for their unstinting love, trust, and encouragement. Whatever I may accomplish in my life honors them, and so it is to them that I dedicate this book.

ABBREVIATIONS

Corr	*The Correspondence of Henry David Thoreau*, ed. Walter Harding and Carl Bode (New York: New York University Press, 1958)
CW	*The Collected Works of Ralph Waldo Emerson*, ed. Robert Spiller, 3 vols. to date (Cambridge: The Belknap Press of Harvard University Press, 1971–)
Dial	*The Dial: A Magazine for Literature, Philosophy, and Religion*, 4 vols. (1840–1844)
EEM	Henry D. Thoreau, *Early Essays and Miscellanies*, ed. Joseph J. Moldenhauer et al. (Princeton: Princeton University Press, 1975)
EmL	*The Letters of Ralph Waldo Emerson*, ed. Ralph Rusk, 6 vols. (New York: Columbia University Press, 1939)
J1	Henry D. Thoreau, *Journal, Volume 1: 1837–1844*, ed. Elizabeth Hall Witherell et al. (Princeton: Princeton University Press, 1981)
J2	Henry D. Thoreau, *Journal, Volume 2: 1842–1848*, ed. Robert Sattelmeyer (Princeton: Princeton University Press, 1984)
J3	Henry D. Thoreau, *Journal, Volume 3: 1848–1851*, ed. Robert Sattelmeyer et al. (Princeton: Princeton University Press, 1990)
JIII–XIV	*The Journal of Henry David Thoreau*, ed. Bradford Torrey and Francis H. Allen, 14 vols. (Boston: Houghton Mifflin, 1906)
JMN	*The Journals and Miscellaneous Notebooks of Ralph Waldo Emerson*, ed. William H. Gilman et al., 16 vols. (Cambridge: The Belknap Press of Harvard University Press, 1960–1982)
MFL	*The Letters of Margaret Fuller*, ed. Robert N. Hudspeth, 5 vols. to date (Ithaca: Cornell University Press, 1983–)
MW	Henry D. Thoreau, *The Maine Woods*, ed. Joseph J. Moldenhauer (Princeton: Princeton University Press, 1972)
RP	Henry D. Thoreau, *Reform Papers*, ed. Wendell Glick (Princeton: Princeton University Press, 1973)

W	*The Writings of Henry David Thoreau*, 20 vols. (Boston: Houghton Mifflin, 1906)
Wachusett	Henry D. Thoreau, "A Walk to Wachusett," *Boston Miscellany of Literature and Fashion* 3.1 (January 1843): 31–36
Walden	Henry D. Thoreau, *Walden*, ed. J. Lyndon Shanley (Princeton: Princeton University Press, 1971)
Week	Henry D. Thoreau, *A Week on the Concord and Merrimack Rivers*, ed. Carl F. Hovde et al. (Princeton: Princeton University Press, 1980)

Prophet in the Marketplace

INTRODUCTION

> We live in the greatest commercial era that the world has yet known. And Literature,—which has been alternately the companion and foster-child of the Augustan warrior, the convent religionist, and the feudal landowner,—now makes its home with the Merchant, and already begins to assail its old protectors amid the new associations it has formed. The seat of commerce is, therefore, the centre of literary power. The political capital of the country may shift its position from Washington to St. Louis, and the junction of the Missouri and Mississippi become, in a few months thereafter, the focus of public sentiment; but the metropolis of our book-world, on this side of the Atlantic, will still remain where Commerce congregates the mass of the wealth and intelligence of the country, from every point of the Union; and where the author from the far interior will seek his most available mart.
>
> —Charles Fenno Hoffman, *The Literary World*, August 7, 1847

> Who will not confess that the necessity to get money has helped to ripen some of his schemes?
>
> —Thoreau, JIII: 282 (February 6, 1852)

HENRY THOREAU'S enduring reputation, for which he has been both celebrated and criticized, has been as an inflexible and high-minded eccentric who stood apart from society, living to the beat of a different drummer. He was, according to this perception, a romantic individualist who was indifferent to, and therefore refused to condescend to, whatever audience might choose to read what he wrote. While there is undeniably a good deal of truth in this representation, it is not entirely accurate, and it is certainly not complete. Such a portrait obscures the fact that his principles of self-reliance, however genuine, were always qualified by his literary ambitions: as a public writer and as a moral reformer Thoreau simply could not afford to ignore the public; on the contrary, he was anxious to engage in a relationship with American society and elicit some response from it. Working from the premise that Thoreau desired not to withdraw from American society but to forge for himself a distinctive place in it, I examine in this study the ways in which Thoreau's public aims and the literary marketplace itself acted as shaping influences on his writing.

Thoreau's transcendentalist assumptions about the role of the writer indeed created a deep-seated ambivalence about his relation to the public. He found himself caught between his desire for independence from the community and the simultaneous need to engage its attention. His desire for philosophical and moral self-sufficiency was not rooted in misanthropy, but in his ambition to assume the role of American prophet (a role that appealed to most of the other New England transcendentalists as well). This ambition required that the seer emerge from the isolation of his private vision to become the public bard or "sayer." Whether as a Jeremiah rebuking the sins and backslidings of the populace or as a Moses catching a Pisgah sight of a new life in the promised land, the prophet had to come down from the mountaintop to impart his vision to the people.

For Thoreau, the act of publishing (whether in print or in lectures) was the descent necessary to the fulfillment of his prophetic role. Despite his protestations to the contrary, he was hardly indifferent to the public's response to this work. In a voice that derived its authority from spiritual withdrawal, the prophet and reformer directly exhorted an audience that alone could gratify his ambitions. Thoreau's ambivalence about the proper relationship between author and audience led to a similar ambivalence in his ideas about the proper form of prophetic discourse. Thoreau's development as a writer can, in fact, be seen in terms of his efforts to find a mode of discourse that was both faithful to his private vision and intelligible to the community.

Furthermore, Thoreau had an economic as well as a moral stake in the success or failure of his work. As a public writer who published works during his lifetime through conventional commercial channels, Thoreau was intent not only on finding an audience for his writings but, whenever possible, on being paid for them as well. Thus, in spite of his principles, his personality, and his literary persona, Thoreau found himself grudgingly implicated in the complexities of the literary marketplace. If material success (profit) was always secondary to moral success (prophecy), nevertheless these two impulses came into curious alignment at points—even while they remained distinct and created complex tensions in the writing itself. In either case, whether as prophet or professional, Thoreau found it necessary to attend to the literary marketplace and the prevailing literary tastes in order to bring his works before the public. This meant dealing with the middlemen, the entrepreneurs of the literary world (magazine editors, lyceum directors, and book publishers), and it meant dealing more directly with that diverse public whom he had to please, as well as provoke, with his writings and lectures.

This complex of cultural facts underlying Thoreau's career has largely been neglected in Thoreau scholarship. Thoreau's biographers—notably Canby and Harding—have ably documented many of the facts of Thoreau's professional career, but they have not brought these to bear upon our critical understanding of his works. Critical studies of Thoreau have for the most part elected to dwell on intellectual history and the more private, interior reaches of Thoreau's mind. While some, including Sherman Paul's invaluable study *The Shores of America*, have dealt with Thoreau's problem of "vocation," none has developed this issue into a treatment of Thoreau and the business of writing. Paul's subtitle, *Thoreau's Inward Exploration*, suggests that he regards Thoreau's philosophical and literary development as essentially independent of the vagaries of his professional career, his intellectual and moral crises as isolable from his public identity. Similarly revealing is the title of the only real successor to Paul's book to date, Robert D. Richardson, Jr.'s *Henry Thoreau: A Life of the Mind*. Works concerned more specifically with Thoreau's psychology, such as those by Richard Lebeaux and Richard Bridgman, have been even more inclined to underestimate the significance of Thoreau's professional life in shaping his language, his attitude toward society, and his sense of himself.

The mythologizing of Thoreau into a writer who somehow stood outside of and remained untouched by the cultural conditions of his profession (a myth that Thoreau himself is largely responsible for creating) pervades Thoreau scholarship but has had an especially strong impact on critical treatments of his *Journal*. In 1958, Perry Miller argued acerbically that "in all the literature of the world, here is the case of a sensible man who found nobody so interesting to talk with as himself."[1] Miller's judgment has been echoed, much more sympathetically, in recent studies of Thoreau's *Journal* by William Howarth and Sharon Cameron, who consider the *Journal* to be Thoreau's major literary achievement. While some exciting work is being done on the literary dimension of the *Journal*, one perhaps inadvertent effect of such claims for the primary status of the *Journal* has been to further discount the interaction between the writer and his culture and, ironically, to contribute to Thoreau's disfranchisement from the culture he was so eager to influence and reform. H. Daniel Peck's insightful study, *Thoreau's Morning Work* (1990), which I was able to read only after completing this study, is an important advance in its treatment of the "intertextuality" of the journals and the published books, emphasizing "the ways in which they may be considered as emergences from one another."[2] I believe my own discussion complements Peck's work by treating the *Journal* in the context of Thoreau's complex considerations of audience and by reasserting its importance in relation to the published work.

Scholarship on the profession of writing in America has so far failed to include Thoreau. In his ground-breaking study of the subject, William

Charvat dismissed not only genuinely private writers like Emily Dickinson from consideration, but also "such authors as Thoreau and Whitman," arguing that because they "never succeeded on an economic plane," they were not among "those writers for whom both art and income were matters of concern, and whose work, accordingly, revealed the often conflicting pressures of the will to create and the need to create for a buying public."[3] Charvat's definition of professionalism is arbitrarily narrow, however: the fact that Thoreau attempted but largely failed to address a public audience makes a study of his relation to the literary marketplace pertinent not only to an understanding of his own career but to an understanding of the nature and boundaries of the marketplace itself. Michael Gilmore's suggestive essay "*Walden* and the Curse of the Trade" comes closest to my own study in its basic assumption that Thoreau "had far more interest in popular success than has commonly been supposed."[4] The following study documents and contextualizes much of what Gilmore intuits from Thoreau's use of the language of the marketplace; it takes Thoreau's evolution as a professional writer, rather than a single text, as its subject.

The fact that Thoreau suffered major professional failures is indisputable, but the actual effect of those failures has not been fully recognized. Thoreau's varied attempts to avoid, overcome, reinterpret, or reconcile himself to failure are clearly manifested in the works themselves and are an important source of the very richness of language and thought we find there. In the present study, therefore, I argue that Thoreau's involvement in his profession had a profound (and ultimately positive) effect upon both the man and his works. The changing and maturing textual strategies that we can trace through Thoreau's career are explicable and fully comprehensible only when we acknowledge that Thoreau did not write in isolation or indifference, but that his works were shaped by his ongoing interaction with American readers and the literary marketplace which controlled that interaction. In order to examine Thoreau's career in its cultural context, I juxtapose an analysis of the aesthetic principles that informed his writing with a consideration of the means by which Thoreau conducted the "business of life" that was *business*. By taking into account the economics of writer and reader in nineteenth-century America that affected his career—by treating the act of writing as a dynamic interchange between author and audience—I hope to clarify our understanding of the man and his works.

Because I see the relation between Thoreau and his audience as dynamic and interactive, my book adheres rather closely in structure to the chronology of Thoreau's career. Each chapter attempts to demonstrate the ways in which individual works are the product of a complex interaction among the author, the audience (both intended and actual), and the literary marketplace that mediated between them. While each chapter includes close readings of individual texts (in which particular attention is paid to questions of genre, narrative persona, diction, figurative language and wordplay, and the like, as they illuminate the dynamics of the implied author-reader relationship), a corresponding emphasis is placed on extratextual issues that clarify and document the status of each work in Thoreau's career and in the larger literary scene.

This study is not a comprehensive survey of Thoreau's entire career; rather, I focus primarily on the period between 1837, the year he both began keeping his journal and first appeared in print, and 1849, when his first book, *A Week on the Concord and Merrimack Rivers*, was published and proved to be a disastrous commercial failure. This by no means ended Thoreau's professional career, but it did mark a turning point. With the publication of his first book, Thoreau had exhausted the available commercial literary outlets—lectures, periodicals, and books; he had also practiced the full range of literary forms that he would employ in his career. Consider that by 1849 Thoreau had tried his hand at the moral essay, the literary essay, the familiar essay, the nature essay, the political essay, the book review, verse, translation, and travel narrative; he had published in both popular magazines and coterie journals; he had lectured throughout New England and had published his first book. Thus, while limiting my study chronologically, I have not limited my examination of the full range of the extratextual factors that shaped his career, and I have in fact been enabled to examine these in greater detail than would otherwise have been possible.

This is not to say that after 1849 Thoreau's professional and literary position became static. On the contrary, I indicate in the concluding chapter that between 1850 and 1862 Thoreau became perhaps even more acutely sensitive to his audience as well as more pessimistic in his expectations. But if any useful distinction can be made between a writer's apprenticeship and his maturity, it is that a writer refines in maturity the literary territory he has discovered and staked out in his apprenticeship; and it is with that process of discovering the territory that this study is primarily concerned.

PART I

New Views

Chapter 1

"THAT PUBLIC GROUND BETWEEN GOD AND CONSCIENCE": THOREAU'S APPRENTICESHIP AND THE EARLY *DIAL*

HENRY THOREAU was too young to take part in the original ferment of New England transcendentalism in the late 1820s and early 1830s, and it is unlikely that he would have taken much interest in the narrowly theological debates of those early years. But by 1837, when Thoreau graduated from Harvard, the implications of transcendentalism were being extended well beyond the boundaries of the church, and Thoreau had clearly begun to align himself with the "new views." The force of transcendentalism rested in its fundamental claims for the authority of the *intuition*, the innate capacity for the immediate apprehension of truth, without mediation. The individual's intuitive faculty superseded all external claims for the authority of religious or secular institutions, of Scripture or tradition. While Thoreau was not part of the Unitarian establishment, then, he was nevertheless attracted to the broadly antiauthoritarian drift of the transcendentalists' message. Thoreau had always been something of an outsider at Harvard (by virtue of both his socioeconomic status and his personality), and in his senior year he was necessarily faced with all the anxieties of entering the adult world. Undoubtedly, the transcendentalists' views appealed to his youthful need to assert his self-worth through a spirit of rebellion, especially as these views seemed to legitimize and grant a high moral seriousness to such feelings. But because transcendentalism for Thoreau was not principally a matter of church reform, as it was for his mentors, he faced a dilemma in terms of vocation even greater than that which they had faced.

The first group of New England transcendentalists, however radical their "new views," had derived their public authority largely by virtue of their status within Boston society and the Unitarian church in particular (converging, as they did, at Harvard). Frederick Henry Hedge, George Ripley, Ralph Waldo Emerson, and William Henry Channing were all from prominent, well-connected families in and around Boston; those who did not have status by birth, such as James Freeman Clarke and Theodore Parker, acquired it by going through the divinity school, where they made important personal and professional connections in addition to acquiring the institutional authority of the clergy.[1] Among the first generation of transcendentalists, those most easily disregarded or ridiculed were those without any institutionally sanctioned status: Bronson Alcott and the two leading women, Margaret Fuller and Elizabeth Peabody. Fuller, who was unable to follow friends like Clarke and W. H. Channing into the university and divinity school, could only express to these friends her frustration and "sense of 'unemployed force'" (MFL 2: 126, 353).

Yet the inevitable result of the transcendentalists' flouting of institutional authority was that the Unitarian establishment eventually disfranchised them, and when this happened, the generation of upcoming transcendentalists was left with no public forum, no popular authority at all. Ironically, Emerson's "Divinity School Address" in 1838 marked the final blow. In his violent reaction to the address, Andrews Norton denied any complicity in bringing Emerson to Harvard: "No one can doubt for a moment of the disgust and strong disapprobation with which it must have been heard by the highly respectable officers of that Institution. . . . The preacher was invited to occupy the place he did, not by the officers of the Divinity College, but by the members of the graduating class. These gentlemen, therefore, have become accessories, perhaps innocent accessories, to the commission of a great offence; and the public must be desirous of learning what exculpation or excuse they can offer."[2] Perry Miller has commented that Norton's "blasting not only the orator but the graduates who chose him was so unprecedented an act that it could have been inspired by nothing less than pure rage,"[3] but Norton's strategy was shrewder and more calculated than Miller implies. By using the graduating students as a buffer, Norton effectively distanced the Unitarian establishment from any association with Emerson and transcendentalism. He was able to make it appear that Emerson's own views were, as he averred, insignificant in themselves, because he presented Emerson as an obnoxious outsider with no claims to the toleration for free speech the transcendentalists had been accorded when the debate was regarded as an internal one. This opened the way for the previously tolerant *Christian Examiner* and *Christian Register* to renounce Emerson, and they soon closed their pages to the transcendentalists. Ironically, it was virtually impossible after Emerson's address for anyone who was moved by his position to enter the divinity school. In fact, enrollment in the divinity school suffered something of a crisis at this time,[4] and by the end of 1840, Harvard seemed to have gotten rid of almost all traces of transcendentalism: in December of that year, a disinterested Henry Wadsworth Longfellow responded to one correspondent's charge of "pantheism at Cambridge" by exclaiming, "Why, there is in all Cambridge only one Transcendentalist,—and he a tutor! In the theological school there is none of it; the infected class is gone. The students are now inclined to rigid *Puseyism*."[5] Emerson himself was not invited again to speak at Harvard for thirty years.

The distinction between first- and second-generation transcendentalists is crucial then, not merely in terms of available vocations, but more importantly in terms of the modes of public discourse available to them as writers whose aim was, as Emerson had proclaimed in "The American Scholar," "to cheer, to raise, and to guide men." In a college essay for March 1837, Thoreau had argued that the writer "who addresses his fellow men through the medium of the press" had greater potential for public influence than the preacher, whose influence was "almost despotic" but "narrow and circumscribed" (EEM 86–87). Given this view, it is perhaps not surprising that Thoreau first appeared in print in the local newspaper. He had gone to the Concord poorhouse to interview Anna Jones, one of Concord's last survivors of the Revolutionary era. She was too ill to make the interviews particularly fruitful, but when she died on November 12, Thoreau wrote an obituary notice that was printed anonymously in Concord's *Yeoman's Gazette* on November 25. The fact that his first publication was a newspaper obituary is appropriate, for an obituary notice represents the peculiar conjunction of the minister's and the journalist's roles.

Thoreau's notice tends to be awkward where it is not merely conventional, but it faintly strikes the note of Emerson's American scholar. "After a youth passed amid scenes of turmoil and war," Thoreau writes, "she has lingered thus long amongst us as a bright sample of the Revolutionary woman. She was as it were, a connecting link between the past and the present—a precious relic of days which the man and patriot would not willingly forget" (EEM 121). The search for a distinctly American identity and heritage was, of course, a national pursuit; but Thoreau's interest in Anna Jones, and his treatment of her as an American type—the "Revolutionary woman"—seems to be a modest response to Emerson's assertion in "The American Scholar" that "the millions that around us are rushing into life, cannot always be fed on the sere remains of foreign harvests. Events, actions arise, that must be sung, that will sing themselves" (CW 1: 82). Further, Thoreau's characterization of Anna Jones as a "connecting link between the past and the present" not only memorializes her as an emblem of the Revolution, but exhibits the rudiments of what would become habitual verbal and ideological constructions in Thoreau's writing.[6]

An anonymous obituary notice in a village newspaper, in spite of its intriguing possibilities, was nevertheless hardly an adequate means of fulfilling Emerson's call for an American scholar. The newspapers, which in truth catered to the most ephemeral and material interests of society, suffered the attacks of nearly all the transcendentalists, attacks launched perhaps most persistently by the mature Thoreau. And without the institutionally recognized status and credentials of an Emerson, Thoreau was not yet in a position to approach the public from the lecture platform. Thoreau had high ambitions, and Emerson encouraged them; but his very ambition made those conventional outlets which were accessible inadequate. Thoreau would not appear in print again until the establishment of the *Dial* in 1840, a situation that left him with the same sense of "unemployed force" which Fuller experienced as a disfranchised woman in a man's world.

Thoreau had also begun keeping a private journal at this time, and he still had this as an outlet, of course; there he began to work out the nature of his identity as a writer. He thought of himself as a transcendental "Poet," which for the transcendentalists was essentially synonymous with "genius," "seer," and "prophet." His early journal entries, when not comments on his reading, tend to be impersonal, abstract, and aphoristic passages under generalized headings such as "Revolutions," "Heaven on Earth," "Influence," "Fear," and the like. Often, his subject is the Ideal itself, in various guises. The result was a kind of calculated vagueness, characteristic of many of the transcendentalists, and frequently charged against them as their primary fault.

The problem of focusing on the ideal, however, lay deeper than a matter of style alone; it created a fundamental problem of identity as well. This idealization of his role as writer only exacerbated Thoreau's sense of disjunction between the private and public, the passive and active selves. In a journal entry for March 5, 1838, headed "What to Do," Thoreau asked himself, "But what does all this scribbling amount to?" What had pleased him in the writing appeared "stale, flat,—and unprofitable" when he read it afresh. And if he could not record his inspirations in his writing, how much more difficult to translate them into his life. The larger problem, then, was how to make *any* action worthy of his vision:

> What may a man do and not be ashamed of it? He may not do nothing surely, for straightway he is dubbed Dolittle—aye! christens himself first—and reasonably, for he was first to duck. But let him do something, is he the less a Dolittle? Is it actually something done—or not rather something undone—Or if done, is it not badly done —or at most well done comparatively? . . .
>
> And is he doomed ever to run the same course? Can he not wriggling, screwing, self-exhorting,—self-constraining, wriggle or screw out something that shall live—respected, intact, intangible, not to be sneezed at? (J1: 33–34)

What emerges most clearly from this passage is the sense of his frustrated ambition to do something of merit. Thoreau's idealism resulted in his making tremendous, perhaps impossible demands on himself. Here, one gets a sense of the fear and even terror that he must have felt when he contemplated the possibility of failing to make something great of his life, especially when he was not even sure what criteria for greatness were applicable. On the one hand, Thoreau clearly wants to produce something that the world will recognize as valuable—he does not want to be perceived as a "Dolittle." But to produce something that has merit only in the world's eyes is no achievement and makes him a "Dolittle" still by absolute standards.

Out of the fear of his own ambitions for public recognition, the fear that such ambitions would compromise his spiritual integrity, Thoreau came to perceive the public as his antagonist. Yet because he felt the need for an active social role in the world, he could not abandon or entirely disregard that public.

On March 14, a week after his entry on "What to Do," he composed a lecture on "Society," which was delivered at the Concord Lyceum on April 11, 1838—his first public lecture. Emerson had held out for the American scholar the promise that the sincere and self-confident orator would find himself to be "the complement of his hearers," and that his most private thought would be revealed as the most public (CW 1: 103). Thoreau's lecture, itself a variation on Emerson's theme of self-trust, could hardly have struck a responsive chord in its audience, however. The didactic, imperative tone Thoreau adopted must have exacerbated the audience's negative reaction to a lecture that characterized the public as "only working oxen and neat cattle" (J1: 36). "Let not society be the element in which you swim, or are tossed about at the mercy of the waves," he exhorts, "but be rather a strip of firm land running out into the sea, whose base is daily washed by the tide, but whose summit only the spring tide can reach" (J1: 39). Moreover, this exhortation is really an expression of Thoreau's own anxiety, barely disguised as public discourse; it is a self-directed warning to remain insulated from the world. Not surprisingly, then, Thoreau did not lecture again until 1843.

In the privacy of his journal, Thoreau could write at a greater distance from the public, less threatened by its influence. Relinquishing the role of interpreter, he also resigns himself to alienation from a world that fails to comprehend his message. On January 29, 1840, Thoreau wrote in his journal, "The social condition of genius is the same in all ages. Aeschylus was undoubtedly alone and without sympathy in his simple reverence for the mystery of the universe" (J1: 107). Both Thoreau's ambition and his sense of the threat that the world posed to his principles led him to seek the solace and sanctuary provided by his journal, in which the transcendentalist poet was a solitary hero.

Publicly, Thoreau's problem of vocation was at least temporarily resolved in the summer of 1838, when, along with his brother John, Thoreau opened a private school in Concord. The school operated until April 1, 1841, when it closed because of John's poor health.[7] His years of teaching allowed him, in effect, to postpone his emergence as a public writer until he could discover his true audience and the proper vehicle for expression. While the Thoreau school did provide this opportunity for delay, however, it was never more than that. In his journals for these years there is not a single reference to his teaching; as Thoreau would later explain in *Walden*, "As I did not teach for the good of my fellow-men, but simply for a livelihood, this was a failure" (*Walden* 69).

Significantly, Thoreau defined success here in social terms as acting "for the good of my fellow-men." If it seems ironic that this criterion could not be met by teaching, while it could be by retreating to the shores of Walden Pond, we must recognize that the fulfillment of his experience was not in the retreat itself, but in the publication of that experience in the pages of his books—first *A Week on the Concord and Merrimack Rivers*, then *Walden*. Similarly, Thoreau's "retreat" into the pages of his private journal could not remain an end in itself but constituted further preparation for public expression.

In 1839, work began toward the establishment of a periodical that would provide a forum for the expression and defense of transcendentalism, and Thoreau's early works are not really comprehensible without an understanding of the context that the *Dial* provided for them. The idea for the journal had been revived in the "Transcendental Club" after George Ripley had printed a pamphlet defending their views against the attack of Andrews Norton, and the group as a whole felt the need for a regular outlet for their works. As Emerson viewed it, the journal would be "for the exposition of absolute truth" (EmL 2: 225). No one, however, was anxious to undertake the chore of actually editing such a journal. Emerson had written to his brother William, "I will never be editor, though I am counted on as a contributor. We have a power of fine people who would write a few numbers of such a book, who write nowhere else. My Henry Thoreau will be a great poet for such a company, and one of these days for all companies" (EmL 2: 225). Emerson's commitment to the cause and to his disciples—among whom Thoreau was foremost—eventually affected his choice to go back on his word and to assume the *Dial*'s editorship in 1842. The very idea of public-oriented discourse, however, was a problem for virtually all the transcendentalist writers, and Thoreau's own ambivalence about his sense of audience must be seen as simply one manifestation of a profound and pervasive ambivalence inherent in transcendentalist thought.

As early as 1833, Frederick Henry Hedge—a member of the original "Transcendental Club"—staked out one position regarding the relationship between the transcendentalist writer and the public in an essay defending Coleridge and the German transcendentalists against charges of obscurity: "To those only is he obscure who have no depths within themselves corresponding to his depths." Hedge explained that the primary condition of the transcendentalist was an intuitive perception of truth, and therefore "the effect of such writing upon the uninitiated, is like being in the company of one who has inhaled an exhilarating gas. We witness the inspiration, and are astounded at the effects, but we can form no conception of the feeling until we ourselves have experienced it."[8]

Hedge's simile ironically confirms the apparent absurdity of transcendentalist writing, but the simile is particularly appropriate in that it plays on the meaning of "inspiration," a trope the transcendentalists routinely used to describe this primary intuitive perception. Following through with this figure, Hedge regards the writing of the transcendentalists as the "expression" of that "inspiration." But there is a crucial distinction between language as "expression" and language as communication. The expression of an inspiration is a complementary activity that *completes* rather than *initiates* an action; it is essentially self-referential, and its function is therefore not to mediate between the initiated and the uninitiated. Communication is incidental at best, and, as Hedge suggests, perhaps impossible. Transcendentalist epistemology leads naturally to the notion of an esoteric language of expression, and subsequently to the transcendentalist writers' recurrent indifference toward an "uninitiated" public. This made a particularly attractive defensive posture, to which many of the transcendentalists had recourse. Others, however, embraced transcendentalism not so much as a systematic philosophy as for its potential to serve the aims of democracy and of religious and social reform. To the extent that this was true, a condescending indifference to those outside the pale was an unsatisfactory position, and it came under increasing strain, on both theoretical and practical grounds.

What is in question here is the authority of language, and a language of authority. The transcendentalists' intuitive perception of truth is both absolutely authoritative, because self-confirming, and at the same time devoid of any external authority for precisely the same reason—because truths *must* be self-confirming. Emerson confronted this in "The Divinity School Address" when, having declared that truth was a matter of "intuition," he explained, "It cannot be received at second-hand. Truly speaking it is not instruction, but provocation, that I can receive from another soul. What he announces, I must find true or reject" (CW 1: 80). Up to a point, this only confirms the isolation of the individual writer; but by placing up against the authority of the writer's intuition the corresponding authority of the reader or hearer's "interior consciousness," Emerson transforms what appears as elitism in Hedge into a radical egalitarianism, without compromising the epistemological premises of transcendentalism. Because one cannot truly instruct, the minister's or scholar's conventionally didactic, homiletic, and pedagogic mode of discourse is both presumptuous and ultimately ineffective; but because the genuine expression of truth should provoke a corresponding intuitive recognition in one's audience, Emerson's distinction between language of instruction and language of provocation promised possibilities as well as limitations for a social or public function of transcendentalist discourse.

For several of the New England transcendentalists, however, even Emerson's version did not go far enough in the democratization of transcendentalist writing, and they found his imperious self-trust fraught with dangers. Not surprisingly, the chief dissenters were those transcendentalists most involved with and committed to religious and social reform—notably Orestes Brownson, George Ripley, and Theodore Parker. In an 1838 essay, Ripley had summarized the dissenting position when he cautioned that "the most sublime contemplations of the philosopher can be translated into the language of the market; and unless they find a response in the native feelings of humanity, there is probably some error in the doctrine or some defect in its exposition. . . . The office of the true scholar in our republic is to connect himself in the most intimate and congenial relations with the energetic and busy population of which he is too often merely an insignificant unit."[9]

Orestes Brownson (who had withdrawn from the gathering of the "Transcendental Club" after their meeting in May 1837 and in 1838 established the *Boston Quarterly Review*) took on Emerson's version of the American scholar directly in an 1839 review. He criticized Emerson and his supporters, saying, "They bid the scholar make all things subsidiary to himself. . . . he must scorn to create for a purpose, . . . to work for an end beyond the work itself." Instead, Brownson argues, "American scholars we shall have; but only in proportion as the scholar weds himself to American principles and becomes the interpreter of American life."[10]

Emerson and his followers, on the other hand, remained extremely suspicious of the writer who "wedded himself" *too* fully to the life—and language—of the nation, thereby becoming merely the mouthpiece for its extant values and institutions and betraying the genuine source of universal truths.

These tensions among the transcendentalists were inevitably heightened when efforts were now begun to produce the *Dial*, and the result was a great deal of caution and reserve on the part of all involved. Emerson explained in a letter of December 12, 1839, to Fuller, "I believe we all feel much alike in regard to this journal; we all wish it to be, but do not wish to be in any way personally responsible for it" (EmL 2: 242). In fact, there was not even the consensus of feeling that Emerson imagined. Brownson had visited Alcott in October 1839 and proposed a merger of the *Dial* with his *Boston Quarterly Review*, but Alcott disapproved of Brownson's narrowly partisan stance and told Emerson and Fuller that they should produce an independent journal wherein contributors would be free to express "the purest thoughts and tastes."[11] Hedge, on the other hand, became nervous about the proposals for a transcendentalist journal not sanctioned by the Unitarian church, and when Fuller pressed him to become a contributor, he confessed his fears and disclaimed any association with transcendentalism (MFL 2: 113n, 124–25; EmL 2: 270–71). For very different reasons, even Emerson was reluctant to commit himself fully to the journal: "For the sake of the brilliant possibility I would promise honest labor of some sort to each number for a year, but I should wish to leave myself the latitude of supreme indifference, nay abhorrence of such modes of working forever after" (EmL 2: 243).

By the time the *Dial* came into being, both its aims and its list of potential contributors had shifted considerably from those envisioned by the liberal Unitarian clergymen who had first contemplated a new journal. Fuller became the editor of the *Dial*, with semiofficial assistance from Ripley and Emerson. The difficulty even these three had in reaching a consensus about the purpose and tone of the journal is evident in their correspondence about an introductory essay for the inaugural issue. Apparently at the urging of Ripley, Fuller first drafted an introductory essay, which of course would be her prerogative as the editor, but Emerson, who thought it was "written with talent and strength," nevertheless had a number of reservations about it. It was, he felt, too defensive: "This paper addresses the public, and explains; it refers to the contemporary criticism; it forestalls objection; it bows, though a little haughtily, to all the company." What is remarkable here, and perhaps a little hard to grasp, is that Emerson regarded all of these characteristics as faults, implying that "it is not quite confirmed in its own purpose." By stooping to the public, by deigning to explain, it threatened to compromise their "Universal aims." Taking a higher tone, Emerson did not see the need for a formal introduction at all: "If there be need of a new journal, that need is its introduction; it wants no preface."

> With the old drowsy Public which the magazines address, I think we have nothing to do;—as little with the journals & critics of the day. If we knew any other Journal, certainly we should not write this. This Journal has a public of its own; its own *Thou* as well as *I*; a new-born class long already standing waiting for this voice & wondering at its delay. (EmL 2: 285–86)

Emerson wanted the preface to proclaim the ideal and to rise above the merely topical and ephemeral. Therefore, he thought Fuller's introduction might more properly be incorporated into her "Essay on Critics," which she had written for the first number: "These statements concerning the modern periodical literature &c. are all just, and I think would be more graceful in another essay than the Preface." Emerson concluded his remarks by returning any final decision to Fuller but added, "If you wish me to solve any of my own problems I would even now try to write an essay on These Men & This Work. I say this as expiation for my petulance" (286).

Fuller took Emerson's criticism graciously but still foresaw difficulties: "It is no wish of mine to have an introduction or to write it, and all that you say on that score had occurred to me,[12] but Mr. Ripley and the publishers both thought it very desirable. I shall show Mr. R. what you have written and talk with him once more—those parts you thought too fierce, he thought not sufficiently so. I know not whether I can find the golden mean between you" (MFL 2: 132). Fuller accepted Emerson's offer of an introductory essay of his own, and when he sent it to her on April 27, he commented, "I have not had the smallest success & have learned not to send a capricious offer another time"; yet because he knew that his views were not shared by everyone, he cautioned Fuller (in spite of his own disparaging remarks about his introduction) that "if anything in this or other paper of mine is used, it must not be 'modified'—I mean by any insertion—without making me a party to the word *before printing*" (EmL 2: 292–93). When Emerson's essay was, in turn, subjected to criticism, the lack of consensus among them had become ludicrous, and on May 8 Emerson wrote to Fuller, "I hope ere this you have digested your chagrin concerning the Introduction I sent you Nay have fairly got Mr. Ripley at work to try his hand in drafting a Declaration of Independence. When he has tried, suppose we apply to Dr. Channing—indeed I would send the requisition all round the Table to every member, & then print the Dial without any, & publish the Rejected Introductions in a volume" (EmL 2: 294). In the end, Ripley wrote a prospectus for the *Dial*, Emerson wrote the address "The Editors to the Reader" to introduce the first number, and this was immediately followed by Fuller's "A Short Essay on Critics."

Ripley's prospectus, first issued on May 4, 1840 and reprinted in the inside cover of each number of the new journal, attempted to satisfy all concerned parties. "The purpose of this work," it states, "is to furnish a medium for the freest expression of thought on the questions which interest earnest minds in every community." Yet this did not mean that the journal would engage directly in the social and theological debates of the day; as Ripley goes on to explain, "It aims at the discussion of principles, rather than at the promotion of measures; and while it will not fail to examine the ideas which impel the leading movements of the present day, it will maintain an independent position with regard to them." The journal's "independent position," then, was not merely independent of particular movements, but independent of all movements—a position that ultimately seemed to be too ineffectual to the more active reformers among the transcendentalists. Yet even the nonactivists envisioned the journal as an instrument of social progress and moral reform, and so wanted the *Dial* to appeal to the widest possible audience. Thus the prospectus also claims that the *Dial*'s "contents will embrace a wide and varied range of subjects, and combining the characteristics of a Magazine and a Review, it may present something both for those who read for instruction, and those who search for amusement." More specifically, what Ripley meant here is that, like the monthly magazines, the *Dial* would include verse and prose miscellanies, but that like the reviews it would be published quarterly and would also include long reviews and scholarly essays. Their ambition was to make the *Dial* a popular journal, and they thus recognized the desirability of approaching a popular format. But the editors had taken on a quixotic task, for while they vaguely hoped to attract a broad reading public, they had not really worked out the means by which their abstract ideas could be made either instructive or amusing.

In his address "The Editors to the Reader," Emerson elaborates the aims of the journal by reiterating the position he had taken in his "American Scholar" address. His emphasis is on public influence: the purpose of the journal is to give expression to that which "lifts," "restores," "purges," and raises men. The series of verbs here (comparable to the American scholar's aim "to cheer, to raise, and to guide men") is striking and significant in its emphasis on action, on effecting public change. The aim of the journal was, in fact, nothing less than universal moral reform: "It has all things to say and no less than all the world for its final audience" (*Dial* 1.1: 3). Yet at the same time, the journal would hold itself aloof from all reform movements, and Emerson echoed Ripley's assertion that it would offer no creed but would represent a "search for principles." Emerson then shifts his focus abruptly away from public to private, and from active to passive: the contributions to this journal would not come from "the pens of practiced writers"—that is, of those who made it their business to attend directly to the public audience—but "from the beautiful resources of private thought. . . . from the secret confession of genius afraid to trust itself to ought but sympathy." That is, Emerson still held to his belief that the public would respond to the writing of those who looked inward only and refused to consider the public itself when they wrote. Recognizing that the new views would arouse controversy, he nevertheless argues that the "spirit of the time. . . . is too confident in its tone to comprehend an objection, and so builds no outworks for possible defence against contingent enemies. It has the steps of Fate, and goes on existing like an oak or a river, because it must" (*Dial* 1.1: 3). This is Emerson's correction of the defensiveness he had found in Fuller's introduction; but while he portrays this idealism as a kind of heroism, and in spite of his use of active verbs to describe the journal's aims, his method of effecting public influence was actually a passive one: the writing itself was fundamentally private—inward-looking and self-contained—while the audience in reading it was *to be* lifted, *to be* restored, *to be* purged, and *to be* raised. Emerson claimed that "our means correspond with the ends we have indicated," but in fact there remained an unbridged gap between means and ends.

While Emerson's address promotes a reliance on reform through the example of individual experience and private discourse, Fuller's "A Short Essay on Critics" implicitly acknowledges that the inspired utterance may need "translating" into some kind of public discourse (the vernacular) in order to affect the world. Certainly her task was more difficult than his, for she was attempting to justify public-oriented discourse within the context of a philosophy that sanctions the authority of Reason over Understanding and that regards the apprehension of truth as a matter of "provocation" rather than "instruction." Her method is justification through definition: "Essays entitled critical are epistles to the public through which the mind of the recluse relieves itself of its impressions. . . . Or they are articles, got up to order by the literary hack writers, for the literary mart, and the only law is to make them plausible" (*Dial* 1.1: 5). The latter type of critical essay may, of course, be dismissed out of hand. The former apparently defines criticism in a way that justifies it, but it is a rather remarkable characterization. Nominally, critical essays mediate between the work of art and the public, and Fuller claims that "next to invention is the power of interpreting invention" (7). Yet the thrust of Fuller's characterization is to assure that the critic (like the artist) remains unaffected, untainted even, by the public to whom the critical essays are presumably addressed. The critic is characterized as a "recluse," whose proper condition is outside any social sphere.

Developing an essentially Coleridgean model of criticism, Fuller identifies three classes of critics: the "subjective" critics pass judgment on the authority of personal taste merely, and their writing characterizes their own values rather than those of the artist under review. The "apprehensive critics" "can go out of themselves and enter fully into a foreign existence" and are thereby able to "reproduce the work of which they speak" in the spirit in which it was written. The "comprehensive" critics, who are the true critics, are also apprehensive, but they are able to "judge [the artist's] work" not only "by its own law," but also by universal laws, because such a critic "perceives the analogies of the universe, and how they are regulated by an absolute, invariable principle" (7). This, presumably, is why the "comprehensive" critic is a recluse. As such, however, the critic cannot truly mediate between artist and public. Critical essays are not a response to public demand, are not really didactic or pedagogic in intent, and do not take into account the language, conventions, and values of the audience. The "apprehensive" powers that are *necessary* for the critic to enter fully into the spirit of the artist and his work are denied to the critic in relation to the public audience: "If he adapts his work to us . . . we will not talk with him. . . . We will go to the critic who trusts his genius and trusts us, who knows that all good writing must be spontaneous" (10). Rather than interpret, Fuller's critic simply repeats at one remove the artist's own process of withdrawal and submission to "spontaneous" intuited "impressions." In "trusting" the public, the critic becomes, in effect, indifferent to the essay's influence upon that public. When Fuller says the critic's mind "relieves itself" through critical essays, she is drawing upon the romantic language of inspiration/expression, but there is a perhaps unconscious scatological pun here—capturing the transcendentalists' antagonism toward audience by characterizing public discourse as an unpleasant but necessary bodily function to expel waste.[13]

Fuller's essay is a sophisticated and ingenious exposition of transcendental critical theory. The ideas in her essay were not entirely new; in an 1838 essay in the *New York Review*, for example, George Allen had drawn heavily on Coleridge in his proposals for what he called "reproductive criticism"—virtually identical to what Fuller calls "apprehensive criticism." Yet for Allen criticism remains, above all, "a guide to the study of Art. . . . written to supply a demand,"[14] and the critic's work is fundamentally educational, a matter of public service. Fuller's "comprehensive" criticism further elevates the status of criticism by allowing the critic, as well as the artist, direct access to absolute universal values, but in doing so, it precludes her reclusive critic's serving as a link between artist and audience; the idealism of her "comprehensive criticism" only seems to broaden the gap between them.

In practice, Fuller's literary criticism belies her theory of critic as "recluse." In the preface to her translation of *Eckermann's Conversation with Goethe* (1839), for example, she is acutely aware of Goethe's popular reputation in America, and she takes on current criticism of him directly and systematically in order to mediate effectively between the artist and the public. Her work as editor of and critic for the *Dial*, and especially her later work as literary critic for the *New York Tribune*, actually assured her continued sensitivity to the social context of literature and of the critic's role. Here, however, her essay embodies the deeply rooted theoretical tension between the transcendentalists' ambitions for public influence and their self-imposed isolation from that public.

Thoreau had been grappling with many of the same issues in the privacy of his journal, building up the same kind of defensive wall around the sanctity of the private voice, while hoping ultimately to find an audience and a public function as well. Like so many of his fellow transcendentalists, Thoreau's image of himself as a writer was that of a prophet. On the one hand, this meant that he must withdraw from the world in order to be divinely inspired, and throughout the summer of 1840 he kept returning in his journal to the elusive, mysterious, and untranslatable qualities of that divine voice. On April 8, 1840, Thoreau wrote in his journal: "How shall I help myself? By withdrawing into the garret. . . . Completely silent and attentive I will be this hour, and the next, and forever.—The most positive life that history notices has been a constant retiring out of life—a wiping ones' [*sic*] hands of it—seeing how mean it is, and having nothing to do with it" (J1: 121). On June 28, he wrote, "The profane never hear music—the holy ever hear it. It is God's voice—the divine breath audible" (J1: 144). On July 2, he recorded, "I am not taken up, like moses [*sic*], upon a mountain to learn the law, but lifted up in my seat here, in the warm sunshine and genial light" (J1: 147).

Precisely because he did conceive of himself as a kind of prophet, however, Thoreau's "withdrawal" was not to find silence, but to find his own voice, and then an audience for it. As early as February, 1839, Thoreau had begun showing his poems to Emerson (EmL 2: 182), who responded warmly, describing one of them as "the purest strain, and the loftiest, I think, that has yet pealed from this unpoetic American forest" (JMN 5: 241). By November of that year, Thoreau began submitting poems to Emerson explicitly for consideration for the first number of the *Dial*, which Emerson hoped would be ready by the following spring (EmL 2: 234, 242, 243). From that point on, Emerson acted as intermediary between Thoreau and the *Dial*'s editor, Fuller. Probably early in 1840 Thoreau recorded in his notebook the following list of topics, presumably for lectures or essays: "Love, Sound & Silence, Horace, Greek Poetry, The Brave Man, Memoirs of a Tour—A Chit-Chat with Nature, Music, Hindoo Scripture."[15] Clearly, Thoreau was anxious to break into print again. In the beginning of March 1840, Emerson reported to Fuller that he had received "a fine critique of Persius" from Thoreau (EmL 2: 259), and by the end of the summer Thoreau gave Emerson an ambitious metaphysical essay or prose poem on "The Brave Man," which he now called "The Service" (EmL 2: 280–81, 285). Thoreau's journal entry on withdrawing into silence was therefore written at the very time he was submitting his writing for public scrutiny; his contemplated withdrawal seems not so much a result of indifference to the world as a result of his ambitions and his consequent fears of public failure.

His fears were not entirely unfounded, for Fuller had responded to his submissions rather critically and unsympathetically, in spite of Emerson's almost invariable recommendations. Nevertheless, the first number of the *Dial* included both his poem "Sympathy" and his first effort at transcendental criticism, "Aulus Persius Flaccus." In "Persius" Thoreau assumes the stance of Fuller's "comprehensive" critic, who judges a work in relation to "absolute, invariable principle." As such, he is critical not only of Persius but of satire in general. True poetry is the expression of divine inspiration, not the "unmusical bickering with the follies of men," and even the greatest art is but a faint echo of its source. "Most of all," he writes, "satire will not be sung. A Juvenal or Persius do not marry music to their verse, but are measured fault-finders at best; stand but just outside the faults they condemn, and so are concerned rather about the monster they have escaped, than the fair prospect before them" (EEM 122). Ironically, Thoreau's reputation would ultimately be based largely upon his own brilliance as a satirist, but at this point his transcendental idealism provided no justification for a form of discourse that addressed the world so directly. The satirist, Thoreau claims, is "*particeps criminis*," a partner in crime, because he is himself too thoroughly involved in the merely temporal and mundane. Thoreau then describes a hierarchical "order in the development of Genius" involving three steps, from "Complaint" to "Plaint" to "Love." The lowest (that of Persius) is untouched by the ideal; the second is an ennobled form of "regret" that comes from "the enjoyment of a superior good," and this may, he says, even characterize the "highest strain of the muse." But the third order of Genius is one that attends exclusively to the ideal, is unaffected by the follies of the actual world, and is "as impersonal as nature herself" (123). And this, Thoreau claims, is the "severest satire"; its self-contained and exemplary virtue, its supreme indifference to vice, constitute a standing rebuke.

Given this critical orientation, Thoreau has little interest in Persius's satires except where the author transcends the occasion and utters some universal truth, "since that which he says best at any time is what he can best say at all times" (124). Thoreau goes on to quote and comment upon a handful of such lines, using them as jumping-off points for his own plunges into transcendental abstraction. Turning one of Persius's lines against him, for example, Thoreau asserts that the wise man *ought* to live his life extemporaneously, careless whither his feet bear him, "for he lives out of an eternity that includes all time" (126). Anticipating Emerson's line in "Self-Reliance"—"A foolish consistency is the hobgoblin of little minds"—Thoreau asserts that "all questions rely on the present for their solution. . . . If this is what the occasion says, let the occasion say it" (126). Thoreau concludes his essay by asserting the transcendentalist dictum that "the artist and his work are not to be separated," that what literature reveals, inexorably, is "character," and this is what we invariably judge.

The essay as a whole seems rather disjointed. Only scant attention is actually paid to Persius's satires, which function not so much as the subject of his essay as the occasion for expressing his generalized ideas on the relation of art, criticism, and life. Consistent with the implications of transcendentalist epistemology (and, perhaps, imitative of Emerson), Thoreau's language tends to be metaphorical, and his sentences highly aphoristic and epigrammatic. He does not really develop a critical argument here; rather, he presents a series of discrete assertions, which are often parallel or complementary in import rather than sequential and logical. Nevertheless, the essay has its own principles of coherence, and Thoreau's ideas on art and criticism in general are fully consistent with the positions taken by Emerson and Fuller. The idealism underlying his objections to satire neatly parallel the *Dial*'s stated desire to address "principles" rather than to promote "measures," to give expression to elevating influences rather than to engage in partisan disputes.

It is not surprising, then, that Emerson had been particularly enthusiastic about this essay. Although Thoreau was at first reluctant to make any revisions in it, Emerson told Fuller he thought it "so fresh and original a piece of criticism, that it will quite pay the pains of a little blotting and sandpaper" (EmL 2: 281). Thoreau soon changed his mind and reworked the essay carefully, quite possibly with Emerson's assistance, and when Emerson reported to Fuller that he had read the revised essay, he urged her to include it in the first number, calling it a "piece of character" (EmL 2: 290). He repeated his view when he sent the essay itself to Fuller the next day: "I want you to print the Persius in the first number. Can you not, will you not if it is good?" (EmL 2: 292). Fuller replied to Emerson on the following day, agreeing to include "Persius" in the first number.[16]

Other important *Dial* contributors were far from enthusiastic about the essay, however. James Freeman Clarke, who thought it was by Theodore Parker, found it poorly written.[17] Theodore Parker, in turn, thought it a "foolish article," imitative of Emerson. "I hope he will writte [*sic*] for the newspaper more and less for the Dial. I would recommend him to the editor of the New World to keep the youth out of mischief" (EmL 2: 324n).

With the exception of her approval of "Persius," Fuller seems to have shared Parker's low opinion of Thoreau. Although the *Boston Morning Post* chose to reprint Thoreau's poem "Sympathy" from this first issue of the *Dial*,[18] Fuller subsequently rejected most of Thoreau's submissions to the journal, printing only four of his poems and no more of his prose during the two years of her editorship. While those poems she did print seem to have been admitted largely because of Emerson's persistent urgings, for the most part Fuller guarded her control over the *Dial* rather jealously and shaped its character to her own views.[19] Emerson's claim, in his address to the readers, that contributions would be gleaned from "the portfolios which friendship has opened to us" (*Dial* 1.1: 4), did not extend to Thoreau until Emerson himself became the editor.

"The Service," Thoreau's most ambitious composition during the *Dial*'s first two years, never found its way into print at all during his life. The subject of his essay was the "brave man," whose heroism consisted in his unwavering and single-minded "service" to the divinity within him, and his heroic resistance to the ways of the world. The essay, which was completed in the summer of 1840, is a careful compilation of related journal passages written mostly since December 1839, and with concentrated effort in July and August of 1840. The martial imagery which governs the essay works, verbally, as a means of reconciling the worlds of contemplation and action—that is, of reconciling his own divided self, his spiritual and worldly ambitions. The reconciliation is only verbal, however; the "action" of the essay's elaborate metaphysical conceits remains abstract and metaphorical, the heroism remains that of willful spiritual withdrawal and isolation.

In content, "The Service" reworks ideas that are central to almost all of Thoreau's early writing, giving Emerson's ideal of transcendental self-reliance his own peculiar stridency and internal tension. Like the independent individual of his lecture "Society," and like the true poet of his "Persius" essay who "never turns to rebuke falsehood," the brave man is characterized by his absolute self-trust, his self-possession and sublime indifference to external influences. These motifs are not only familiar already in Thoreau's writing but consistent with (if not derivative of) positions expressed by both Emerson and Fuller, and ideologically there is little here to which they would have objected. What is most distinctive about the essay, and the source of both its strengths and its weaknesses, is Thoreau's ambitious, experimental use of language and structure to create a transcendentalist essay;

"The Service" expresses transcendental values not only in its delineation of the heroic character but in its form as well.

Even more than was the case in "Persius," its organizing principle is associational rather than narrative or expository; it is built around image clusters and extended metaphors. The governing image, implied in the title, is that of the soldier in the service of higher laws, a version of the Arthurian Galahad whose spiritual purity is both his strongest armor against worldly temptation and the means to a transcendent vision. This imagery runs through all three of the essay's subdivisions, "Qualities of the Recruit," "What Music Shall We Have?" and "Not How Many but Where the Enemy Are," but each of these sections is further governed by its own dominant metaphors or image clusters.

Thoreau begins the first section, "Qualities of the Recruit," by delineating his own allegorical mythology: "The brave man is the elder son of creation, who has stept buoyantly into his inheritance, while the coward, who is the younger, waiteth patiently till he decease. He [the brave man] rides as wide of the earth's gravity as a star, and by yielding incessantly to all the impulses of the soul, is constantly drawn upward and becomes a fixed star" (RP 3). This armature of myth does not generate an allegorical narrative, however; rather, it introduces several images that Thoreau will explore and develop in the essay. The astronomical imagery here leads to a cluster of images relating to the cosmic system and the "sphericity" of celestial bodies that dominates this first section; and the "impulses of the soul" hints at the theme he will pick up in the second section, "What Music Shall We Have?"

Sphericity is wholeness—literally, integrity—and (influenced by his reading in Sir Thomas Browne and the metaphysical poets) Thoreau plays upon as many variations of this image as he can contrive. Images of celestial spheres, orbs, and arcs pile upon one another before Thoreau actually explains his elaborate symbolic metaphysics of "sphericity" itself: the coward, or weak person is "flat," "but the brave man is a perfect sphere"; "only by resigning ourselves implicitly to the law of gravity in us, shall we find our axis coincident with the celestial axis, and by revolving incessantly through all circles, acquire a perfect sphericity." "What shame then," Thoreau concludes, "that our lives, which might so well be the source of planetary motion, and sanction the order of the spheres, should be full of abruptness and angulosity, so as not to roll nor move majestically" (RP 6–7). The verbal excesses here—the strained metaphysical conceits and the awkward neologisms—suggest the powerful influence of fellow transcendentalists like Emerson and Alcott. But the section is held together by the insistent, if extravagant, use of astronomical imagery, which is extended through the remainder of the first section.

The second section of the essay, "What Music Shall We Have?" interweaves images of soldiers, music, and the cosmos within his mythic contrast between the "brave man" and "the coward." "The brave man is the sole patron of music," he begins. "It is his voice. His language must have the same majestic movement and cadence, that philosophy assigns to the heavenly bodies." Thoreau moves this into a cluster of martial images—the soldier, war, chivalry, heroism, and crusades—and he brings these together with his music symbolism, saying, "If the soldier marches to the sack of a town, he must be preceded by drum and trumpet, which shall identify his cause with the accordant universe" (9). Music is the "universal language," "God's voice," and to attend to it, to harmonize with it, he says, is to achieve "true sphericity," reasserting the imagery of his first section (10). Toward the end of the section, Thoreau writes, "A man's life should be a stately march to an unheard music, and when to his fellows it seems irregular and inharmonious, he will be stepping to a livelier measure, which only his nicer ear can detect" (11). This is only one of a sequence of very similar statements in this section; the last variant of it would not be formulated until *Walden*'s famous "different drummer" passage.

While the first two sections of the essay define and celebrate the ideal, the correspondence between the music of the spheres and the hero's own "sphericity," the final section focuses more on the disjunction between the actual and the ideal, and this shift constitutes Thoreau's call to battle. Both the astronomical and the martial imagery here establish links with the earlier sections, but the celebratory tone of the earlier sections is now modified by an element of direct criticism and a tone of lament—the "regret" or "plaint" that comes from "the perception of a higher good," as he had explained in his "Persius" essay. The edge of frustration, dissatisfaction, and impatience here also makes this the most personal section of the essay.

> When my eye falls on the stupendous masses of the clouds, tossed into such irregular greatness across the cope of my sky, I feel that their grandeur is thrown away on the meanness of my employment. In vain the sun through morning and noon rolls defiance to man, and, as he sinks behind his cloudy fortress in the west, challenges him to equal greatness in his career; but from his humbleness he looks up to the domes, and minarets, and gilded battlements of the eternal city, and is content to be a suburban dweller outside the walls. (12)

In the first section, Thoreau had proclaimed a correspondence between the eye of the brave man and "the whole concave of the heavens"; here he begins by confessing that he feels not a correspondence but a sense of his own insignificance and inadequacy when confronting "the cope of my sky." Even though Thoreau immediately shifts to an impersonal construction and generalizes his sense that man has lost, or abdicated, his true divine estate, the passion of Thoreau's call to heroic action seems to have its source in his own self-doubts and his frustrated sense of his unemployed force.

This shift, from the ideal to the inadequacies of the actual leads to both a sharper degree of criticism and an intensified call to action. The battle imagery that dominates this section is correspondingly more vigorous and graphic than earlier in the essay. We need, Thoreau says, "some of that testy spirit of knight errantry," and if we find no worthy worldly foe, then "with our trusty swords and double handed maces, hew and mangle some unreal phantom of the brain" (12–13). Scornfully he chides mankind for cowardice in the face of the personified enemy "Falsehood": "The very dogs that bay the moon . . . do evince more heroism than is tamely barked forth in all the civil exhortations and war sermons of the age" (13). In the first section of the essay, Thoreau wrote that the brave man "deals not so much in resolute action, as healthy and assured rest"; but such serenity could be established only through a self-discipline that was militant, vigorous, and relentless.

Thoreau's martial imagery in this section is eclectic, but it is predominantly medieval/Arthurian, for his disinherited hero (his alter ego) is on a quest for spiritual redemption and, to succeed, is to transform his estate from the barren wasteland into the eternal city. Having vented his frustration, Thoreau converts his "discontent" into an exhortation to virtue—that is, to strenuous self-reform: "Of such sort, then, be our crusade, which, while it inclines chiefly to the hearty good will and activity of war, rather than the insincerity and sloth of peace, will set an example to both of calmness and energy. . . . Nor let our warfare be a boorish and uncourteous one, but a higher courtesy attend its higher chivalry" (17). Thoreau's hortatory and visionary conclusion would be reworked in both "Sir Walter Raleigh" and *A Week on the Concord and Merrimack Rivers*, and it indirectly anticipates the conclusion of *Walden* as well: "We are dreaming of what we are to do. Methinks I hear the clarion sound, and clang of corselet and buckler, from many a silent hamlet of the soul. The signal gun has long since sounded and we are not yet on our posts. Let me make such haste as the morning, and such delay as the evening" (17).

While the dominant imagery of "The Service" is that of knight errantry, Thoreau's own role and voice are essentially those of the prophet. The first two sections in effect constitute the prophet's withdrawal from the world into the insular serenity of contemplation; in these sections he is trying only to articulate his vision of the ideal, unconscious of audience—at least rhetorically—and without ulterior motive, so he uses declarative sentences almost exclusively in these sections. The third section, on the other hand, represents the prophet's descent from the mountaintop, as it were, back to the world where he must both rebuke and inspire the people.[20] Appropriately, Thoreau frequently uses imperatives in this section, imperatives that range in tone from the humility of a prayer to the more assertive and imperious authority of a commandment.[21] Most often Thoreau's imperatives are constructed in the first person plural (e.g., "Let us make such haste as the morning"), which captures exactly the peculiar relation of the prophet to his audience: his authority to use the imperative—to rebuke and command—comes from his privileged insight, which sets him apart from the community; but the first person plural reasserts his participation in the community, implicitly requesting the people to *join* with him in some action.

Thoreau's experiment with transcendental prose is by no means always well controlled. In pulling together various strands from his journal on the basis of theme and imagery, he is often oblivious to conflicting elements, such as the awkward shifts in tone between his expansive metaphysical conceits and his sometimes pedantic use of classical allusions; the extended metaphors themselves too often are strained to the point of obscurity or absurdity; and too often the poetic gives way to the didactic or the merely vapid. Nevertheless, "The Service" was an experiment deeply responsive to the ideological and critical values of his transcendentalist mentors and peers. Thoreau's aphoristic sentences, his high level of abstraction, and his elaborate, recurring metaphysical conceits are all intended to liberate language from the actual and familiar world in order to echo, however faintly, transcendent truths.

That Fuller rejected the essay is not entirely surprising, but the decision seems somewhat capricious when one considers some of the contributions she did accept and the fact that she was often hard-pressed to find enough material of any kind to fill some of the issues of the *Dial*. The responses that Thoreau's essay generated from Emerson and Fuller illuminate the complexity of the underlying tensions in transcendentalist aesthetics and criticism.

Emerson sent a draft of the essay to Fuller in early August of 1840 with this comment:

> I read it through this morning and see that it may give you some hesitations. There is too much manner in it—as much as in Richter—and too little method, in any common sense of that word—yet it has always a spiritual meaning even when the literal does not hold: and has so much brilliancy and life in it that in our bible for The Young America, I think it ought to find a place. I wish it were shorter. But the three divisions of the piece may be marked in the typography; and nobody need read it who cannot transpierce the imagery. (EmL 2: 287)[22]

Emerson's ambivalence not only about Thoreau's essay but about the purpose of transcendental writing is clear in these comments. On the one hand, he found the essay satisfactory in spiritual terms, as the sincere expression of individual inspiration, and thus valued it for their "bible for The Young America." On the other hand, however, Emerson was acutely aware of its limits as effective public discourse; the spiritual was evoked at the expense of the literal, and by neglecting the literal, Thoreau lost the necessary point of contact with an audience.

Emerson's criticism of its lack of "method," by which he seems to mean logical structure, also reflects his thinking about audience response to the ideas rather than about the ideas themselves; this becomes clearest in his concern with the length and typography of the piece—thoroughly pragmatic considerations of form that have nothing to do with the quality of the thoughts but everything to do with their effectiveness as public statement. Emerson's final recommendation was based on his sense that priority must be given to the original inspiration, yet he continued to feel frustrated over Thoreau's obvious inability—and the inability of the *Dial* generally—to attract a popular audience.

Emerson correctly anticipated Fuller's response to "The Service," though his comparison of Thoreau's excessive "manner" to Richter may, in fact, have been a subtle strategy to enlist her tolerance. In the first number of the *Dial* Fuller had printed two of her own poems on Richter, the second of which, titled "Some Murmur at the 'Want of System' in Richter's Writing," provided a defense similar in several respects to that which Emerson was offering on Thoreau's behalf:

> A labyrinth! a flowery wilderness!
> Some in thy "slip-boxes" and "Honey-moons"
> Complain of —*want of order*, I confess,
> But not of *system*, in its highest sense.
> Who asks a guiding clue through this wide mind,
> In love of Nature, such will surely find;
>
> . . . .
>
> Nature's wide temple, and the azure dome,
> Have plan enough for the free spirit's home!
>
> (*Dial* 1.1: 135)

In any case, Emerson failed to persuade Fuller. He had optimistically told her that "there is surely enough time for you to send this paper back to Thoreau for any corrections" (EmL 2: 287)—that is, time for inclusion in the October *Dial*; but in fact, it was December before Fuller got around to sending the essay back to Thoreau, and then it was to reject it. It "is rich in thoughts," she conceded, "and I should be *pained* not to meet it again. But then the thoughts seem to me so out of their natural order, that I cannot read through it without *pain*. I never once feel myself in a stream of thought, but seem to hear the grating of tools in the mosaic. It is true, as Mr. E says, that essays not to be compared with this have found their way into the *Dial*. But then these are more unassuming in their tone, and have an air of quiet good-breeding which induces us to permit their presence. Yours is so rugged that it ought to be commanding" (Corr 41–42).

Fuller's response actually turns her defense of Richter against Thoreau. Her objection to his "mosaic" method of composition is that its artificiality betrays the "natural order" of the thoughts; she had defended Richter's apparent lack of order, on the other hand, by asserting that it was precisely a "natural" order which he followed. As she had written in her essay on critics, "all good writing must be spontaneous," and Thoreau's essay clearly was not.

Fuller's critique, like Emerson's, is perceptive and just, but it reflects an ambivalent attitude toward the authority of language and the relation of style and audience. Both Fuller and Emerson concede the richness of "thought" in the essay, yet this somehow seems inadequate to them, even while they sanctify the authority of individual inspiration. While the editorial address to the readers claimed that the *Dial* would rely upon "the beautiful resources of private thought," these were nevertheless judged in terms of their potential for *public* effectiveness; and Fuller was implicitly backed into the rather awkward position of informing Thoreau that works inferior in thought to "The Service" were nevertheless more publishable.

Thoreau's early efforts were, indeed, neither quite "commanding" nor "unassuming." Thus he came across to Fuller (as he had to Parker in the "Persius" essay) as a rather pretentious adolescent whose proud assertion of his differentness annoyed rather than inspired. Both Fuller and Parker were tempted to put him in his place and steer him toward a more unassuming, more conventional prose.

In Thoreau's mind, however, inspiration had nothing to do with the "unassuming" tone of "quiet good-breeding." As if he had anticipated Fuller's letter rejecting "The Service" (or perhaps having already heard Emerson's and/or Fuller's initial reactions to it), Thoreau wrote in his journal on October 6, 1840: "I have not read any just literary criticism yet. . . . The flowing drapery of genius is too often tucked up and starched lest it offend against the fashions of the time. What is sacrificed to time is lost to eternity. . . . I want no politeness nor ceremony in books. . . . Our thoughts as well as our bodies are dressed after the latest Parisian fashion" (J1: 185; cf. J1: 188–89).

Such heroic idealism did not, of course, effect a reconciliation of private and public discourse. Although Fuller invited Thoreau to revise and resubmit "The Service," he apparently chose not to do so. If, as Thoreau wrote, "what is sacrificed to time is lost to eternity," it was also true that what was dedicated to eternity was lost to the times, for the essay remained unpublished during Thoreau's lifetime. In light of Fuller's unsympathetic response to his submissions to the *Dial*, Thoreau beat a defensive, and somewhat indignant retreat into the idealized realm of private discourse. In January 1841, Thoreau wrote in his journal:

> We should offer up our *perfect* thoughts to the gods daily—our writing should be hymns and psalms. Who keeps a journal is a purveyor for the Gods. There are two sides to every sentence; the one is contiguous to me, but the other faces the gods, and no man ever fronted it. . . . Consequently it demands a godlike insight—a fronting view, to read what was greatly written. (J1: 220)

In the pristine environment of his private journal, Thoreau's audience is the gods, not the public; there, his purpose is purely expressive rather than pragmatic—to write "hymns and psalms," not to wake his neighbors up (cf. n.13). His sentences have two sides, but *only* two sides—contiguous to himself and the gods. That is, his expression is "*perfect*" precisely because each of his sentences "faces the gods" directly and does not condescend, i.e., does not deviate in the direction of its aim, to accommodate any external audience, who must necessarily perceive such language *im*perfectly, from an oblique angle. A reader must therefore assume a "godlike position" himself in order to get a "perfect" "fronting view" of such language. Even as he writes about the ideal nature of his journalizing, however, Thoreau cannot remain satisfied with its merely private character; the last sentence of this entry, in which he considers how such writing must be read, betrays Thoreau's underlying public ambitions. He resolves his dilemma not by accommodating the public, but by insisting that the reader accommodate him—by assuming a "fronting view."

In a longer journal entry for January 22, Thoreau seems to be responding even more directly to Fuller's complaint that she never felt herself "in the stream of thought":

> I hear it complained of some modern books of genius, that they are irregular, and have no flow, but we should consider that the flow of thought is more like a tidal wave than a prone river, and is the effect of a celestial influence, or sort of ground swell, it may be, and not of any declivity in its channel. . . . The one obeys the earthly attraction, the other the heavenly attraction. The one runs smoothly because it gravitates toward the earth alone, the other irregularly because it gravitates toward the heavens as well.
>
> The reader who has been accustomed to expend all his energy in the launching—as if he were to float down stream for the whole voyage—may well complain of nauseating ground swells, and choppings of the sea, when his frail shore craft gets amidst the breakers of the ocean stream—which flows as much to sun and moon, as lesser streams to it—If he would appreciate the true flow that is in these books, he must expect to see it rise from the page like an exhalation—and wash away the brains of most like burr-millstones. They flow not from right to left, or from left to right, but to higher levels, above and behind the reader. (J1: 225–26)

Whatever "modern books of genius" Thoreau had in mind here, he clearly regarded this as a defense of his own writing. Thoreau later integrated this passage into the text of *A Week on the Concord and Merrimack Rivers*, where it functions as a guide to the reading of that book. Here Thoreau's point is to reject criticism like Fuller's on the grounds that she misapprehends his true audience; at the same time, he is trying to find a means of accommodating a public, not by writing *to* them, but by showing them *how* to read the works of genius.

While Thoreau could justify the "ruggedness" of his prose, Fuller's criticism of his mode of composition still needed to be countered. Was his "mosaic" method a betrayal of his inspiration after all? Thoreau himself had, like so many of the transcendentalists, shared Fuller's sense that inspired writing was spontaneous. As early as March 1838 he had written in his journal, under the heading "Composition," that "the nearer we approach to a complete but simple transcript of our thought—the more tolerable will be the piece, for we can endure to consider ourselves in a state of passivity—or in involuntary action; but rarely our efforts, and least of all our rare efforts" (J1: 35). In composing his essays, however, Thoreau had felt that the collecting of separate journal entries would give his thoughts greater coherence. Now he wondered again if this was tampering with his true response, taking entries out of their context for the sake of an effect. In a journal entry for February 6, 1841, Thoreau reflected again on his mode of composition, elaborating on Fuller's remarks:

> When I select one here and another there and strive to join sundered thoughts, I make but a partial heap after all—Nature strews her nuts and flowers broadcast, and never collects them into heaps. . . . Fate has surely enshrined [a single and casual thought] in this hour and circumstance for some purpose—What she has joined together let not man put asunder.—Shall I transplant the primrose by the river's brim—to set it beside its sister on the mountain? *This* was the soil it grew in—*this* the hour it bloomed in—if sun wind and rain came *here* to cherish and expand it—shall not we come here to pluck it?—Shall we require it to grow in a conservatory for our convenience? (J1: 253)

Emerson, who also composed his lectures and essays as "mosaics" drawn from his journals, had confronted this dilemma several years earlier and had defended his method in a journal entry of 1837, noting, "Let not a man decline being an artist under any greenhorn notion of intermeddling with sacred thought. I put like things together" (JMN 5: 335). The crucial distinction Emerson implicitly made here was between the *seer*, who could afford to respect the integrity of the original transcripts of his thoughts for himself, and the *artist*, who sought *public* influence. The fact that Thoreau continued to use his "mosaic" method in composing his public essays suggests the extent of his ambition to achieve public recognition and influence. Ironically, Thoreau eventually extracted this February 6 passage from his journal, too, and worked it into the complex mosaic of *A Week on the Concord and Merrimack Rivers*.

Thoreau thus vacillated between the public and private dimensions of his art. On February 7, 1841, for example, he wrote, "I would have men make a *greater* use of me—Now I must belittle myself to have dealings with them" (J1: 257). He longed to serve the world as a poet-prophet, but he saw that he could be "useful" only if he compromised himself by explaining. Thus he was again driven to a position of imperturbable aloofness from the world.

On February 10, 1841, he wrote: "Our thoughts and actions may be very private for a long time—for they demand a more catholic publicity to be displayed in than the world can afford. Our best deeds shun the narrow walks of men, and are not ambitious of the faint light the world can shed on them, but delight to unfold themselves in that public ground between god and conscience" (J1: 263).

In the midst of this uncertainty about his identity as a writer, Thoreau moved (in April 1841) into the Emerson household, where he earned his room and board as a handyman and laborer. The Emerson home was the hub of transcendental activity, and shortly after Thoreau moved in, Emerson invited Fuller to stay with them for a few weeks. Here she met Thoreau for the first time, but if Emerson hoped that the meeting might result in a greater understanding between the editor and the writer, he did not succeed; Thoreau was toying with the idea of becoming a farmer, and Fuller felt this would be his most fruitful course (MFL 2: 210). She apparently offered her criticism of Thoreau's poem "With Frontier Strength Ye Stand Your Ground" during this visit, and Thoreau dutifully revised it, but a month later she rejected the revision. Thoreau persisted with this poem, but Fuller apparently continued to balk at the "ruggedness" of Thoreau's writing, and Emerson wrote to her regarding Thoreau's poem on September 8: "Henry Thoreau says that if you will send him his 'Mountains' he will try to scrape or pare them down or cover the peaks with a more presentable greensward" (EmL 2: 445; cf. 2: 70). On October 18, Fuller wrote to Thoreau again rejecting the poem: "There is a want of fluent music," she complained, and she closed her letter with the pointed wish, "May Truth be irradiated by Beauty!" (MFL 2: 243). While she urged that he revise it still further for the *Dial*, the poem was never published there.

Emerson still had high hopes for Thoreau, however: in June he had written to his brother William, "Thoreau is a scholar and a poet and as full of buds of promise as a young apple tree" (EmL 2: 402), and he hoped to cultivate Thoreau to fruition. While Thoreau himself was repeatedly tempted to retreat from the public and be satisfied with his private vision, Emerson was encouraging him to grapple with the world. During the summer of 1841, Thoreau wrote out another list of writing topics: "Merrimack & Musketaquid, Sound & Silence, Bravery, Concord, Friendship, Books & Style, Seeing, Obligation, Dying, Devil, Journal."[23] In September 1841 Emerson wrote to Fuller, "H. T. is full of noble madness lately, and I hope more highly of him than ever. I know that nearly all the fine souls have a flaw which defeats every expectation they excite but I must trust these large frames as of less fragility—than the others. Besides to have awakened a great hope in another, is already some fruit is it not?" (EmL 2: 447).

Even at the height of his enthusiasm for Thoreau, Emerson had doubts about the younger writer's ability to convey his vision to the public. Emerson's ambivalence centered upon the question of who was responsible when the poet failed to engage the public. In a journal entry for October 24, 1841, Emerson recorded:

> And yet though we pine for great men, we do not use them when they come. Here is a Damascus blade of a man such as you may search through nature in vain to parallel, laid up on the shelf in our village to rust and ruin. It seems as if they were never quite available for that very idea which they represent. H. [Thoreau] is a person of extraordinary health and vigor, of unerring perception, and equal expression; and yet he is impracticable and does not flow through his pen or (in any of our legitimate aqueducts) through his tongue. (JMN 8: 118)

This passage begins by extolling Thoreau's merit as a superior man and blames the public for not recognizing him as such; but by the end of the passage, the failure is Thoreau's. He has failed to find the language needed to engage the public, and the responsibility is his.[24]

Thoreau himself would not have disagreed entirely with Emerson's estimate of him, though he was more apt to see his uncompromising and "impracticable" art as a sign of his heroism. In September of 1841, shortly before Emerson made his journal entry, Thoreau wrote to Lucy Brown, describing his situation. He noted he was "in the mid-sea of verses" and, while unsatisfied with most of them, hoped for eventual success. "I am as unfit for any practical purpose—I mean for the furtherance of the world's ends—as gossamer for ship-timber; and I, who am going to be a pencil-maker tomorrow, can sympathize with God Apollo, who served King Admetus for a while on earth. But I believe he found it for his advantage at last,—and I am sure I shall, though I shall hold the nobler part at least out of the service" (Corr 46).

Emerson fully understood Thoreau—he had earlier applied the Apollo-and-Admetus metaphor to himself (JMN 5: 12 [1835]); but now he was at least encouraging this uncompromising young Apollo to find an Admetus to serve, and he took practical measures on his behalf: Emerson found an appropriate enough Admetus figure in Rufus W. Griswold, to whom he recommended Thoreau's verse for the first edition of Griswold's *Poets and Poetry of America*. In a letter of September 25, 1841, Emerson wrote, "Unless I am greatly mistaken, Mr. Thoreau already deserves and will more and more deserve your attention as a writer of American Poetry."[25] Early in October Thoreau followed through by sending Griswold three of his poems that had been printed in the *Dial* (Corr 54), but Griswold seems not to have desired the services of this Apollo, and none of Thoreau's poems appeared in the collection. Neither did Fuller, as the *Dial*'s editor, seem eager for his poems.

Thoreau's career as a poet held little promise, so Thoreau sought another practicable outlet for his literary ambitions. Perhaps also under Emerson's guidance, Thoreau began a more or less systematic reading of early English poets, apparently toward the end of compiling an anthology or history of these poets: he copied long extracts of their work from Emerson's commonplace book, and at the end of November Emerson advanced Thoreau fifteen dollars to pay for a trip to the Harvard library "in account of his book."[26] This turned out not to be quite the right work for him either, however. It was only with some difficulty that he received permission to use the library, and then he recorded in his journal:

> When looking over the dry and dusty volumes of the English poets, I cannot believe that those fresh and fair creations I had imagined are contained in them. . . . I can hardly be serious with myself when I remember that I have come to Cam. after poetry—and while I am running over the catalogue, and collating and selecting—I think if it would not be a shorter way to a complete volume—to step at once into the field or wood, with a very low reverence to students and librarians. . . . On running over the titles of these books. . . . I am oppressed by an inevitable sadness. (Jl: 337–38)

Though Thoreau made sporadic efforts to pursue this project over the next several years, his heart was clearly not in the work. This was just another manifestation of Apollo drudging for Admetus. Thoreau regarded his true service as to the gods, not to man—and surely not to students and librarians—so, for the time being at least, he was satisfied to record his truest feelings in his journal occupying "that public ground between god and conscience."

Chapter 2

"THE VALUE OF A FACT": THE *DIAL* UNDER EMERSON AND THE "NATURAL HISTORY OF MASSACHUSETTS"

AT THE END of 1841, Thoreau's inclination was to withdraw and remain aloof from the public arena, but his position altered with the events of 1842. In addition to the steady pressure from Emerson to become a more "practicable" writer, the death from lockjaw of Thoreau's older brother John on January 12, 1842, brought new pressures on Thoreau to assume an acceptable role in society. Two years before John's death, Thoreau had written in his journal, "On the death of a friend, we should consider that the fates through confidence have devolved on us the task of a double living—that we have henceforth to fulfil the promise of our friend's life also, in our own, to the world" (J1: 114). Whatever the origins of this notion, Thoreau seems to have taken it seriously. John, who was Henry's best friend as well as his older brother, had always been the more sociable and popular of the two, and while John lived, the younger brother was left relatively free to pursue his more private and idiosyncratic course. He could therefore allow himself the self-indulgent pose of the sensitive spirit too fine for the world. But now Henry was the only son in the Thoreau family, and this resulted in both a sense of survivor guilt[1] and an increased sense of ambition—the need to fulfill the promise of John's life in his own. After a case of sympathetic lockjaw, which brought Thoreau himself close to death, and a month of silence in his journal, Thoreau's entries took on a new intensity and sense of mission.

On February 20, 1842, Thoreau wrote in his journal that "the death of friends should inspire us as much as their lives" (J1: 369). Yet Thoreau's sense of guilt, as the survivor, complicated his desire to "fulfil the promise" of John's life. To assert his own will now might seem like the usurpation rather than the fulfillment of John's place, and his guilt manifested itself in a desire for passivity and self-effacement. On March 11, Thoreau wrote:

> I must receive my life as passively as the willow leaf that flutters over the brook. I must not be for myself, but God's work and that is always good. . . . My fate cannot but be grand so. . . . I feel as if [I] could at any time resign my life and the responsibility of living into Gods [*sic*] hands—and become an innocent free from care as a plant or stone. (J1: 371)

Yet such "innocent" passivity did not satisfy his other impulse—to assume a more active public role, not as a usurper, but out of love and honor for John. His journal entry therefore moves toward a resolution of these conflicting impulses by demanding, if he submit himself to God's will, that God then use him:

> My life my life—why will ye linger? Are the years short and the months of no account? How often has long delay quenched my aspirations—Can God afford that I should forget him—Is he so indifferent to my career—Can heaven be postponed with no more ado—.
>
> Why were my ears given to hear those everlasting strains—which haunt my life—and yet to be prophaned much more by these perpetual dull sounds! . . .
>
> Why God did you include me in your great scheme? Will ye not make me a partner at last? (J1: 371–72)

Although Richard Lebeaux reads this passage as a Hamlet-like death wish,[2] it more clearly manifests Thoreau's sense of himself as a prophet: implicitly, Thoreau is asking for a covenant with God. John was taken from the world, and in spite of Henry's sympathetic illness, he has been made to live. He will submit himself entirely to God's will, but in return God must agree to *use* him for some great purpose. Thoreau is not asking why his life itself "lingers" but, having been chosen to live, why his "aspirations" and his "career" linger unfulfilled.

That Thoreau wished not for death but for a mission is made more explicit in a letter Thoreau wrote to Emerson on the same day, March 11, 1842. Emerson, too, was in mourning—his son Waldo had died on January 27—and Thoreau offered his transcendental consolation: "How plain that death is only the phenomenon of the individual or class. Nature does not recognize it, she finds her own again under new forms without loss. Yet death is beautiful when seen to be a law and not an accident." In terms that he would later use in the "Spring" chapter of *Walden* (and which Whitman would use in "Song of Myself"), Thoreau goes on to celebrate at length the organic law by which death is a source of life. Thoreau's most revealing remark, however, is the brief commentary he appends to his extended affirmation of natural law: "After I have imagined thus much will not the Gods feel under obligation to make me realize something as good" (Corr 64–65). Here, clearly, is Thoreau's sense of a covenant. He has submitted to God's will: he can accept and even celebrate death without guilt by transcending his mean egotism and assuming an identification with the universal "innocence" of nature. But having "imagined thus much"—having made the transcendental leap of faith required to reconcile himself to those laws of Nature—Thoreau demands the gods' acknowledgment in return; they are "under obligation" to make him "realize" his aspirations.

In a journal entry for March 19, Thoreau reasserts the link he had made in his letter to Emerson among his imagination, his continuing life, and his fate by regarding the stars in the sky as an objective correlative for his own condition. He cannot fathom their use any more than he can fathom that of his own apparently "low and grovelling" life, but his very ability to perceive the "equally useless" stars, and thus to identify with them, gives him the right to imagine that he, too, is "reserved for a high destiny": "My fate is in some sense linked with that of the stars—And if they are to persevere to a great end—shall I die who could conjecture it?" (J1: 382).[3] The imagination both contemplates and creates nature, and so contemplates and creates his own destiny. In "conjecturing" the analogy between the stars and himself, Thoreau expresses his personal ambition within the larger context of passive acceptance. He is awaiting not just a sign of *grace*—that sign came when he survived John and is implicit in his ability to imagine that he and the stars are "fellow-creatures"; he is awaiting, rather, a sign of *mission* and divinely appointed purpose.

Yet Thoreau's spiritual resistance to the world had resulted in his practical alienation from it. With the Concord school closed, his brother John dead, and Fuller as the unsympathetic editor of the *Dial*, Thoreau had virtually no outlet for his prophetic and missionary impulses, no contact with the community he now longed to serve. Up to a point, Thoreau could cultivate this isolation to confirm the integrity of his private vision. On March 24, 1842, he wrote in his journal: "Those authors are successful who do not *write down* to others, but make their own taste and judgment their audience. By some strange infatuation we forget that we do not approve what yet we recommend to others.—It is enough if I please myself with writing—I am then sure of an audience" (J1: 388). Yet Thoreau's journal entries following John's death more often suggest that he dreaded this solitude. Disfranchised as he was from the community, of what purpose was his vision? If Thoreau, as prophet, ascended the mountain for a heavenly vision (and Thoreau here assumes he writes from the heights, not willing to "write down" to others), there was nevertheless something terrifying in this isolation. It was, in fact, not enough to be his own sole auditor, and as long as that was the case he felt his life to be "low and grovelling." Thus, he could not remain complacent, and on the day following this expression of his aloof indifference to the public, he wrote, "I shall not be so cheap to myself if I see that another values me" (J1: 391). His sense of moral purpose and special destiny inevitably move him toward an ultimately more social stance. While the meditations of this period reveal an intensification of his inward vision, they also reveal a complementary intensification of his need to make that vision public. The next day, March 26, Thoreau wrote at length of this need for a public:

> I must confess I have felt mean enough when asked how I was to act on society—what errand I had to mankind—undoubtedly I did not feel mean without a reason—and yet my loitering is not without defence—

> I would fain communicate the wealth of my life to men—would really give them what is most precious in my gift. . . . I have no private good—unless it be my peculiar ability to serve the public—this is the only individual property. (J1: 393)

Thoreau emerges, then, from this period of grief and isolation with a significantly different attitude toward the world. Although for years he had been grappling in the pages of his journal with the difficulties of remaining aloof, untainted, and unrelated to the world and the public, this journal passage expresses his profound need to "communicate," to "give," to "serve the public." The extent to which Thoreau had revised his attitude is clearly suggested when we remember that, in September, 1841, he had compared himself to Apollo serving King Admetus and promised, "I shall hold the nobler part, at least, out of the service"; now, in a journal entry of March 30, he summarizes his revised position by asking himself, "If I could help infuse some life and heart into society—should I not do a service?" (J1: 397).

Under Fuller, the *Dial* provided only occasional opportunities for Thoreau to fulfill his "errand" to mankind; but at precisely this time, when Thoreau was most eager for public expression, Emerson took over the *Dial*'s editorship. In March 1842, Fuller wrote to Emerson that she could no longer continue in the job (MFL 3: 53–54), and by March 21 Emerson replied to her that he would assume the responsibility (EmL 3: 35). The very existence of the *Dial* was in jeopardy.[4] Emerson wrote to Frederick Henry Hedge on March 23, "Poor Dial! It has not pleased any mortal. No man cried, God save it!" (EmL 3: 36). And to his brother he wrote that the *Dial* was "at its lowest ebb and must greatly increase" or end entirely (EmL 3: 39). Nevertheless, once Emerson assumed the editorship, the *Dial*'s doors were open to Thoreau,[5] and Emerson renewed his efforts to find for him a "practicable" mode of expression.

Emerson was not slow to find such an opportunity.[6] On April 10, 1842, he wrote to Fuller that he had just received a series of "Scientific Surveys" commissioned by the state of Massachusetts,

> and this day I have, as I hope, set Henry Thoreau on the good track of giving an account of them in the Dial, explaining to him the felicity of the subject for him as it admits of the narrative of all his woodcraft boatcraft & fishcraft . . . as private secretary to the President of the Dial, his work and fame may go out into all lands, and, as happens to great Premiers, quite extinguish the titular master. (EmL 3: 47)

As Emerson makes clear, the "felicity of the subject" lay not only in Thoreau's particular affinity for the subject but also in the subject's potential to attract a popular audience. Current interest was high in the popularization of natural science, and Emerson himself had made the transition from Unitarian minister to lay preacher in 1833 by delivering a series of natural science lectures. As the editors of Emerson's early lectures point out, "It was more than coincidence that popular interest suggested the three alternatives to formal religion that he was most ready to explore: nature, the lives of great men, and literature."[7] By lecturing successfully on popular topics, Emerson cultivated and established his credibility with an expanded, secular audience. Only then, when he was in demand as a lecturer, did he begin explicitly to introduce his more abstract, transcendental ideas to the public. Apparently, Emerson felt that by asking Thoreau to review the state surveys he might help Thoreau serve a similarly effective apprenticeship with the public.

Thoreau took Emerson's suggestion, and his "Natural History of Massachusetts" was printed in the *Dial* for July 1842. Thoreau does not really review the state surveys; rather, as Emerson suggested, he uses them as the occasion for collecting his own journal observations on local natural history. Over the next several years Thoreau in fact proceeded, under Emerson's tutelage, to try his hand at each of Emerson's popular topics—nature, great men, and literature. Nature, of course, proved to be the subject for which he had a special genius, and the "Natural History of Massachusetts" therefore constitutes a significant step in his writing career. It is not only Thoreau's first nature essay; it is, more broadly, Thoreau's first attempt to adapt a popular literary form to his transcendentalist aims—an attempt to find a genuinely public mode of discourse through which he might reach a broad reading public and thereby "help infuse some life and heart into society."

Significantly, the opening paragraphs of the "Natural History of Massachusetts" establish a genial, almost intimate relationship with the reader. "Books of natural history make the most cheerful winter reading," Thoreau begins. "I read in Audubon with a thrill of delight, when the snow covers the ground, of the magnolia, and the Florida keys, and their warm sea-breezes . . . and owe an accession of health to these reminiscences of luxuriant nature" (W 5: 103). The setting, tone, and persona Thoreau adopts here—of the rather urbane, idle bachelor engaged in a pleasant winter reverie in his study—place the "Natural History" within the conventions of the familiar essay. Derived from Lamb and Hazlitt and popularized in America by Irving, the familiar essay dominated the periodical literature of England and America and established the reputations of such contemporaries of Thoreau's as Nathaniel P. Willis, Donald Mitchell ("Ik Marvel"), George William Curtis, and James Russell Lowell. Thoreau's style is informal, and the mood established by the opening winter reverie is comfortable, nostalgic, even sentimental. Initially, at least, Thoreau emphasizes the pleasures of the study as much as the pleasures of nature: it is *reading* and *reminiscing* that generate delight and establish the genial mood here. Nature, in turn, is presented as neither sublime nor transcendental here, but as picturesque, pleasing, consoling. Thoreau's persona is that of neither a prophet nor a woodsman, but a gentleman indulging his fancy.

Thoreau sustains the mood by inserting after the opening paragraph his poem "Within the Circuit of This Plodding Life." This is also a winter reverie, in which the speaker, "High in my chamber in the frosty nights," remembers "the shimmering noon of summer past" (103–4). In metaphysical terms, the setting of the poem is in what Thoreau calls the "verdure of my mind"—where, through a kind of metaphysical photosynthesis, the imagination converts natural facts into symbols and thereby nourishes itself. But the literal setting of this reverie reinforces the character of Thoreau's persona and the comfortable, nostalgic tone of the familiar essay.

While Thoreau is interested in using a familiar and accessible mode of discourse to engage his audience, his underlying message is still that of a transcendental prophet, however, not an idle gentleman of leisure; he aims at moral reform and thus cannot be truly complacent. He must insist, finally, on a superior insight that is neither bound nor influenced by social institutions. Thus Thoreau introduces, rather cautiously at first, an opposition between society and nature. Recalling the image of health in nature that he had introduced in his opening paragraph, he now develops the complementary image of a diseased society: "There is a singular health in these words, Labrador and East Maine," he writes, "which no desponding creed recognizes. . . . The merely political aspect of the land is never very cheering; men are degraded when considered as members of a political organization. On this side all lands present only symptoms of decay" (104).

By developing the complementary images of health and decay, nature and society, Thoreau raises his reflections to a higher level of seriousness and gives his essay an edge sharper than that of his opening paragraph. Sherman Paul has argued that this opposition between nature and society was the result of Thoreau's "darkened" views of society,[8] but it is worth recalling that just two weeks before Emerson commissioned this essay, Thoreau had written in his journal that his only "private good" was his "peculiar ability to serve the public." Nature is, indeed, initially established as the polar term for society in this essay, but the result is that Thoreau no longer needs to set *himself* up as the polar term. In his lecture "Society" and in "The Service," Thoreau had been forced, in effect, to propose as an alternative to the meaner aspects of society the militantly self-reliant individual—that is, himself. By substituting nature as the polar term, Thoreau avoids this kind of direct confrontation and its consequent alienation. Without really changing his underlying view of the mass of men, he can, in fact, align himself with his audience and propose that, together, they turn to the concrete facts of nature for inspiration. "In society you will not find health, but in nature," he writes, as he warms to his subject; "society is always diseased, and the best is the most so. There is no scent in it so wholesome as that of the pines, nor any fragrance so penetrating and restorative as the life-everlasting in high pastures" (105). Thoreau's criticism of society is a rhetorical counterpoint to his celebration of nature. He suggests, through a cluster of contrasting metaphors, that without the salutory influence of nature, man is always subject to despair, and that nature can provide the truest and most universal consolation: "The doctrines of despair, of spiritual or political tyranny or servitude, were never taught by such as shared the serenity of nature" (105). Thoreau's point is that health and joy are immediately accessible in nature, to all people, and they are therefore universal, in contrast to the partial—and paltry—consolations offered by the institutions of a civilization divorced from nature.

> We fancy that this din of religion, literature, and philosophy, which is heard in the pulpits, lyceums, and parlors, vibrates through the universe, and is as catholic a sound as the creaking of the earth's axle; but if a man sleep soundly, he will forget it all between sunset and dawn. It is the three-inch swing of a pendulum in a cupboard, which the great pulse of nature vibrates by and through each instant. (106)

To the "din" of civilized discourse Thoreau contrasts the "serene and retired spirit" required to contemplate nature, reminding us how "silent and unambitious" life is against this backdrop of universal harmony (107). Thus Thoreau develops two pairs of images contrasting the condition of civilization and nature—sickness versus health and noise versus silence—in order to disengage his readers gradually from their attachment to a social environment and draw them to the source of health and joy in nature itself. His comments on society contrast a partial and anthropocentric view of the world with the more profoundly satisfying and universal perspective provided by nature.

Thoreau is not rejecting civilization per se, however: the paragraph that begins by denouncing the "din" of civilization and elevating the private and serene life in nature moves rapidly into a portrayal of scientific study as heroic. "What an admirable training is science for the more active warfare of life! Indeed, the unchallenged bravery which these studies imply, is far more impressive than the trumpeted valor of the warrior" (106). The particular value of science is that it is the highest manifestation of reason—that which seems to set man apart from and superior to nature—and at the same time it is dedicated to nature, submissive to its authority. The scientist is a soldier whose victories do not alienate man from nature but reconcile them. "Science is always brave; for to know is to know good; doubt and danger quail before her eye. . . . But cowardice is unscientific; for there cannot be a science of ignorance. There may be a science of bravery, for that advances; but a retreat is rarely well conducted; if it is, then it is an orderly advance in the face of circumstances" (107). The language here is that of "The Service," but instead of the "brave" individual who resists the world, Thoreau celebrates scientific endeavor *for the sake of the world*, thus further aligning himself with the community and the idea of civilization as progress.

This paragraph concludes the essay's introductory section. Significantly, the essay has not, up to this point, left the familiar and reassuring sphere of the study. Even as he develops the contrast between nature's health and society's disease, Thoreau retains sight of his initial topic of cheerful winter reading—"I would keep some book of natural history always by me as a sort of elixir, the reading of which should restore the tone of the system" (105). Thus Thoreau's transition into the body of his essay—"But to draw a little nearer to our promised topics" (107)—carries a double meaning: not only does his essay turn toward the material covered in the state survey, but the narrator himself "draws a little nearer" to nature, leaving the study to observe it directly. Thoreau's language, too, now emphasizes active engagement—expansion, extension, exploration: "Entomology *extends* the limits of being in a new direction, so that *I walk in nature* with a sense of greater space and freedom. . . . *I explore*, too, with pleasure, the sources of the myriad sounds which crowd the summer noon" (107; emphasis mine).

Following the structure established by the state reports, Thoreau briefly but systematically takes up the insects, birds, quadrupeds, fishes, reptiles, amphibians, and vegetation of the state. Mere classification, however, is not the aim of either the familiar essayist or the transcendentalist; concrete details initiate speculation and reflection. The observation of the "shrill roll-call of the harvest fly," for example, functions as a springboard for his assertion that nature is our contact with the eternal and a source of historical unity: "There were ears for these sounds in Greece long ago, as Anacreon's ode will show"—and he goes on to quote that ode in his own translation. When he shifts to birds, he begins with the bald fact, drawn from the state surveys, that Massachusetts has about 280 species, but he then adds, by way of commentary, "Those which spend the winter with us have attained our warmest sympathy" (108). Both the subjective response and the wordplay are typical of the familiar essay, but they also reiterate his more transcendental concern with the relation between natural facts and the imagination.

As Thoreau characterizes familiar Massachusetts birds, introducing them according to their appearance in the seasonal cycle, they take on an emblematic quality, manifesting the universality of each particular experience: "At length the summer's eternity is ushered in by the cackle of the flicker" (111). But Thoreau is careful to keep his transcendental message embedded subtly in the concrete observations. He concludes his section on birds, for example, by writing, "These are the sights and sounds which reach our senses oftenest during the year. But sometimes one hears a quite new note, which has for background other Carolinas and Mexicos than the books describe, and learns that his ornithology has done him no service" (114). In his original journal entry, for March 4, 1840, Thoreau had written: "I learned to-day that my ornithology had done me no service—The birds I heard, which fortunately did not come within the scope of my science—sung as freshly as if it had been the first morning of creation, and had for background to their song an untrodden wilderness—stretching through many a Carolina and Mexico of the soul" (J1: 115).

The revisions Thoreau made here all suggest a new attentiveness to his audience and a shrewder assessment of their expectations and demands. In the journal passage, Thoreau makes it quite clear that he hears an ideal rather than an actual music, and that he is traveling in the regions of the soul. In the essay version, he is deliberately more ambiguous, and the empirical world is less easily dismissed. In both versions, Thoreau evokes images of unexplored territory, but whereas the original puts science and the soul at odds with each other, and clearly chooses the latter ("fortunately," he says, the bird songs "did not come within the scope of my science"), the revised version does not preclude the possibility that he is still referring to physical geography, to the actual world: "other Carolinas and Mexicos than the books describe" may be fruitfully explored by the scientist-hero as well as the romantic idealist.

By retaining his hold on the value of empirical data, Thoreau retains his hold on the world he shares with his readers. This attentiveness to his audience is evident in other revisions of journal passages incorporated into the essay as well.

One of Thoreau's most effective passages, for example, describes his trailing a fox across the snow, yet in revising the original journal entry he omitted those passages in which he presented himself as most wild and thus most at odds with his audience.[9] In the essay version, Thoreau not only focuses more fully on the fox than on himself, but the remarks introducing this section make the fox itself appear more familiar than in the journal entry: "Perhaps of all our untamed quadrupeds, the fox has obtained the widest and most familiar reputation, from the time of Pilpay and Aesop to the present day" (117). With this addition, Thoreau introduces his reader simultaneously to a wild animal and to the reader's own cultural traditions: the fox is an "untamed quadruped," but it has been domesticated by the imagination in shared cultural myths and legends. By pointing to Pilpay and Aesop, Thoreau reinforces one of the recurrent themes of his essay—that the value of nature lies in the imaginative experience of it, not in the mere cataloging of facts. The imagination's domestication of nature begins with individual experience, but Thoreau's rhetorical strategy here is to reverse the direction: Before recounting his own observations of a wild fox, he reminds his readers of their shared cultural perception of the animal as symbol or type—the virtually universal "reputation" of the fox.

Having established this common ground, Thoreau begins to penetrate back to the primary experience from which the "familiar reputation" is derived. First he establishes the immediacy of the experience for the reader

("His recent tracks still give variety to a winter's walk"), and then he narrates his personal encounter with the fox in nature: "I tread in the steps of the fox that has gone before me by some hours, or which perhaps I have started, with such a tiptoe of expectation as if I were on the trail of the Spirit itself which resides in the wood, and expected soon to catch it in its lair" (117). Thoreau sustains the sense of immediacy and keeps the reader engaged by alternating between first person singular and second person ("I am curious to know what has determined its graceful curvatures"; "sometimes you will see the trails of many together"), though the passage increasingly gives way to a detailed, objective third-person description of the fox itself. Thoreau's narrative role is that of a guide, consciously mediating between civilization and nature, between the public and the private.

From his detailed and absorbing description of trailing the fox, Thoreau turns abruptly to a consideration of fishes, and he again begins with a bald statement of facts—the number of genera and species cited in the state reports. The transition is awkward and reveals the ways in which the state reports both helped and interfered with the structure of Thoreau's composition, but by this point we have discerned Thoreau's method, and we are prepared for him to move from scientific fact to a more personal and imaginative response to nature, as when he proclaims, "I am the wiser in respect to all knowledges, and the better qualified for all fortunes, for knowing that there is a minnow in the brook. Methinks I have need even of his sympathy, and to be his fellow in a degree" (118). This movement from objective to subjective response, from taxonomy to claims of fellow feeling with the minnow, manifests the transcendentalists' epistemological valuation of Reason over Understanding, and Thoreau repeats this structural movement throughout the essay. But, again, a comparison of this essay passage with the journal entry from which it was derived reveals the care Thoreau took to temper his transcendental extravagance. From the original entry, Thoreau deleted the sentence "I fancy I am amphibious and swim in all the brooks and pools in the neighborhood, with the perch and bream, or doze under the pads of our river amid the winding aisles and corridors formed by their stems, with the stately pickerel" (J1: 109). Like the omitted passage in the description of his trailing the fox, this is a vivid, evocative sentence, which fully conveys Thoreau's imaginative engagement with nature; but, as with the other omitted passage, this one reveals a more extravagant, pantheistic author than Thoreau cares to expose. Instead, he resumes his controlling rhetorical stance by withdrawing from immediate experience of nature to that mediated by literature. He compares his own delights to those "as might have inspired the muse of Homer and Shakespeare" and then—by bringing us back to the narrative present—reminds the reader that he is, after all, still the gentleman of leisure in his study or parlor: "now, when I turn the pages and ponder the plates of the Angler's Souvenir" (119). Here, his enthusiasm for fish is neither mystical nor eccentric but is aligned with a genteel and familiar tradition.

Thoreau began his essay by establishing nature and society as polar terms, but now immersed in nature he deftly articulates their reconciliation:

> Next to nature, it seems as if man's actions were the most natural, they so gently accord with her. The small seines of flax stretched across the shallow and transparent parts of our river are no more intrusion than the cobwebs in the sun. I stay my boat in mid-current, and look down in the sunny water to see the civil meshes of his nets, and wonder how the blustering people of the town could have done this elvish work. The twine looks like a new river-weed, and is to the river as a beautiful memento of man's presence in nature, discovered as silently and delicately as a footprint in the sand. (119)

Water is, for Thoreau, the element of transcendence, and thus it is particularly appropriate as the medium in which to portray this reconciliation. Water, evaporating in the summer heat and freezing in the winter cold, is in its liquid state the mediating link between gas and solid in which polarities are dissolved; it is an emblem of the true unity underlying apparent multiplicity, and it symbolizes the reconciliation of air and land, spirit and matter, nature and society. As he had written in his journal in December 1840, "Water seems a middle element between earth and air. The most fluid in which man can float" (J1: 199). If Thoreau seems uneasy still with the "blustering people of the town," he nevertheless perceives a transformation, a harmony between man and nature, in the fluid water. Here, human culture is naturalized: fishing seines are not emblems of man's intrusion into and exploitation of nature; they are emblems of his participation in nature. Here the pastoral movement, begun in the opening lines of the essay, is fulfilled. The initial remarks disengage the reader from civilization, bringing him into contact with nature, and now the two are reconciled there. The "din" of man *out* of nature—of "religion, literature, and philosophy"—is implicitly contrasted with the "silently and delicately" discovered beauty of "man's presence *in* nature."

In the following paragraphs, Thoreau explicitly traces the metamorphosis of water as winter gives way to spring: "When the ice is covered with snow, I do not suspect the wealth under my feet," but with the spring thaw, "every icicle, which has tinkled on the meadow grass so long, trickles down its stem, and seeks its level unerringly with a million comrades. The steam curls up from every roof and fence" (119). Anticipating the "Spring" chapter of *Walden*, Thoreau describes the breaking up of the ice, celebrating the inundation of the landscape as the ice, "full of content and promise," is joyously released in the burgeoning, flowing water of ponds, streams, and rivers.

Thoreau's language, too, seems released here, and his expansive prose gives way to fanciful versification:

> The river swelleth more and more,
> Like some sweet influence stealing o'er
> The passive town; and for a while
> Each tussock makes a tiny isle,
> Where, on some friendly Ararat,
> Resteth the weary water-rat.
>
> (120)

Here the deluge is not an act of retribution but an annual baptism, immersing the town in water that dissolves the boundaries between man and nature—a phenomenon which Thoreau's poem goes on to celebrate with the comic exuberance of his painfully bad rhymes ("Our village shows a rural Venice, / Its broad lagoons where yonder fen is").

In this section of the essay we move from mere observers of nature to participants in it, and Thoreau goes on to instruct his reader in the art of spearfishing. Just as Thoreau's method in describing the flora and fauna of the state has been to begin with bald facts and then develop his imaginative engagement with the genus or species under consideration, so too Thoreau first treats the activity of spearfishing in its practical and material aspects, cataloging in considerable detail all the equipment needed; "and then," he adds, "with a fire crackling merrily at the prow, you may launch forth like a cucullo into the night." With this simile, we are also launched forth into the realm of the imagination. "And much speculation does this wandering star afford to the musing nightwalker," Thoreau explains, as he extravagantly compares the fisherman with his fire not only to a wandering star and nightwalker, but also to Charon crossing the Styx, to a jack-o'-lantern, to Prometheus ("light-bringer"), and to Diana ("or some sister-moon"). Here, on the silent water at night, his fire an emblem of his own imagination, the fisherman "enjoys the opportunity which so many have desired, for the roofs of a city are indeed raised, and he surveys the midnight economy of the fishes . . . —a scene not unlike what the human city would present" (122). Thoreau's earlier observations on the fishermen's seines had, in effect, naturalized civilization; here, the fish themselves are "civilized," and the blurring of distinctions between nature and society is complete.

Thoreau never entirely loses sight of the immediate, material object of this expedition, and so he provides detailed instructions on how to catch actual fish, too; "but," he adds, "these last accomplishments he will soon learn to dispense with, distinguishing the real object of his pursuit, and find compensation in the beauty and never-ending novelty of his position" (122–23). Thoreau would echo and develop this same view in "Higher Laws"

(*Walden* 212–13). In both cases he begins by addressing the utilitarian interests of his audience, grounding his transcendental vision of beauty firmly in practical and tangible commodity. The reader may follow him as far as he will: he can still go home with a string of fish, but Thoreau would have him aim higher. At midnight, the fisherman "may have to steer his way home through the dark by the north star, and he will feel himself some degrees nearer to it for having lost his way on the earth" (123; cf. *Walden* 171).

Following the structure of the state reports, but persisting with his own methodology of working from concrete observation to imaginative response, Thoreau goes on to take up briefly the reptiles and then the vegetation of the state. Throughout, he seeks evidence of the universal in the particular. In his consideration of vegetation, for example, Thoreau observes the strikingly similar forms of foliage and frost crystals, and he digresses into a rather lengthy speculation on the universality of the foliate structure—repeated in ice crystals, plants, coral, feathers, minerals—and discerns the operations of "but one law. . . . As if the material were indifferent, but the law one and invariable" (127).[10]

Only in the final pages of the essay does Thoreau turn to the books under review: "The works we have placed at the head of our chapter, with as much license as the preacher selects his texts, are such as imply more labor than enthusiasm" (129–30). This ironic glance at his method reveals his sense of his true relation to his material, for his "review" is as much a sermon as it is a familiar essay. But he has dropped the oracular and hortatory voice of his earlier "sermons" and is now entirely genial, not above making a slight joke at his own expense.

The scientific reports themselves "deal much in measurements and minute descriptions, not interesting to the general reader"—to whom Thoreau's essay is addressed—but they are of real value nevertheless. "Let us not underrate the value of a fact; it will one day flower in a truth" (130). This is Thoreau's message. It is, as well, his method in the essay: he begins always with some concrete fact or observation, and each one is made to "flower in a truth" as it evokes a response from the author's imagination. On the one hand, this is simply a vitalization of Emerson's formula that "Nature is the Symbol of Spirit." "The imagination," Emerson explained, "may be defined to be the use which the Reason makes of the material world" (CW 1: 31).[11] Yet Thoreau's advice not to underrate the value of a fact is double-edged and addresses both the materialist and the idealist. The materialist public underrated facts because they valued them only on the level of commodity, not realizing that they could "flower" into universal and eternal truths; but the transcendentalists had underrated the "facts" of the material world in their desire for an unmediated perception of those truths.

In *Nature* Emerson had explained that when the "animal eye" is stimulated by "the eye of Reason," "outlines and surfaces become transparent, and are no longer seen; causes and spirits are seen through them" (CW 1: 30). Clearly this defines the principles underlying Thoreau's essay as well; but too often the transcendentalists—including Thoreau up to this point—were concerned only with recording the "causes and spirits," which were necessarily rendered as abstractions; "outlines and surfaces" were invisible to the eye of Reason and so they were loath to record them. Thoreau discovered in the "Natural History," however, that by first recording the tangible and material world perceived by "the animal eye," he could come to terms with his audience: they met at the "fact." By beginning with the shared perception of the actual, Thoreau hoped to bring his readers to a shared perception of the ideal, of the universal truths borne by the particular facts. Emerson's *Nature* had been attacked by Francis Bowen in the *Christian Examiner* because, Bowen wrote, Emerson's philosophy "rejects the aid of observation, and will not trust to experiment. The Baconian mode of discovery is regarded as obsolete, induction is a slow and tedious process, and the results are uncertain and imperfect. General truths are to be attained without any previous examination of particulars, and by the aid of a higher power than the understanding."[12] Thoreau did not reject the aid of observation here, and he paid careful attention to particulars, but he concluded his essay—as if in belated response to Bowen—by reasserting the primacy of Reason over Understanding, shifting the emphasis from fact to truth, from knowledge to wisdom: "It is with science as with ethics—we cannot know truth by contrivance and method; the Baconian is as false as any other, and with all the helps of machinery and the arts, the most scientific will still be the healthiest and friendliest man, and possess a more perfect Indian wisdom" (131).

The "Natural History of Massachusetts," then, does not depart significantly from the Emersonian transcendentalism with which Thoreau began his writing career, but it does reflect a dramatic shift in his sense of the writer's role, and especially of his relation to his audience. The fact that this is Thoreau's first nature essay is ultimately less significant than the fact that this is the first essay in which the pose of reclusive seer gives way to that of the truly public writer, accommodating his audience in order to guide them to a clear perception of his theme. There is no need to sacrifice those readers who "cannot transpierce the imagery," because the images are rooted in the common ground of "fact."

In a "Preliminary Note" to the essay in the *Dial*, Emerson wrote that he had invited the author "to give us such comments as he had made on these books, and, better still, notes of his own conversation with nature in the woods and waters of this town," so that "Isaak Walton and White of Selborne might not want a successor, nor the fair meadows, to which we also have owed a home and the happiness of many years, their poet" (*Dial* 3.1: 19). Emerson's prefatory note thus reinforces Thoreau's own efforts to write in a popular mode by portraying him as writing in the genial tradition of Walton and White. Yet Thoreau scholars have tended to place misleading emphasis upon the antisocial comments in the "Natural History," presenting the essay as far more misanthropic than it actually is. Paul, for example, suggests that, in repudiating society and the "din" of civilization, Thoreau "repudiated Emerson, Alcott and the *Dial*," and he concludes that neither his transcendentalist friends nor "New England" could "accept the social renunciation of Thoreau's preference for nature."[13] In fact, however, Thoreau's essay disturbed neither his fellow transcendentalists nor the general reader; on the contrary, it won for Thoreau the kind of popular approval that had eluded him until now.

It is true that Emerson was not as pleased with the essay as he might have been, but this was not because of its critique of society. On July 19, 1842, Emerson wrote to Fuller—who had apparently expressed her by now familiar objections to Thoreau's work—"I am sorry that you, and the world after you, do not like my brave Henry any better. I do not like his piece very well, but I admire his perennial threatening attitude, just as we like to go under an overhanging precipice. It is wholly his natural relation and no assumption at all" (EmL 3: 75). Emerson actually seems to have been disappointed in the "Natural History" because it was not otherworldly enough for his "bible for The Young America." Emerson's favorite piece in the July number of the *Dial* was Charles King Newcomb's highly abstract and almost unintelligible piece of transcendental prose, "The Two Dolons." Newcomb's piece is an interesting contrast to Thoreau's, for it too is about the spiritual life in nature, but there is so little of the actual world in it that it immediately became, along with Alcott's "Orphic Sayings," a favorite example for the popular press of the absurd extravagances of transcendentalism. Yet these were just the qualities Emerson admired. In asking Newcomb to send his piece to the *Dial*, he wrote, "I shall prize it and every rich word of the Imagination spoken in solitude and long unintelligible except to hermits" (EmL 3: 55). After the July number was published, Emerson replied to Theodore Parker's objection to the excess of "*Dialese*" in some of the pieces, asserting that "the maddest piece in the number, odious as its license of composition is to me, is yet on some accounts to me the best and the most valued—I mean 'Dolon'" (EmL 3: 71). And in the same letter to Fuller in which he confessed he did not care for Thoreau's piece, he described Newcomb's as "native gold" (EmL 3: 75).[14]

Confronted with both the actual and the ideal, then, Emerson preferred the ideal. Yet Emerson would not have taken Thoreau's remarks on the "din" of civilized arts as a repudiation of himself or the *Dial*, since Emerson took much the same point of view. In his early lecture on "The Naturalist" (delivered May 7, 1834), Emerson said, "Whatever theology or philosophy we rest in, or labor after, the students of Nature have all agreed that in

Nature nothing is false or unsuccessful. . . . A willow or an apple is a perfect being; so is a bee or a thrush. The best poem or statue or picture is not." Further on in the same lecture, he warmed to his subject in much the same way Thoreau did: "We are the cossets of civilization, a refinement which consists very much in multiplying comforts and luxuries . . . and has the bad effect that crutches have of destroying the use of the limbs they are meant to aid. . . . In cities we are in danger of forgetting our relation to the planet and the system."[15] Both Emerson and Thoreau use images of disease to characterize civilization and images of health to characterize nature. For both Emerson and Thoreau the central theme is the same: the study of nature is man's only access to universal truth—all other means are partial and limited.

While Emerson and Fuller were not particularly impressed by the "Natural History," Alcott's response to Thoreau's essay was one of unqualified admiration. In a letter of August 2, 1842, he wrote, "Yesterday saw 'the Dial' . . . and read it with truest delight. That [torn] of Thoreau's is worthy of Isaac Walton himself, and the woods [torn] of Concord are classic now."[16] Thoreau's essay is, in fact, the only piece Alcott specifically singles out for praise in the letter.

Indeed, the "Natural History" was precisely the kind of essay that could attract the general reader, and especially the New Englander, whose natural environs Thoreau described so admirably and so admiringly. The naturalist played a prominent role in the fervent nationalism of the period. That the state of Massachusetts commissioned studies of indigenous flora and fauna attests to the link between nature and nation, and Thoreau clearly perceived his own essay—as did Emerson and Alcott—as contributing to the celebration of the American landscape. Emerson shrewdly compared Thoreau's essay to White's *Natural History of Selborne* because he recognized the eagerness with which readers would respond to someone who could do for the New England landscape what White had done for the English countryside. Emerson suggests in his introductory note that Thoreau will not only be a successor to White but, in effect, a competitor—the poet of *our* place, "the fair meadows, to which *we also* have owed a home and the happiness of many years (emphasis mine)." This undercurrent of literary nationalism is equally apparent in Alcott's delighted proclamation, and Thoreau himself places his observations in this context by alluding to the most popular naturalists of the American landscape, Audubon and Wilson.

Moreover, Thoreau's critique of society in the "Natural History" was in fact a conventional romantic view of man's relation to nature, which found expression not only in Emerson's lectures but throughout the popular press. If Thoreau's persona comes across as something of a misanthrope, it must be recognized that such a pose had characterized the personae of the most popular familiar essays and sketches of the day, from Irving's Geoffrey

Crayon to the narrators of Hawthorne's sketches: these retiring bachelors remain genial while assuming a romantic melancholy that looks back to Burton for its model (both Irving's *Sketchbook* and Thoreau's *Journal* open with epigraphs from Burton). A degree of misanthropy is indulged in temporarily for the sake of a disinterested view of humanity and for the deeper sentiments afforded by solitary contemplation. With its opening scene of "cheerful winter readings," Thoreau's essay (like virtually all the essays and sketches in this tradition) might have taken for its title that of Donald Mitchell's tremendously popular volume, *Reveries of a Bachelor*. Carl Bode has suggested that Mitchell's pseudonym "Ik Marvel" was probably a combination of Isaak Walton and Andrew Marvell[17]—a name that would equally suit Thoreau's persona here. Thoreau's persona in the "Natural History" assumes essentially the same attitude as the narrator of Hawthorne's 1838 sketch "Foot-Prints by the Sea-Shore," who begins by confessing his need for "sometimes stealing from the sultry sunshine of the world, to plunge into the cool bath of solitude. At intervals, and not infrequent ones, the forest and the ocean summon me . . . forth from the haunts of men."[18] While Thoreau's essay perhaps lacks the grace, urbanity, and unity of mood that characterize the sketches of Irving, Hawthorne, and others, we must nevertheless recognize that neither Thoreau's persona nor his view of man and nature would have startled a New England reader.

The extent to which Thoreau had in fact closed the gap between himself and the popular audience whom he wished to reach might also be illustrated through comparison of "Natural History" to a similar piece, entitled "Natural Science . . . Lessons of Town and Country," which had appeared in the popular *Knickerbocker Magazine* of New York in 1840.[19] Like Thoreau's essay, the *Knickerbocker* piece is nominally a review but might more accurately be described as a familiar essay written on the occasion of its author's reading recently published books[20]—in this case, White's *Natural History of Selborne* (originally published in 1789, but just reprinted by Carey and Lea in Philadelphia) and the "Reports of the Fishes, Reptiles and Birds of Massachusetts," commissioned by the Massachusetts legislature. The first point to be made, then, is that both the subject and the form of Thoreau's essay were clearly agreeable even within the pages of New York's most popular and most "urban" magazine—one that frequently condemned the transcendentalists and the *Dial*.

The writer of the *Knickerbocker* essay also uses nature and society as polar terms (though he does not repudiate one for the other); and like Thoreau, he praises the scientific study of nature for its ability to provide a more universal perspective, "to free [the mind] from unworthy prejudices; to bring it out of that state in which we are so apt to regard our world of thoughts as the universe; and the opinions we have espoused of the truth, as the only one worthy of the name. In other words, to dogmatize, whether in religion, literature, morals, or politics" (99). Thoreau's apparently antisocial and misanthropic remarks about "the din of religion, literature, and philosophy" thus do not transgress the boundaries of the popular romanticism of the day.

Furthermore, the writer of the *Knickerbocker* essay—like Thoreau in his concluding remarks—makes the distinction between "knowledge" and "wisdom" (Thoreau's "facts" and "truths"), suggesting that only the latter is valuable, for the former may easily degenerate into mere mechanical expediency. "For these reasons it is, that the country, in its freedom from a thousand noxious influences, is so favorable to becoming *wise*. There is an air in the cities, more pestilent than pent up vapors. It is the atmosphere of vice"—and this issuing from Broadway! Like Thoreau's comment on the fisherman "distinguishing the real object of his pursuit," this writer remarks, "Many a citizen, who goes to the country in search of green fields and a purer air, does not know that he wants spiritual things far more" (99). The spiritual use of nature, then, and the superiority of "wisdom" to "knowledge," must not be seen as the exclusive province of the transcendentalists. And while the *Knickerbocker* essay goes on to remind the reader of both the potential evils of the country (those coming "from leisure unimproved") and the positive influence of cities, there is nothing in Thoreau's essay that would have offended even the urban sensibilities of the *Knickerbocker*'s wide readership.

Thoreau's essay, then, while admittedly more strident and uncompromising in tone, was nevertheless generally consistent with the popular and pervasive romantic view of nature, issuing even from relatively conservative quarters. What most fully distinguished Thoreau's essay from Emerson's *Nature* (or Newcomb's "Dolon") in the popular mind—and so consequently exempted it from their contempt for transcendentalism—was his attention to "facts," to detailed observations of actual phenomena that alone justified moral abstractions upon nature. The distinction is made forcefully in an 1845 review essay on "The Poetry of Bryant" by the popular critic and essayist Henry T. Tuckerman. Tuckerman praises the poet for his love of nature and his precision, and adds:

> There is no mystical love in the tributes of his muse. All is clear, earnest and thoughtful. Indeed, the same difference that exists between true-hearted, natural affection, and the metaphysical love of the Platonists, may be traced between the manly and sincere lays of Bryant and the vague and artificial effusions of transcendental bards. The former realizes the definition of a poet which describes him as superior to the multitude only in degree, not in kind. He is the priest of a universal religion; and clothes in appropriate and harmonious language sentiments widely felt and cherished. He requires no interpreter. There is nothing eccentric in his vision.

His poetry thus grounded in common experience, Bryant is then given license to draw out moral truths from carefully observed facts, and Tuckerman suggests that this is his true genius: "Some elevating inference or cheering truth is elicited from every scene consecrated by his muse"; "he traces a natural phenomenon, or writes in melodious numbers, the history of some familiar scene, and then with almost prophetic emphasis, utters to the charmed ear a high lesson or sublime truth."[21]

That Thoreau's essay was regarded in essentially the same light, and thus exempted from censure as one of "the vague and artificial effusions of transcendental bards," is borne out by virtually every response the essay elicited from those outside the circle of transcendentalists. Nathaniel Hawthorne, who had just moved into the Old Manse in Concord, came to value Thoreau as a writer specifically on the basis of the "Natural History of Massachusetts." On September 1, 1842, Hawthorne recorded in his notebook a rather long sketch of Thoreau; he was particularly impressed by his familiarity with nature and praised the "Natural History" for being

> so true, minute, and literal in observation, yet giving the spirit as well as the letter of what he sees, even as a lake reflects its wooded banks, showing every leaf, yet giving the wild beauty of the whole scene,—then there are passages in this article of cloudy and dreamy metaphysics, partly affected, and partly the natural exhalations of his intellect;—and also passages where his thoughts seem to measure and attune themselves into spontaneous verse, as they rightfully may, since there is real poetry in him. There is a basis of good sense and moral truth, too, throughout the article, which is also a reflection of his character; for he is not unwise to think and feel, however imperfect in his own mode of action. On the whole, I find him a healthy and wholesome man to know.[22]

Hawthorne identifies precisely those aspects of the essay which made it accessible to the general reader, and which were largely missing in his earlier pieces: the minute and literal observations, and the "basis of good sense and moral truth." When, in October of 1842, Hawthorne was solicited by Epes Sargent for contributions to his new monthly magazine, Hawthorne generously recommended Thoreau as a potential contributor, again on the basis of the "Natural History." Hawthorne was fully aware of Thoreau's eccentric relation to society, describing him to Sargent as "withal a wild, irregular, Indian-like sort of fellow, who can find no occupation that suits him"; yet Hawthorne goes on to say:

> He writes; and sometimes—often, for ought I know—very very well indeed. He is somewhat tinctured with Transcendentalism; but I think him capable of becoming a very valuable contributor to your Magazine. In the Dial for July, there is an article on the Natural History of this part of the country, which will give you an idea of him as a genuine and exquisite observer of nature—a char-

> acter almost as rare as that of a true poet. A series of such articles would be a new feature in Magazine-literature, and perhaps a popular one; and, not improbably, he might give them a more popular tone than the one in the Dial. Would it not be worthwhile to try Mr. Thoreau's pen? . . . The man has stuff in him to make a reputation of; and I wish you might find it consistent with your interest to aid him in attaining that object. In common with the rest of the public, I shall look for character and individuality in the Magazine which you are to edit; and it seems to me that this Mr. Thoreau might do something towards marking it out from the ordinary catalogue of such publications.[23]

Hawthorne might well be considered too much of a recluse himself to provide an accurate index of the public's response to the essay, were it not for the striking similarity between his praise for Thoreau's virtues and Tuckerman's for Bryant's. Moreover, contemporary reviews of the *Dial* make it clear that Thoreau had indeed found a subject and a mode of discourse with a broad general appeal. The *New York Daily Tribune* (edited by Horace Greeley, a strong supporter of the transcendentalists and the *Dial*, and therefore perhaps the least objective of the reviewers) called the "Natural History" "excellent . . . written in the spirit of a poetic philosopher."[24] The *Boston Morning Post*, less sympathetic to the *Dial*, called Thoreau's essay "a very good article," while it blasted Newcomb's "Dolon" as a piece of "Transcendentalism run to seed" by "a mind diseased," and "worse than the Orphic Sayings."[25] And even the *Knickerbocker Magazine*, often harsh in its attacks on the *Dial*, conceded that the July issue as a whole was "an excellent number," and singled out the "Natural History" as "an admirable article. . . . The writer is evidently an enthusiastic lover of nature. All her sights and sounds are to him familiar things; and all her birds, quadrupeds, fishes, are with him objects of quiet, accurate study."[26]

While Sargent failed to act upon Hawthorne's recommendation of Thoreau, Hawthorne's perception of the potential popularity of essays like the "Natural History" was accurate and prophetic. By the end of the next decade, nature sketches would be standard fare in most of the popular magazines and were especially prominent in the *Atlantic Monthly*, which printed Thoreau's own late nature essays. As the genre grew, Thoreau's "Natural History" remained influential. As late as 1849, and as far away as England, the "Natural History" was cited by the English journal *Reasoner* as "a model of nature study."[27] Thomas Wentworth Higginson was an early admirer of Thoreau's nature writing, and his own very popular nature sketches (also published largely in the *Atlantic Monthly*) frequently acknowledge their debt to Thoreau. Higginson's "My Out-door Study," printed eighteen years after Thoreau's first nature essay, suggests its enduring influence: "Even the driest and barest book of Natural History is good and nutritious, so far as it goes, if it represents genuine acquaintance; one can find summer in January by poring over the Latin catalogues of Massachusetts plants and animals in Hitchcock's Report."[28]

Thus, while Emerson himself was not fully satisfied with the "Natural History," he had indeed set Thoreau on the "good track," as he had hoped. For Thoreau discovered that his careful observation of natural facts could serve as an acceptable means of conveying to a wider audience his essentially spiritual, transcendental vision. The significance in this is not only that Thoreau could express the transcendental view of nature—as Emerson had in his first great essay—but that attention to concrete facts and detailed observations allowed him to work on both a material and a spiritual level; the reader could appreciate his work in either way, or both. And by allowing a literal reading of his works—as he did not, for example, in "The Service"—he could begin to think about writing for a far broader audience than the *Dial*'s.

PART II

The Wider World

Chapter 3

"THE POET ACTIVE": WRITING BEYOND THE *DIAL*

As THE NEW editor of the *Dial*, Emerson began to call upon Thoreau regularly both as a contributor and as an assistant to the editor. Thoreau undoubtedly appreciated these opportunities to appear in print, but his involvement with the *Dial* was a mixed blessing: by responding to Emerson's various requests and to the conception of the *Dial* generally, Thoreau ultimately diverted his energies away from the kind of writing with which he had actually begun to bridge the gap between the transcendental visionary and the public.

Other than the "Natural History," Thoreau's contributions to the *Dial* during the first year of Emerson's editorship consisted of poetry, translations, and selections from ancient writers. Emerson had always been more favorably impressed by Thoreau's poetry than Fuller was, and now Emerson included eight of Thoreau's poems in the October 1842 *Dial*, many of them dating back to 1840 and 1841. Once printed, these verses received a fairly cordial response from sympathetic readers. Greeley's *Tribune*, for example, which regularly praised the *Dial*, reprinted "Rumors from an Aeolian Harp," calling it "one of the most favorable specimens" in the October number.[1] Even Fuller expressed tempered praise for Thoreau's poems in this number (MFL 3: 97). Nevertheless, Thoreau's prospects as a poet, even in the pages of the *Dial*, were limited. When Thoreau submitted more poems in November, Emerson confessed that, while they possessed a "rude strength," they were, after all, only "poetry of the second degree" (JMN 8: 257). Clearly, Thoreau aspired to something greater than this. Walter Harding suggests that it may have been around this time that Thoreau, discouraged, burned a great number of his poems.[2] In any case, the January 1843 *Dial* contained none of Thoreau's poetry, and the only other Thoreau poems subsequently printed in the *Dial* appeared in the number that Thoreau edited himself.

Thoreau's only contribution to the January 1843 number was a translation of *Prometheus Bound*, which he had begun in 1839 and which Emerson now commissioned him to complete for the *Dial*. It was a reasonably good piece of scholarship, and, rather surprisingly, Thoreau's translation was recalled six years later in two reviews of Henry William Herbert's 1849 verse translation of the work; but the *North American Review*'s comments reveal not only the limitations of Thoreau's translation, but also, and more significantly, the disadvantage he suffered in the eyes of conservative scholars simply by writing for the *Dial*:

> There has been one translation of the Prometheus Fettered published in this country before Mr. Herbert's. It was written for that whimsical and short-lived monthly [*sic*]—the Dial—by Mr. Henry Thoreau, a scholar of talent, but of such pertinacious oddity in literary matters, that his writings will never probably do him any justice. This translation was executed with ability, but not being in the poetical form, is scarcely subject to criticism as a work of art, and cannot be brought into fair comparison with Mr. Herbert's.[3]

For the same number of the *Dial* in which the translation appeared, Emerson also enlisted Thoreau to compile extracts from "The Laws of Menu" for the series of "Ethnical Scriptures" that Emerson began when he took over the journal. The translations of classics and of "Ethnical Scriptures" reflect a shared interest among the transcendentalists in ancient religion, mythology, and bardic language, but their inclusion also represents a policy of editorial caution on Emerson's part: they were seen as a reliable kind of filler for the *Dial*, which he could fall back on rather than print new pieces of questionable quality. Emerson had explained his strategy for putting the *Dial* back on its feet to Fuller in a letter of March 21, 1842: "My main resource is to adopt the expedient of Selection from old or foreign books almost with the liberality to which Alcott would carry it—certainly to make Synesius or Lucian or Chaucer speak whenever a dull article is offered and rejected" (EmL 3: 35; cf. 36–37). Thoreau's contributions were more than mere scholarly hackwork, for he had an abiding interest in the literature of classical Greece and of the Orient (especially the Hindu scriptures), but it is also true that Emerson found it expedient to draw upon Thoreau's interest and abilities as a translator and compiler rather than encourage him to develop as an original writer. Emerson's professional use of Thoreau as an editorial assistant, like his private use of Thoreau as a kind of day laborer, was well-meaning and in many ways generous, but such patronage ironically made Emerson a type of Admetus to Thoreau's Apollo.

Thoreau's contributions to the *Dial* were useful and serious exercises that appealed to his own tastes, but they did little to advance his literary career. Moreover, these contributions—and the *Dial*'s contents in general—had little real potential for expanding the journal's meager readership. Horace Greeley's *Tribune*, while dutifully puffing the *Dial* as "the very best Magazines [*sic*] in the country" in its review of this January 1843 number, also graphically pointed out the severe limitations of its audience appeal. The magazine, it said, "is fitted mainly for the perusal of scholar-like tastes and reflective habits, and for such it contains matter of interest and instruction." Of Thoreau's translation it noted, "Faithful adherence to the text is what is mainly attempted. The version is literal—and will attract and reward the interest of classical students."[4] In a letter to his wife Lidian of January 20, 1843, Emerson reported Henry Hedge's similar assessment, writing that Hedge "rejoices in [Thoreau's] *Prometheus*, and believes the Dial a valuable *book,* however it fare as a journal" (EmL 3: 129). Since the conservative intellectual community (the readers of the *North American Review* or the *Christian Examiner,* for example) shunned the unorthodoxy of the *Dial,* and the high tone of the *Dial* made it inaccessible or uninteresting to the general reader, the transcendentalists failed to engage the wider audience they desired.

The transcendentalists' dilemma was perhaps best expressed in Emerson's own contribution to the January 1843 *Dial,* "The Transcendentalist" (part 3 of his "Lectures on the Times"). Emerson concedes that "the two lives, of the understanding and of the soul, which we lead, really show very little relation to each other, never meet and measure each other: one prevails now, all buzz and din; and the other prevails then, all infinitude and paradise; and, with the progress of life, the two discover no greater disposition to reconcile themselves." Yet, Emerson continues, society should nevertheless tolerate and find a place for the transcendentalists—

> collectors of the heavenly spark with power to convey the electricity to others. Or, as the storm-tossed vessel at sea speaks the frigate or "line-packet" to learn its longitude, so it may not be without its advantage that we should now and then encounter rare and gifted men, to compare the points of our spiritual compass, and verify our bearings from superior chronometers . . . will you not tolerate one or two solitary voices in the land, speaking for the thoughts and principles not marketable or perishable? (*Dial* 3.2: 312–13)

Melville, in his novel *Pierre,* articulated this dilemma in strikingly similar terms through Plotinus Plinlimmon's "Horologicals and Chronometricals," but Melville's novel bitterly demonstrates that the world would refuse Emerson's plea for toleration. Thoreau recognized this as his own dilemma, as well—his central problem as a writer, with which he had been grappling since his first journal entries. But as Emerson realized, the inability to reach a broad audience was inherent in the transcendentalists' position, and not just a problem of individual talent.

While the transcendentalists did offend and repel orthodox religionists on strictly theological grounds, their real problem with the general public was not their theology but their language.[5] This is especially clear when we turn to the response of the contemporary press not strictly engaged in any of the theological controversies generated by transcendentalism. The *Knickerbocker*'s review of the first number of the *Dial,* which was particularly scornful of Emerson's and Fuller's opening pieces, said: "There are good *thoughts* in several of the 'Dial' papers, but they are smothered in 'words, words.' This school of literary euphuists cannot last: the imitative pupils, especially [the reviewer perhaps had Thoreau's "Persius" in mind here], are destined to a speedy dissolution."[6] The *Knickerbocker* held Alcott's "Orphic Sayings" in particular contempt. Rejoicing at their absence from the *Dial*'s second number, the *Knickerbocker* reviewer said of them, "The main impression of the reader was, that the writer had gone out of his wits, and that he had no great journey to go, to get past their confines."[7] The "Orphic Sayings" quickly became the object of jokes like this throughout the periodical press, and when more were printed in the January 1841 *Dial*, the *Knickerbocker* again blasted them, saying Alcott "seems to consider German *fog* a necessary appendage of profound thinking."[8]

This criticism extended to almost all the *Dial* writers. In an 1841 essay on Emerson in *Arcturus*, William A. Jones wrote of the transcendentalists, "The tone of the sect is at once mystical, aphoristic, oracular. . . . But their oracles are not always veracious. . . . It is easy to speak falsely in enigmas; it is almost impossible to lie in plain phrase. Much of this censure applies to Mr. Emerson, as the exponent and grand master of the school. He has less, however, of these defects than his friends and followers, writers in the 'Dial'."[9] Thus, in their efforts to find a language that would reveal the universal and ideal truths they perceived, the transcendentalists succeeded only in generating a mode of discourse so far removed from the vernacular that their revelations were regarded as an unreal fog rather than the "electricity" of the "heavenly spark."

Even Carlyle, so sympathetic to the thoughts in the *Dial* (and so often linked with it by critics of both its ideas and style), was made uncomfortable by its language. Virtually all of his letters to Emerson commenting on the *Dial* harp on this theme. Of the first number he complained: "For me it is *too* ethereal, speculative, theoretic . . . I will have all things condense themselves, take shape and body, if they are to have my sympathy. I have a *body* myself; in the brown leaf, sport of the autumn winds, I find what mocks all prophesyings."[10] Carlyle registered similar complaints against subsequent numbers of the *Dial*,[11] and when, in the summer of 1842, Emerson asked Carlyle to contribute a piece to the *Dial*, Carlyle hedged in his answer and wrote, "I love your *Dial*, and yet it is with a kind of shudder. You seem to me in danger of dividing yourselves from the Fact of this present universe."[12]

Thoreau had managed in one essay, at least, to escape the criticism and frustration over the abstract, oracular, and unintelligible language of the transcendentalists. The "Natural History of Massachusetts" satisfied to a large extent the demand for concreteness and thus provided Thoreau with a means of making his principles marketable without Emerson's special pleading on behalf of their "superior chronometers." Thus encouraged, by the end of 1842, Thoreau was in a frame of mind to go beyond the confines of the *Dial* and to charge the marketplace more aggressively. In January of 1843 (the same month his "Prometheus" and Emerson's "The Transcendentalist" appeared in the *Dial*), Thoreau's "A Walk to Wachusett" was printed in the *Boston Miscellany of Literature and Fashion*, and on February 8, 1843, Thoreau delivered his lecture "Sir Walter Raleigh" at the Concord Lyceum.

The publication of "A Walk to Wachusett" marks a significant development in Thoreau's professional career: it was his first endeavor within the popular genre of travel writing; it was the first time Thoreau wrote anything for publication outside the *Dial* (excepting his 1837 obituary notice); and it was the first time he submitted anything with the expectation of being paid for it. The content of "A Walk to Wachusett" shows Thoreau moving in a markedly different direction from his *Dial* contributions, but the context in which Thoreau's work appeared before the public must also be taken into account if we are to understand his career as a writer, so it is worth considering what sort of publication offered to print "A Walk to Wachusett." As its name suggests, the *Boston Miscellany of Literature and Fashion* was a far different sort of publication from the *Dial: A Magazine for Literature, Philosophy, and Religion*. Seeking a broad popular audience, the *Boston Miscellany* was modeled in part on the highly popular Philadelphia monthly magazines *Graham's* and *Godey's Lady's Book*, and, following them, it "was one magazine outside of Philadelphia which paid contributors well, or attempted to."[13] Liberal payments could attract the best, or most popular, writers of the day, but in order to finance this practice the magazine needed to be assured of a wide circulation; and this meant, at the very least, tempering the high-quality literary material with whatever could guarantee large sales.

The *Boston Miscellany* was established in 1842 by the publishers Bradbury and Soden, who wanted to expand their magazine market to Boston from New York.[14] It was first edited by Nathan Hale, Jr., and then, in 1843, by Henry T. Tuckerman. Numbering among its contributors James Russell Lowell, Nathaniel P. Willis, and Nathaniel Hawthorne, it was, throughout its short life, a significant outlet for the Boston literary circle of romantic writers. The magazine had genuine literary merit but its aim was popular, and variety was essential to the life of the magazine. Thus a great deal of attention was paid to giving it an attractive appearance, the tone was kept light, and each number included colored fashion plates. The situation of the magazine was later summarized by Edward Everett Hale, brother of the editor:

> If Mssrs. Bradbury and Soden had been questioned, they would have said, what was true, that there was no class of readers who could sustain creditably a purely literary magazine. . . . But they would have said that there were a great many factory-girls in the country for whom there was no journal of fashion. They would have said that these girls could be relied upon to float a literary magazine, if in each number there was a love-story which they would be glad to read. And I remember there was a great glee in the counting-room when it was announced that a thousand copies of the magazine had been sold in Lowell.[15]

Hale notes that both his brother and James Russell Lowell, uncomfortable with the inclusion of fashion plates, insisted on maintaining forty-six pages of literary material to two pages of fashion in each number. But the principle of "floating" a literary magazine seemed sound, and the magazine as a whole was clearly designed to attract a popular audience.

The growing importance of periodical publications in the first half of the nineteenth century cannot be overemphasized, and any writer seeking a commanding reputation needed to publish in them. In an 1844 essay in the *Democratic Review*, William A. Jones observed, "Periodical literature certainly flourishes in this country, if no other kind of writing may be said to be in vogue. . . . Articles have, in a measure, superseded books."[16] Margaret Fuller, in an 1846 essay on American literature, declared that "the most important part of our literature . . . lies in the journals, which . . . form at present the only efficient instrument for the general education of the people."[17] Furthermore, both Jones's and Fuller's essays express the generally recognized distinction between the types of periodical publications: quarterly reviews (such as the *North American Review* and the *Christian Examiner*), monthly magazines (such as the *Knickerbocker*, *Graham's*, *Godey's*, and the *Boston Miscellany*), and newspapers (both weeklies and dailies).

For Fuller, "the Magazines take the lowest rank. Their object is principally to cater for the amusement of vacant hours, and, as there is not a great deal of wit and light talent in this country, they do not even this to much advantage." "The Reviews are more able," she suggests, and while they are not comparable to those of Europe, "at least a vast amount of talent and culture is brought to bear upon all the departments of knowledge."[18] Jones, with a different bias, takes a more generous view: "Invention, wit, humor, fancy, imagination; tales, sketches, characters, criticism, poetry and politics, find their appropriate niches in a Magazine; while the Review admits only of essays and criticism, historical sketches and philosophical discussion. . . . Invariably a lighter character and vein is expected in Magazine writing, than in periodicals of greater pretension. Even its gravest disquisition should be eminently readable."[19] The magazine therefore had an especially powerful attraction for those with their eye on the marketplace. Edgar Allan Poe, hoping to establish a magazine of his own, had written to potential contributors in 1841:

> I need not call your attention to the signs of the times in respect to Magazine literature. You will admit the tendency in that direction. The brief, the terse, and the easily circulated will take the place of the diffuse, the ponderous, and the inaccessible. Even our Reviews are found too massive for the taste of the day—I do not mean for the taste of the merely uneducated, but also for that of the few.[20]

Given this pressure from the marketplace, critics were careful to insist upon certain standards. Jones recommends a middle road for the magazines: they must not contain too much humor, there must be no foppishness, and they should address topics of genuine substance. Distinguishing among the magazines themselves, Jones heartily condemns the ladies' magazines as filled with "inanity itself and the veriest nonsense," and he says that "the foolish notion of prefixing plates of the fashions, to a literary periodical where they are entirely out of place . . . tends to damn this class of publications still more effectually." In spite of this last stricture, he viewed the *Boston Miscellany* as having been "the most classic Magazine in New England."[21] Though the magazine was short-lived, it was, with its balance between quality and popularity, a favorite with the reviewers. The New York weekly *Brother Jonathan* described it as assuming "a character of more loftiness than many other magazines" and called it "decidedly one of the best monthlies in this country"; Greeley's *Tribune* similarly called it "one of the most elegant and excelent [*sic*] of the many similar publications of the day"; and the weekly *Boston Notion* described it as "destined to become the most valuable and popular of American Monthlies."[22] The fact that Thoreau sought and found publication in the *Boston Miscellany* suggests how far he had come from his earliest essays in adjusting his vision to the demands of the marketplace.

"A Walk to Wachusett" was just the thing for the *Boston Miscellany*, for with this essay Thoreau joined in the vogue for picturesque travel, through which the writers and painters of the day played a crucial role in making tourism—particularly to scenes of natural beauty—a major recreational activity for genteel and increasingly not-so-genteel Americans.[23] Thoreau's essay is an account of a walking trip Thoreau had made in July 1842 in the company of Margaret Fuller's younger brother Richard.[24] Among the mountains of the northeastern United States, Wachusett had nothing like the appeal of Mount Holyoke, on the Connecticut River, or the Catskills or the White Mountains—all of which had been the subject of innumerable paintings and literary sketches and drew thousands of tourists each year (including Thoreau, who had already visited the White Mountains with John in 1839, and who would explore the Catskills with Ellery Channing in 1844); but Mount Wachusett was a familiar sight on the landscape, and excursions to its summit were quite popular (Hawthorne climbed Wachusett in 1845, for example, accompanied by George William Curtis and George Bradford).[25]

While "A Walk to Wachusett" addresses some characteristically Thoreauvian themes, its subject, its tone, and the particular application of its themes even more obviously conform to conventions of picturesque travel narratives. Far more explicitly than in the "Natural History," Thoreau links his observations of the local landscape to the issue of literary nationalism, an issue that was virtually unavoidable in popular American travel literature. In composing the essay Thoreau did draw upon material from earlier journal entries, but the essay is not essentially a "mosaic" composition as were "The Service" and the "Natural History"; Thoreau composed "A Walk to Wachusett" by elaborating, commenting upon, and interpreting the rather straightforward factual account with which he began, and this, too, is consistent with the typical form of the picturesque or romantic travel sketch. There is a seriousness of purpose and vision that perhaps noticeably distinguishes Thoreau's essay from the typical example of the genre: the essay is governed by the thematic oppositions between east and west and between the plains and the mountains, which emerge naturally from his literal account, and the excursion is presented as a symbol of both our nation's westward migration and a pilgrimage to more celestial heights; the two motifs are merged so that the view from Wachusett provides not only a grand panorama of the landscape but a vision of a spiritualized national destiny. Yet even in this Thoreau is not so much departing from convention as he is exploring more explicitly than usual the issues implicit in those conventions. In his 1835 "Essay on American Scenery," the extraordinarily popular landscape painter Thomas Cole explained the appeal of mountain scenery by reminding his readers that "prophets of old retired into the solitudes of nature to wait the inspiration of heaven. It was on Mount Horeb that Elijah . . . heard the 'still, small voice'—that voice is YET heard among the mountains!"[26] And as John F. Sears has recently argued, American tourist attractions generally functioned as "sacred places": both the religious pilgrimage and the scenic tour "provide escape from . . . ordinary social relationships, hierarchies, and restraints. . . . They both promise spiritual renewal through contact with a transcendent reality (the shrine of the saint or the sublime waterfall). . . . In a pluralistic society [tourist attractions] provided points of mythic and national unity."[27] This is precisely what Thoreau had in mind in celebrating Wachusett.

Thoreau's epigraph—"The needles of the pine, / All to the west incline"—implies his theme of our westward national destiny, but in the opening paragraph, Thoreau concedes that the mountains on the western horizon sent his imagination back to the Old World:

> Summer and winter our eyes had rested on the dim outline of the mountains to which distance and indistinctness lent a grandeur not their own, so that they served equally to interpret all the allusions of poets and travellers; whether, with Homer, on a spring morning, we sat down on the many-peaked Olympus, or, with Virgil, and his compeers, roamed the Etrurian and Thessalian hills, or with Humboldt measured the more modern Andes and Teneriffe. (Wachusett 31; cf. W 5: 133)[28]

The mountains are alluring because informed by these rich associations, but Thoreau also recognizes that only "indistinctness" allows him to make such associations and find in them "a grandeur not their own." While Thoreau will continue to build upon their archetypal, exemplary status, particularly through classical allusions, he is also determined to discover their own, distinctive grandeur and so celebrate the American landscape.

Thoreau thus follows this opening sentence with a poem addressed to the mountain. Although the earliest version of this poem had been written in 1841, even before Thoreau made his excursion to Wachusett (several versions of it had been rejected by Fuller for the *Dial*), here it introduces each of the central themes Thoreau develops in his essay. The poem begins by associating the mountain with "frontier strength," that rugged self-reliance which Americans had adopted as their national character and which Thoreau had adopted as his own. The mountains appear on the horizon like "some vast fleet," the simile linking them with heroic discovery, and especially with the discovery of America and the western progress of civilization. Thoreau celebrates the mountains' "western leisure," and while he uses the imagery of "western trade" without irony, the "high emprise" of this "vast fleet" is spiritual, not commercial: he imagines these mountain ships sailing westward toward "a shore amid the skies," where "through your defiles windeth the way to heaven."

Thoreau's goal, then, is both a symbolic and an actual mountain, and before embarking on the narrative of the journey itself, Thoreau reminds his readers that "the landscape lies far and fair within, and the deepest thinker is the farthest travelled" (31). This introductory section is more insistently symbolic than is typical in the travel sketches of the day, certainly, but literary allusions and interjected verse were conventional in the accounts of picturesque travelers, who understood that the interest in their accounts consisted as much in the responses of their poetic sensibilities as in the faithful description of the places visited.[29] Moreover, even while Thoreau insists that true landscapes are interior ones, his excursion is not like *Rasselas*, to which he alludes; if he is part allegorist, he is also part practical tour guide. When he begins his account proper, Thoreau cheerfully records the particulars of their progress across the actual landscape—passing "rapidly through Acton and Stow" and resting on the banks of "a tributary of the Assabet, in the latter town"—and recording the names of the indigenous birds they heard along the way—"the red-eye, the thrushes, the phoebe, and the cuckoo" (31).

Even more explicitly than the "Natural History," "A Walk to Wachusett" enacts a withdrawal from the community into nature, where Thoreau achieves some greater insight into universal truths. In the portion of the essay that describes their journey through the region between Concord and Wachusett, however, Thoreau celebrates the human as well as the natural landscape in America, proclaiming both to be the worthy subject of a great national literature. As the travelers pass through a region of hops fields, for example, Thoreau suggests that this crop "supplies the want of the vine in American scenery, and reminds the traveller so often of Italy, and the South of France," providing an equally worthy emblem of the pastoral harmony between man and nature. It is with obvious pleasure that Thoreau comments on the communal activity of "the women and children, and the neighbors from far and near" who come together to work in the fields, and he suggests that "the culture of the hop, with the processes of picking, drying in the kiln, and packing for the market, as well as the uses to which it is applied, so analogous to the culture and uses of the grape, may afford a theme for future poets" (32; cf. W 5: 136–37). Throughout the essay Thoreau romanticizes the local landscape by treating it explicitly as comparable to that celebrated in the classic works of Western literature, and most particularly in Virgil's *Georgics*.

In suggesting these analogies, Thoreau is not merely creating an image of pastoral harmony between human society and nature, however; he is in fact engaging in what seems to have been the principal controversy over the value of the American landscape—its apparent lack of poetic *associations*. The vogue for picturesque landscapes was built largely on the aesthetics of associationalism propounded by Archibald Alison in *Essay on the Nature and Principles of Taste* (1790), and travelers were keenly aware of the American landscape's inferiority to Europe's on this score. In *Scenes in My Native Land* (1845), Lydia Sigourney quotes—in order to refute—an earlier traveler's succinct statement of the argument: "A fine landscape without associations, is like a fair woman without a heart. . . . This constitutes the charm of travelling in a classic clime. The mountains may not be richer, or the mountains more lofty, but every dell and stream are consecrated. Therefore a new country must be inferior to the old. Its loftiest associations lead but to the labors of the colonist, or his wars upon the wild beasts that were there before him."[30] In *Traits of American Life* (1835), Sarah J. Hale had similarly complained that the American landscape held greater rewards for the naturalist or philosopher than for the sentimental traveler:

> The barrenness, the vacancy, painfully felt by the traveller of taste and sentiment, arises from the want of intellectual and poetic associations with the scenery he beholds. Genius has not consecrated our mountains, making them high places from which the mind may see the horizon of thought widening and expanding around, over past ages,—they are nothing but huge piles of earth and rocks, covered with blighted firs and fern; the song has not named our streams—they are only celebrated for affording fine fish, good mill-seats or safe navigation. . . . We want writers who can throw enchantment around rural scenes and rural life.[31]

And Thomas Cole, in his 1835 "Essay on American Scenery," also grappled with "those who through ignorance or prejudice strive to maintain that

American scenery . . . being destitute of those vestiges of antiquity, whose associations so strongly affect the mind, . . . may not be compared with European scenery":

> We have many a spot as umbrageous as Vallombrosa, and as picturesque as the solitudes of Vaucluse; but Milton and Petrarch have not hallowed them by their footsteps and immortal verse. He who stands on Mount Albano and looks down on ancient Rome, has his mind peopled with the gigantic associations of the storied past; but he who stands on the mounds of the West, the most venerable remains of American antiquity, *may* experience the emotion of the sublime, but it is the sublimity of a shoreless ocean un-islanded by the recorded deeds of man.[32]

There were several possible responses to this apparent deficiency, and most writers who were inclined to champion the American landscape—including Thoreau—drew upon more than one of them. One could argue (as Cole, Hale, and Sigourney all do) that the American landscape *was* sufficiently rich in historical and legendary associations; American travel literature and landscape description regularly drew upon Indian legends, battles between colonists and Indians, and other dramatic episodes from the colonial and Revolutionary era, either in passing allusions or in extended anecdotal digressions. Thoreau made greatest use of this in *A Week on the Concord and Merrimack Rivers*, but he does so in "A Walk to Wachusett" as well, when, in his brief account of their return journey, he notes, "This, it will be remembered, was the scene of Mrs. Rowlandson's capture, and of other events in the Indian Wars" (Wachusett 36).

Or, as Thoreau does with the hops fields and throughout the essay, one could claim that associations between the American scene and Europe or the classical ages are legitimated by analogy rather than direct historical identification—the sensitive and educated observer naturally associated the scene before him or her with scenes stored in the imagination, and these enrich the perception even as they transcend time and place, and so render the American scene the equal of *any* it evokes. Fuller's observations of sugar making at Sault Sainte Marie in *Summer on the Lakes, in 1843*, for example, strikingly echo Thoreau's here: "Our huskings and hops-gatherings—the hops gathered where groups of men and girls are pulling down and filling baskets with gay festoons, present as graceful pictures as the Italian vintage."[33] More often, the genteel traveler evoked European scenery or the classics as a mere display of erudition or worldliness, and often with an at least implied condescension to American provinciality. American painters were more successful than writers, generally, in lending a classical aura to manifestly American rural scenes, and for Thoreau (like Fuller) as well, those associations allowed him to discover the universality of his experience: when the travelers rest on a hilltop and read Virgil as they gaze at Wachusett on the horizon, Thoreau reflects on the fact "that Virgil, away in Rome, two thousand years off, should have to unfold his meaning, the inspiration of Italian vales, to the pilgrim on the New England hills. This life so raw and modern, that so civil and ancient, and yet we read Virgil, mainly to be reminded of the identity of human nature in all ages" (Wachusett 32; cf. W 5: 138).

Perhaps the most satisfying possibility in terms of literary nationalism was to claim, as Cole also does, that "American associations are not so much of the past as of the present and the future."[34] Looking at the barren American landscape, the viewer could imagine the glorious future it held for civilization as it was tamed and settled in the westward progress. This vision alike informed Cole's picturesque landscapes and his friend Bryant's poem "The Prairies" and is central as well to "A Walk to Wachusett." A final response, and one that had gained increasing authority among painters and writers alike, was to substitute the aesthetics of the sublime for those of the picturesque and celebrate the very rawness and wildness of the landscape, transcending the domesticating influence of historical associations. This would later be Thoreau's strategy in "Ktaadn," but Wachusett did not provide Thoreau with a sublime wilderness, and this essay must be read in the context of the previously described responses to the landscape.

Attracted by the universality of experience, Thoreau nevertheless retains his command of the particulars and never abandons his role as a tour guide across the actual New England landscape. He keeps us apprised of his progress, and we can trace his route with considerable accuracy from Acton and Stow through hops country, then to Bolton and "the highlands overlooking the valley of Lancaster" by noon, where he not only reads Virgil but describes "the lay of the land hereabouts" in detail. By late afternoon they reach Sterling and the banks of the Stillwater, where they spend the night at a farmer's inn. The next day they follow the Stillwater four miles to the base of Wachusett, then climb to the summit where they pitch their tent and spend the night. He tells us the summit is "nineteen hundred feet above the village of Princeton, and three thousand above the level of the sea" (Wachusett 33), and he meticulously records all the flora and fauna observed on and around the summit. In the morning he describes the view and locates Wachusett for us in relation to the other mountains of New England and then briefly describes their descent at noon and their return through Stillwater and Sterling to Lancaster, Nashua, Stillriver Village, and Harvard, where they spent the night, again at a farmhouse. In the morning he and his companions part, Fuller going to Groton, Thoreau to Concord.

Yet each incident along the way is treated, in the typical fashion of the picturesque travel sketch, as the subject for some moral reflection; and while these perhaps sometimes come across as facile, sometimes as contradictory, there is generally a satisfying thematic consistency to Thoreau's reflections, governed primarily by the image of "westering," which is clearly related to, but also dissents from, the more conventional "future" associations of the American landscape. Even the west of Massachusetts evokes the frontier for Thoreau, and this "west" takes on strong moral overtones. Thus he relishes the "truer and wilder pronunciation" of a farmer they encounter: "It made us ashamed of our tame and civil pronunciation, and we looked upon him as born and bred farther west than we" (32; cf. W 5: 137). Of Stillwater, Thoreau says, "We fancied that there was already a certain western look about this place." He is prepared to be impressed by the fact that the business of western life seems too consuming to allow for the niceties of eastern hospitality—his landlord is busy with fieldwork and his landlady has the milking yet to do—and Thoreau appreciates his enforced self-reliance. "But I must confess," he adds, "it did somewhat disturb our pleasure, in this withdrawn spot, to have our own village newspaper handed us by our host, as if the greatest charm the country offered to the traveller was the facility of communication with the town. Let it recline on its own everlasting hills, and not be looking out from their summits for some petty Boston or New York in the horizon" (33). Thoreau's disappointment here might easily be dismissed as that of the genteel traveler whose rather foolish illusion of a western adventure has been violated by this reminder of his proximity to his native town, and who therefore peevishly chastises the town for taking away the "charm" of his fancied excursion. Certainly at the beginning of this passage Thoreau's language is that of the genteel traveler. Yet Thoreau's remarks have a more serious and visionary dimension. This introduces some awkwardness in Thoreau's tone, for he is invariably tempted to shift from the genial narrative mode to the hortatory, imperative mode of the prophet ("Let it recline on its own everlasting hills"); but this shift makes it clear that he is not merely a disappointed tourist: he is in earnest when he calls Boston and New York "petty" and criticizes this village for not fulfilling its role in the nation's westward destiny. That destiny, he suggests, is *not* to bring the materialism and urban decadence of some petty Boston or New York" into the west; rather, he proposes that as men move west, they should acquire the independence of "frontier strength" and become to some extent naturalized in the land to make America truly a New World.

Although Thoreau occasionally rises to the hortatory jeremiad, his vision is nevertheless consonant with the popular romanticism of the day, and "A Walk to Wachusett" is closely akin to the popular rural landscape paintings of the day: with cleared land, a cow or two, or some rural youth or maid in the foreground, and the unsettled wilderness and mountain scenery dominant in the background, these landscapes, like Thoreau's essay, explore the ways in which the wilderness informs an idealized, pastoral American character. In describing their early-morning departure from the Stillwater farmhouse where they spent the night, Thoreau deftly sketches a lovely—

and conventional—picturesque landscape: "[We] left the inn the next morning in the grey twilight, after it had been hallowed by the night air, and when only the innocent cows were stirring, with a kind of regret. It was only four miles to the base of the mountain, and the scenery was already more picturesque" (33).

As they approach the mountain, Thoreau's vision grows more "wild," and he increasingly disengages himself from the world below. As they travel upstream along the Stillwater River, Thoreau laments its rapid descent—literally and figuratively—into a "career of usefulness," preferring the more picturesque though nonutilitarian beauty of the mountain stream "breaking at the bottom of a deep ravine, filled with pines and rocks" (33; cf. W 5: 142). Though he had celebrated the picturesque hops harvesting, now their act of picking raspberries along the way implicitly contrasts with such commercialized cultivation and, integrating the literal and the symbolic, becomes a ritual of purification in preparation for their ascent of Wachusett, "thus propitiating the mountain gods, by a sacrifice of their own fruits. The gross products of the plains and valleys are for such as dwell therein; but surely the juices of this berry have relation to the thin air of the mountain tops" (33; cf. W 5: 142). Upon the summit of Wachusett, Thoreau intensifies this polarity between mountains and plains. The mountaintop, he says, is "infinitely removed from the plain . . . so withdrawn and solitary it seems" (34). As he and his companion watch the sunset from the mountain ridge, Thoreau declares, "It was a place where gods might wander, so solemn and solitary, and removed from all contagion with the plain" (34).

In spite of his apparent antagonism toward "the plain," it is not really wilderness solitude that Thoreau either seeks or finds on the mountain. Conscious, still, of the lack of historical or poetic associations with this scene, Thoreau and his companion read Virgil and Wordsworth on the summit, and Thoreau speculates hopefully, "Who knows but this hill may one day be a Helvellyn, or even a Parnassus, and the Muses haunt here, and other Homers frequent the neighboring plains?" (34). His own endeavor to commemorate this place in verse reiterates this prospective vision as it undercuts the polarity he had established between mountain and plain, between nature and man:

> Not unconcerned Wachusett rears his head
>   Above the field, so late from nature won,
> With patient brow reserved, as one who read
>   New annals in the history of man.
>
> (34)

The *American* poet must therefore *necessarily* be a prophet as well, and this withdrawal and ascent constitute the archetypal act of purification required of the prophet. As the sun sets, Thoreau and his companion watch all the land below them fall into shadows until, Thoreau observes, "the sun's rays fell on us two alone, of all New England men" (34). Here, it seems, is the sign of grace, of his special destiny, that Thoreau had longed for in his journal entries of spring 1842. Yet even as withdrawal and solitude seem to be necessary conditions for his prophetic vision, the vision of a special destiny is collective rather than personal. From their superior position, they discern a fire on Mount Monadnock, "which lighted up the whole western horizon, and by making us aware of a community of mountains, made our position seem less solitary" (34). In this "community of mountains," Thoreau symbolically images a nation of mountain-men, self-reliant, but equally graced and united by their high destiny.

Wachusett is illuminated by the moon and planets, and Thoreau reflects that "it was a satisfaction to know that they were our fellow-travellers still, as high and out of our reach, as our own destiny. Truly the stars were given for a consolation to man. We should not know but our life were fated to be always grovelling, but it is permitted to behold them, and surely they are deserving of a fair destiny" (34). We have already seen this passage, in the journal for March 19, 1842, but it has undergone a significant transformation when worked into public discourse. In the journal entry (written before Thoreau's excursion), the stars held out the promise of his own special destiny against his private doubts and fear of death. Here, the shift to first-person plural renders that special destiny communal, embracing the whole race. While Thoreau warns the villages that they may fail to fulfill their highest destiny, his vision nevertheless holds out the possibility and hope that the nation as a whole may discover that its fate is related to the stars.

Thoreau's private vision is both socialized and nationalized. In the morning, the sun, which had shone on them alone the previous evening, is now seen to "rise up out of the sea, and shine on Massachusetts." The sun's blessing is bestowed not only on the natural landscape but on the political state. The view, he concedes, had "little of the sublimity and grandeur which belong to mountain scenery"; rather, it is picturesque and so appropriately incorporates the human as well as the natural landscape. In the clear morning air they could see "how the earth . . . answered to the heavens in breadth, the white villages to the constellations in the sky" (35). Just as the individual's destiny corresponds to that of the stars, so the destiny of the "white villages"—the society of the plains—corresponds to that of the constellations. The panoramic view emphasizes the picturesqueness, not the contagion of the plains, as "on every side, the eye ranged over successive circles of towns, rising above one another, like the terraces of a vineyard, till they were lost in the horizon" (35). Thoreau also observes the topography of the natural landscape—especially the mountain ranges to the north and west—but as he discerns the valleys of the Merrimack and Connecticut Rivers, he reflects, "These rival vales, gradually extending their population and commerce along their respective streams, to what destiny who shall tell?" (35; cf. W 5: 147).

Thoreau naturalizes the westward migration of men by comparing it to the migration of birds, and he goes on to suggest the role the mountains will play in shaping our western destiny:

> A mountain chain determines many things for the statesman and philosopher. The improvements of civilization rather creep along its sides than cross its summit. How often is it a barrier to prejudice and fanaticism! In passing over these heights of land, through their thin atmosphere, the follies of the plain are refined and purified. As many species of plants do not scale their summits, so many species of folly do not cross the Alleghanies; it is only the hardy mountain plant that creeps quite over the ridge, and descends into the valley beyond. (35; cf. W 5: 148)

Only those spiritually pure pass over the mountain summits, and what he ironically refers to as the "improvements of civilization" are left behind. Thoreau does not reject the virtues of commerce entirely in this essay, but in suggesting that the mountains distill and purify the civilization which is to cross over to the new world of the west, Thoreau proclaims his higher, more spiritual vision of our national destiny. In later works (most fully in "Walking"), after Thoreau had grown disillusioned in the face of the "grovelling" character of Americans in their rush for California's gold and the imperialism of the Mexican War, he would voice his vision of "westering" in the terms of the jeremiad, accusing the nation of failing to fulfill its destiny, and calling for lamentation and repentance. Here, however, Thoreau is hopeful that the actual and the spiritual west might become one.

The mountain vision realized, the companions descend and, "having returned to the abodes of men, turned our faces to the east again" (35). Though he had insisted that the mountains refined "the follies of the plain," he is nevertheless struck once more by the picturesqueness of this landscape upon his return: "There is an unexpected refinement about this scenery; level prairies of great extent, interspersed with elms and hop-fields, and groves of trees, give it almost a classic appearance" (36). As Thoreau continues his journey eastward, however, his imaginative powers gradually fade, and he vividly describes the contraction of thought on the plains: "At length, as we plodded along the dusty roads, our thoughts became as dusty as they; all thought indeed stopped, thinking broke down, or proceeded only passively in a sort of rhythmical cadence of the confused material of thought" (36). This is the danger in descending from the heights.

In an effort to recover the mountain vision, Thoreau regards his excursion as a moral allegory and offers as "consolation to the most way-worn traveller"—that is, to his reader—the symbolic correspondence of the journey to life itself, "now climbing the hills, now descending into the vales. From the summits he beholds the heavens and the horizon, from the vales he looks up to the heights again" (36). The penultimate paragraph of the *Boston Miscellany* text returns to a straightforward narration of their night at Harvard and the companions' separation in the morning (including a tribute to the generosity and hospitality of the farmer and his wife with whom he had stayed), but in the final paragraph, the narrator again draws back from the literal excursion and, in the hortatory voice of a preacher, uses that excursion as the text of his sermon:

> And now that we have returned to the desert life of the plain, let us endeavor to impart a little of that mountain grandeur into it. We will remember within what walls we lie, and understand that this level life too has its summit, and why from the mountain top the deepest valleys have a tinge of blue; that there is elevation in every hour, as no part of the earth is so low that the heavens may not be seen from, and we have only to stand on the summit of our hour to command an uninterrupted horizon. (36)

While the modern reader is perhaps particularly sensitive to the artificiality of such facile moral tags, we should recognize that the literary conventions of the day countenanced, if they did not dictate, their inclusion (we can find analogous moral tags, for example, at the end of many of Hawthorne's sketches). The moral lessons themselves were so conventional that no reader would have taken offense; only the tone was perhaps not right for the picturesque excursion. When Thoreau later revised the essay for inclusion in *Excursions*, he reversed the order of the last two paragraphs, thus ending with the literal account of his return to Concord rather than with the moral allegory (W 5: 151–52). Such a shift seems to integrate the moral commentary somewhat more fully into the essay, but in either case "A Walk to Wachusett" reveals an author still experimenting with, and uncertain of his audience's responsiveness to, the relation between natural "facts" and spiritual "truths."

Nevertheless, the basic strategy of "A Walk to Wachusett," which he would improve upon in subsequent essays, allowed him to bring his transcendental themes before the general reading public more successfully than in any of his earlier compositions. Because "A Walk to Wachusett" is the account of an actual, leisurely walking tour, it is both a coherent narrative and an essay in which, as William A. Jones admonished, his "gravest disquisitions" were made "eminently readable." The narrative structure allowed Thoreau to speak with the familiar voice of the gentleman of leisure; he covers solid ground, passes through familiar towns, and shares with his readers his impressions of a popular local tourist spot. In this context, his moralizing and philosophical passages are brought into conformity with the popular romanticism of the day. Further, Thoreau's vision in "A Walk to Wachusett" is itself far more social and conciliatory than in his earlier pieces: by identifying his personal destiny with the nation's destiny, he renders his individualism less militant and antagonistic, more exemplary; he adopts a more generous view of society itself; and he addresses the popular issues of literary nationalism and the westward migration. In particular, his essay conforms to the most popular mode of travel and nature writing, in which the emphasis is on the viewer as well as the viewed, and the landscape is valued precisely as a source of moral and aesthetic associations.

All these factors helped Thoreau make the transition from the narrow confines of the *Dial* to the more popular magazines. Perhaps no essay of this kind was capable of creating a great stir with the public, but it could help establish a respectable reputation. Bradbury and Soden actively promoted the *Boston Miscellany* in the literary marketplace, and advertising notices of this January issue were printed in both Boston and New York papers (in which it was called "The Boston Miscellany and Lady's Monthly Magazine"). Boston's *Morning Post* carried the ad every day for the first three weeks of January, and though it listed only the better-known contributors by name, it did include "A Walk to Wachusetts" [*sic*] in its list of the contents.[35] *The New York Tribune* ran a similar ad for the January issue on December 19, 23, and 24, 1842; this notice did not identify any of the contributors, but it too listed "A Walk to Wachusett" as one of this issue's selections.[36] Although the *Morning Post*, which generally praised the *Boston Miscellany*, failed to review this issue, the *Tribune* did do so. The reviewer comments briefly on the pieces by better-known writers (not greatly impressed by any of them) and then says, "The magazine contains several other articles, of a good degree of literary merit, of which 'The Walk to Wachusett' is perhaps the best."[37]

Thoreau had been anxious to reach a broader public, and with the publication of "A Walk to Wachusett" he was apparently beginning to succeed. Unfortunately, the *Boston Miscellany* folded after the February 1843 number, and ironically Thoreau was never paid for the essay, though the fact that the *Boston Miscellany* was reportedly a well-paying magazine must have attracted him to it. The lack of payment was not due to Thoreau's indifference, certainly; he sought payment for over half a year and enlisted the help of several friends. On February 17, Lidian Emerson wrote to her husband (away on a lecture tour), "Did I tell you that Bradbury & Soden have refused to pay Henry more than two thirds of the money they promised for his 'Walk to W,' and that they postpone the payment even of that? Will it not do for you to call on your return through Boston and demand it for him?"[38] There is no record of Emerson's doing so at this time, but Elizabeth Peabody did intercede with Bradbury and Soden on Thoreau's behalf in February (Corr 93) and failed to get results. Four months later, Thoreau wrote to Emerson from Staten Island, "Bradbury told me, when I passed through Boston [in the first week of May 1843], that he was coming to New York the following Saturday, and would then settle with me, but he has not made his appearance yet. Will you, the next time you go to Boston, present that order for me which I left with you?" (Corr 112). On June 15, Emerson replied to Thoreau that he would be going to Boston the next day, where "I shall carry the order to the faithless booksellers" (Corr 118); but by July 7, Thoreau wrote to his mother, "I did not get my money in Boston and probably shall not at all" (Corr 121). When Emerson wrote to Thoreau on July 20, he explained the outcome of his efforts on Thoreau's behalf:

> I am sorry to say that when I called on Bradbury & Soden nearly a month ago, their partner in their absence informed me that they could not pay you at present any part of their debt on account of the B. Miscellany. After much talking, all the promise he could offer, was, "that within a year it would probably be paid," a probability which certainly looks very slender. The very worst thing he said was the proposition that you should take your payment in the form of B. Miscellanies! I shall not fail to refresh their memories at intervals. (Corr 126)

Hearing this, Thoreau gave up and replied to Emerson on August 7, 1843, "Pray don't think of Bradbury and Soden any more 'For good deed done through praiere / Is sold and bought too dear I wis / To herte that of great valor is'" (Corr 134).

Though Thoreau recognized the futility of further efforts and let the matter die, his correspondence makes it quite clear that he was not indifferent to payment and that he could reconcile his idealism with the implicit materialism of the professional author. The idea of being paid for their writing at all was a matter the transcendentalists needed to come to terms with—especially for those who had begun their careers as clergymen. But Emerson himself had set the precedent and had dealt with the question explicitly in a journal entry for March 3, 1836: "The philosopher, the priest, hesitates to receive money for his instructions,—the author for his works. Instead of this scruple let them make filthy lucre beautiful by its just expenditure" (JMN 5: 120). Fuller, in her essay "American Literature," would make this distinction: "No man of genius writes for money; but it is essential to the free use of his powers, that he should be able to disembarrass his life from care and perplexity," and she goes on to lament the impoverished and powerless position of the author in the American literary marketplace.[39] Thoreau too could come to terms with his professionalism and reconcile the apparent irony of benefiting from the commercialism against which he preached; but having come to terms with this, he still faced the problem of actually getting paid. Thoreau's difficulties with the *Boston Miscellany* turned out to be only the first of many he had with editors and publishers once he determined upon entering the marketplace, and his problems in the marketplace ultimately turned him even more sharply against it.

At this time, however, the twenty-six-year-old Thoreau was still full of the optimism, hope, and ambition he had felt since the spring of 1842, when he had written, "I have no private good, unless it be my peculiar ability to serve the public." He had been acting upon that idea since then, not only in the more social character of his writing, but in a variety of activities in the Concord community. In the summer of 1842 he had helped Emerson establish a public reading room, the Concord Athenaeum, in Concord's First Parish Church (among the papers and journals they donated were not only the *Dial* but the *Boston Miscellany*).[40] The most direct way of engaging the public, though—both to "serve" them and for professional advancement—was through the lyceum system. Thoreau had been involved with the Concord Lyceum for several years, actually, and in November of 1842 he was elected one of its directors. Accepting the office only reluctantly, he set up an admirable lecture series that included as speakers an impressive list of leading reformers and transcendentalists: Emerson, James Freeman Clarke, Horace Greeley, Wendell Phillips, Orestes Brownson, Charles Lane, Theodore Parker, and Thoreau himself. Thoreau had even managed to stay under the lyceum budget, spending exactly $100 and returning $9.21 to the lyceum treasury. He later confided with justifiable pride: "How much might be done for a town for $100: I myself have provided a select course of twenty-five lectures for a winter, together with room, fuel and lights, for that sum,—which was no inconsiderable benefit to every inhabitant."[41]

Thoreau's own lecture, delivered on February 8, 1843, was "Sir Walter Raleigh." Unlike some of the other speakers in the series, Thoreau steered clear of controversial social issues (Wendell Phillips lectured on slavery, for example, only after a motion to prevent him from doing so was defeated). Thoreau was an idealist and moral reformer, but his aim now was to further his career; he could not serve a society that refused to listen to him, and the "Raleigh" lecture, in both form and content, reveals how fully Thoreau had come to socialize his vision since his last lyceum lecture—his 1838 lecture, "Society." Whereas "Society" was an abstract moral essay in which Thoreau assumed the role of a secular preacher declaring, on his own authority, the proper relation between the individual and society, "Sir Walter Raleigh" was in the more conventional form of the Life of a Great Man—a form that significantly enabled Thoreau himself to assume the more modest role of scholar.

Thoreau's "Natural History" had been the first of several works in which he followed the example of Emerson's secular literary apprenticeship by addressing, in turn, the popular topics of natural history, biography, and literature; "Raleigh" represents the second of these stages, and it follows the model of Emerson's 1835 series of six lectures on Great Men ("a topic," the editors of Emerson's early lectures point out, "which was almost equally familiar [with natural science] to lyceum audiences").[42] Thus Emerson shared Thoreau's hopes for the success of the "Raleigh" lecture, and he wrote to Lidian on January 20, 1843, "Do not fail to tell me every particular concerning Henry's lecture when that comes—and the brightest star of winter shed its clear light on that night!" (EmL 3: 129). Thoreau himself seems to have been cautiously hopeful that the lecture might augur well for his career; three days after delivering it he wrote to Emerson: "I lectured this week. It was as bright a night as you could wish. I hope there were no stars thrown away on the occasion" (Corr 84). Their references to stars here were, on one level, quite literal and pragmatic: a lecturer hopes for a clear, bright night so that the townspeople would be encouraged to venture out to the lecture hall.[43] But both Emerson and Thoreau wryly imply that the stars may have a more profound influence upon the fate of his career—in the lecture itself Thoreau quotes Raleigh at length in defense of astrology, or "star learning": "Why should we rob the beautiful stars of their working powers? . . . those uncountable glorious bodies [were] set in the firmament . . . for instruments and organs of his divine Providence" (EEM 202–3).

The lecture seems in fact to have been at least moderately well received. Lidian Emerson was genuinely enthusiastic in her report to her husband:

> Henry[']s lecture pleased me much—and I have reason to believe others liked it. Henry tells me he is so happy as to have received Mr. [John S.] *Keyes*'s suffrage and the Concord paper has spoken well of it. I think you would have been a well pleased listener. I should like to hear it two or three times more. Henry ought to be known as a man who can give a Lecture. You must advertise him to the extent of your power. A few Lyceum fees would satisfy his moderate wants—to say nothing of the improvement and happiness it would give both him & his fellow creatures if he could utter what is "most within him"—and be heard.[44]

Thoreau was especially happy to have "Mr. Keyes's suffrage" because Keyes had led the opposition to Wendell Phillips's lecture on slavery. For Thoreau to have won Keyes's support, then, further attests to the wisdom in Thoreau's choice of lecture topics in terms of his ambitions for professional success. He would have agreed fully with Lidian on his need not only to "utter what is 'most within him,'" but also to "be heard." The *Concord Freeman*'s report was not as enthusiastic as Lidian Emerson's, but Thoreau's was, rather surprisingly, the sole lecture of the series to be noted in the paper (even though the reporter was able to provide only a second-hand account). "Mr. Thoreau's Lecture . . . is spoken of as a production very creditable to its author,"[45] the reporter notes; and while he goes on to take issue with Thoreau's choice of Raleigh as a heroic model, it is clear that, unlike "Society," the lecture was recognized and taken seriously as dealing with a conventional topic in an appropriate and "creditable" manner.

Perhaps encouraged by the public response to the lecture, Thoreau revised "Sir Walter Raleigh" shortly afterward into essay form and apparently submitted it to Emerson, but the *Dial* folded in 1844, before the essay could be printed. By that point, Thoreau realized that the literary biography was a genre not particularly well-suited to his purposes, and "Sir Walter Raleigh" was never published during his lifetime. The essay is, finally, not an especially impressive or memorable composition, but it is a very revealing production of this period in his career.[46] Perhaps even more significant than Thoreau's adoption of a conventional, "practicable" literary form (and thus underscoring the range of genres with which Thoreau was experimenting at this time) is the fact that "Raleigh" explicitly articulates a heroic model markedly different from that of such earlier works as "Society" and "The Service."

Several critics have noted that "Raleigh" is related thematically to "The Service": as Paul writes, "The martial fantasy of *The Service* . . . was now given the foundation of actual fact,"[47] and Raleigh is presented as the historical type of the abstract "spheral man." Thoreau's concern at this point in his career, however, was not with the individual's heroic resistance to society but with his heroic effort to integrate himself with and to serve society, and in this sense "Raleigh" differs significantly from "The Service." In that earlier essay, the world itself was the "enemy" of the "recruit" whose duty was to serve the cause of higher laws: "A man's life," he wrote, "should be a stately march to an unheard music, and when to his fellows it seems irregular and inharmonious, he will be stepping to a livelier measure, which only his nicer ear can detect" (RP 11). This is a familiar, recurring theme in Thoreau, of course, but in "Raleigh" the emphasis shifts to the man who, without abandoning or compromising his highest spiritual duty, can act in harmony with his fellow men. Thoreau says of Raleigh, "He speaks from England as his castle and his, as no other man's, is the voice of the state, for he does not assert the interests of an individual but of a commonwealth" (EEM 182). Raleigh is the hero who united, in action, self-fulfillment and public good.

This is far from recommending mere conformity, since the hero is the man who does not *follow* the interests of his society but *determines* its interests—"he especially possessed those prevalent and popular qualities which command the admiration of men" (178). But Thoreau does not count it a fault in him that he was not "a saint or a seer in his generation, but 'one of the gallantest worthies that ever England bred'" (178–79). Thoreau's theme of the self-reliant and militantly heroic life is still present, but here (as in "A Walk to Wachusett") he now identified the hero's individual destiny with the national destiny. Thus, he takes a special interest in Raleigh as an explorer of the New World and as "the man of the most general information and universal accomplishment of any in England" (195). On the other hand, his praise for Raleigh is not unqualified, and he writes, "We can least bear to consider Raleigh as a courtier" (183), because this is precisely when Raleigh seems to compromise his higher duty for a baser one. Thoreau again makes the individual's higher duty clear when he writes of Raleigh's imprisonment that "in writing the history of the world he was indeed at liberty; for he who contemplates truth and universal laws is free, whatever walls immure his body" (197). But it is significant that, even when imprisoned, Raleigh takes as his subject the history of *the world*—that his heroism is in his efforts to ally himself with his society and his culture.

This crucial shift in emphasis between "The Service" and "Sir Walter Raleigh" is reflected in the very different form and language of the two works. In "The Service" Thoreau was writing for "the gods," and he could therefore afford to lose those readers who could not "transpierce the imagery"; in "Sir Walter Raleigh," on the other hand, he was writing, and in fact speaking, directly to an audience of his fellow men and he had a keen interest in winning their approval.

The language of "Sir Walter Raleigh," therefore, is no longer abstract, poetic, and oracular, but distinctly concrete. We need only juxtapose the opening sentences of "The Service" and "Sir Walter Raleigh" to see the difference. "The Service" begins, "The brave man is the elder son of creation, who has stepped buoyantly into his inheritance, while the coward, who is the younger, waiteth patiently till he decease" (RP 3). "Sir Walter Raleigh" begins, "Perhaps no one in English history better represents the heroic character than Sir Walter Raleigh; for Sidney has got to be almost as shadowy as Arthur himself" (EEM 178). In both essays Thoreau focuses immediately on his theme of the representative brave or heroic man, but in the earlier essay the hero is an abstraction drawn from his private mythology. The language of "The Service" is highly figurative, epigrammatic, and oracular. Thoreau's voice is impersonal and detached, and he affects an intentionally archaic, scriptural diction. Thoreau's prophetic voice announces the hero who exists out of space and out of time. In "Raleigh" Thoreau chooses history over mythology; he finds Raleigh a more appropriate representative of the heroic character than Sidney precisely because he is more concrete and less subject to the vague and "shadowy" abstractions of Arthurian legend. As a lecturer, Thoreau does not assume the mantle of a prophet but speaks as a fellow citizen; his language is straightforward and literal, and the informality and implicit modesty of beginning the essay with the word "perhaps" contrasts sharply with the severe oracular pronouncement with which he begins "The Service." As in his nature and travel essays, Thoreau's lecture responds to contemporary criticism of the transcendentalists' writing by grounding his moral and philosophical observations firmly in the actual.

After rehearsing the facts of Raleigh's life for his auditors, and discussing the nature of his heroism, Thoreau devotes the latter part of the essay to a discussion of Raleigh's style as a writer. Many of his observations are taken from earlier journal entries that were only later linked specifically to Raleigh, but they express repeatedly the lessons he had been learning himself about the value of facts and concrete experience to convey a thought forcefully and effectively. "Raleigh might well be studied if only for the excellence of his style. . . . You have constantly the warrant of life & experience in what you read. . . . The sentences are verdurous and blooming as evergreen and flowers, because they are rooted in fact and experience, but our false and florid sentences have only the tints of flowers without their sap or roots" (211). Here Thoreau himself offers an admirable corrective to the "fog" and "literary euphuism" of which the critics complained in the transcendentalists, and it is this concreteness that would continue to set him apart from them, even while he would occasionally get lost in the same "fog" himself.

In an extended passage that actually has very little to do with Raleigh, but a great deal to do with Thoreau's own evolving sense of language and style, Thoreau argues that "the necessity of labor, and conversation with many men and things, to the scholar, is rarely well remembered" (212). Asserting more rigorously a theme he had learned from Emerson's "American Scholar," this nevertheless articulates an attitude far different from that which he expressed in his 1841 description of himself as "unfit for any practical purpose—I mean for the furtherance of the world's ends—as gossamer for ship-timber." Now he writes, "The scholar may be sure he writes the tougher truth for the calluses on his palms. They give firmness to the sentence" (212). While these comments speak to Raleigh only indirectly, Raleigh is nevertheless a fit representative of Thoreau's scholar-hero, for "as he was heroic with the sword, so was he with the pen" (197).

In celebrating "the steady and cheerful bravery of Raleigh" (217), Thoreau seems willing to sacrifice some of the purity of the transcendentalist's spiritual aloofness—the almost tragic inactivity that Emerson describes in "The Transcendentalist." Near the end of his "Raleigh" essay Thoreau explains, "For the hero too has his religion, though it is the very opposite to that of the ascetic. It demands not a narrower cell but a wider world. He is perhaps the very best man of the world; the poet active, the saint enterprising; not the most godlike, but the most manlike" (218). At an earlier date Thoreau had called for more godlike readers; he would do so again, as well, but here he calls for more manlike heroes and writers.

This essay articulates a crucial shift, then, in Thoreau's ideal and in his sense of his relation to the public. That it is not, finally, an especially interesting or successful essay may be attributed to several factors. First, Thoreau had difficulty extracting his heroic ideal from a historical figure without running into characteristics he did *not* want to valorize. I noted earlier the advantages Thoreau found in choosing history over mythology, but

Thoreau then found himself excepting or excusing too many parts of Raleigh's career: his life as a courtier, his revenge against Essex, the period of despair during his imprisonment when he contemplated suicide. Thus, while Thoreau began his essay by choosing Raleigh over Sidney as his exemplary hero because of Raleigh's greater historical concreteness, he ends his essay with what amounts to a retraction: "When we reconsider what we have said in the foregoing pages, we hesitate to apply any of their eulogy to the actual and historical Raleigh, or any of their condemnation to that ideal Raleigh which he suggests. . . . With all his heroism, he was not heroic enough" (216). Thoreau found Raleigh an only partially satisfactory model, for the biographical facts did not always conform to his ideal. Thus Thoreau was finally rather limited in what he wanted to say about Raleigh, and the essay is alternately redundant, or filled with long quotations from Raleigh's writing, or taken up with repeated apologies or excuses for Raleigh's less desirable traits.

Further, if "The Service" was too abstract and ethereal (the *Concord Freeman* would never have called *it* a "creditable" performance), "Raleigh" is perhaps too mundane and conventional. In his desire to appeal to popular tastes, Thoreau seems to have been almost too cautious, and the essay lacks the "heavenly spark" that Emerson spoke of and which makes "The Service," with all its faults, in some respects the more interesting essay. "The Service" lacks solid ground, but it also has moments of poetic flight that successfully convey the transcendental ecstasy. In expressing a private vision, "The Service" takes risks that might win Thoreau both scorn *and* the title of prophet. There was simply no place for such risks in "Sir Walter Raleigh," and while this made it a more acceptable conventional work, it ultimately failed to satisfy Thoreau's own highest ambitions.

Yet the abstract mythology of "The Service" was also unsatisfactory; Thoreau had learned, in part from Raleigh, the value of language "rooted in fact and experience." Neither biography nor moral abstractions met this requirement, and Thoreau eventually returned to the facts of his own life, imparting to them a mythic dimension. Thus it was "A Walk to Wachusett" and not "Sir Walter Raleigh" that pointed the way to Thoreau's great later works. Nevertheless, in both of these productions of early 1843 Thoreau demonstrates a socialization of his vision and a corresponding shift in his writing style to more familiar and more accessible modes of discourse. He was discovering—though not yet mastering—techniques by which he could convey his transcendentalism through familiar and popular literary genres.

Chapter 4

"NOW GOES OUR BRAVE YOUTH": THOREAU IN NEW YORK

"A WALK TO WACHUSETT" and the "Raleigh" lecture constituted Thoreau's initiation into the literary world outside of the *Dial*, but since Emerson had taken over as its editor, Thoreau had also become increasingly involved with the *Dial*'s production—an involvement that reached its peak when Emerson left Concord on a lecture tour from January to mid-March 1843, leaving the editing of the April number in Thoreau's hands. His own contributions to the April number were all of the sort not likely to find their way into print outside the *Dial*. Following Emerson's requests, and paralleling his work for the January number, Thoreau included a translation from the Greek and more extracts of "Ethnical Scriptures." This time his translations were of poems thought to be by Anacreon, for which he also wrote a brief introduction, and his extracts were taken from the sayings of Confucius. Perhaps taking advantage of his editorial freedom, Thoreau also included three of his poems ("To a Stray Fowl" and his two "Orphics," "Smoke" and "Haze") and a short essay entitled "Dark Ages."

"Dark Ages" is an abstract, transcendental meditation on history, drawn from his journal. Thoreau's theme, which informs so much of his work in one guise or another, is the transcendentalist's conception of the ahistorical nature of truth, which is always available to the individual intuition, as distinguished from mere historical facts, which, in themselves, have no interest: "the *past* cannot be *presented*; we cannot know what we are not. But one veil hangs over past, present, and future, and it is the province of the historian to find out not what was, but what is" (EEM 144). Like Thoreau's early compositions, "Dark Ages" is an abstract and aphoristic "mosaic," yet it is a strikingly succinct statement of the transcendentalist view of history. It was drawn from a collection of miscellaneous but loosely connected comments upon history and ancient literature put together after the spring of 1842 and many of which were transcribed from his earlier journal volumes.[1] After the last paragraph of the section used in "Dark Ages," and suggesting that it may in fact have been intended as part of a much larger and more ambitious project, the journal continues, "But enough on this subject; the reader will have learned by this time that we do not intend to be hampered by what is called the history of this people" (J1: 418). Thoreau had already drawn upon these entries for his introduction to and selection from "The Laws of Menu" in the January *Dial*, and he had also extracted from among the "Dark Ages" entries a paragraph on the "dark ages" of New England that he included in "A Walk to Wachusett." While no larger project on ancient literature was ever completed, much of this journal material, including "Dark Ages," was later incorporated into A *Week*.

Thoreau's contributions to the April *Dial* drew a mixed response in the *New York Tribune*'s review. The reviewer did not consider any of the *Dial*'s poetry "surpassing" but singled out Thoreau's poem "Haze" as being among the best in the number. Commenting on his translations, the reviewer reiterated more emphatically the criticism lodged against the *Prometheus Bound* in the previous number: "Mr. Thoreau contributes some translations from Anacreon, which would be excellent but for the attempt to render them literal—an attempt which destroys their value for the general reader and renders them interesting to scholars only."[2] The reviewer looked with greater favor upon Thoreau's introduction to the translations because of its more popular appeal, and he quotes a passage from this. Indeed, Thoreau's introduction strikes just the right magazine tone. He presents his translations as the product of a perhaps accidental but pleasant encounter with remembered poets: "We lately met with an old volume from a London bookshop, containing the Greek Minor poets, and it was a pleasure to read once more only the words—Orpheus,—Linus,—Musaeus, —those faint poetic sounds and echoes of a name, dying away on the ear of us modern men" (*Dial* 3.4: 484). In truth, some of Thoreau's translations date from 1838, and it was no chance encounter but Emerson's urging that turned Thoreau back to the Greek minor poets.[3] Thoreau did not fabricate the occasion exactly, but he capitalized on its most romantic possibilities and so leaves the reader to infer (erroneously, of course) that he had been browsing in the London bookshop himself when he came across this volume with such pleasing associations (he had, in fact, borrowed the book from Alcott's English friend Charles Lane). Thoreau's persona wears his scholarship lightly, and in creating the mood of nostalgic reverie he again recalls Irving's Geoffrey Crayon. He goes on to celebrate the pleasures of the study as the refuge of the sensitive spirit, where he can indulge his imagination free from the hustle and bustle of the modern world: "We know of no studies so composing as those of the classical scholar. When we have sat down to them, life seems as still and serene as if it were very far off. . . . Distracting cares will not be allowed to obstruct the field of his vision." The odes of Anacreon are similarly recommended for their refinement and delicacy, "like gems of pure ivory. . . . They charm us by their serenity and freedom from exaggeration and passion, and by a certain flower-like beauty" (485). Thoreau had earlier included his translations of two Anacreon odes in the "Natural History," but here he presents the poet in the context of a popular romanticism that had even greater potential appeal for the magazine audience of the day.

In general, however, both Thoreau's contributions and the April number as a whole conformed to the *Dial*'s established design and tone. The issue was, after all, shaped largely by Emerson in spite of his absence, and Thoreau would not have introduced significant changes even if he had been given an entirely free hand. The *New York Tribune*'s review praised the *Dial*, as always, while issuing another plea for public support of the journal, which was by now in grave trouble. Failing to engage the general reader, the transcendentalists characteristically, and futilely, relied on special pleading on their behalf—whether Emerson's or the *Tribune*'s. Typical of such gestures was Charles Lane's contribution to this April *Dial*, a long review essay on Alcott's works in which Lane attempts to "translate" the often unintelligible words of the "prophet" Alcott: "It is the true critic's endeavor to bridge the waters which separate the prophet from the people, to compass the distance which divides the *understanding* in the auditor from the *intuition* in the utterer. The inspired oracle never indulges in a vain expression" (*Dial* 3.4: 417). Yet such special pleading on behalf of the transcendentalists failed to overcome the most obvious objection to these "prophets." As Henry James, Sr., complained to Emerson about Lane's essay, "What divine sanction have we to go forth to the great race and proclaim *him a prophet*? . . . Let his words prove him so—which is the convincing way. . . . The truth must reach them at some time, by some truer Jeremiah—why should he send his attendants forth when his voice failed to arrest the people, to sound the praises of that voice?"[4]

Indeed, the public was not responding to the *Dial*, and Elizabeth Peabody (who had taken over publication from the bankrupt Weeks & Jordan) informed Emerson that the journal was no longer paying expenses and that the subscription list was lower than ever, around 220 (EmL 3: 154, 157, 165). Although he was highly pleased with Thoreau's editing, Emerson contemplated making the April number the final one (EmL 3: 148–49, 151, 154, 157). Though he resolved to continue the *Dial*, Emerson saw the need to conform to the practices of the marketplace; on April 20, he wrote to Fuller that he would try to assure "its publication on the first day of each quarter, which seems so important to booksellers. & I will try what can be done for more efficient publishing." Yet he was also reluctant to capitulate to the marketplace and added, "We are not magazine makers, but wish to represent &, by representing, further the best culture of New England. If possible, if possible, the Dial could look beautiful to you, my friend, & to me, I could well forgive its slender popularity" (EmL 3: 166).

The fact that the *Dial* could still please its own small group of contributors and sympathizers was a temporary consolation at best, and one that could not be sustained long. In March, Emerson informed Fuller that Lane and Alcott were anxious for the *Dial* to continue, "But Elizabeth Hoar is sure that its principal contributors will work just as well, & with some present reward, *out* of the Dial" (EmL 3: 159–60). Hoar's suggestion was already in the minds of several of the *Dial*'s principal contributors, who were beginning to seek other outlets. Fuller was about to embark on a western journey that would result in her book *Summer on the Lakes*, and by 1844 she would be in New York working for Greeley's *Tribune*. Emerson was seeking a publisher for a volume of Ellery Channing's verses and was also in the process of arranging for the inclusion of some of Channing's poems, as well as a piece of his own, in the Philadelphia annual *The Gift* for 1844.[5]

Thoreau had extolled the "poet active" as hero in his "Raleigh" lecture, and now he was himself anxious to seek a wider world of activity. While he remained loyal to the *Dial*, he realized that it could neither support him financially nor serve as an adequate vehicle for his broader literary ambitions. These ambitions had already brought him to the *Boston Miscellany* and before the lyceum audiences again; now it led him to seek opportunities further afield. In January, Hawthorne had invited him to tea with John L. O'Sullivan, who was visiting from New York where he edited the *Democratic Review*. Of this initial meeting, Thoreau reported to Emerson that although O'Sullivan "did not strike me," he nevertheless "made a point of asking me to write for his Review, which I shall be glad to do" (Corr 77).

Because Thoreau shared Emerson's belief that the idealist reformer should remain above narrowly partisan political views, he was rather suspicious of O'Sullivan, even though the *Democratic Review* was generally sympathetic toward the transcendentalists. When Emerson met with O'Sullivan in New York (a week after Thoreau's meeting at Hawthorne's), Emerson reported to Fuller: "Today I dined with Mr. O'Sullivan . . . but the man is politico-literary and has too close an eye to immediate objects. *Washington* is supposed in every line of the 'Demo. Review' " (EmL 3: 146–47). Both Thoreau and Emerson would eventually make use of O'Sullivan's services, however, and Thoreau began to think more and more of New York as his wider world.

On March 1, while he was in the midst of editing the April *Dial*, Thoreau wrote to Emerson in New York that he was "meditating some other method of paying debts than by lectures and writing which will only do to talk about—If anything of that 'other' sort should come to your ears in New York will you remember it for me?" (Corr 89).[6] Recognizing the prospects for his younger disciple in New York, Emerson wasted little time following up Thoreau's suggestion. Emerson's brother William proposed that Thoreau come to his house in Staten Island to act as tutor for his young son Willie. By March the terms of the arrangement were being worked out: Thoreau was to have board and lodging, with his own room, plus one hundred dollars per year. Since Thoreau's interests were largely financial, Emerson also inquired about additional work for him—perhaps clerical work in William's offices—but this would be only temporary, "pending the time when he shall procure for himself literary labor from some quarter in New York." Thoreau was anxious to embark and proposed that he could begin April 1. Everyone seemed pleased with the arrangement, and Emerson added "Lidian and Elizabeth [Hoar] are charmed with the project, & think it auspicious on both sides only Lidian cannot spare Henry" (EmL 3: 158–59).

Thoreau did not actually leave for Staten Island until the first week in May (delayed most likely by ill health, which had plagued him sporadically for some time), and during the interval his anxiety about the move no doubt increased. The very fact that everyone regarded it as a professional opportunity to be seized must have heightened his fear of failure. Emerson had written in his journal in March, "Young men, like H.T. owe us a new world & they have not acquitted the debt" (JMN 8: 375). Now, on the eve of Thoreau's departure, he wrote to his brother, "And now goes our brave youth into the new house, the new connexion, the new City. I am sure no truer & purer person lives in wide New York; and he is a bold and profound thinker though he may easily chance to pester you with some accidental crotchets and perhaps a village exaggeration of the value of facts" (EmL 3: 158–59). Emerson sent Thoreau to New York, in effect, as an emissary of Concord transcendentalism, and his comments suggest both his high hopes and his reservations about Thoreau's adequacy to the task.

When Thoreau called on Hawthorne to announce his intended move, Hawthorne recorded in his journal,

> I am glad, on Mr. Thoreau's own account, that he is going away; as he is physically out of health, and, morally and intellectually, seems not to have found exactly the guiding clue; and in all these respects, he may be benefitted by his removal;—also, it is one step toward a circumstantial position in the world. On my account, I should like to have him remain here, he being one of the few persons, I think, with whom to hold intercourse is like hearing the wind among the boughs of a forest-tree; and with all his wild freedom, there is high and classic cultivation in him too.[7]

One more close friend, Elizabeth Hoar, gave Thoreau a pen and inkstand as a parting memento, writing that she hoped they "may be made sometimes the interpreter of friendly thoughts to those whom you leave beyond the reach of your voice,—or record the inspirations of Nature, who, I doubt not, will be faithful to you who trust her in the sea-girt Staten Island as in Concord woods and meadows" (Corr 98).

This generosity of his friends had a double edge. On their own accounts, they would have liked him to stay—Emerson undoubtedly valued his assistance both with the *Dial* and in his household, Lidian and Elizabeth Hoar would feel his absence, Hawthorne enjoyed his company—but for his own sake they urged him to go. Thoreau had initiated the move himself, recognized his opportunity, and no doubt hoped for success; but now it was becoming a less private matter, and though his friends wished for success for his sake, he would come to feel that he needed to succeed for *their* sakes as well. All these pressures—his own ambition as a writer, his desire to serve the public as the "poet active," his sense of responsibility to his family, friends, and mentor and his simultaneous desire to establish his independence from them—made his move to New York a critical test for Thoreau, and the strain was apparent throughout his stay there. When the venture resulted in failure, it became a momentous failure and modified his entire professional career: Thoreau would never again leave the environs of Concord for anything other than brief excursions, and though he placed later pieces in magazines of the urban centers, he never again attempted to do his work in the cities.

Thoreau did not resign himself easily to defeat, but his situation proved to be less than ideal and his opportunities limited. Transportation from Staten Island to New York City was too difficult for frequent trips—especially when he was in need of money (he was already in debt to R. W. Emerson for his traveling expenses); his relation with the William Emersons was stiffly cordial at best, and he was not especially attracted to the boy Willie (Corr 112, 114); he suffered from a cold and then from chronic drowsiness while in Staten Island; and he was basically too much a countryman and a transcendentalist to think well of the city. Nevertheless, all these disappointments might have been overlooked had his real test, in the literary marketplace, proven successful. More than at any other point in his career, Thoreau actively sought to enter the literary marketplace directly and put himself at its disposal, but ultimately they could not accommodate each other.

The city disappointed and even offended Thoreau at times, but he approached it as a writer, alert to the life around him and eager to turn it to his account. Thoreau's first letter home, describing his arrival in Staten Island, includes an amusing and insightful sketch of the cabmen hustling for fares written almost as if he intended to work it into a sketch for the magazines. In this and subsequent letters, Thoreau described his fascination with the people (even when, at times, he despised them), with the imposing aspects of commerce (when seen from a distance), and his ultimate dislike of the city, especially its rigid, institutional aspects, which seemed to him devoid of life. Typical of his letters is that which he wrote to his sister Helen on July 21: "I am well enough situated here to observe one aspect of the modern world at least—I mean the migratory—the western movement. Sixteen hundred immigrants arrived at quarantine grounds on the fourth of July, and more or less every day since I have been here" (Corr 142). The immigrants fascinated Thoreau because they were the new pioneers. New York itself was the gateway to the western adventure he had celebrated in "A Walk to Wachusett," though Thoreau felt New York might be corrupting that adventure from the outset. To Emerson he wrote on August 7, "I study the aspects of commerce at its Narrows here, where it passes in review before me, and this seems to be beginning at the right end to understand this Babylon" (Corr 133).

Although Thoreau scholars have emphasized the fact that he was often unhappy and homesick in New York, Thoreau made a concerted effort to understand the character of the city. While Thoreau published only two pieces in New York, they both reflect this involvement in the world and his desire to address his countrymen.

Thoreau failed in New York's literary marketplace not so much because he had nothing to say about or to the people of the city, but because the marketplace itself could not easily accommodate or support a new, relatively unknown writer. In one sense, of course, New York was the most logical place for a writer to address the wider world. In 1839, Longfellow had written enthusiastically, "New York is becoming more literary. It will soon be the center of everything in the country;—the Great Metropolis. All young men of talent are looking that way; and new literary projects in the shape of Magazines and Weekly papers are constantly started, showing great activity, and zeal, and enterprise."[8] By 1840 New York was indeed the leading American magazine center, with 50 percent higher circulation than either Boston or Philadelphia, and it also led in bookselling and publishing.[9] But even Longfellow soon learned that New York's literary scene was also full of obstacles.

Thoreau's first difficulty was in making contacts for publication. Emerson did what he could for him in this regard, though in the end it was not much—his own connections in New York were limited and he had never published there himself. Emerson arranged for Thoreau to meet two young New York friends, Giles Waldo and William Tappan, whom Thoreau liked well enough (they brought him to their "English alehouse" his first week there [Corr 107]), but as they were neither easily accessible from Staten Island nor influential in the literary world, they afforded little service to Thoreau. Emerson also wrote to Henry James, Sr., whom he had met in New York during his 1842 lecture tour; he asked James to meet with Thoreau and, with an eye to Thoreau's literary prospects, added, "If you meet Mr. [Parke] Godwin . . . mention Thoreau to him, as one of our main contributors to the *Dial*, and as one who would be very glad of literary employment and would make on many subjects very valuable papers. He hopes to make his pen useful to him through journals or booksellers."[10] James did meet with Thoreau, and each was much impressed with the other, but James shortly left the city for the summer and embarked for Europe in October, so he too was of little use to Thoreau.

James does not seem to have recommended Thoreau to Parke Godwin, but that was not likely to have proved a fruitful connection in any case. Like most of the transcendentalists' friends and sympathizers in New York, Godwin was a confirmed supporter of Fourierist association (he later became a Brook Farmer and the editor of its journal *The Harbinger*), a position that Thoreau unambiguously rejected. Thoreau did meet, briefly, the leader of the American Fourierist movement, Albert Brisbane, and on several occasions he met with William Henry Channing, who was just establishing in New York a society for "Christian Union" and who was about to produce a new journal, *The Present*, also strongly biased in favor of association movements. Channing had long been acquainted with many of the *Dial* transcendentalists, especially with Fuller, and had been a contributor himself; but as perhaps the most active social reformer and communitarian among all the transcendentalists, Channing was at the opposite end of the transcendentalist spectrum from Thoreau and Emerson. In New York, Thoreau approached the associationists with considerable reserve and was not initially impressed with either Brisbane or Channing. As he became better acquainted with Channing, he modified his judgment of him and conceded, "I like the man all the better, though his schemes the less" (Corr 143). As he explained in a letter to his sister Helen after seeing the first issue of *The Present*, "My objection to Channing and all that fraternity is that they need and deserve sympathy themselves rather than are able to render it to others. . . . To speak or do any thing that shall concern mankind, one must speak and act as if well, or from that grain of health which he has left" (Corr 147).[11] Thoreau held these views with such strength that both the theme and language of this letter would be echoed in several of his published compositions.

Horace Greeley impressed Thoreau more favorably than did Channing or Brisbane, although Greeley, too, was an associationist. Thoreau described him as "a hearty New Hampshire boy as one would wish to meet. And says, 'now be neighborly'—and believes only or mainly, first, in the Sylvania Association somewhere in Pennsylvania—and secondly and most of all, in a new association to go into operation soon in New Jersey, with which he is connected" (Corr 128). As editor of the *Tribune*, Greeley had been a faithful supporter of the *Dial*, and he thought well of Thoreau's writing. Within the next several years, Ellery Channing, Margaret Fuller, and George Ripley would each come to work for Greeley on the *Tribune*, but there is no indication that Thoreau was either offered or interested in a position there. In the long run, Greeley was probably the most valuable professional contact Thoreau ever made aside from Emerson. An unwavering believer in Thoreau's genius, he acted, after 1846, as Thoreau's unofficial literary agent, placing his pieces, securing his payments, announcing his works and lectures in the *Tribune*, and untiringly offering professional advice; but their relationship yielded no tangible results during Thoreau's stay in New York.

Thoreau had spent most of May getting settled at William Emerson's, recovering from a cold he had contracted, and getting acquainted with New York and Emerson's friends there. Thoreau had hardly settled in when Emerson anxiously requested material for the July *Dial*, so Thoreau complied by sending him several poems and an essay he was just completing—"A Winter Walk." Ironically, Emerson found enough material for the July issue and printed nothing of Thoreau's. By this time, Thoreau had turned his attention to the New York literary marketplace, and the language he used to describe his efforts reveals how thoroughly he now thought of himself as a professional writer out to capture a public. On June 8 he wrote to his mother, "As for money matters I have not set my traps yet, but I am getting the bait ready" (Corr 114). Here is a note of deliberate calculation not previously found in Thoreau, and if it implies a certain contempt for the marketplace, it also suggests his new determination to succeed there.

Determined to earn some material remuneration for his work, Thoreau began his assault on the marketplace with a surprisingly pragmatic attitude. He still needed to be disabused of his illusions about the opportunities available in the New York marketplace, however. By the end of August he reported to his mother:

> I may yet accomplish something in the literary way—indeed I should have done so before now but for the slowness and poverty of the Reviews themselves. I have tried sundry methods of earning money in the city of late but without success. Have rambled into every bookseller or publisher's house and discussed their affairs with them. Some propose to me to do what an honest man cannot—Among others I conversed with the Harpers—to see if they might not find me useful to them—but they say that they are making fifty thousand dollars annually, and their motto is to let well alone. I find that I talk with these poor men as if I were over head and ears in business and a few thousand were no consideration with me—I almost reproach myself for bothering them thus to no purpose—but it is very valuable experience—and the best introduction I could have. (Corr 134–35)

Emerson, who had been requesting more Greek translations for the *Dial* (he never printed Thoreau's poems, but "A Winter Walk" would appear in the October number), seems to have been a little shocked by Thoreau's determined assault on the marketplace. He wrote to Thoreau on September 8: "We were all surprised to hear, one day lately, from G. Waldo, that you were forsaking the deep quiet of the Clove for the limbo of the false booksellers, and were soon relieved by hearing that you were safe again in the cottage in Staten Island. I could heartily wish that this country, which seems all opportunity, did actually offer more distinct and just rewards of labor to that unhappy class of men who have more reason and conscience than strength of back and arm" (Corr 136). Thoreau must have been rather surprised himself at Emerson's scruples about the "false booksellers," and he replied quite defensively, "I was absent only one day and a night from the island, the family expecting me back immediately. I was to earn a certain sum before winter, and thought it worth the while to try various experiments." He had even tried selling subscriptions to the *American Agriculturalist* to earn some money, explaining to Emerson his hard-learned lesson: "Literature comes to a poor market here, and even the little that I write is more than will sell. I have tried the *Democratic Review*, the *New Mirror*, and *Brother Jonathan*. The last two, as well as the *New World*, are overwhelmed with contributions which cost nothing, and are worth no more. *The Knickerbocker* is too poor, and only the *Ladies' Companion* pays" (Corr 139).

In a letter to his mother on October 1, he returns to the striking metaphor of his earlier letter home to explain the condition of the marketplace: "My bait will not tempt the rats; they are too well fed. The *Democratic Review* is poor, and can only afford half or quarter pay—which it *will* do—and they say there is a Ldy's Companion that pays—but I could not write anything companionable." In spite of his obvious frustration, he comments upon his situation with considerable humor: "It is very gratifying to live in the prospect of great successes always, and for that purpose, we must leave a sufficient foreground to see them through" (Corr 141).

Thus, in spite of—in fact, *because* of—all the literary activity in New York, the marketplace was inhospitable to the writer himself. Thoreau's hope and that of his mentors, that he might earn his living by his pen in New York, was in fact a naive one; almost no writer could expect to do so, and especially not an unknown writer. In 1839, for example, the *Knickerbocker* could not afford to pay Longfellow for a poem, in spite of its claims of paying contributors well. When Longfellow tried the following year to find someone in New York to print George W. Greene's *Letters from Rome*, he explained to Greene that he had not even written to the *Knickerbocker*, "because it has been in trouble, and not able to pay anybody." He then adds,

> I wrote to [Epes] Sargent, to negotiate with whomsoever would pay best. . . . I got an answer, showing that nobody pays now-a-days. He writes . . . "The Ladies' Companion pays for Tales and poetry, but I . . . learn that there is little chance for any higher composition. The fact is that all our publishers *whether of books or of periodicals, are desperately poor at present. Money is not to be had*." And this is very true. . . . Most publishers will not look at a book; and are working off the obligations they had on hand.[12]

By 1843, the *Knickerbocker* could still afford to pay only its best-known contributors and, as Thoreau discovered, did not pay others at all. The practice of paying according to reputation was fairly commonplace, and the *Knickerbocker*'s attitude was that which Sarah J. Hale, editor of Philadelphia's *Godey's* (which also had a reputation for high payment for contributors), finally spelled out in the pages of her magazine: "We want it distinctly understood that, unless by previous understanding to that effect, no articles published in this magazine will be paid for. Young writers and those who have not acquired a literary reputation must remember that the mere insertion of their articles . . . is quite a compensation in itself."[13]

Magazines at this time had not yet begun the practice of selling advertisements, so they relied entirely on money generated by sales; thus even the magazines with large circulations were often in financial trouble, especially because delinquency in subscription payments was widespread. *The Ladies' Companion*, for example, which Thoreau understood paid contributors, claimed a subscription list of 22,500 in 1840 but was in debt in 1843 due to delinquents.[14] The ladies' magazines were subjected to severe criticism from the rest of the periodical press in any case, and Thoreau was not alone in finding he "could not write anything companionable."[15]

The weekly papers such as the *New Mirror*, the *New World*, and *Brother Jonathan* relied primarily on reprinted material, especially English and other foreign works that were unprotected by international copyright laws and therefore cost them nothing in royalties. Because such material was so abundant and so popular, the weeklies did not need to pay for those original contributions they did publish, as Thoreau discovered. The practice of reprinting unprotected material affected the whole publishing business, of course, not just the weeklies. It was, as John Tebbel notes in his history of American book publishing, an "age of piracy" in which many book publishers, too (to the detriment of American authors), "saw little profit in setting laboriously from a handwritten manuscript when it was so easy to reprint a foreign book, on which they could also be assured they would not have to pay royalty."[16] The crisis in the literary marketplace that lay behind Thoreau's and Longfellow's experiences, however, came with the establishment of *Brother Jonathan* in 1839 and the *New World* in 1840. These were the "mammoth weeklies," which, by combining the use of oversized sheets with the lower postal rates for newspapers, were suddenly able to compete directly with both magazine and book publishers. The magazines could no longer hold their advantage over newspapers whose larger format allowed for lengthier entries, and the *New Mirror* (a weekly that did not adopt the "mammoth" format) complained,

> We are at a loss . . . to discover the justice of a system by which newspapers, large enough to paper a moderate-sized room, are rated at one and a half cents over one hundred miles, while periodicals, composed certainly of more substantial, and generally more useful material, are charged two and a half cents for the same distance for every sixteen octavo pages; the whole sixteen being in size about one-half that of the ordinary sixpenny papers.[17]

When the mammoth weeklies began reprinting as "supplements" cheap editions of entire (uncopyrighted) novels they had serialized, a publishing price war began that nearly destroyed the literary market.[18] The *New York Herald* wryly editorialized: "The terrible contest and competition now going on among the publishers of cheap literature will produce two or three results: first, the ruin of all publishers; second, the fortunes of all the venders in the large cities; and third, the spread of literary taste among the people. All these results are positive and certain."[19] The *New World* defended its "cheap editions" by appealing to the consumer, claiming that the public should be grateful for the *New World*: "You are not going to desert promising young fellows like ourselves, trying to get along in the world, and whom you have hitherto taken good care of, for any overgrown rich men. . . . In other words, you are not so green as to give a dollar for what you can get for eighteen pence or a shilling; not you!"[20]

Particularly hard hit by the competition from the mammoth weeklies were the book publishers who had previously relied heavily on foreign reprints, such as Harper's. It is thus particularly ironic that Thoreau reported, "They say that they are making fifty thousand dollars annually, and their motto is to let well alone." The truth is that 1842 had been the worst year in Harper's history: they added only thirty-six new books to their list that year, and their warfare with the weeklies reached its low point when someone from the *New World* broke into Harper's bindery to steal the new G.P.R. James novel; they set the place on fire and the bindery was destroyed.[21] The end of the price wars came with postal reforms of 1843, but recovery was slow. The mammoth weeklies lingered on until 1845, and it was not until the end of the decade that Harper's emerged as the largest publisher in the world.

The point is that no matter how pragmatic he might be, Thoreau could not win an assault on a marketplace which operated against the interests of the writers themselves. In 1842, *Brother Jonathan* had shamelessly and transparently defended the commercial exploitation of writers by editorializing that the professional writer was somehow un-American:

> The man who would be literary, must earn his living first—daily provide his wants—pursue an honest occupation. . . . His necessities thus provided for, literature may be to him the most delightful and ennobling amusement. We want no such profession in our country as purely literary men. . . . There is no room in a republic for any such diploma pedants. We need practical writers, or none at all.[22]

Ultimately, such an attitude threatened to undermine the entire literary marketplace; by April of 1843—on the eve of Thoreau's arrival—*Brother Jonathan* conceded, "Literature is now a drug; all the markets are overstocked."[23] Thoreau's timing for entering the New York literary world was comically bad. Even in 1846, Nathaniel Parker Willis, himself the best-paid magazinist in the country, wrote to an aspiring writer, "As to writing for the magazines, that is very nearly done for as a matter of profit. The competition for notoriety alone gives editors more than they can use. . . . The literary avenues are all over crowded, and you cannot live by the pen, except as a drudge to a newspaper."[24]

In the end, Thoreau's only contact that yielded results was with John L. O'Sullivan's *Democratic Review*, which eventually published two of Thoreau's pieces. The *Democratic Review* also had its problems with subscription payments; it too had suffered serious losses in 1842,[25] in spite of a healthy circulation, and, as Thoreau reported, could "only afford half or quarter pay" (a fact Hawthorne also discovered, much to his chagrin).[26] Nevertheless, payments were at least more equitably distributed than at many magazines, and Thoreau could expect to be paid as well and as promptly as other contributors.

The *Democratic Review* was perhaps also the magazine best suited for Thoreau in other respects. As its full title indicates, the *United States Magazine and Democratic Review* tried to combine the features of the quarterly review and the monthly magazine, and it did so in practice, not merely in a wishful prospectus, like the *Dial*. Like the magazines, it was published monthly and included poems, stories, and sketches; but it did not go wholly over to popular forms and retained some of the weightier tone of the reviews, with their typically longer, more serious articles. It was thus less ponderous than quarterlies like the *North American Review* or the *New York Review*, while it was more serious in tone than either the *Knickerbocker Magazine* or the *Boston Miscellany*, for example, and certainly more serious than the monthly ladies' magazines or the weeklies. The *Democratic Review* included among its principal contributors Bryant, Whittier, and Hawthorne, and also published works by Longfellow, Lowell, Catherine Sedgwick, Joseph Neal, H. T. Tuckerman, and W. A. Jones. It thus catered sufficiently to popular tastes to insure a circulation of 3,500 in 1843,[27] and while this was nowhere near that of the most popular magazines (such as *Godey's* or *Graham's*), it was a very respectable figure—and certainly a vast improvement over the *Dial*'s 220 subscribers.

The *Democratic Review* was the principal organ of the loosely knit "Young America" group, which included, among others, O'Sullivan, Evert A. Duyckinck, W. A. Jones, Cornelius Mathews, and, later, Herman Melville. Politically, their magazine supported liberal and reform-minded democrats and "loco-focos"; in literature, they were calling for distinctively American works. Thus the *Democratic Review* was generally sympathetic to Emerson and the New England transcendentalists, though it was critical of their more mystical effusions and of Emerson's apolitical, quietist tendencies. As one critic has commented, "The *Democratic Review* and the

Young Americans writing for it were as transcendental as Democrats could be."[28] In all, it was a magazine of the highest quality, which commanded the respect of the liberal and conservative press alike. Edgar Allan Poe (who had been befriended by Duyckinck) conceded in 1843, "Were it not for its ultraism in politics, we should consider the *Democratic Review* the most valuable journal of the day."[29]

But the politics of the magazine were also something of a problem. While the *Democratic Review*'s position was progressive, both Emerson and Thoreau were uncomfortable with the fact that, first, it engaged in partisan politics at all; second, that it advocated a Jacksonian democracy which they feared catered to, rather than elevated, the masses; and, third, it supported communitarian experiments, which they felt both threatened the principles of individualism and self-reliance and were often misguided in their emphasis on utilitarian, materialist principles.

These last objections were not insurmountable, however, and Thoreau was glad to have an editor interested in his writing. The first piece of "bait" Thoreau prepared for the magazine was a review of John Adolphus Etzler's *The Paradise within the Reach of All Men, without Labor, by Powers of Nature and Machinery, an Address to All Intelligent Men.*[30] Originally, Emerson had asked Thoreau to review this utopian tract, which combined Etzler's schemes for mechanical reform with the principles of Fourierist association, for the April 1843 *Dial*; at that point, however, Thoreau had done no more than make some very brief notes (Corr 85, 88). It is not clear exactly when Thoreau completed the review, but some time between mid-June and early July he submitted it to the *Democratic Review*.[31]

Entitled "Paradise (to Be) Regained," Thoreau's lengthy review amounts to a manifesto of the anticommunitarian and antimaterialist vision of self-reform that he shared, in its essentials, with Emerson; and as such, it was bound to meet objections from both the communitarian transcendentalists associated with the *Dial* and from the New York communitarians, such as Brisbane, W. H. Channing, Parke Godwin, Horace Greeley—and O'Sullivan. Initially, O'Sullivan rejected the review, explaining,

> I am very sorry that with so much in it that I like very much there are others in the paper you have favored me with which have decided me against its insertion . . . if you would not object I think it very likely that some addition & modification made with your concurrence would put your review of [Etzler's book] into the shape to suit my peculiar notion on the subject. Articles of this nature are not in general published in the D R on the responsibility of the individual name of the author, but under the general impersonality of the collective "we"—(the name of the author being usually indicated in pencil on the Index in the copies sent to the editors of newspapers). This system renders a certain pervading homogeneity necessary, inviting often the necessity of this process of editorial revision, or rather communication. (Corr 130 [July 28, 1843])

What O'Sullivan meant by this was simply that the *Democratic Review* took a sympathetic view of the Fourierists and various other communitarian experiments, and was therefore unwilling to let Thoreau's criticism represent the magazine. Later in his career, Thoreau would bristle at such editorial interference, and he could be merciless in his damnation of editors and journals alike; but at this point he was apparently able to take the commercial aspects of publication, and O'Sullivan's rejection, in stride. This seems particularly ironic, since O'Sullivan's explanation that such articles did not speak for the individual but must reflect the common opinion of the editors was a form of the collective activity Thoreau criticized in his review (and elsewhere) as a threat to the self-reliance on which he based his principles of reform. In any case, he informed his mother that the piece had been turned down because "they could not adopt the sentiments," adding, "However, they were very polite, and earnest that I should send them something else, or reform that" (Corr 132 [August 6]). Conveying the same information to Emerson, he observed only that "O'Sullivan wrote me that articles of this kind have to be referred to the circle, who, it seems are represented by this journal, and said something about 'collective we,' and 'homogeneity'" (Corr 134 [August 7]).

Unwilling to modify his views, Thoreau nevertheless managed to get O'Sullivan to change his mind. On September 14 he informed Emerson, "O'Sullivan is printing the manuscript I sent him some time ago, having objected only to my want of sympathy with the Communities" (Corr 139). "Paradise (to Be) Regained" was published with little, if any, revision, as the lead article in the November number.[32] This attests to O'Sullivan's open-mindedness as an editor and to his apparent regard for Thoreau's article, for "Paradise (to Be) Regained" was, in fact, an eloquent rebuttal of much that the *Democratic Review* stood for. Thoreau defended the position of the transcendentalist self-reformer as opposed to the activist organization reformer, much as Emerson had done, in general terms, in "Man the Reformer" (1841) and in his "Introductory Lecture on the Times"; but Thoreau argued the position in more concrete terms, using Etzler's proposals as a foil.

Thoreau begins his review by attributing current interest in Etzler's book "to the recent spread of Fourier's doctrines. It is one of the signs of the times" (19), and Thoreau's review indeed penetrates beyond the particulars of Etzler's schemes to analyze the principles of associationist reformers in general.[33] He quotes the whole of Etzler's opening paragraph,[34] which begins, "Fellow Men! I promise to show the means of creating a paradise within ten years, where everything desirable for human life may be had by every man in superabundance, without labor, and without pay" (19). Etzler's grandiose proposals for harnessing the energy of the sun, wind, and water for use in industry, agriculture, transportation, and habitation are strikingly prophetic of our late twentieth-century realities and near-realities;

and Thoreau acknowledges a certain power in Etzler's book: "It did expand us a little. It is worth attending to, if only that it entertains large questions" (19). But while he is duly impressed by the expansiveness of Etzler's vision, he immediately calls into question the direction in which his idealism is channeled: "It would seem from this and various indications beside, that there is a transcendentalism in mechanics as well as in ethics. . . . While one scours the heavens, the other sweeps the earth. One says he will reform himself, and then nature and circumstances will be right. . . . The other will reform nature and circumstances, and then man will be right" (20). Thoreau begins on a note of cautious, even skeptical, disinterestedness here, withholding overt assertions of his own commitment to moral self-reform. As he elaborates on the aims of the mechanical reformer, however, he becomes increasingly ironic, parodying the pretensions of those who would "reform nature and circumstances":

> Talk no more vaguely, says he, of reforming the world—I will reform the globe itself. What matters it whether I remove this humor out of my flesh, or the pestilent humor from the fleshy part of the globe? Nay, is not the latter the more generous course? At present the globe goes with a shattered constitution in its orbit. Has it not asthma, and ague, and fever, and dropsy, and flatulence, and pleurisy, and is it not afflicted with vermin? . . . No doubt the simple powers of nature properly directed by man would make it healthy and paradise. (20)

It was after having written this that he explained to his sister that he objected to "Channing and all that fraternity" because "they want faith and mistake their private ail for an infected atmosphere." In "Paradise (to Be) Regained," however, Thoreau conveys this criticism through the indirection of irony, and he extends his impersonation of the mechanical reformer until it reaches a broadly comic reductio ad absurdum: "Let us not succumb to nature. We will marshall the clouds and restrain the tempests; we will bottle up pestilent exhalations. . . . We will wash water, and warm fire, and cool ice, and underprop the earth. We will teach birds to fly, and fishes to swim, and ruminants to chew the cud. It is time we had looked into these things" (21).[35]

Thoreau persists in this ironic, commonsensical vein when he turns from the calculated rhetoric of this introduction to a consideration of Etzler's particular schemes for harnessing the power of nature to effect these reforms. Thoreau is responsive to both the magnificent and the ludicrous in Etzler's fantastic, minutely detailed plans. The point Thoreau subtly builds toward, though, is that Etzler's book is both wildly visionary and pathetically narrow in its merely utilitarian materialism. The basis of his criticism, then, is not merely the solid ground of common sense, but the even more extravagant vision of the transcendentalist who "scours the heavens." After explaining Etzler's detailed computations for harnessing natural resources and applying that energy to the production of elaborate machines for agriculture, transportation, habitation, and clothing, Thoreau summarizes: "Thus is Paradise to be Regained, and that old and stern decree at length reversed. Man shall no more earn his living by the sweat of his brow. All labor shall be reduced to 'a short turn of some crank'" (39).

If the particulars of Etzler's engineering schemes were fantastic to nineteenth-century readers, they were nevertheless based on two related principles that were, in varying degrees, accepted by reformers and conservatives alike, and Thoreau's criticism was ultimately aimed at these underlying assumptions. First, Thoreau rejected the principle of utilitarianism, which, seeking the greatest good for the greatest number, regards society as a whole, rather than the individual, as the proper object of reform. Etzler had proposed the construction of Fourierist phalansteries, communities of exactly sixteen hundred people who would be housed in apartmentlike complexes that Etzler designed in great detail; these were to provide what he described as "the most convenient lodgings, with the greatest comforts and enjoyments, by the least trouble, to the greatest sum of individuals in the smallest space."[36] Second, Thoreau rejected the principles of materialism as they were applied to social reform—that is, the belief that improvements in the material environment would effect improvements in the moral and intellectual conditions of those within the environment, both by direct influence and by providing the leisure and means for such improvement. This view implies, of course, that the material environment, rather than the individual character, should be the immediate object of reform. Etzler justifies the luxurious accommodations that he projects for each of the phalansteries by explaining, "Love and affection may there be fostered and enjoyed without any of the obstructions that oppose, diminish, and destroy them in the present state of men" (RP 39).

This happened to be the principle of reform supported by the *Democratic Review*, as well. William A. Jones voiced the collective view of his peers in an 1844 review: "To render man physically comfortable, and to give him sufficient occupation, of whatever sort circumstances demand, is the primary duty of society; but immediately next to that, to seek to elevate and refine, deepen and expand, the characters of all men."[37] But this was precisely the source of Thoreau's disagreement with the reformers, and thus, having completed his presentation of Etzler's designs, Thoreau begins his rebuttal in earnest, asserting his own values now, without indirection or irony. Men may or may not be able to harness physical energy to these ends,

> but there is a certain divine energy in every man, but sparingly employed as yet, which may be called the crank within,—the crank after all,—the prime mover in all machinery,—quite indispensable to all work. Would that we might get our hands on its handle! In fact no work can be shirked. It may be postponed

> indefinitely, but not infinitely. Nor can any really important work be made easier by co-operation or machinery. . . . We are rather pleased after all to consider the small private, but both constant and accumulated force, which stands behind every spade in the field. This it is that makes the valleys shine, and the deserts really bloom. (RP 40)

While Thoreau certainly advocated his own kind of leisure, he also shared the philosophy of work espoused by Carlyle and Emerson (as in "Man the Reformer," for example); man's object ought not to be to eliminate the need for work, but to find one's own proper work and perform it for its own sake. Furthermore, Etzler's scheme to reform nature and man's physical circumstances implied that man's will is superior to the laws of nature—a position the transcendentalists found morally offensive. Moreover, as Thoreau explains, Etzler announces that his scheme requires time, money, and other men, while for Thoreau,

> the true reformer does not want time, nor money, nor co-operation, nor advice. What is time but the stuff delay is made of? And depend upon it, our virtue will not live on the interest of our money. . . . And as for advice, the information floating in the atmosphere of society is as evanescent and unserviceable to him as gossamer for clubs of Hercules. There is absolutely no common sense; it is common nonsense. (41)

Herein lies the force of Thoreau's title, "Paradise (to Be) Regained," for the weight of Thoreau's criticism of reformers such as Etzler is concentrated in the parenthetical "(to Be)." They must wait for the proper "capital"—whether it be time, money, or men—and this "will prolong the ten years to ten thousand at least" (43). The material reformers begin at the wrong end and thus never begin at all. This would be the burden, too, of the "Economy" chapter of *Walden*, where he sought to demonstrate how little "capital" was really needed to begin, and concluded that "the man who goes alone can start today; but he who travels with another must wait till the other is ready, and it may be a long time before they get off" (*Walden* 72).

From the principles of utilitarian materialism, Etzler followed Fourier in concluding that to implement social reform, man must depend upon collectivism: "It will now be plainly seen," Etzler argues, "that the execution of the proposals is not proper for individuals"; rather, man must "constitute societies. Man is powerful but in union with many. Nothing great, for the improvement of his own condition, or that of his fellow men, can ever be effected by individual enterprise" (RP 41). This was the underlying principle upon which all the communitarian utopias were based, but to which Thoreau reacts: "Alas! this is the crying sin of the age, this want of faith in the prevalence of a man. Nothing can be effected but by one man. He who wants help wants everything. . . . We must first succeed alone, that we may enjoy our success together. . . . In this matter of reforming the world, we have little faith in corporations; not thus was it first formed" (42).

Thoreau was reacting not just to Etzler's book here, but to his whole experience in New York. He had been struck by the tremendous potential of the crowds and the daily influx of new immigrants to create a new world in America but had been driven to lament to Emerson, "When will the world learn that a million men are of no importance compared with *one* man?" (Corr 111–12); and he had explained to his sister that he objected to the communitarians because "they need and deserve sympathy themselves rather than are able to render it to others." The communitarians lacked faith, and, as he wrote in his review of Etzler, "Faith, indeed, is all the reform that is needed; it is itself a reform" (RP 43).

By expressing his criticism of the material reformers through his essentially ironic and skeptical commentary on Etzler's program, Thoreau establishes a basis from which he can make his final transition to the positive assertion of his own vision of moral reform:

> The chief fault of this book is, that it aims to secure the greatest degree of gross comfort and pleasure merely. . . . Undoubtedly if we were to reform this outward life truly and thoroughly, we should find no duty of the inner omitted. . . . But a moral reform must take place first, and then the necessity of the other will be superseded, and we shall sail and plough by its force alone. (45–46)

Having explicitly inverted the principles of the materialist reformers, Thoreau concludes his essay by abandoning completely the cautious, ironic skepticism with which he began, asserting his own prophetic, transcendental voice. His language becomes aphoristic—"Where an angel travels it will be paradise all the way, but where Satan travels it will be burning marl and cinders" (46). He quotes from the Vishnu Sarma (a saying he had selected for the "Ethnical Scriptures" in the July 1842 *Dial*): "He whose mind is at ease is possessed of all riches. Is it not the same to one whose foot is enclosed in a shoe, as if the whole surface of the earth were covered in leather?" (46). He becomes hortatory and oracular—"He who is conversant with the supernal powers will not worship these inferior deities of the wind, the waves, tide, and sunshine" (46). Thoreau rises to transcendental expansiveness: "Love is the wind, the tide, the waves, the sunshine. Its power is incalculable . . . it can make a paradise within which will dispense with a paradise without" (47).

If Thoreau began the review as a Yankee skeptic, he ends it as a Yankee preacher; like Melville's Father Mapple, who preaches in the language of the whaling trade, Thoreau preaches his spiritual message in Etzler's own language of mechanical reform. His vision is controlled by the analogy between finite physical forces and the infinite forces of the spirit—and since the latter are infinite, they hold the promise of an infinitely higher kind of reform:

> As the mechanical forces have not yet been generously and largely applied to make the physical world answer to the ideal, so the power of love has been but meanly and sparingly applied, as yet. It has patented only such machines as the almshouses, the hospitals, and the Bible Society, while its infinite wind is still blowing, and blowing down these very structures, too, from time to time. Still less are we accumulating its power, and preparing to act with greater energy at a future time. Shall we not contribute our shares to this enterprise, then? (47)

Thoreau's transcendentalist faith and his vision of moral reform based on a rigorous, spiritual self-reliance are stated explicitly and powerfully here; nevertheless, they were not likely to gain widespread approval. While many readers might not have shared the *Democratic Review*'s sympathy with Fourier and communitarian experiments, Thoreau's wholesale rejection of Etzler's utilitarian and materialist principles undoubtedly isolated him from larger interests on all sides.

The fact that O'Sullivan eventually agreed to print the review, thus implicitly letting it represent the views of the magazine itself, suggests that Thoreau's arguments were compelling and his rhetorical strategy effective. Still, O'Sullivan was unlikely to publish other such direct assaults on principles supported by the magazine. When O'Sullivan initially rejected the article, he nevertheless asked Thoreau to submit something else (Corr 130). Thoreau interpreted this as a request for something "purely literary I suppose" (Corr 134), and he complied. In "The Landlord," which was actually printed before the Etzler review, in the October number of the *Democratic Review*,[38] Thoreau tried his hand at a form of the familiar essay that was new to him; his subject was neither nature nor travel, but the "character" of the landlord as a type. Thoreau was experimenting here in a mode that he did not attempt again—and perhaps because of this it has been subjected to an unusual amount of critical scorn.

When it appeared in print Thoreau wrote to his mother, "I see that they have printed a short piece which I wrote to sell in the Dem Review" (Corr 142). Seizing upon this remark, Thoreau critics have almost invariably dismissed the essay as a failed piece of hackwork, an effort to cater to the magazine audience, which Thoreau was constitutionally unable to do.[39] Yet it is idle to dismiss "The Landlord" simply because it was written "to sell"; Thoreau's very removal to New York was motivated chiefly by his desire to earn his own way by his pen, and payment was a major consideration in his approach to all the publishers and editors there. Seen in this context, his comment to his mother may more reasonably be regarded as a cautious note of the success he hoped for than as a note of disparagement. The "Walk to

Wachusett" had gone to the *Boston Miscellany* and the Etzler review to the *Democratic Review* rather than to the *Dial* because, in both cases, Thoreau hoped to be paid. This is no less true of the pieces he would subsequently offer to other popular magazines. As a transcendentalist writer, Thoreau did not abandon his aim of being an instrument of moral reform, but when he entered the literary marketplace his specific interests as a professional writer were to get his work published, to appeal to a large audience, and to get paid. The question of audience appeal was, moreover, essential to his interest as a reformer, and "The Landlord" was an effort to find a form for his writing that could fulfill all of these aims.

The Etzler review had been accepted only with difficulty because it did not conform to the magazine's editorial opinions; as O'Sullivan had explained to him, "Articles of this nature are not in general published in the D R on the responsibility of the individual name of the author." As a "purely literary" piece, however, "The Landlord" belonged to the "magazine" rather than the "review" side of the journal and was therefore a signed contribution: "By Henry D. Thoreau" appears clearly beneath the title. This was useful not only in promoting Thoreau's reputation, but also in circumventing the constraints of having to represent the editors' views. Writing something "purely literary" did not mean that Thoreau set aside his own views in order to pander to popular tastes. While "The Landlord" is a literary sketch, it nevertheless treats implicitly several of the issues he had treated explicitly in "Paradise (to Be) Regained."

As Marie Law Hamilton noted in her study of the nineteenth-century English familiar essay, "The character sketch provided an admirable means of lending concreteness to the general observations of the essayist, of emphasizing the moral he wished to bring home, and of providing the wit and humor necessary to hold the reader's attention."[40] The character sketch, and the familiar essay in general, had become popular in America for precisely the same reasons, and, at a time when Thoreau was especially interested in reaching a broad audience, this was a form potentially well suited to his needs. Thoreau had recognized the value of concreteness with the "Natural History of Massachusetts," but in "Sir Walter Raleigh," with its focus on human, moral characteristics, he discovered that historical and biographical facts were less tractable than natural facts. As a character type, Thoreau's landlord is mythic rather than historical, yet he is sketched with a degree of concreteness Thoreau had not been able to give his "brave man" in "The Service." Thoreau's use of wit and humor in "The Landlord" is also an extension of his recent experiments with the light tone of the familiar essay. Thus while Thoreau did not write in this mode again, "The Landlord" is not as anomalous as it has seemed to many Thoreau scholars; rather, it is one of several related experiments from this period in which Thoreau explored the potential of various popular literary forms to carry the burden of his consistently transcendentalist themes.

Thoreau's opening paragraph establishes the tone of the familiar essay, indulging in fanciful speculation on an apparently trivial topic, yet clearly leading to some moral point:

> Under the one word "house" are included the school-house, the almshouse, the jail, the tavern, the dwelling-house; and the meanest shed or cave in which men live contains the elements of all these. But no-where on the earth stands the entire and perfect house. The Parthenon, St. Peter's, the Gothic minster, the palace, the hovel, are but imperfect executions of an imperfect idea. Who would dwell in them? . . . that should be the most sacred roof which shelters most of humanity. Surely, then, the gods who are most interested in the human race preside over the Tavern, where especially men congregate. Methinks I see the thousand shrines erected to Hospitality shining afar in all countries, as well Mahometan and Jewish as Christian, khans and caravansaries and inns, whither all pilgrims without distinction resort. (W 5: 153)

The wit and humor lie in the juxtaposition of the very triviality of the subject and the large claims the writer makes for it—elevating the commonplace tavern to the status of a shrine. It is, in fact, the essence of the genre of the sketch to make the most of small things. Irving's *Sketchbook* might be taken as the paradigm: "Geoffrey Crayon" offers a mock apology in his preface for the "idle humor" that, he says, "has led me aside from the great objects studied by every regular traveller who would make a book" and has therefore resulted in sketches only of "nooks, and corners, and by-places."[41] Similarly, H. T. Tuckerman took as the epigraph for his 1850 collection of familiar essays, *The Optimist*, the line from Richter, "That I may show the whole world that we ought to value little joys more than great ones; the night gown more than the dress coat."[42] Even closer to Thoreau's sketch is Tuckerman's somewhat later familiar essay "Inns," in which he writes, "In the East a monastery, in the Desert a tent, on the Nile a boat, a *hacienda* in South America, a kiosk in Turkey, a *caffe* in Italy, but in Britain an inn, is the pilgrim's home, and one not less characteristic. The subject as suggestive of the philosophy of civilization is worth investigation."[43]

Whereas Tuckerman's essay remains quite superficial, however, Thoreau's speculations are neither as idle nor as trivial as they first appear. While several critics have suggested that Thoreau's subject matter in "The Landlord" was wrong for him—that he had, in effect, no business writing about taverns and innkeepers—Thoreau's subject is really a rather ingenious one, through which he addresses issues of central concern to him. In "Paradise (to Be) Regained" Thoreau had recoiled from Etzler's scheme for social reform in which Fourierist communities would be housed in huge and extravagant apartmentlike complexes. By speculating fancifully on the "ideal house" here, Thoreau creates a model through which he makes his claims for all those values he saw ignored or rejected by Etzler and by his materialist and utilitarian society in general.[44]

Thoreau's claim that the most sacred house is that which "shelters most of humanity" is an ironic jab at the utilitarians, for Thoreau's standard of measure has nothing to do with the merely numerical calculations of men like Etzler. Thoreau's fanciful claims for the tavern as a "shrine" for "pilgrims" have a serious undercurrent, since the tavern offers not what he had found in Etzler's book, "the greatest degree of gross comfort and pleasure merely," but the real source of social and moral reform—what he called "Love" in "Paradise (to Be) Regained," and "Hospitality" in "The Landlord." In "Paradise (to Be) Regained," Thoreau concluded that "the power of love has been but meanly and sparingly applied, as yet. It has patented only such machines as the almshouses, the hospitals, and the Bible Society, while its infinite wind is still blowing, and blowing down these very structures, too, from time to time" (RP 47). In "The Landlord," the tavern is the emblem of the institution founded out of perfect hospitality, or love, and it therefore replaces these structures. Especially, it replaces the church, which is also only an "imperfect execution of an imperfect idea" and cannot accommodate, as the tavern can, "all pilgrims without distinction." Thoreau concludes his essay by making the comparison explicit: "To conclude, the tavern will compare favorably with the church. The church is the place where prayers and sermons are delivered, but the tavern is where they are to take effect, and if the former are good, the latter cannot be bad" (W 5: 161–62).[45]

In Thoreau's sketch, the landlord represents the "perfect man": "The Landlord is a man of more open and general sympathies, who possesses a spirit of hospitality which is its own reward, and feeds and shelters men from pure love of the creatures" (153). While Thoreau is quite earnest about this spirit of hospitality, he nevertheless characterizes his ideal landlord with comic extravagance and seasons his portrait with puns to retain the genial tone: "He must have no idiosyncrasies, no particular bents or tendencies to this or that, but a general, uniform, and healthy development, such as his portly person indicates, offering himself equally on all sides to men" (157). Thoreau's pun on the "portly" shape of the landlord is partially at least a self-directed irony, a comic reduction of the abstract virtue of "sphericity" that he had celebrated in "The Service." Moreover, Thoreau has also sketched an ideologically different sort of "spheral man" from that of "The Service." While both the "brave man" and the landlord attain their "sphericity" by opening themselves up to the influence of the universal spirit, the brave man is militantly individualistic in resisting the influence of the world, whereas the landlord—even more than Sir Walter Raleigh—is the example of the man of the world, the *absolutely* social being, whose "sphericity" is manifested not in militant heroism but in absolute sympathy:

> Talking with our host is next best and instructive to talking with one's self. It is a more conscious soliloquy. . . . "High-ho!" exclaims the traveler. Them's my sentiments, thinks mine host, and stands ready for what may come next, expressing the purest sympathy by his demeanor. . . . He is wiser than to contradict his guest in any case; he lets him go on; he lets him travel. (160)

There is an extravagance in Thoreau's characterization of the landlord and a playfulness in his language that prevents the reader from taking his virtues entirely seriously; but Thoreau was quite serious about the value he placed on the landlord's broad humanity. In *Walden,* Thoreau would characterize his friend Alcott's "hospitable intellect" in terms clearly adapted from those used to describe the landlord, imagining Alcott, too, as the keeper of "a caravansary on the world's highway," where all pilgrims are welcome (*Walden* 268–69).

In "The Landlord" Thoreau explicitly rejects the "peaked and inhospitable [man] of genius," who "says, by all possible hints and signs, I wish to be alone—good-bye—farewell. But the landlord can afford to live without privacy" (W 5: 157). Undoubtedly, there was a good deal of conscious self-criticism in this, for Thoreau had written in his journal three years earlier, "The most positive life that history notices has been a constant retiring out of life—a wiping one's hands of it—seeing how mean it is, and having nothing to do with it" (J1: 121). He was perhaps addressing some of his friends back in Concord as well—those other transcendentalists, who, as Emerson had described them, "shun general society; they incline to shut themselves in their chamber in the house . . . and to find their tasks and amusements in solitude" (CW 1: 208). In contrast, the landlord "never wants to be alone, but sleeps, wakes, eats, drinks, sociably, still remembering his race" (W 5: 158). In "Raleigh" Thoreau had praised the hero as "not the most godlike, but the most manlike"; in "The Landlord" he rephrased this more humorously: "If he is not the most upright, let us allow him this praise, that he is the most downright of men" (159).

Thoreau's landlord is an archetype of the democratic man, representing the most social side of Thoreau's vision—the side most important to him in his venture into the city, where he had come to address the mass of men. But he is a transcendental democrat and so stands in opposition to both the capitalist and the communitarian. He "loves all men equally" (154), but precisely because he loves them *equally,* he insists on the integrity of each individual and knows that each man must reform himself. The tavern "shelters most of humanity" because it accommodates rather than constrains the freedom and independence of those sojourners who pass beneath its roof. Here, people come together without being reduced to mere members, as they are in the Fourierist communities, and the spirit of hospitality prevails with nothing asked in return: "The traveler steps across the threshold, and lo! he too is a master"; "Here at length we have free range, as not in palaces, nor cottages, nor temples, and intrude nowhere" (155, 156).

The tavern itself contrasts pointedly with what Thoreau had called the "crystal palaces" of Etzler's utopia. The landlord's tavern is "no gay pavilion, made of bright stuffs, and furnished with nuts and gingerbread"; rather, "it is as simple and sincere in its essentials as the caves in which the first men dwelt, but it is also as open and public" (155). It is simple because the spiritual man has no need for superfluous material comforts. As Thoreau explained in "Paradise (to Be) Regained," if a moral reform takes place first, "then the necessity of the other will be superseded." In contrast with the elaborate compartmentalization of Etzler's phalansteries, in which "any member may procure himself all the common articles of his daily wants, by a short turn of some crank, without leaving his apartment" (RP 37), Thoreau's tavern is as open as nature—as open as the man of nature—and at its center is the hearth, as at the center of the man is his heart, the seat of spiritual life. "All the secrets of housekeeping are exhibited to the eyes of men, above and below, before and behind. . . . And why should we have any serious disgust at kitchens? Perhaps they are the holiest recess of the house. . . . Here the real and sincere life which we meet in the street was actually fed and sheltered" (W 5: 156).

Thoreau proposed his ideal house not only as an alternative to Etzler's utopian dreams, but as a reaction to the actual life of the society he found in the city. To Thoreau, the typical Victorian house of his well-to-do contemporaries was just as good—and just as bad—as the apartments envisioned by Etzler. In a journal entry of October 21, 1843, Thoreau reflected upon the "hollow glazed life . . . which some couples lead—with their basement parlor with folding doors—a few vistors cards and the latest annual." People "do not live" but merely "reside" in such houses; "There is no hearth in the center of the house—The atmosphere of the apartments is not yet peopled with the spirit of its inhabitants, but the voices sound hollow and echo and he sees only the paint and the paper" (J1: 478). The accumulation of material comforts was not the way to moral reform. Thoreau could see that it only contributed to the compartmentalization of life and alienated people not only from nature, but from each other—and finally from themselves, concealing the "real and sincere life" of the heart.

Repelled by such hollow, compartmentalized lives, Thoreau was fascinated by the tremendous crowds of immigrants he saw pouring daily into

New York, doing their domestic chores out in the open, on the quays and pavements—masses of people on their way west, who moved on "for the most part without having *landed* here" (Corr 128; cf. 141–42). These were the American sojourners who most interested Thoreau and on whom he seems largely to have placed his hopes for the creation of the new world. New York itself was a kind of giant tavern or way station—the first stop in America for the waves of travelers on the great road west—and in "The Landlord" Thoreau seems to be advising the city itself on how best to fulfill its obligation and role as "landlord."

Thus Thoreau's sketch was not aimed merely to please the public but contained, implicitly, serious social criticism that informed his later works as well. His critique of American housing in the "Economy" chapter of *Walden* develops and often closely echoes passages in "The Landlord"; conversely, many of the ideal attributes of the tavern became a reality in his hut by the pond and are even more closely paralleled—with many striking verbal echoes—in the idealized house Thoreau describes in the "Housewarming" chapter (*Walden* 243–44).

If "The Landlord" does not quite reveal Thoreau's highest genius, it nevertheless can claim a genuine and effective element of wit and humor, a reasonably well-sustained level of informality and geniality, and serious themes presented in an entertaining and positive key. That is, it exhibits Thoreau as a "practicable" writer in the marketplace. While such sketches were not likely to be treated at any length by reviewers, the *New World* did identify "The Landlord" in its notice of the October *Democratic Review* as among the "lighter miscellaneous articles" that it found "very interesting."[46]

After "The Landlord" appeared in print, Thoreau wrote to his sister Helen, "I did not send the Dem Rev because I had no copy, and my piece was not worth fifty cents" (Corr 147). Walter Harding has commented, "Few now would dispute his judgment,"[47] but Thoreau's remark may reflect his pecuniary judgments as much as his literary ones—after all, the half-pay the *Democratic Review* could offer for "The Landlord" was only twenty dollars and Thoreau was still in debt. Interestingly, Thoreau saw fit to inform his mother and sister of the essay's publication, and both his references to it—as a piece he wrote "to sell," and as one not worth fifty cents to send—involve money; yet Thoreau does not seem to have mentioned "The Landlord" at all in his correspondence with Emerson, who certainly took an active interest in the progress of his literary career. It seems that Thoreau was pleased enough to let his family know he was achieving a modicum of commercial success—however deprecatory his terms—while he was perhaps too conscious of Emerson's lofty standards and expectations to call attention to an apparently slight piece of entertainment. Yet Thoreau reworked both themes and particular passages from "The Landlord" into later works—

most notably *Walden*; so the essay proved, in the long run, to be of greater worth than Thoreau was prepared to acknowledge at this point.

. . .

"Paradise (to Be) Regained" and "The Landlord" were the only pieces Thoreau published in New York at this time. There is no record of payment from the *Democratic Review*, but almost certainly Thoreau was paid no more than forty dollars for both essays. Thoreau had sent "A Winter Walk" to Emerson for the *Dial*, so it did not become part of the "bait" he set before the literary marketplace in New York. Nevertheless, the essay is worth considering in some detail at this point, not only because it was completed during Thoreau's stay in New York, but because the very fact that he chose not to sell it there reflects Thoreau's ambivalent professional judgments and ambitions.

Emerson had requested that Thoreau send him (with less than three weeks' notice) "something good by the 10th of July certainly, if not before" (Corr 102). Clearly Emerson hoped that Thoreau would be able to establish his own, independent career in New York (he had added in this letter, "I am sure you are under sacred protection, if I should not hear from you for years Yet I shall wish to know what befalls you on your way"); but by relying so heavily on Thoreau for assistance with the *Dial*, he was in fact impeding that independence. Thoreau responded to the request by sending some poems and, having rushed to meet the deadline, a draft of "A Winter Walk," saying, "I have very hastily written out something for the Dial, and send it only because you are expecting something,—though something better. It seems idle and Howittish, but it may be of more worth in Concord, where it belongs" (Corr 112).

The essay was "worth more" in Concord only in the sense that, like the "Natural History," it was an account of the local landscape drawn from his journal entries; in a pecuniary sense, however, the essay would have been "worth more" to Thoreau in New York, where he might sell it to a paying magazine. And "A Winter Walk" seems to have been written with a more popular magazine in mind. More than in the "Natural History of Massachusetts," Thoreau consciously shaped his observations into a popular form by working them into an imagined excursion of a single day, from dawn to evening, and by using a familiar first-person narrative voice. Hawthorne had suggested to Epes Sargent that Thoreau might write nature sketches like the "Natural History" but "in a more popular tone," and he quite likely made the suggestion to Thoreau himself. While "A Winter Walk" draws largely upon journal entries from the winters of 1840–1841 and 1841–1842, Thoreau's first attempt to pull these together into a familiar essay was not until late summer or fall of 1842[48]—after Hawthorne had read and responded to the "Natural History" in the *Dial* (and at roughly the same time he composed "A Walk to Wachusett"). Thoreau may have had the *Boston Miscellany* in mind for "A Winter Walk" as well as for "A Walk to Wachusett," but the *Boston Miscellany* had ceased publication with the February 1843 issue; by the time Thoreau finished his sketch there was no longer a paying monthly magazine in the Boston area to send it to.[49] For the lack of a New England alternative, Thoreau was now pleased to send it to Emerson and the *Dial*, but he also felt compelled to apologize for its "idle and Howittish" tone.

The fate of "A Winter Walk" and Emerson's and Thoreau's correspondence regarding it are fraught with ironies; and the tact, delicacy, and indirectness with which each tried to accommodate the other's wishes without clarifying his own perhaps suggest how ill-suited both men were for dealing with the *business* of writing. Thoreau sent his essay to Emerson rather than to a paying magazine in New York because Emerson requested something from him on short notice. When Emerson saw that he did not need it for the July *Dial* after all, he could not simply return it, so he offered to keep it for the October number, "subject however to your order if you find a better disposition for it" (Corr 188)—thus giving Thoreau an opportunity to recall it and submit it to a paying magazine after all. Thoreau was unwilling to take back now what he had freely given, however, so his reply was equally noncommittal, forcing Emerson to decide whether to keep it: "As for the 'Winter Walk' I should be glad to have it printed in the D. if you think it good enough, and will criticize it—otherwise send it to me and I will dispose of it" (Corr 125). In some respects, Thoreau clearly would have liked his essay to appear in the *Dial*, not only because of its local interest but because his early submissions had so often been turned down that it must have been a kind of triumph to him to be published there, even without remuneration. He felt he had alternatives, however. Thoreau's letter corresponds approximately with the time he submitted "Paradise (to Be) Regained" to O'Sullivan, so he could talk of "dispos[ing] of it" elsewhere rather casually. It would be another three weeks before he received O'Sullivan's rejection notice, and a month before he discovered just how straitened the literary marketplace was in New York.

In the meantime, Emerson solicited translations of Pindar from Thoreau while still remaining noncommittal about the fate of Thoreau's essay, writing on July 20 only that "I will soon send you word respecting the 'Winter Walk'" (Corr 127). A week later, "Paradise (to Be) Regained" was rejected by O'Sullivan, who nevertheless requested that Thoreau send him something else: "Especially should I like some of those extracts from your journal, reporting some of your private interviews with nature, with which I have before been so much pleased" (Corr 130). O'Sullivan was probably referring to the "Natural History," which Hawthorne must have called to his attention when the three of them met the previous January. Thoreau now had a complete essay that exactly suited O'Sullivan's request, but it was sitting on

Emerson's desk in Concord. When Thoreau informed Emerson of O'Sullivan's rejection of the Etzler review, he added only that O'Sullivan invited him to submit "other matter—purely literary I suppose" (Corr 133–34). If Thoreau had quoted O'Sullivan more precisely, Emerson might well have been compelled to send back "A Winter Walk"—he had not yet committed himself to printing it in the *Dial*, after all, and he could hardly deny his protégé the double advantage of being paid and addressing a larger audience than the *Dial*'s. But Thoreau's remark gave only the vaguest suggestion of O'Sullivan's interest, which Emerson might apply to Thoreau's essay but only by being the first to suggest that Thoreau take back "A Winter Walk." Emerson would not send the sheets for the October number to the printer for another five weeks, so he certainly had time to return the essay; but he was discovering that there was a paucity of good material for the *Dial*,[50] so in spite of the fact that he did not particularly care for Thoreau's essay, he decided to edit it into shape himself for the October issue. Emerson sent word to Thoreau on September 8:

> I mean to send the Winter's Walk to the printer to-morrow for the Dial. I had some hesitation about it, notwithstanding its faithful observation and its fine sketches of the pickerel-fisher and of the woodchopper, on account of *mannerism*, an old charge of mine,—as if, by attention, one could get the trick of the rhetoric; for example, to call a cold place sultry, a solitude public, a wilderness domestic (a favorite word), and in the woods to insult over cities, whilst the woods, again, are dignified by comparing them to cities, armies, etc. By pretty free omissions, however, I have removed my principal objections. I ought to say that Ellery Channing admired the piece loudly and long. (Corr 137–38)[51]

Thoreau, who could accept Emerson's editorial intervention as he could no one else's, thanked Emerson for the pains he had taken with the manuscript (Corr 139), and "A Winter Walk" was duly printed in the October *Dial*,[52] the same month another "purely literary" piece, "The Landlord," appeared in the *Democratic Review*. Pleased to see his essay in the *Dial*, Thoreau nevertheless lost, by consigning it there, an important piece of "bait" with which to attract New York's paying magazines. Because Thoreau was a painfully slow writer, this loss was all the more significant; it was a poor professional decision for someone determined "to earn a certain sum before winter." More puzzling than the fate of "A Winter Walk," however, is the fact that Thoreau did not eventually comply with O'Sullivan's request for some similar nature sketch. There was still journal material to be mined, but perhaps he felt that his "private interviews with nature" did not satisfy his own ambitions for addressing the *Democratic Review*'s audience. Ironically, it was Hawthorne who had acted on the possibilities of writing nature sketches "in a popular tone": his "Buds and Bird Voices," which may have been inspired by his response to the "Natural History" and which owed at least one nature note directly to Thoreau, was published in the *Democratic Review* for June 1843.[53]

"A Winter Walk" combines, and improves upon, all the elements of popular writing with which he had experimented in his earlier pieces. Thoreau uses concrete and detailed nature descriptions like those which, in the "Natural History," had pleased Hawthorne for being "so true, minute and literal in observation," but he now embeds these (as he had to a lesser extent in "A Walk to Wachusett") in a lively personal narrative. He uses the excursion structure of "A Walk to Wachusett," beginning and ending in the familiar surroundings of "home," and it is made even tighter structurally by being compressed here into the account of a single day. And his use of a diction and rhetoric aimed at establishing the engaging, intimate, and genial tone of the familiar essay is more successful and sustained than in any of his earlier compositions.

The essay's opening description of the serene stillness of a winter night is leisurely, attentive to details; the diction (especially the modifiers, but also the verbs) creates a mood of comfortable domesticity in nature:

> The wind has gently murmured through the blinds, or puffed with feathery softness against the windows, and occasionally sighed like a summer zephyr lifting the leaves along, the livelong night. The meadow mouse has slept in his snug gallery in the sod, the owl has sat in a hollow tree in the depth of the swamp, the rabbit, the squirrel, and the fox have all been housed. The watch-dog has lain quiet on the hearth, and the cattle have stood silent in their stalls. (W 5: 163)

The images of comfort are made all the more inviting by Thoreau's contrast between the cheerful serenity of the sleeping creatures and "forlorn nature at her midnight work," and between the snugness of the "gallery," "house," "hearth," and "stall," and the vast reaches of silent space when he describes the faint creaking of a hinge as "the only sound 'twixt Venus and Mars" (163). But Thoreau's emphasis, both rhetorically and thematically, is on the domesticity of all of nature and on the "remote inward warmth" that endures even on a long winter night. The contrasts dissolve in the summer-in-winter metaphor already implied here and underscored by his description of the midnight snowfall: "But while the earth has slumbered, all the air has been alive with feathery flakes descending, as if some northern Ceres reigned, showering her silvery grain over all the fields" (163).

As in both "A Walk to Wachusett" and the "Natural History," Thoreau first views nature from the familiar confines of "home," but here there is a far greater emphasis on domesticity itself: "We sleep, and at length awake to the still reality of a winter morning. The snow lies warm as cotton or down upon the window-sill; the broadened sash and frosted panes admit a dim and private light, which enhances the snug winter cheer within"

(163). For modern readers of Thoreau, the picturesque and sentimental imagery of these opening pages may seem excessive and distracting, but for better or worse, it was just such characteristics that brought Thoreau's writing into line with the popular writing of the day. If these conventions distract from the work as a natural history essay, they add what the nineteenth-century reader demanded—the element of authorial *personality*. More than in any of his earlier compositions, Thoreau succeeds here in creating that sense of intimacy and immediacy which is the essence of the familiar essay: "The floor creaks under our feet as we move toward the window to look abroad through some clear space over the fields" (163–64). The narrative point of view is the critical element in establishing this familiar tone. The essay is narrated in the present tense and in the first person (primarily in the first-person plural, as here, but also with repeated use of direct address to the reader), both of which create a sense of *presence* and command the reader's participation; the reader becomes the narrator's companion on this excursion.

Thus gradually is the reader escorted from familiar environs to the wonders of nature out-of-doors. From the window, "we see the roofs stand under their snow burden. . . . The trees and shrubs rear white arms to the sky on every side." Then, "silently we unlatch the door, letting the drift fall in, and step abroad to face the cutting air" (164). Initially, this out-of-doors twilight world is presented as mysterious, even somewhat threatening: "A lurid brazen light in the east proclaims the approach of day, while the western landscape is dim and spectral still, and clothed in a Tartarean light, like the shadowy realms. They are Infernal sounds only that you hear,—the crowing of cocks, the barking of dogs, the chopping of wood, the lowing of kine, all seem to come from Pluto's barnyard and beyond the Styx" (164). Here, the domestic is made to seem exotic, mysterious, and a tour of the neighboring landscape is made to appear an exploring expedition of high adventure; but Thoreau's underlying theme is in fact the opposite of this: that to explore even the apparently hostile winter landscape is but to go out into a larger but equally hospitable "home" provided by all of nature.

In the early morning, then, we move leisurely outward, farther away from familiar domestic scenes to nature in its pristine form. "Opening the gate, we tread briskly along the lone country road, crunching the dry crisped snow under our feet" (164). Observing smoke ascending from chimneys, Thoreau interjects his poem "Smoke in Winter," in which the smoke is personified as the dweller's "early scout, his emissary" into the outer world, while the dweller "crouches still beside the hearth, / Nor musters courage to unbar the door." Venturing forth "upon its heavenward course," the wreath of smoke discovers that Nature is benevolent after all, "And greets its master's eye at his low door, / As some refulgent cloud in the upper sky" (165). As if possessing a new faith, Thoreau again describes the sound of chopping wood, the baying of dogs, and the crowing of cocks; now they are not "infernal sounds" but "come clear and bell-like. . . . and even the ordinary rural sounds are melodious, and the jingling of ice on the trees is sweet and liquid" (165–66).

Once fully out-of-doors, Thoreau elaborates his major themes: the purity and health of winter and the "subterranean fire"—the spiritual life—that exists both in man and in nature. And because Thoreau perceives a correspondence between the inner fire in nature and in man, he sees all of nature as his larger home: "At length, having reached the edge of the woods, and shut out the gadding town, we enter within their covert as we go under the roof of a cottage, and cross its threshold, all ceiled and banked up with snow" (168–69). The rhetorical trick of calling everything wild domestic can be, as Emerson complained, heavy-handed ("What would human life be," Thoreau asks, "without forests, those natural cities?"); but this domestication of nature, and the images Thoreau uses to evoke this theme throughout the essay, are also familiar conventions of the romantic picturesque.

Further, Thoreau brings the reader into the scene by direct address: "In this glade covered with bushes of a year's growth, see how the silvery dust lies on every seared leaf and twig. . . . Observe the tiny tracks of mice around every stem, and the triangular track of the rabbit" (169). The narrator is always present as our genial walking companion. He points out the minute details of the scene and also indulges in fanciful speculations along the way. The abstractions are made palatable through the narrator's familiarity—they are not moral imperatives, but speculations designed to entertain us as he guides us along. Thus the transcendental abstractions are embedded in paragraphs that almost invariably begin by reasserting the immediate presence of the narrator and the actual scene:

> Let us go into this deserted woodman's hut. . . . (172)
>
> See how many traces from which we may learn the chopper's history! (173)
>
> And now we descend again, to the brink of this woodland lake. . . . (174)
>
> Again we have wandered through the arches of the wood, until from its skirts we hear the distant booming of the river. . . . (176)
>
> Before night we will take a journey on skates along the course of this meandering river. . . . (177)
>
> Far over the ice, between the hemlock woods and snow-clad hills, stands the pickerel fisher. . . . (180)
>
> But now, while we have loitered, the clouds have gathered again, and a few struggling snowflakes are beginning to descend. (181)
>
> Now commences the long winter evening around the farmer's hearth. . . . (183)

Upon this narrative armature, then, Thoreau can develop his serious themes and moral values. As in the "Natural History," Thoreau moves from the town to the woods in order to propose his vision of man's more spiritual life in nature. Here the movement away from the village finds its fulfillment and complement in the discovery of a woodman's hut (analogous to the discovery of the fishermen's seines in the "Natural History"). Thoreau's description of the hut is a masterful evocation of the life that was lived there, rich in detail and made a felt experience through his use of present tense and direct address. Like a detective reading the clues of life, he examines each artifact, or "fact," and makes it yield its "truth"—evidence of man's health in nature. Thoreau's whole essay is, in fact, about how to read correctly the clues found in nature, and the particular natural facts of the Concord landscape are a microcosm revealing all the laws of nature to those who know how to see.

From the cabin Thoreau leads us to a hilltop, where we again see a column of smoke rising "from some invisible farmhouse" below, as we did when first stepping out onto the road; and again the smoke is an emblem—"a hieroglyphic"—which "suggests more intimate and important things than the boiling of a pot. Where its fine column rises above the forest, like an ensign, some human life has planted itself,—and such is the beginning of Rome, the establishment of the arts, and the foundation of empires, whether on the prairies of America or the steppes of Asia" (174).

From the hilltop we descend to the edge of "a woodland lake," and Thoreau proceeds to read *its* history, "in the lapse of its waves, in the rounded pebbles on its shore, and in the pines which grow down to its brink" (174). Though unnamed here, this is in fact Walden Pond, and Thoreau's description of it as "the earth's liquid eye, a mirror in the breast of nature," is repeated and expanded in "The Ponds" chapter of *Walden*. "Reading" the lake for the truths it might yield, Thoreau notes that it has no apparent outlet or inlet, but he adds: "It has not been idle, though sedentary, but, like Abu Musa, teaches that 'sitting still at home is the heavenly way; the going out is the way of the world.' Yet in its evaporation it travels as far as any" (174). The lake becomes an image of the self and its evaporation (like the smoke ascending from the cabin) an image of his imagination, or spirit—his more ethereal nature. In "A Walk to Wachusett" Thoreau had given his reader notice before the excursion began that "the landscape lies far and fair within, and the deepest thinker is the farthest travelled"; here too Thoreau alerts his reader to the fact that all excursions are interior, and the object of discovery in the exploration of nature is the self. Thoreau is simply taking to its logical conclusion the principle of romantic travel literature in general, the interest of which, as I have noted, resided in the perceiving mind more than in the thing perceived. *Walden*, of course, would be the ultimate expression of this—a travel book in which the narrator literally stayed "at home" and advised his reader to "be a Columbus to whole new continents and worlds within you, opening new channels, not of trade, but of thought" (*Walden* 321).

"A Winter Walk" takes us over the Concord landscape that Thoreau would return to again in *A Week* and *Walden*, finding much the same significance there as he would in those books, just as it also looks back to the "Natural History" and "A Walk to Wachusett." These connections are especially strong when Thoreau describes bodies of water—either the lake or the river, to which he turns next. There, "we see all things from a new and wilder side. . . . It is the outside and edge of the earth" (W 5: 178). Thoreau had similarly described the hilltop on which they rested in "A Walk to Wachusett" as "such a place as one feels to be on the outside of the earth" (W 5: 138). Having stepped outside the bounds of human institutions, we acquire a perspective from which to perceive the universal truths expressed by nature. As in the "Natural History," water is the reconciler of opposites, and upon the river, in the figure of an ice-fisherman, man and nature merge. The fisherman is "himself a finless fish" (W 5: 180); "He belongs to the natural family of man, and is planted deeper in nature and has more root than the inhabitants of towns" (181).

Having taken the reader out into nature for a "new and wilder" view of life, Thoreau brings the essay to a conclusion by retracing his steps, at nightfall, to the secure and familiar surroundings of home and hearth, and even before we are actually indoors Thoreau enlists the conventional imagery of picturesque domesticity again. "Our hearts are warm and cheery, like cottages under drifts, whose windows and doors are half concealed, but from whose chimneys the smoke cheerfully ascends" (182). The essay ends indoors, with familiar images of "a warm corner by the chimney-side" (182) and "warm stoves and fireplaces" (183).

"A Winter Walk" is a paean to the "subterranean fire," the inner life, of which we become fully aware only in winter's outward cold. It is another image for the spirit of "Love" in "Paradise (to Be) Regained" and "Hospitality" in "The Landlord," each a symbol of his unwavering faith in the universe. Thus, in the penultimate paragraph Thoreau explicitly contrasts this fully sufficient source of inner faith with the inadequate forms of faith currently manifest in society.

> The good Hebrew Revelation takes no cognizance of all this cheerful snow. Is there no religion for the temperate and frigid zones? We know of no scripture which records the pure benignity of the gods on a New England winter night. . . . The best scripture, after all, records but a meagre faith. . . . Let a brave, devout man spend the year in the woods of Maine or Labrador, and see if the Hebrew Scriptures speak adequately to his condition and experience, from the setting in of winter to the breaking up of the ice. (183)

Thoreau had similarly concluded "The Landlord" by comparing the tavern favorably with the church. Thoreau's irreverence is protected here (though perhaps just barely) by the license accorded the familiar essayists' fancy; the extravagant claims for the value of winter call for the indulgence of his reader/companion, who shares with him, after all, this special knowledge of northern winters. "A Winter Walk" is, like the rest of Thoreau's writing, a testament of his own particular faith. Significantly, Thoreau ends his essay by proclaiming that faith not in oracular and prophetic pronouncements but in the image of a familiar domestic scene, "the long winter evening around the farmer's hearth, when the thoughts of the indwellers travel far abroad, and men are by nature and necessity charitable and liberal to all creatures" (183).

It is not really surprising that, in spite of Emerson's reservations about the essay (as well as Thoreau's own), "A Winter Walk" was Thoreau's most popular essay to date, for if it is a vehicle for Thoreau's transcendentalist faith in nature, it is also a veritable catalog of conventional images of picturesque New England—from the barnyard at dawn, to the smoke ascending from the rustic cabin, to the ice-laced branches, to the abandoned woodsman's cabin, to skating on the river, to the solitary fisherman, to the snug farmer's hearth. The essay evoked an immediate positive response from the popular press and remained influential. Greeley's *Tribune* reviewed the October 1843 *Dial* favorably overall and had high praise for "A Winter Walk" in particular, reprinting a long, seven-paragraph extract from it.[54] The *Knickerbocker Magazine*'s review of the *Dial* called it "a very excellent and lifeful number of that greatly-improved magazine," and "A Winter Walk" was one of four pieces it singled out for particular praise. Of Thoreau's essay the reviewer wrote, "Well pleased should we have been to accompany our observant and thoughtful essayist, when he fetched his 'Winter Walk.' Mark his delicate appreciation of the little acccessories of the season. We thank him for awakening vivid glimpses of the past, that go strait [*sic*] to the fresh scenes of boyhood." Interestingly, he quotes the paragraph on the "slumbering subterranean fire" in nature, one of the most "transcendental" passages of the essay—and that quotation constitutes the longest extract in the review. So it is especially significant that the writer concludes with the observation "There is much less of the new style of verbal affectation in the present than in preceding numbers of 'the Dial,' and it is just in this proportion the more readable and attractive."[55] Even embedded in the obscure pages of the *Dial*, the essay attracted attention, and years later it was recalled by both Thomas Wentworth Higginson and James Russell Lowell in their own familiar essays on winter—essays that were to a large extent modeled on Thoreau's.[56] Thus "A Winter Walk" provided a model for popular outdoor sketches long after the *Dial* ceased to exist.

The publication of "A Winter Walk" in the *Dial* signaled the end of Thoreau's experiment in New York. He returned home briefly at Thanksgiving, at which time Emerson arranged for him to deliver a lecture at the Concord Lyceum, and by December he was back in Concord to stay. There is every indication that "A Winter Walk" could have been published in the paying *Democratic Review*, but it is even clearer that Thoreau could not have earned his keep in New York on its meager pay and his meager output. He did not write enough to keep pace with magazine publishing even if the magazines had been more willing to print his works or able to pay enough for them to make it worth his while. Yet his failure in New York was due as much to circumstances as to his character. I have suggested the almost overwhelming obstacles presented by the New York literary marketplace in 1843; and it is perhaps worth noting that Emerson, who avoided many of these impediments by lecturing rather than publishing in New York, had in fact been quite as unhappy in New York as Thoreau, explaining his feelings in a letter to Fuller: "I was born to stay at home, not to ramble. . . . These kindly but too determined persons, the air of Wall street, the . . . crowd in Broadway, the endless rustle of newspapers all make me feel not the value of their classes but of my own class—the supreme need of the few worshippers of the muse—wild & sacred—as counteraction to this world of material ephemeral interest" (EmL 3: 20). Emerson sent Thoreau to New York with high hopes, but one suspects that he hoped, in part, that the younger and more practical Thoreau—his former handyman—would perform the missionary duties of transcendentalism in the city as his surrogate. This is not to deny Emerson's truly high regard for and service to Thoreau, which seem indisputable, but it should help explain why Thoreau himself, under less congenial conditions than Emerson had experienced there, found New York such a trial. Thoreau's failure in New York did not signal the end of his literary ambitions, but it did profoundly alter the course of his professional career; back in Concord, Thoreau would need to reassess his sense of himself as a writer and his relation to the literary marketplace.

PART III

A Strategic Retreat

Chapter 5

"FAVORED BY THE GODS": WRITING FROM WALDEN POND

WHEN THOREAU returned to Concord from Staten Island, he settled in again with his parents and spent the year 1844 working in his father's pencil business to pay off the debts he had incurred the previous year. Emerson did much to mitigate Thoreau's sense of failure, both by his continued solicitation of material for the *Dial* and by seeking new literary outlets for his disciple. By returning to the security offered by that discipleship, however, Thoreau also seems to have retreated somewhat from the literary independence he had begun to exercise. When Emerson learned that Thoreau would be returning from Staten Island for Thanksgiving, he urged him to bring back something to read at the Concord Lyceum (Corr 149). As I noted in chapter 1, Thoreau had been engaged since 1841 in a sporadic but more or less systematic study of early English poets, and he had returned to this project with considerable energy while in New York, where he frequented the libraries to read Ossian as well as Renaissance poets. Thoreau does not seem to have made any serious efforts toward compiling a book on the English poets, but he could at least mine this material for lectures, so on November 29, 1843, Thoreau delivered a lecture, "Ancient Poets" (Homer, Ossian, and Chaucer). This lecture seems to have been intended, like the "Sir Walter Raleigh" lecture, to establish Thoreau's reputation by retracing the steps of Emerson's own early lectures. Just as "Raleigh" followed the model of Emerson's 1835 series of lectures on "Great Men," Thoreau's "Ancient Poets" bears striking similarities to Emerson's 1835–1836 series, "English Literature."

Thoreau treats both Homer and Ossian as exemplifying the primitive energy and original value of poetry and the poet. When he considers the age of Chaucer, Thoreau says, "We cannot escape the impression, that the Muse has stooped a little in her flight, when we come to the literature of civilized eras. . . . The bard has lost the dignity and sacredness of his office" (EEM 162). Emerson, in his lecture on Chaucer, had similarly lamented the decline in the status of the poet from bard to mere decoration that began in the Middle Ages: "The English poets of the Middle and Modern age were forced to quit the raised platform from which elder bards had talked down to the multitude and win their attention by the study of the taste and genius of the people. To get any audience at all they were forced to amuse the people."[1] Emerson's lament acquired a particularly poignant resonance for would-be bards and prophets contributing to the *Dial,* and both Emerson and Thoreau hoped, of course, to restore to the poet his original dignity and prophetic role; but both writers, in tracing a decline from the golden age of bardic poetry and myth, were expressing what had by this time become a romantic commonplace. Thoreau knew from his Harvard days, for example, Friedrich von Schlegel's *Lectures on the History of Literature,* which outlined the historical descent of literature from "the elevated character of heroic times . . . into the common life and citizenship of ordinary men."[2]

Emerson subsequently published an edited version of the lecture as "Homer. Ossian. Chaucer." in the January 1844 *Dial* and even paid Thoreau ten dollars—apparently the only time Thoreau was paid for contributions to the *Dial.*[3] The *New York Tribune*'s laudatory review of that number found Thoreau's lecture particularly admirable; yet the reviewer damns Thoreau even as he praises him, by describing him as "a young disciple and companion of Emerson, in whom the true spirit of the author's philosophy is reproduced."[4]

Indeed, Thoreau had little to say that Emerson had not already said eight years earlier. In the long run, it would do little good to retrace the steps of Emerson's own apprenticeship if Thoreau could do no more than echo his mentor. While Thoreau subsequently revised this lecture further for inclusion in A *Week* (as he did with so much of his early writing), he did not use any other of his commonplace book material on the English poets for independent pieces, and Thoreau effectively abandoned the project in 1844.[5]

Thoreau's other contributions to the January 1844 *Dial* had even less potential to advance his career. Emerson printed the translation from Pindar that he had solicited—though Thoreau discovered that he wished Pindar "was better worth translating" (Corr 133); and Thoreau also seems at least to have had a hand in preparing the extracts from "The Preaching of Buddha" and from "Hermes Trismegistus" for the "Ethnical Scriptures." For the final number of the *Dial,* in April 1844, Emerson printed some of the remaining poems of Pindar and Thoreau's review, the "Herald of Freedom," of Nathaniel P. Rogers's antislavery weekly periodical. Only this last contribution exhibits Thoreau as an independent writer.

The "Herald of Freedom" is a minor piece, filled largely with quotations from Rogers's editorials, but it is interesting in several respects. Most obviously, the review's staunch support for Rogers's antislavery activity demonstrates Thoreau's increasing willingness to engage in social questions of the day. This is not a new departure for Thoreau so much as the development of a tendency suggested as early as his lecture "Sir Walter Raleigh," but in "Herald of Freedom" Thoreau commits himself more fully than in any of his previous pieces to a particular political stance—specifically, Rogers's no-organization position toward the antislavery movement. Significantly, though, Thoreau praises and defends Rogers as much for the vigor, simplicity, and clarity of his style as for his politics, and in fact suggests a close relationship between the two. Rogers's "genuine yankee style," he says, "reminds us occasionally, as does all free, brave, and original writing, of its great master these days, Thomas Carlyle" (RP 50). Thoreau expresses his admiration for Rogers's equally forthright character and prose style in terms recalling "the poet active, the saint enterprising" of his "Raleigh" essay, who continued to serve as Thoreau's own ideal self-image even after his failure in New York.

It is perhaps appropriate then, that Thoreau's review appeared in the *Dial*'s final number, for it suggests the extent to which the *Dial* had outlived its purpose. Emerson had sedulously attempted all along to keep the *Dial* aloof from specific social issues and focused on universal moral verities, but by 1844 it was becoming increasingly clear to the transcendentalists that such a stance could not engage the American public. Greeley's *Tribune*, faithful to the end, printed what amounted to a eulogy for the *Dial*, but in praising it, also implicitly revealed the cause of its failure:

> "The Dial" holds the same relation to our current periodical literature that the Poet or Prophet does to the money-getting, pork-producing characters of everyday life. On its fair pages the idealist, the advocate of novel and startling theories (so they be generous and informed by love) is permitted to utter his free thoughts. We know no magazine more valuable to a strong mind, more fascinating to a refined one. . . . "The Dial" was filled with admirable papers by R. W. Emerson, C. Lane, W. E. Channing, H. D. Thoreau, and others of the noblest intellects and most genial spirits in New England.[6]

Emerson himself recognized the need for these writers to move beyond what were now the confines of the *Dial*. He had perhaps recognized this in sending Thoreau off to New York, and though that venture had failed, the *Dial* was still not a satisfactory alternative. When the *Dial* finally ceased publication, Emerson announced to his friend William Henry Furness, "Its last number is printed; & having lived four years, which is a Presidential term in America, it may respectably end. . . . It is time that each of the principal contributors to it, should write in their own names, and go to their proper readers."[7]

Thoreau's problem now was finding a way to reach his "proper readers," for with the end of the *Dial* and his experience in New York, there seemed to be few outlets for his work. One rather surprising opportunity occurred when Thoreau was included in a series of lectures on reform issues at Boston's Amory Hall during the spring of 1844.[8] Emerson read his "New England Reformers" there on March 3, and he was almost certainly responsible for getting Thoreau on the program; the following week, on March 10, Thoreau delivered his "Reformers," a lecture that developed the theme of individual moral reform which informed both "Paradise (to Be) Regained" and "Herald of Freedom." Even while Thoreau was becoming increasingly direct in his treatment of social issues, however, he deliberately stood apart from organized reform movements of the day—many of which were represented in this lecture series. As part of this series, Thoreau's lecture was advertised widely in the Boston papers,[9] and as his first lecture outside of Concord this was an important event in Thoreau's career; but because the position toward reform that he shared with Emerson was so anomalous, it did not help set Thoreau's career in any clear direction. There seems to have been virtually no response or comment upon his lecture either in the local press or among his transcendentalist friends, or even in Thoreau's own journals and correspondence.

At the end of April 1844, after the last *Dial* had been printed, Thoreau took a boat trip up the Sudbury River with Edward Hoar (during which they accidentally set fire to the Concord woods), and in late July he made an excursion to Saddleback Mountain in the Berkshires and then, joined by Ellery Channing, on to the Catskills. September was taken up with helping his father build a new house. But these desultory activities only deferred the time when he would need to come to terms with his literary vocation. After the *Dial* ceased publication, Thoreau did not appear either in print or on the lecture platform for a full year. Emerson seems to have been disappointed with Thoreau's lack of accomplishment. He had almost nothing to say about Thoreau in his journals during 1844 and 1845, and his one extended comment on him reveals his ambivalent attitude toward his disciple. "Henry is a good substantial child. . . . The only man of leisure in the town," he wrote, but he added a revealing note of mixed respect and disappointment: "If I cannot show his performance much more manifest than that of the other grand promisers, at least I can see that with his practical faculty, he has declined all kingdoms of this world. Satan has no bribe for him" (JMN 9: 103).

Yet Thoreau was not quite ready to renounce "all kingdoms of this world" in the way Emerson's remark implies. Thoreau's poem "The Offer," written during the summer of 1844,[10] poignantly expresses his frustration with his current state of inactivity and his resolute ambition:

> I make ye an offer,
> Ye gods hear the scoffer,
> The scheme will not hurt you,
> If ye will find goodness I will find virtue.
> Though I am your creature,
> And child of your nature,
> I have pride still unbended,

And blood undescended,
Some free independence,
And my own descendents.
If ye will deal plainly,
    I will strive mainly,
If ye will discover
    Great plans to your lover,
And give him a sphere
    Somewhat larger than here.

(J2: 93)

Reminiscent of his journal entries following John's death, Thoreau's poem is an even more explicit proposal to enter into a covenant with the gods. His pride was indeed "still unbended" in this expression of his frustrated ambition to become an American prophet: he will serve the gods faithfully if they will "discover great plans" to him and provide a larger sphere in which to enact them.

His sense of that covenant had all along been linked somehow with his brother John; and he had long been struggling to find some appropriate form for his desultory notes on the two-week trip they had made together in 1839, boating north on the Concord and Merrimack Rivers into New Hampshire and then hiking to the summit of Mount Washington in the White Mountains. Thoreau now returned to the few notes he had made in 1842 and began in earnest drafting the book that would eventually become *A Week on the Concord and Merrimack Rivers*.[11] It is hard to say precisely why Thoreau began *A Week* at this particular point. In part, he may have felt that without any ready outlet for his writings in the periodical press it was necessary to take on a book-length project to enact his "great plans." He may also have been encouraged in the project by the publication in June 1844 of Fuller's *A Summer on the Lakes, in 1843*, a similarly desultory and digressive travelogue. And Thoreau's own recent excursion with Ellery Channing may have reinvigorated his interest in the account—the ascent of Saddleback on this later trip would eventually be incorporated into his book manuscript. One additional factor was crucial in enabling Thoreau to concentrate on an ambitious writing project: in September of 1844, Emerson bought a piece of land on the shores of Walden Pond, and it was not long before Thoreau was making plans to take up residence there. The move to Walden Pond would, to a considerable extent, free Thoreau from his immediate need to earn a living and would thus enable him to produce the most ambitious works of his career.

Even before moving into his cabin, Thoreau completed a lecture, "Concord River," which he read at the Concord Lyceum on March 25, 1845. This was Thoreau's only lecture during the 1844–1845 lecture season[12] (which regularly ran roughly from October to early May), and Thoreau was not paid for lecturing at the Concord Lyceum; but "Concord River"—which was eventually incorporated into the first two chapters of A *Week*—dealt with a topic of local interest, and reading it may have provided further impetus for sustained work on the book.

Thoreau also appeared in print once between the end of the *Dial* and his move to the pond. Two weeks before Thoreau's lecture, Wendell Phillips had given a lecture, "Slavery," at the Concord Lyceum, and Thoreau responded with a letter to the editor of the *Liberator*, praising Phillips's lecture. The prospect of a Phillips lecture stirred up considerable controversy within the Concord Lyceum each time he was proposed, and this time the conservative curators resigned rather than invite him. Thoreau became one of the replacements who were responsible for extending the invitation, and his letter was therefore most likely a calculated follow-up, defending Phillips's right to speak and confirming the success of the lecture itself.[13] Thoreau's letter (which was printed in the *Liberator* for March 28, 1845) thus makes a modest addition to Thoreau's growing body of compositions concerned explicitly with social reform. Moreover, as his first and only "letter to the editor" consciously intended for publication, it was also a resourceful means of maintaining a modicum of public visibility, even as he was about to withdraw to prepare a more ambitious project for publication.

Thoreau spent the remainder of that spring preparing for his move to Walden, and when he took up residence there in July, he felt as if his "offer" to the gods had been accepted; ten days after moving to his cabin he wrote,

> Sometimes when I compare myself with other men methinks I am favored by the Gods. They seem to whisper joy to me beyond my deserts and that I do have a solid warrant and surety at their hands, which my fellows do not. . . . I am especially guided and guarded.
>
> And now I think of it—let me remember—
>
> What was seen true once—and sanctioned by the flash of Jove—will always be true, and nothing can hinder it. I have the warrant that no fair dream I have had need fail of its fulfilment. (J2: 159–60; cf. *Walden* 131)

As if to fulfill his end of the covenant, Thoreau began work on literary projects with an energy unmatched by any of his earlier efforts.

His first priority was his account of the 1839 river trip with John. With very few notes from the actual excursion, he ransacked the whole of his journal for other, related material and for self-contained meditations and sketches that might be interpolated to flesh out the narrative. By the end of 1845, Thoreau had completed a skeletal first draft.[14] Thoreau did not think of this as a finished composition—it consists of only 111 manuscript leaves, and much of the narrative was still in hurriedly written fragments—but it was a sufficient framework upon which to build a book. He wrote it as a day-by-day account, but already he had determined to limit his narrative to the river journey, omitting the week's hike through the White Mountains. Perhaps this was Thoreau's first fatal decision about this book, for he eliminated precisely that part of his excursion of greatest interest to tourists, painters, and other writers. Nevertheless, once that interlude in their journey was eliminated, the symmetrical and potentially symbolic narrative structure of a single week became evident. Moreover, as slight as this draft is, Thoreau had already begun to use the river narrative as a vehicle for extended digressions, meditations, and reflections on various topics.

With this rough draft under way, Thoreau turned to other literary projects. In addition to completing this draft of *A Week*, he also began shaping the record of his life at the pond into lecture material (see J2: 187) and drafted a lecture on Thomas Carlyle, all during the second half of 1845. He finished his Carlyle lecture by the middle of the next lecture season and read it at the Concord Lyceum on February 4, 1846, giving it the title "The Writings and Style of Thomas Carlyle."

Carlyle had generated considerable interest among both the transcendentalists and the larger reading public. Emerson had been Carlyle's literary agent in America, arranging for the publication of his books here, and Carlyle had long been identified—for better or worse—as one of the chief exporters of the "German fog" of transcendental philosophy and language. A writer of acknowledged status, however controversial, Carlyle made a fairly promising subject for a lyceum lecture. As a critical review of a contemporary writer, the lecture marks yet another new genre for Thoreau (though we might consider "Herald of Freedom" and "Wendell Phillips" as exercises anticipating this full-scale critical analysis), but Thoreau had long been familiar with Carlyle's writing and drew for the lecture upon entries made in his journal as early as 1842.

This was Thoreau's only lecture of the season, just as "Concord River" had been his only lecture the previous year, but in both cases Thoreau began reworking them almost immediately into publishable form. This was a slow and difficult process for Thoreau, but by midsummer he had completed his Carlyle essay, now titled "Thomas Carlyle and His Works."

The essay begins with a brief biographical sketch, clearly intended to accommodate what Thoreau understood to be the interest of the general reader, and thus to broaden the popular appeal of the piece. "Thomas Carlyle is a Scotchman," Thoreau's essay begins, "born about fifty years ago, 'at Ecclefechan, Annandale,' according to one authority" (EEM 219). Thoreau's authority here, and for the bulk of the biographical sketch, was George Gilfillan's *Sketches of Modern Literature, and Eminent Literary Men (Being a Gallery of Literary Portraits)*, just published by D. Appleton & Co. (New York) in 1846 (J2: 216–17). This book, most likely unavailable to Thoreau until after his lecture on Carlyle in February, was invaluable to him in providing material for his essay's introductory sketch, which is to a considerable extent simply a string of quotations from Gilfillan's book. Yet the impatience and the irony with which Thoreau presents this material suggest that while he recognized the popularity of "literary portraits," he was also satirizing them, exposing the triviality and irrelevance of such concern for the accidental *facts* of a man's life rather than for the enduring *truths* he discovered and recorded. Thus Thoreau rapidly outlines the events of Carlyle's early life and career but implicitly dismisses them as "the usual middle passage of a literary life." Thoreau draws heavily upon Gilfillan's account to set up an intimate sketch of the author at home: "You may imagine him living in altogether a retired and simple way, with small family, in a quiet part of London, called Chelsea, a little out of the din of commerce, in 'Cheyne Row,' there, not far from the 'Chelsea Hospital.' 'A little past this, and an old ivy-clad church, with its buried generations lying around it,' writes one traveller, 'you come to an antique street running at right angles with the Thames, and, a few steps from the river, you find Carlyle's name on the door'" (EEM 220). In embellishing this account, however, Thoreau undermines it, wryly poking fun at our concern for the trivialities of the writer's routine. He pictures Carlyle surrounded by his books and papers, "now, perhaps, looking out into the street on brick and pavement, for a change, and now upon some rod of grass ground in the rear; or, perchance he steps over to the British Museum, and makes that his studio for the time. This is the fore part of the day; that is the way with literary men commonly" (221). "In the meanwhile," Thoreau continues, "people are calling to *see* him, from various quarters, very few worthy of being *seen* by him, 'distinguished travellers from America,' not a few, to all and sundry of whom he gives freely of his yet unwritten rich and flashing soliloquy" (221). Finally Thoreau's irony exposes his masquerade; he abandons the effort to sketch Carlyle's life—nominally because he lacks further information but in fact because this account has so little to do with Carlyle's greatness. "How after all, he gets his living; what proportion of his daily bread he earns by day-labor or job-work with his pen, what he inherits, what steals—questions whose answers are so significant, and not to be omitted in his biography—we, alas! are unable to answer here" (222).

Instead, he turns to that which is indeed noteworthy about Carlyle, beginning with his impact upon America. "When we remember how these volumes came over to us. . . . and what commotion they created in many private breasts, we wonder that the country did not ring . . . from the Atlantic to the Pacific, with its greeting. . . . Through him, as usher, we have been . . . made acquainted with what philosophy and criticism the nineteenth century had to offer" (222–23). Thoreau acknowledges that to the older generation, especially, Carlyle's writings have seemed an abomination, perverse and impenetrable, abounding "only in obstinate mannerisms, Germanisms, and whimsical ravings of all kinds," yet "to many a clear-headed boy, they are the plainest English" and Carlyle speaks especially to those "in the most perceptive and recipient season of life" (224–25).

In discussing characteristics of Carlyle's works Thoreau becomes increasingly engaged; his analysis is generalized, rather impressionistic, and ultimately quite personal as he tries to reach some fair estimate of the man. "We have not attempted to discriminate between his works," he explains toward the end of the essay, "but have rather regarded them all as one work, as is the man himself. We have not examined so much as remembered them. To do otherwise, would have required a more indifferent, and perhaps even less just review, than the present" (258). In these general terms, his estimate of Carlyle is perceptive, but his approach perhaps inevitably reveals even more about Thoreau himself. In trying to provide a balanced assessment of Carlyle's strengths and weaknesses Thoreau often seems to contradict himself, and at these impasses, especially, Thoreau exposes his ambivalence about his own literary values—which at this time he was reassessing and modifying.

He identifies Carlyle's style as "eminently colloquial . . . the rhythms and cadences of conversation endlessly repeated"; and he becomes Carlyle-ish himself as he expands his characterization:

> It resounds with emphatic, natural, lively, stirring tones, muttering, rattling, exploding, like shells and shot, and with like execution. So far as it is a merit in composition, that the written answer to the spoken word, and the spoken word to a fresh and pertinent thought in the mind, as well as to the half thoughts, the tumultuary misgivings and expectancies, this author is, perhaps, not to be matched in literature. (226)

Thoreau valued the forcefulness of colloquial language and had similarly championed the raw vigor of the language of the American West and Nathaniel Rogers's "genuine yankee style," which he likened to Carlyle's; but his qualification here, "So far as it is a merit in composition," bespeaks deep reservations as well. What Carlyle gains in vigor he loses in depth and resonance. Thoreau imagines Carlyle must be "a rare talker"; however, "he does not trace back the stream of his thought, silently adventurous, up to its fountain-head, but is borne away with it, as it rushes through his brain like a torrent to overwhelm and fertilize" (229). The result is that "his works are not to be studied, but read with a swift satisfaction. . . . The first impression is the truest and deepest, and there is no reprint, no *double entendre*, so to speak, for the alert reader" (241).

Thoreau praises Carlyle's humor as "a main attraction in these books" and notes that "especially the transcendental philosophy needs the leaven of humor to render it light and digestible" (235). The more serenely transcendent one's vision, the broader the range of one's humor; "To the thinker, all the institutions of men, as all imperfection, viewed from the point of equanimity, are legitimate subjects of humor," and Carlyle's humor "is always subordinate to a serious purpose" (235–236). Yet having made these claims, he goes on to suggest that even "the deepest humor will not keep. . . . In the oldest literature, in the Hebrew, the Hindoo, the Persian, the Chinese, it is rarely humor, even the most divine, which still survives, but the most sober and private, painful or joyous thoughts, maxims of duty, to which the life of all men may be referred. After time has sifted the literature of a people, there is left only their SCRIPTURE, for that is WRITING, *par excellence*" (238). He says that Carlyle's style is "one of the most important features of the man"—"so diversified and variegated!"—and claims that while "others speak with greater emphasis to scholars . . . none so earnestly and effectually to all who read" (228, 230, 234); yet he also says that "Carlyle must undoubtedly plead guilty to the charge of mannerism. . . . There is no mannerism in Scriptures. . . . Of this universal speech there is very little" (239–40). He says Carlyle "has the earnestness of a prophet" and that "his writings are a gospel to the young of this generation" (235), yet later he says that "Carlyle is not a *seer*, but a brave looker-on and *reviewer*" (246).

For all Thoreau's ambivalence about Carlyle's colloquialism, his humor, and his mannered style, Thoreau seems to admire without qualification Carlyle's use of "exaggeration"—a term that perhaps comprehends all of these other characteristics. "He who cannot exaggerate is not qualified to utter truth," he writes. "Moreover, you must speak loud to those who are hard of hearing, and so you acquire the habit of shouting to those who are not" (265). This of course anticipates Thoreau's celebration of "extra-vagance" in the "Conclusion" to *Walden*, just as Thoreau's critique of Carlyle generally reflects the reassessment of literary values that occupied these crucial years at the pond. Certainly one can see the use of more vigorous, colloquial speech, of humor, and of exaggeration in *Walden*, which he was beginning to write at this time; and if these traits are less apparent in *A Week*, that is at least in part because that book collected so much of his earlier writing. Yet Thoreau learned as much from the assessment of Carlyle's weaknesses as he did from the discovery of his strengths: Thoreau believed in the ultimate superiority of the written to the spoken word, and while he increasingly adopted the more vigorous language of speech, he even more assiduously cultivated "*double entendre* . . . for the alert reader." Thoreau found something admirable in Carlyle's ability "to address himself to his own age" (233), but he faulted him for not having "addressed himself more entirely to his true audience posterity" (250). Thoreau desired to address both audiences, and while Carlyle provided a valuable model for addressing his contemporary readers, when Thoreau turned his eye toward posterity his model was the sober serenity of Scripture—"WRITING, par excellence"—in comparison with which Carlyle appeared rather thin and ephemeral.

The tension between his desire to address his contemporaries and to address posterity parallels the tension between his impulse toward action, on the one hand, and contemplation on the other. Thoreau's desire to combine these is suggested in his comparison between Carlyle and Emerson, two men whom he considers "the complement of each other." Carlyle, he says, "has more sympathy with heroes, or practical reformers, [Emerson] with the observers or philosophers; put these worthies together, and you will have a pretty fair representation of mankind" (251). The contrast is telling, for it not only helps Thoreau characterize Carlyle but suggests the extent to which he was beginning to distance himself from Emerson: by characterizing him thus he establishes both the extent and the limits of Emerson's influence as model and mentor. Indeed, Thoreau was particularly preoccupied at this time with the question of how to combine these characteristics in his own nature—and ultimately in his writing. In a journal entry during the spring of 1846 (while he was working on this essay) Thoreau had written, "The struggle in me is between a love of contemplation and a love of action—the life of a philosopher & of a hero. . . . To make a perfect man—the soul must be much like the body not too unearthly and the body like the soul. The one must not deny & oppress the other" (J2: 240). Shortly afterward, he returned to the subject, observing,

> Certainly I am not living that heroic life I had dreamed of—And yet all my veins are full of life—and nature whispers no reproach—The day advances as if to light some work of mine—and I defer in my thought as if there were some where busier men—It was morning & lo! it is now evening—and nothing memorable is accomplished—Yet my nature is *almost* content with this—It hears no reproach in nature. (J2: 242)

Yet the serenity and leisure of inaction grated on him, too, especially since he saw himself as having a special destiny to fulfill. In his journal, he sought a reconciliation between action and inaction by turning to the Bhagavad Gita; his journal for late June is filled with long quotations from this work: "The man is praised, who, having subdued all his passions, performeth with his active faculties all the functions of life, unconcerned about the event. Perform the settled functions: action is preferable to inaction. The journey of the mortal frame may not succeed from inaction" (J2: 253–54; cf. 255–61). Much of this debate eventually found its way into A *Week*; and in his essay on Carlyle, he sought to reconcile action and inaction by comprehending the complementary traits he attributed to Carlyle and Emerson. Together, he said, these two cover a fairly comprehensive spectrum of humanity, but he notes exceptions: "To say nothing of Christ, who yet awaits a just appreciation from literature, the peacefully practical hero, whom Columbus may represent, is obviously slighted; but above and after all, the Man of the Age, come to be called working-man, it is obvious that none yet speaks to his condition, for the speaker is not yet in his condition" (EEM 251). Here Thoreau defined the role he might fulfill without being a mere imitator of either Carlyle or Emerson. If, through failure, Thoreau had been forced to come to terms with getting a living—hoeing beans at Walden Pond—he perhaps also found himself in precisely that condition to address the "Man of the Age," the "working-man." In *Walden* he would mythologize this figure into the native type of "the peacefully practical hero," and certainly the "Conclusion" establishes Columbus as his representative man. But it is, of course, an *inward* exploration he celebrates there, and in his account of cultivating his bean fields especially we discover that he has not forgotten the lesson of the Bhagavad Gita, for it is a labor both heroic and transcendent.

Ironically, Thoreau's work on Carlyle brought him back to himself, to his own life at the pond as the authority that justified his addressing the public. While transforming his Carlyle lecture into an essay Thoreau also returned to A *Week*, filling it out by drawing upon passages from earlier, unpublished compositions including "The Service" and "Sir Walter Raleigh."[15] By July 1846, Thoreau had begun reading from his book manuscript to Alcott, who described it in his diary as "a pastoral Book now ready for the Press,"[16] and to Emerson, who wrote enthusiastically to Charles King Newcomb, "In a short while, if Wiley & Putnam smile, you shall have Henry Thoreau's 'Excursion on Concord & Merrimack Rivers,' a seven days' voyage in as many chapters, pastoral as Isaak Walton, spicy as flagroot, broad & deep as Menu. He read me some of it under an oak on the river bank the other afternoon, and invigorated me" (EmL 3: 338). Thoreau himself must have been the source of Alcott's and Emerson's impression that the book was ready for press, but it was his essay on Carlyle, not A *Week*, that he tried to publish at this time. Thoreau kept his book manuscript, revising and expanding it considerably over the next year. Perhaps he felt he could afford to do so now that his Carlyle essay was finished: in early August he sent the essay to Greeley, asking him to place it, if he could, in a paying magazine.

A few weeks earlier—in late July—Thoreau had spent the night in jail for refusing to pay a poll tax, and by the end of August Thoreau would leave on his first excursion to the Maine woods; but in the midst of these acts of rebellion against and withdrawal from society Thoreau was still trying to succeed in the *business* of writing in the marketplace. Greeley had most likely first offered to be of service when Thoreau met with him in New York in 1843; when he now received Thoreau's manuscript, he readily took on the role of Thoreau's unofficial literary agent. In his reply to Thoreau, Greeley gave him a forthright appraisal and some sound professional advice. "I *mean* to do the errand you have asked me," he wrote, "and that soon. But I am not sanguine of success, and have hardly a hope that it will be immediate if ever. I hardly know a soul that could publish your article all at once, and 'to be continued' are words shunned like the pestilence." Greeley knew the criteria of the marketplace and saw immediately that Thoreau's essay was too long to suit the paying magazines of the day; he liked the essay very much but told Thoreau it was "too solidly good, I fear, to be profitable to yourself or attractive to publishers." This was advice Thoreau needed to hear if he indeed wanted to "tempt the rats," but Greeley knew his man and realized that to adopt the standards of the marketplace himself was no way to persuade Thoreau, so he added, "Didst thou ever, O my friend! ponder on the significance and cogency of the assurance, 'Ye cannot serve God and Mammon,' as applicable to literature. . . . In my poor judgment, if any thing is calculated to make a scoundrel of an honest man, writing to sell is that particular thing" (Corr 169–70). Thoreau's experience in New York had made him suspicious of the literary marketplace, but Greeley's genuine and unwavering faith in Thoreau won his trust.

Perhaps nothing so clearly illustrates the inestimable service Greeley did for Thoreau as the letter Greeley wrote to George R. Graham, publisher and editor of *Graham's Magazine*, regarding the Carlyle essay. The very elements about which Greeley had confessed his doubts to Thoreau he now turned into virtues, and he presented the piece to the magazine as something it could not afford to pass by:

> Thoreau is a young man, a scholar, poor of course, and sends this to me to get utterance and bread. I know it is unlike the general staple of your Magazine, but I think it will on that account be relished and give a zest to the work. That it is a brilliant as well as vigorous essay, and gives a Daguerrotype of Carlyle and Carlylism which no man living but Emerson could excel, I believe any scholar would say, and I am confident it would attract many new readers to the Magazine. It would make about a sheet or sixteen pages of the Mag. and would probably have to be divided—I hope but once. If you choose to publish it, and pay as much as you pay others for right good prose (where you are not buying a name) I will make it sell a pile of Magazines, anyhow.
>
> I offer it first to you, and ask you to let me have your decision upon it as soon as practicable. Keep the MS. till I send for it, as I may think best to offer it to Godey if you don't want it.[17]

Greeley had just the right combination of disarming frankness and astute salesmanship to enable him to work effectively with such different men as Henry Thoreau and George R. Graham; his letters to each of them are masterpieces of diplomacy. Greeley's final touch here, the veiled threat to sell the piece to the fiercest competitor of *Graham's*, must have made the essay irresistible, and Graham eventually accepted the essay.

There were long delays at every stage of the publication process, however, and Thoreau was anxious to make the essay pay. When Greeley wrote to Thoreau at the end of September informing him that the essay would be published in *Graham's*, he made a point of saying, "Of course it is to be paid for at the usual rate, as I expressly so stated when I enclosed it to Graham"; and after inquiring whether Graham had already written to Thoreau, he reiterates his understanding: "The pay, however, is sure, though the amount may not be large, and I think you may wait until the article appears, before making further stipulations on the subject" (Corr 170). There was no further word on the piece until late October, when Greeley (again, it seems, in response to an inquiry from Thoreau) explained,

> I have to-day received a letter from Griswold, in Philadelphia, who says, "The article by Thoreau on Carlyle is in type, and will be paid for liberally." "Liberally" is quoted as an expression of Graham's. I know well the difference between a publisher's and an author's idea of what *is* "liberally"; but I give you the best I can get as the result of three letters to Philadelphia on this subject. (Corr 171)

The essay turned out not to be "in type," however, and on December 16, 1846, Greeley wrote to Griswold again: "Why don't Graham publish my friend Thoreau's article on Carlyle? He has nothing in the January number that would be read with greater interest. I am disappointed at its non-appearance. Please find out what its prospect is, and advise me."[18]

By this time, however, the new lecture season had begun, and Thoreau wanted "Carlyle" returned to him for lectures now rather than let it sit unused on Graham's desk. Greeley gamely continued to negotiate between the parties while placating Thoreau. Finally, on February 5, 1847, Greeley had an answer for Thoreau:

> Although your letter only came to hand to-day, I attended to its subject yesterday, when I was in Philadelphia. . . . Your article is this moment in type, and will appear about the 20th inst. as the leading article in Graham's Mag. for next month. Now don't object to this, nor be unreasonably sensitive at the delay. It is immensely more important to you that the article should appear thus (that is, if you have any literary aspirations,) than it is that you should make a few dollars by issuing it in some other way. As to lecturing, you have been at perfect liberty to deliver it as a lecture a hundred times if you had chosen—the more the better. It really is a good thing, and I will see that Graham pays you fairly for it. But its appearance there is worth far more to you than money. (Corr 173–74)

"Thomas Carlyle and His Works" was finally published in *Graham's*, in two parts, for March and April 1847; it was, as promised, the lead article, and it appeared beneath his signature, "Henry D. Thoreau." Greeley was right that its appearance in this popular Philadelphia magazine was worth more to his career than the money, though *Graham's* was also the first of the really well-paying magazines. It was aimed at a popular audience of both male and female readers, and its circulation was rivaled only by *Godey's*: in 1842, *Graham's* claimed a circulation of forty thousand, and by 1850 it would claim eighty thousand.[19] Graham cultivated a list of contributors that included the most popular writers of the day, whose names he printed prominently on the title page of each number. In 1847, the year Thoreau's article was printed, the *Graham's* list included Bryant, Cooper, Longfellow, Lowell, Richard H. Dana, James Kirk Paulding, Charles Fenno Hoffman, Joseph C. Neal, Lydia Sigourney, Catherine Sedgwick, "Fanny Forrester," and others. Greeley had impressed upon Emerson the value of publishing in a magazine like *Graham's* as early as 1843, when Emerson recorded in his journal: "Cheap lit. makes new markets. We have thought only of a box audience or at most of box & pit; but now it appears there is also slip audience, & galleries one, two, three; & backstairs, & street listeners, besides. Greeley tells me that Graham's Magazine has 70,000 subscribers. And I may write a lecture, if I will to 70,000 readers" (JMN 8: 343). Significantly, Thoreau would succeed more fully than Emerson in finding a mode of discourse agreeable to the popular periodicals of the day. While this was especially true of his travel and nature writing, the appearance of "Carlyle" in *Graham's* was a major breakthrough for Thoreau into the popular magazines. Though the *Boston Morning Post* characterized Thoreau's essay as "a *rather* toadying article on Carlyle,"[20] Evert Duyckinck praised it in the *Literary World*.[21] In either case, Thoreau's name and work were reaching an incomparably larger audience than he had ever addressed before.

Once the essay was published, it would be another full year before Thoreau was paid for it, and only then because of Greeley's persistence. In the meantime, however, Thoreau was energetically building up his literary stock. In addition to working up accounts of his night in the Concord jail and his excursion to Mount Katahdin, Thoreau was busily expanding the manuscript of *A Week* to nearly twice the length of the first draft. Moreover, he was now ready to try out on the public an account of his life at the pond. Thus, even without his Carlyle essay at hand (which he learned from Greeley he was at liberty to use for lectures while waiting for Graham to print it), Thoreau was able to make the 1846–1847 lecture season the busiest yet of his career. On January 19, 1847, he lectured at the Lincoln, Massachusetts, Lyceum. It was probably for this lecture that Thoreau had asked Greeley to retrieve his Carlyle essay from Graham; but because Greeley's reply postdated the Lincoln lecture, Thoreau's text was most likely the "History of Myself," which he subsequently read at the Concord Lyceum on February 10 and again on February 17.

The "History of Myself" was an early account of his life at the pond that was later incorporated into the first two chapters of *Walden*. The lecture opens with a mock apology for his subject, explaining,

> I should not presume to talk so much about myself and my affairs as I shall in this lecture if very particular and personal inquiries had not been made concerning my mode of life. . . . After I lectured here last winter I heard that some had expected that I would answer some of these questions in my lecture—So I must ask all strangers, and all who have little or no interest in me in this audience to pardon me, if I undertake to answer them in part now.[22]

Thoreau had indeed begun to compose this lecture the previous winter; shortly after he had delivered his Carlyle lecture, he had drafted an introduction in which he explained,

> I expect of any lecturer that he will read me a more or less simple & sincere account of his life—of what he has done & thought. . . .
>
> He who gives us only the results of other men's living though with brilliant temporary success—we may in some measure justly accuse of having defrauded us of our time—We want a man to give us that which was most precious to him—not his lifes [*sic*] blood but even that for which his life's blood circulated what he has got by living. . . .
>
> Yet incredible mistakes are made. . . . When I lectured here before this winter I heard that some of my towns men had expected of me some account of my life at the pond—this I will endeavor to give tonight. (J2: 141–42).

This early draft suggests that Thoreau himself had not been quite comfortable writing his Carlyle lecture; it is not surprising, therefore, that he treated the biographical sketch of Carlyle so ironically when he worked it into the essay. Yet the idea of giving a "simple and sincere account" of his own life, of giving his audience "that which was most precious to him," was hardly a new discovery to Thoreau; recall that in March of 1842 Thoreau had similarly written, "I would fain communicate the wealth of my life to men—would really give them what is most precious in my gift. . . . I wish to communicate those parts of my life which I would gladly live again myself" (J1: 393). Thoreau hit upon the felicitous rhetorical strategy of claiming to be answering his neighbors' questions, but he had clearly been working on the record of his own life for some time. Failure had isolated Thoreau from the community and led him to the pond, where, as he recorded in his journal, he

> went on . . . faithfully minding my business without a partner—till it became more and more evident that my townsmen would not after all admit me into the list of town offices—nor make the place a sinecure—with moderate allowance. . . .
>
> I found at length that as they were not likely to offer me any office in the court house—any curacy or living anywhere else, I must shift for myself. (J 2: 227–28; cf. *Walden* 18–19)

Ironically, it was precisely the fact of his being forced to shift for himself that confirmed Thoreau in his self-reliance and enabled him to speak confidently of what he had learned from his own life. In another passage drafted for this lecture during the winter of 1845–1846, Thoreau wrote,

> I wish to say something tonight not of and concerning the Chinese and Sandwich Islanders as *to* and concerning those who hear me—who are said to live in New England. Something about your condition—especially your outward condition or circumstances in this world—in this town. What it is—whether it is necessarily as bad as it is—whether it can't be improved as well as not. . . .
>
> It is very evident what—a mean and sneaking life you live always in the hampers—always on the limits—trying to get into business—and trying to get out of debt. (J2: 187; cf. *Walden* 4, 6)

Thoreau had led such a life himself, of course—"trying to get into business" in New York and, when he failed, "trying to get out of debt" by working in his father's pencil mill. His move to the pond was not in fact a withdrawal from the world of commerce, for he continued to submit his works to the literary marketplace even from his residence at Walden; but his move certainly altered his relationship with that marketplace. Thoreau's own failures in the public sphere constitute the very basis of his claims, here in his lecture, for independent success; his alienation from the community paradoxically enables him to present himself to that community as an exemplar. This complex and ironic relationship with the public lies at the core of Thoreau's mature work, and the meaning of "failure" and "success" increasingly become the ironic focal point of much of his thought. This tension is apparent in his "History of Myself" in the striking contrast between the self-deprecatory rhetoric of his opening apology for speaking of himself—claiming to do so only out of deference to his neighbors' inquiries—and his aggressive, belligerently self-confident characterization of these same neighbors' "mean and sneaking lives." Only through a careful, responsive attentiveness to his audience can Thoreau make his distinctiveness from the community the basis of his claims to speak in an exemplary voice, as the Man of the Age.

The fact that Thoreau was brought back to read his lecture a second time in Concord suggests that it was well received. Prudence Ward reported on this second lecture in a letter to Caroline Sewall, saying, "Henry repeated his lecture to a very full audience. . . . It was an uncommonly excellent lecture—tho, of course, few would adopt his notions—I mean as they are shown forth in his life. Yet it was a very useful lecture, and much needed."[23] And Emerson wrote to Fuller on February 28, 1847, "Mrs. Ripley and other members of the opposition came down the other night to hear Henry's account of his housekeeping at Walden Pond, which he read as a lecture, and were charmed with the witty wisdom which ran through it all" (EmL 2: 377–78).

Thoreau's own life was now providing an abundance of literary material. Encouraged by the response to his Walden lecture, busy writing about his excursion to the backwoods of Maine, and completing his revision of *A Week*, Thoreau was thus in a position to decline Greeley's suggestion that he follow up his Carlyle essay with similar essays on Emerson and Hawthorne. Greeley had advised Griswold in November 1846 to solicit a biographical sketch of Emerson directly from Thoreau (for use in Griswold's anthology of American prose writers)[24]; though nothing came of that, Greeley recognized the marketability of such material and raised the issue himself in his letter to Thoreau of February 5, 1847 (in which he had promised the "Carlyle" essay would appear in the next month's *Graham's*):

> Just set down and write a like article about Emerson, which I will give you $25 for if you cannot do better with it; then one about Hawthorne at your leisure, etc., etc. I will pay you the money for each of these articles on delivery, publish them when and how I please, leaving you the copyright expressly. In a year or two, if you take care not to write faster than you think, you will have the material of a volume worth publishing, and then we will see what can be done. (Corr 174).

Thoreau had in fact begun to draft sketches of Emerson and Alcott in his journal while he was writing "Carlyle" (J2: 223–24, 226), and Greeley's plan was certainly practical and potentially profitable. If Thoreau were to write such sketches of half the length of his Carlyle essay, as Greeley had suggested, twenty-five dollars would be very reasonable payment, and Greeley could still expect to sell them at a slightly higher rate, retaining an agent's fee for his trouble. Greeley was also right to imply that a book of such sketches might prove profitable. But in writing on Carlyle Thoreau had confronted his discomfort with writing about "the results of other men's living," and although Greeley repeated his request for an essay on Emerson as late as 1852 (Corr 279–80), the essay on Carlyle remained Thoreau's only extended essay on a contemporary writer.

While Thoreau was obviously interested in earning money for his writing, the last thing he wanted to produce now was a book of literary portraits. Instead, he had written *A Week on the Concord and Merrimack Rivers*, which was both a "simple and sincere account" of a passage in his own life and a virtual anthology of his *Dial* compositions (during the winter of 1846–1847 Thoreau added to his manuscript, among other things, material from "Dark Ages" and "Homer. Ossian. Chaucer." as well as a good deal of poetry).[25] Although Emerson's 1846 letter to Charles Newcomb had been premature in announcing that the book would be sent to Wiley & Putnam, in March of 1847 Emerson did write to Wiley & Putnam's literary editor, Evert Duyckinck, recommending Thoreau's book:

> I have represented to Mr. Thoreau, that his best course would undoubtedly be, to send the book to you, to be printed by Wiley & Putnam, that it may have a good edition & wide publishing.
>
> This book has many merits. It will be attractive to *lovers of nature*, in every sense, that is, to naturalists, and to poets, as Isaak Walton. It will be attractive to scholars for its excellent literature, & to all thoughtful persons for its originality and profoundness. The narrative of the little voyage, though faithful, is a very slender thread for such big beads & ingots as are strung on it. It is really a book of the results of the studies of years.
>
> Would you like to print this book into your American Library? It is quite ready, & the whole can be sent to you at once. . . . I am only desirous that you should propose to him good terms, & give his book the great advantages of being known which your circulation ensures.
>
> Mr. Thoreau is the author of an article on Carlyle, now printed & printing in Graham's last & coming magazine, & of some papers in the Dial; but he has done nothing half so good as his new book. He is well known to Mr. Hawthorne also. (EmL 3: 384)

On March 15, Duyckinck replied that he would be glad to read the manuscript (EmL 3: 384n), and on March 27 he printed the following notice in his new journal, the *Literary World*: "Henry D. Thoreau, Esq., whose elaborate paper on Carlyle, now publishing in Graham's Magazine, is attracting considerable attention, has also completed a new work of which reports speak highly. It will probably soon be given to the public."[26]

Thoreau did not actually send his manuscript to Duyckinck until May, an action that began a long and discouraging series of failed efforts to find a publisher for his book, but for the moment, the spring of 1847 must have seemed like the most productive and promising period of his literary career. "Carlyle" was in print; he had lectured successfully on his life at the pond; his book was completed and had already received a prepublication notice; he was busy working on accounts of the Maine woods and his night in the Concord jail; and he was already composing his second book, on his Walden sojourn. Thus he could afford not only to decline Greeley's request for literary portraits, but also to express his lack of interest when the proposal was made to establish a successor to the *Dial*. James Elliot Cabot describes a meeting held at Emerson's house on April 14, to discuss "the project of a new review, more open to new light than the existing organs of public opinion":

> Theodore Parker was the moving spirit, and the Liberals or Reformers generally were well disposed. Mr. Sumner was there, and on the other hand Mr. Thoreau, and the whole range of Boston opinion between them. . . . Everything depended on the editor, and the right man did not offer. Emerson would not take the place, and Mr. Parker was felt not to be in all respects just the person wanted. . . . Thoreau remarked by way of comfort that he did not see why the present reviews were not all-sufficient, thereby intimating that nothing of importance was pressing for utterance.[27]

When Thoreau's "Persius" had appeared in the first number of the *Dial* seven years earlier, Parker had suggested that Thoreau needed the discipline of writing for the commercial press rather than the *Dial* to keep him "out of mischief"; now, ironically, when Parker was pushing for a successor to the *Dial*, Thoreau had an essay printed that very month as the lead article in the nation's most popular magazine and therefore saw no need for a new journal. When the *Massachusetts Quarterly Review* was established that autumn, edited by Parker, Thoreau's estimate of its value and prospects did not change.

Emerson was somewhat premature in telling Duyckinck that Thoreau's book was "quite ready," for Thoreau continued to add new material to the manuscript—in April he wrote the Hannah Dustan episode that was eventually included in "Thursday."[28] He might have lingered over the manuscript even longer than he did (the structure of *A Week* could accommodate a potentially endless number of digressions, and so invited this kind of self-indulgence) but for the fact that in May Emerson wrote to his brother-in-law Charles T. Jackson in an effort to secure for Thoreau a place in Jackson's geological survey expedition to Michigan (EmL 3: 397). Jackson had headed the government-sponsored survey of Maine a decade earlier, and Thoreau was relying rather heavily on the report of that expedition in filling out his own account of "Ktaadn, and the Maine Woods." Thus motivated to complete *A Week*, Thoreau finally sent his manuscript to Duyckinck on May 28, apologizing for the delay, and asking for the specific terms of publication should they accept it. Now that he was sending it out, Thoreau himself was anxious to get it into print, telling Duyckinck, "If you take it—It will be a great convenience to me to get through with the printing as soon as possible, as I wish to take a journey of considerable length and should not be willing that any other than myself should correct the proofs." Therefore he asked that Duyckinck respond "as soon as may be" with "the most favorable terms on which you will print & publish it" (Corr 181–82).

Some background on Wiley & Putnam is necessary at this point to illuminate Thoreau's subsequent negotiations with them. In 1845, Duyckinck had persuaded Wiley & Putnam to back him as the editor of two series, a "Library of Choice Reading" (mostly European imports) and a "Library of

American Books"; it was for this latter series that Emerson recommended *A Week*. When the series was initiated, Duyckinck immediately wrote to Hawthorne (whom he knew through O'Sullivan and the *Democratic Review*), soliciting a contribution. Hawthorne was busy editing his friend Horatio Bridge's *Journal of an African Cruiser*, but he offered this book (which became the first in the American Library Series) and shortly promised him a collection of his own tales. Hawthorne thought Bridge was a "lucky devil" to have his book published here, telling him, "Few authors make their bow to the public under such favorable auspices."[29] Hawthorne was also quite pleased with their offer for his own tales (eventually published as *Mosses from an Old Manse*): for a single volume of twelve to fifteen tales, they would pay a one-hundred-dollar advance and then "eight cents a copy on the edition, fully equal to one half the profits."[30] With Hawthorne secured for the series, Duyckinck then asked him about the prospects of soliciting contributions from Emerson or Thoreau. In a letter of July 1, 1845, Hawthorne replied that Emerson "seems to think it preferable to publish on his own account—which has always been his method hitherto," but added:

> I wish he might be induced to publish this volume in New York. His reputation is still, I think, provincial and almost local, partly owing to the defects of the New England system of publication. As for Thoreau, there is one chance in a thousand that he might write a most excellent and readable book; but I should be sorry to take the responsibility, either towards you or him, of stirring him up to write anything for the series. He is the most unmalleable fellow alive—the most tedious, tiresome and intolerable—the narrowest and most notional—and yet, true as all this is, he has great qualities of intellect and character. The only way, however, in which he could ever approach the popular mind, would be by writing a book of simple observation of nature, somewhat in the vein of White's History of Selborne.[31]

Hawthorne wrote this letter three days before Thoreau formally took up residence at Walden Pond, an experiment his neighbors thought particularly perverse, and this may account in part for Hawthorne's characterization of Thoreau as "the most unmalleable fellow alive." Moreover, Hawthorne was undoubtedly as disappointed as Emerson with Thoreau's failure in New York—especially since O'Sullivan, to whom Hawthorne had recommended Thoreau, failed to get the observations of nature that he had requested for the *Democratic Review*. Hawthorne's reference to Gilbert White suggests that he was recalling Thoreau's "Natural History of Massachusetts" when thinking of how Thoreau might "approach the popular mind." Thoreau was later restored to Hawthorne's favor, but at this point he had not yet written any of his major excursions, and Hawthorne, who under difficult circumstances refused to relinquish his own assault on the literary marketplace, seems disgusted by Thoreau's apparent scorn for and retreat from it.

Not surprisingly, Duyckinck did not pursue his inquiries about Thoreau. He did pursue Emerson rather vigorously, but Hawthorne had reported his views accurately. In August 1845 Duyckinck wrote to Emerson requesting almost any contribution but indicating his particular desire for something new, "written in a popular manner for the best class of readers *virginibus puerisque*" (EmL 3: 297n). Emerson was vaguely attracted by the repeated proposals Duyckinck made through the autumn of 1845 but found various reasons for refusing them. He was tempted to publish a volume of poems in New York, "in the hope of that larger publication which your booksellers can give; but again I have been advised that for a book of poems, Boston was the better shop" (EmL 3: 301–2). When Duyckinck offered specific terms for publishing the *Poems* in his American Library, Emerson found the offer "liberal" yet less than he had expected, and thought that he could do better publishing a more expensive edition in Boston on his own account (EmL 3: 307–8, 350–51). Indeed, Emerson turned down a comparable offer from Appleton in New York and eventually did publish his poems on his own account through James Munroe of Boston. Emerson and Hawthorne both had an eye to their best advantage in the marketplace but came to virtually opposite conclusions. Nevertheless, Emerson had established cordial relations with Wiley & Putnam, and by July of 1846, when he wrote to Newcomb about Thoreau's book, Emerson had negotiated with them for the American publication of Carlyle's *French Revolution* (EmL 3: 315–20).[32] Emerson may, therefore, have told Thoreau he would negotiate with them for his book as well, thus feeling free to name Wiley & Putnam in his letter to Newcomb even before any proposals had actually been made. Neither Emerson nor Thoreau seems to have been aware of Hawthorne's earlier report to Duyckinck on Thoreau and so would have had no reason to expect anything other than a cordial response.

Whatever Emerson's reservations about publishing his own works with Wiley & Putnam, their "Library of American Books" undoubtedly looked like a most attractive place for Thoreau's book in 1846. The series had its first big success that year with Melville's *Typee* (which Thoreau read with great interest), but of even greater relevance to Thoreau was the publication in July of Hawthorne's *Mosses from an Old Manse* and, later that summer, of Fuller's *Papers on Literature and Art*.

Almost a full year elapsed, however, before Thoreau was ready to have Emerson write to Duyckinck on his behalf, and by the time Thoreau actually sent his manuscript, Duyckinck himself was in the midst of a crisis with Wiley & Putnam that jeopardized his position as editor.[33] Duyckinck was thus either disinclined or unable to act swiftly on Thoreau's manuscript. On June 14, 1847, Thoreau wrote to Duyckinck that he would wait two weeks for a decision, but that in the meantime he would like the manuscript returned in order to make some corrections (Corr 173). Thoreau resubmitted the manuscript on July 3, and on July 27 wrote impatiently to Duyckinck, "If Mssrs Wiley and Putnam are not prepared to give their answer now, will you please inform me what further delay, if any, is unavoidable, that I may determine whether I had not better carry it elsewhere—for time is of great consequence to me" (Corr 184). Wiley & Putnam must have replied within a week after receiving this letter, but their terms were not satisfactory: they apparently agreed to publish the book in their series, but only at Thoreau's expense (Corr 191). Thoreau was not, at this point, willing to take such a risk, and for good reason. Though Emerson actually elected to publish at his own expense, Thoreau had neither the reputation nor the capital to make such terms feasible. Moreover, it must have been particularly galling to Thoreau to receive such a poor offer from Wiley & Putnam when he saw them so much more eager to publish his friends' work. Nevertheless, in passing up the "Library of American Books," Thoreau passed up advantages in distribution and publicity he would not easily find elsewhere.

For all of Thoreau's impatience with Duyckinck, nothing came of the proposal for Thoreau to join the Michigan expedition, and his sense of urgency dissipated. Nevertheless, he continued to seek a publisher for A *Week*. When Wiley & Putnam's offer proved unsatisfactory, Emerson then wrote, on August 6, to his friend William Henry Furness, seeking a Philadelphia publisher for the book:

> I think it is a book of wonderful merit, which is to go far & last long. It will remind you of Izaak Walton, and, if it have not all his sweetness, it is rich, as he is not, in profound thought.—Thoreau sent the manuscript lately to Duyckinck . . . who examined it, & "gave favorable opinion of it to W & P." They have however declined to publish it. And I have promised Thoreau that I would inquire a little in N.Y. & Philadelphia before we begin to set our own types. Would Mr. Hart, or Mr. Kay like to see such a manuscript? . . . They shall have it on half profits or any reasonable terms. Thoreau is mainly bent on having it printed in a cheap form for a large circulation.[34]

Ideally, then, Thoreau wanted his book published on terms financially favorable to himself, by an established firm that could distribute it widely, and in a cheap format to promote sales. Any writer would of course look for this first criterion, but the other two, indicating Thoreau's particular interest in reaching a broad readership, distinguish Thoreau's position sharply from Emerson's toward his poems; for Emerson had deliberately elected to publish a smaller and costlier-style edition with Munroe, aimed specifically at a Boston audience, and on his own account. The reasons Emerson rejected Wiley & Putnam's offer were precisely the reasons why Thoreau would have wanted them (or, alternatively, any large New York or Philadelphia publisher) to publish his book.

Furness replied to Emerson that he would see what he could do but was "doubtful of success," and on September 19, he confirmed that Hart was not interested.[35] In the meantime, Emerson had also contacted his Boston publisher, James Munroe & Co., on Thoreau's behalf. Munroe indicated they were prepared to print it, but they apparently assumed they would do so at the author's expense as they did for Emerson's books. On August 28, Thoreau wrote to Munroe,

> Mr. Emerson has showed me your note to him and says he thinks you must have misunderstood him. If you will inform me how large an edition you contemplated, and what will be the whole or outside of the expense—(The book is about the size of one vol. of Emerson's essays)—I will consider whether I will pay one half the same (or whatever of my part one half the profits had failed to pay)—*at the end of six months after the day of publication*, if that is agreeable to you. This arrangement to affect only one edition. The MSS is quite ready and is now in New York. . . . P.S. I should have said above that I decline your proposition as it now stands. (Corr 185)

On August 29, 1847, Emerson wrote to Fuller, "Thoreau's book is not yet published though now on the point of concluding the contract" (EmL 3: 413), but once again his optimism was premature, for Munroe was apparently willing to publish it *only* at Thoreau's expense. Thoreau's letter makes it clear that he was prepared to compromise on the issue of bearing the costs, but he was not yet willing or able to back the book entirely on his own and so rejected the offer.

William Emerson was then asked to inquire on Thoreau's behalf with New York publishers, and on September 29 he wrote to his brother, "Please say to Henry Thoreau, that I gave his last letter immediate attention, and am daily expecting an answer of some sort from the Harpers" (EmL 3: 413n). Emerson sailed for England on October 5 (at which time Thoreau moved into the Emerson household again), before word from Harper's arrived, but on November 14, Thoreau wrote to Emerson, bringing him up to date. All his former urgency was now gone:

> I suppose you will like to hear of my book, though I have nothing worth writing about it. Indeed, for the last month or two I have forgotten it, but shall certainly remember it again. Wiley & Putnam, Munroe, the Harpers, and Crosby & Nichols have all declined printing it with the least risk to themselves; but Wiley & Putnam will print it in their series, and any of them, anywhere, at *my* risk. If I liked the book well enough, I should not delay; but for the present I am indifferent. I believe this is, after all, the course you advised,—to let it be. (Corr 191)

In fact, this was not the course Emerson had advised, and he replied on December 2, "I am not of the opinion that your book should be delayed a month. I should print it at once, nor do I think that you would incur any risk in doing so that you cannot well afford. It is very certain to have readers & debtors here [in England] as well as there" (Corr 195). Emerson's optimism was undoubtedly gratifying to Thoreau, but it was also naive, based as it was only on his own experience of publishing at his own risk. When Emerson published his *Poems* with Munroe in the autumn of 1846, he bore all the expenses of printing the edition of fifteen hundred copies and paid the publishers a 30 percent commission on all retail copies sold, 20 percent on all trade copies sold (EmL 3: 350), but Thoreau could hardly be so confident. In his contract for his own poems, Emerson had also annexed an agreement for the publication of a smaller edition of Ellery Channing's poems on the same terms (EmL 3: 351n). Emerson undoubtedly took a loss on that investment—and he did not offer to underwrite the publication of Thoreau's book.

Whether Thoreau was more skeptical of his book's success than was Emerson or merely smarting from publishers' rejections, he was determined not to publish it on their terms. On December 27, 1847, he noted to James Munroe & Co. (he was writing to transact some of Emerson's business), "I may as well inform you that I do not intend to print *my book* anywhere immediately" (Corr 198).

Chapter 6

"CONTACT! CONTACT!": THE PUBLICATION OF "KTAADN"

THOREAU'S inability to find a publisher for *A Week* was a severe disappointment, but he was buoyed during the winter of 1847–1848 by his steadily improving prospects with the lyceums and the magazines, and so in fact became increasingly self-assured in his professional judgments and grew even more confirmed in his sense of the appropriateness of his literary projects.

Moreover, this was a productive and happy period in his personal life, which also affected his optimism about his professional prospects. In September of 1847 he had left his residence at the pond and, when Emerson left for Europe on October 5, Thoreau returned to the Emerson household. There he did maintenance work on the house and grounds, took care of Emerson's various business dealings, and acted as companion to Lidian and the children. When Thoreau first moved to the pond, he had written, "If I am not quite right here I am less wrong than before" (J2: 156); now he might have said the same thing of his new situation, for midway through his Walden sojourn he had confessed, "When my friends reprove me for not devoting myself to some trade or profession, and acquiring property I feel not the reproach—I am guiltless & safe comparatively on that score—But when they remind me of the advantages of society of worthy and earnest helpful relations to people I am convicted—and yet not I only but they also" (J2: 248–49). By moving into a position of responsibility in the Emerson household, Thoreau immediately gained the advantages of such relations as he desired, while he avoided the need to adopt a profession and acquire property on his own account. Both Thoreau's and Lidian Emerson's letters from this period convey the unmistakable pleasure and satisfaction Thoreau derived from virtually all aspects of his life at the Emerson household.

Although *A Week* lay dormant for the moment, Thoreau was not idle. Fall and winter he was busy working up material for the new lecture season, and by the end of December he was able to report to Emerson, "I have had many good hours in the chamber at the head of the stairs—a solid time, it seems to me. Next week I am going to give an account to the Concord Lyceum of my expedition to Maine" (Corr 199). The lecture seems to have been successful, for he wrote to Emerson on January 12 that he had "read a part of the story of my excursion to Ktadn to quite a large audience of men and boys, the other night, whom it interested" (Corr 204). Thoreau was busy writing other lectures as well; in a letter of February 23, he told Emerson, "Lectures begin to multiply on my desk. I have one on Friendship which is new—and the materials of some others. I read one last week to the Lyceum on The Rights & Duties of the Individual in relation to government—much to Mr. Alcott's satisfaction" (Corr 208).

Thoreau had already delivered a lecture on "the relation of the individual to the state" at the Concord Lyceum on January 26; this earlier lecture (probably the first part of the one reported to Emerson and which, combined with its successor, became "Resistance to Civil Government") had also been admired by Alcott, who recorded that Thoreau read it to "an attentive audience."[1]

Yet, after writing so enthusiastically to Emerson, Thoreau does not seem to have lectured again during the 1847–1848 season. Thus, he read his "Ktaadn" lecture only once and his "Resistance to Civil Government" only twice—all in Concord—and his "Friendship" lecture not at all. Nevertheless, with this material at hand, he began to look for ways of making it pay in print. On March 8, he wrote to James Elliot Cabot, who was assisting Parker with the *Massachusetts Quarterly Review*, about placing an article in their journal. Thoreau first confessed, "My book, fortunately, did not find a publisher ready to undertake it, and you can imagine the effect of delay on an author's estimate of his own work. However, I like it well enough to mend it, and shall look at it again directly when I have dispatched some other things." He then turned obliquely toward the chief point of his letter:

> I have been writing lectures for our Lyceum this winter, mainly for my own pleasure and advantage. I esteem it a rare happiness to be able to *write* anything, but there (if I even get there) my concern for it is apt to end. . . . But I see that I must get a few dollars together presently. . . . Is your journal able to pay anything, providing it likes an article well enough? I do not promise one. At any rate, I mean always to spend only words enough to purchase silence with; and I have found that this, which is so valuable, though many readers do not prize it, does not cost much after all. (Corr 210)

In spite of the calculated offhandedness of his tone and his transparently defensive disclaimers, he was not writing lectures merely for his own pleasure; just a week after Thoreau wrote to Cabot, in fact, Thoreau and Alcott shared their concern whether the lack of public response to their work did not render them ineffective and even somewhat ridiculous.[2] Coincidentally, Thoreau received shortly afterward an admiring letter from H.G.O. Blake of Worcester, Massachusetts; Blake spoke of how powerfully he had been affected by rereading Thoreau's "Persius" in the *Dial* and asked Thoreau to "speak to me in this hour as you are prompted" (Corr 213).

Thoreau's reply to his first disciple further belies the affected indifference of his remarks to Cabot: "I am glad to hear that any words of mine . . . have reached you . . . I have therefore reason to suppose that I have uttered what concerns men, and that it is not in vain that man speaks to man. This is the value of literature" (Corr 214).

Thoreau's primary interest was in reaching an audience to fulfill his role as prophet, but his secondary interest was in reaping at least modest monetary compensation for his writing. He had been writing lectures, but lectures at the Concord Lyceum did not pay, and, as Thoreau told Cabot, he found himself in need of "a few dollars." Moreover, he did not wish to purchase silence, as he asserted to Cabot, but in fact wanted to earn enough to underwrite further public pronouncements. He had learned, at some considerable expense to his ego, that the publication of *A Week* might depend on his ability to cover the initial expenses. His remark to Cabot that he would turn to his book again when he had "dispatched some other things" suggests that he may have been trying to acquire sufficient capital to publish it. Thus, for all the apparent idealism in his letter to Cabot, the one question that really mattered here was whether the *Massachusetts Quarterly Review* paid for contributions. Discovering that it did not,[3] Thoreau submitted his work elsewhere.

When Thoreau subsequently turned his attention to paying magazines, he understood that his most promising work at hand was the account of his Maine excursion, so at the end of March he sent Greeley a long article he had titled "Ktaadn, and the Maine Woods." Greeley promised to take "Ktaadn" and to pay Thoreau for it himself "if I cannot dispose of it more to your advantage within the week ensuing" (Corr 217).

When Thoreau sent his essay to Greeley, he also mentioned that he had never been paid by Graham for "Carlyle." Greeley was surprised at this and promised to take it up with Graham himself when he went to Philadelphia the next week. He missed Graham at that time, but when he returned to Philadelphia a month later, he finally obtained payment for Thoreau. Again he had been unable to meet up with Graham himself, so he explained to Thoreau that, having hunted up the numbers of *Graham's* in which Thoreau's essay appeared,

> I made out a regular bill for the contribution; drew a draft on G. R. Graham for the amount, gave it to his brother here for collection, and to-day received the money. Now you see how to get pay yourself, another time. . . . Had you drawn a draft on him, at first, and given it to the Concord Bank to send for collection, you would have received your money long since. . . . I have made Graham pay you $75, but I send you only $50. (Corr 222–23)

As Thoreau acknowledged in his reply, he would not have obtained any payment for "Carlyle" without Greeley's assistance, so he was delighted to receive the fifty dollars, which was indeed a substantial amount in the literary marketplace of the day. In an article titled "Pay of Authors" in the *Literary World* for April 10, 1847 (the same month Thoreau's "Carlyle" concluded in *Graham's*), the author notes that average pay in periodicals was a dollar to a dollar and a half per page in reviews, two dollars per page in magazines like the *Democratic Review*, and that "the enterprise and competition of Graham and Godey have raised the rates, in special instances, to fifty dollars for a tale by Willis, Poe, or Mrs. Kirkland, a chapter by Cooper, or a poem by Bryant. These are splendid exceptions—days to be marked with a white stone in the lives of American authors."[4] This was, in effect, exactly Thoreau's reaction, and he in fact worried that Greeley had not been sufficiently recompensed for his trouble. Once before, with "A Walk to Wachusett," Thoreau had failed to receive the promised payment for an article. Then the reason was evident, for the *Boston Miscellany* stopped printing the month after Thoreau's piece appeared; but *Graham's* was a tremendously successful magazine with a reputation for high payments, so the reason for Thoreau's difficulty is less clear. As it turns out, Thoreau's problem was again a matter of poor timing: "Carlyle" was published just when George Graham became entangled in serious financial difficulties. In 1846, flush with success, he had overextended himself by buying up three Philadelphia papers, all of which were losing ventures; his problems were compounded by other bad investments, and Graham was forced in 1848 to sell *Graham's* to Patterson & Co., regaining control only in 1850.[5] Graham remained editor throughout this period, and the circulation even increased, so Graham's financial difficulties were not readily apparent; but this was in fact a precarious time for the magazine, and little-known contributors like Thoreau were inevitably the first to suffer from the lack of ready cash. Greeley knew how to obtain Thoreau's payment (a method that would also have worked with the *Boston Miscellany*), but even he did not understand why Thoreau had not been paid sooner.

When Thoreau received the fifty dollars from Greeley, he replied, "My Friend Greeley, I do not know how to thank you for your kindness." He was especially impressed by Greeley's ingenious method of obtaining payment: "I think it might not have occurred to somewhat of a business man. I am not one in the common sense at all—that is, I am not acquainted with the forms—I might have way-laid him perhaps" (Corr 224). Thoreau was indeed "not acquainted with the forms" of business, but he was certainly interested in conducting the business of marketing his writing. He told Greeley, "You prized it well, that was the exact amount," and his delight at being paid is evident throughout his letter.

In the meantime, Greeley was also attempting to place "Ktaadn," and Thoreau was equally pleased with these efforts. Greeley had tried but failed to sell it when he first went to Philadelphia in April, but he decided to pay

Thoreau twenty-five dollars in advance and then take on the risk himself for selling it: "It is rather long for my columns and too fine for the million; but I consider it a cheap bargain, and shall print it myself if I do not dispose of it to better advantage." Having explained what he could do with "Ktaadn," Greeley added, "If you will write me two or three articles in the course of the summer, I think I can dispose of them for your benefit. But write not more than half as long as your article just sent me, for that is too long for the Magazines. If that were in two it would be far more valuable" (Corr 218).

When Greeley wrote again in May, sending Thoreau the money for "Carlyle," he had still not sold "Ktaadn" but asserted, "I have expectations of procuring it a place in a new magazine of high character that will pay. I don't expect to get as much for it as for Carlyle, but I hope to get $50" (Corr 223), so he offered Thoreau the option of selling it to Greeley outright for twenty-five dollars, or waiting to see what Greeley could get for it acting as his agent.[6] Again Greeley added the request for "one or two articles . . . about half the length of this. . . . The length of your papers is the only impediment to their appreciation by the magazines" (Corr 223).

In his letter acknowledging receipt of the fifty dollars from Greeley for "Carlyle," Thoreau indicated that he was quite content to take the twenty-five for "Ktaadn." Interestingly, this letter, which expresses such obvious satisfaction with obtaining payment for his work, begins with a long paragraph explaining how little he actually needed the money:

> For the last five years I have supported myself solely by the labors of my hands—I have not received one cent from any other source, and this has cost me so little time . . . that I have probably enjoyed more leisure for literary pursuits than any contemporary. For more than two years past I have lived alone in the woods, in a good plastered and shingled house entirely of my own building, earning only what I wanted, and sticking to my proper work. The fact is a man need not live by the sweat of his brow—unless he sweats easier than I do—he needs so little. For two years and two months all my expenses have amounted to 27 cents a week, and I have fared gloriously in all respects. . . . How much have we heard about the attainment of knowledge under difficulties of poets starving in garrets—depending on the patronage of the wealthy—and finally dying mad. It is time that men sang another song. There is no reason why the scholar who professes to be a little wiser than the mass of men, should not do his work in the ditch occasionally, and by means of his superior wisdom make much less suffice for him. . . . This money therefore comes as a free and even unexpected gift to me. (Corr 223–24)

This is, of course, a set piece, a rehearsal of the "Economy" chapter of *Walden* (cf. *Walden* 69, 3, 71, especially); also, he seems deliberately to obscure the fact that he is no longer living at the pond. Moreover, it is strikingly at odds, in both style and substance, with the rest of the letter, in which Thoreau addresses the *business* of writing. Not only does he express his satisfaction with Greeley's payments, but he suggests an expedient to accommodate the objections to the length of "Ktaadn": "If more convenient the Maine article might be printed in the form of letters; you have only to leave off at the end of a day, and put the date before the next one" (Corr 224). The epistolary form was highly conventional for travel literature, especially for serial publication in the periodical press; thus, having just proclaimed his relative independence from the marketplace, he now suggests a means of accommodating his work to it. Like his letter to Cabot, this one to Greeley embodies the deep-seated tension between Thoreau's lofty idealism and his practical ambition. In a postscript to this letter Thoreau added, "My book is swelling again under my hands, but as soon as I have leisure I shall see to those shorter articles. So, look out" (Corr 225).

Greeley, in turn, immediately recognized the literary qualities of Thoreau's paragraph on his self-reliance and printed it in the *Tribune* for May 25, in an editorial he titled "A Lesson for Young Poets." He describes Thoreau as "a thorough classical scholar, true poet (though he rarely or never wrote verses,) and never sought to make a livelihood by his writings, though there are not six men in America who can surpass them. We feel indeed honored by his friendship."[7]

Greeley's praise for Thoreau, and Thoreau's paragraph itself, are undoubtedly sincere, but there are at least two underlying ironies here. The subtler and more insidious irony is that this idealistic celebration of the writer's manly self-reliance and independence from the taint of the literary marketplace naively undermined the legitimate interests of the emerging profession of authorship. Thoreau's paean to the simple life is converted, by Greeley's praise for the fact that Thoreau "never sought to make a livelihood by his writings," into an argument strikingly similar to *Brother Jonathan*'s cynical defense of their literary piracy—that "the man who would be literary, must earn his living first. . . . His necessities thus provided for, literature may be to him the most delightful and ennobling amusement." Appealing to the anachronistic type of the gentleman amateur simply left the profits to those shrewd enough to realize that literature had, for better or worse, become a *business*.

The more salient irony of Thoreau's letter and Greeley's printing it is that neither was really renouncing his commercial interests. Greeley was acting at that very moment as Thoreau's literary agent—he sent Thoreau twenty-five dollars for his Maine essay on the day he printed this extract in the *Tribune*, and he then urged Thoreau to see how even this declaration of independence might be marketed successfully. "Don't scold at my publishing a part of your last private letter . . . in this morning's paper," he wrote; "It will do great good." At first Greeley may seem to mean it will do "great good" for the aspiring "Young Poets" who read it, but as he goes on, it becomes clear that Greeley means equally that it may do "great good" for Thoreau's professional career:

> Write me something shorter when the spirit moves (never write a line otherwise, for the hack writer is a slavish beast, *I* know), and I will sell it for you soon. I want one shorter article from your pen that will be quoted, as these long articles cannot be, and let the public know something of your way of thinking and seeing. It will do good. What do you think of following out your thought in an essay on "The Literary Life"? You need not make a personal allusion but I know you can write an article worth reading on that theme when you are in the vein. (Corr 229)

Greeley did not realize that Thoreau had already followed out the thought of his letter in the first draft of *Walden*, which he would use as the material for his lectures in the next lyceum season.

From Greeley's point of view, Thoreau must have seemed oddly unresponsive to his tireless reminders that commercial success depended upon his ability to write short pieces and to produce them regularly. On his side, however, Thoreau was tremendously pleased with his relationship with Greeley, for Greeley had not only provided Thoreau with what was, for him, a considerable sum of money, but he had placed a standing order for whatever else Thoreau might produce. Thus when Emerson wrote enthusiastically from England proposing a transatlantic journal that would bring together Emerson's New England circle with his group of Oxford-based friends, Thoreau responded with the same skepticism he had felt toward the founding of the *Massachusetts Quarterly Review* and offered Emerson a lengthy explanation of his objection to such an undertaking. It would, he feared, merely "excite another short and ineffectual blaze."

> I am more interested in the private journal than the public one, and it would be better news to me to hear that there were two or three valuable papers being written in England & America—that might be printed sometime—than that there were 30,000 dollars to defray expenses—& forty thousand men standing *ready to write* merely, but no certainty of anything valuable being written.

He goes on to recall the first appearance of the *Massachusetts Quarterly Review*: "I read it, or what I could of it, and certainly if one man had written it all a wise publisher would not have advised to print it. It should have been suppressed for nobody was starving for *that*" (Corr 226–27).

Thoreau's idealistic claim to be more interested in the private journal than the public one is a noble half-truth at best. Like his remarks both to Cabot about his unconcern for the fate of his writing and to Greeley about his literary independence, this claim constitutes a platitudinous declaration of his transcendental idealism, but it is equally rooted in what was becoming an almost instinctive defensiveness through which he masked his genuine professional ambitions. In this case, the truth is that Thoreau was so busy with his two books that he had little time for his private journal.[8] Thoreau did not reject the idea of magazine publication; he merely rejected the idea of creating yet another *Dial* or *Massachusetts Quarterly Review*. It was actually his recent commercial successes and not his interest in the "private journal" that enabled him to express himself to Emerson with such self-assurance. Thoreau tipped his hand in his letter to Emerson when he concluded by noting with deliberate casualness, "Greeley has sent me 100 dollars and wants more manuscript" (Corr 227).[9] It was undoubtedly of tremendous importance for Thoreau to let Emerson know that he was beginning to make his way as a publishing writer, that he was beginning to distinguish himself from the "other grand promisers" and need no longer be a disappointment to his mentor.

Thoreau needed to achieve a modicum of success in the marketplace in order to express his superiority to it. Yet in opposing the establishment of a new coterie journal Thoreau demonstrated the extent to which he now saw himself as a public and professional writer. Underwriting a little magazine that could not support itself did not, he discovered, result in the publication of more valuable literature; and if this was the case, then the commercial literary marketplace—whatever its flaws—had at least the advantage of wider circulation and payment for contributions. When Emerson read Thoreau's response, he wrote to Lidian, "Thank Henry for his letter. He is always *absolutely* right, and *particularly* perverse. But I always thank Heaven for him" (EmL 4: 81–82).

Thoreau must have felt vindicated in his response to Emerson's proposal when Greeley succeeded, as he had expected, in selling "Ktaadn, and the Maine Woods" to New York's *Union Magazine*—the "new magazine of high character that will pay." Thoreau's essay was published serially, in five monthly installments, from July through November 1848. It was Thoreau's longest and most important publication before A *Week*, and while he had yet to find a publisher for his book, the appearance of "Ktaadn" must have provided considerable consolation, confirming his viability in the literary marketplace and suggesting the possibility of future successes with the paying magazines.

The *Union Magazine of Literature and Art* was New York's first major effort to imitate and compete with the Philadelphia magazines *Graham's*, *Godey's*, and *Peterson's*. It was first issued in July 1847 and was edited by Mrs. Caroline Kirkland, the popular writer of western sketches. The magazine boasted that it was "Embellished with the Finest Steel, Mezzotint, and Wood Engravings, Music and Colored Fashions," and it was indeed a well-produced and attractive magazine, though it had trouble competing with the already-established Philadelphia publications.[10] Like these Philadelphia magazines, it was a fifty-page, three-dollar-a-year monthly, which listed its prominent contributors and attempted to pay well. It appealed to both male and female readers, and in 1848, the year Thoreau's article appeared, its list of featured contributors included Lydia Sigourney, Frances Osgood, and Catherine Sedgwick, among the popular women writers, and William Cullen Bryant, Fitz Green Halleck, N. P. Willis, Charles Fenno Hoffman, T. S. Arthur, H. T. Tuckerman, William A. Jones, and William Gilmore Simms, among the men. Though not featured on its list, Horace Greeley, George William Curtis, Bayard Taylor, Evert Duyckinck, and the as yet unknown Walter Whitman also contributed during 1848. Bayard Taylor was acting editor of the magazine during the summer of 1848 (while Mrs. Kirkland was in Europe), and it was to Taylor that Greeley sold Thoreau's essay. Taylor later recalled the episode:

> One day Horace Greeley came to me with a thick roll of manuscript, saying, "Now, you must do something for this young man. His name is Thoreau; he lives in a shanty at Walden Pond, near Concord, on $37.21 a year, and he must be encouraged." . . . I had never before heard Thoreau's name and was no less surprised than charmed with the freshness and beauty of his style. The publisher of the periodical agreed to give $75 for the article, and I accepted this offer without consulting the author, as it would meet the latter's expenses for two years to come; and I judged this would satisfy him.[11]

"Ktaadn, and the Maine Woods" was indeed well suited to the interests of a popular audience. Like "A Walk to Wachusett," it falls within that subgenre of travel literature which has the landscape itself as the object of interest; but whereas the earlier excursion took him through pastoral agricultural regions to a modest summit about which "there was little of the sublimity and grandeur which belong to mountain scenery," this is an excursion into the heart of the wilderness to one of the sternest and most imposing peaks in the eastern United States. As in "A Walk to Wachusett," Thoreau is keenly interested in the relation between the landscape and our national character and destiny, but here the wildness of the landscape evokes not picturesque historical and literary associations but the more powerful responses to the sublimity of a landscape untouched by humanity. Thus, it has less in common with the popular genteel travelogues of the day than with the equally popular genre of wilderness exploration and adventure (though the two genres often overlapped). Thoreau seems to have apprehended the somewhat different demands of these genres as he revised "Ktaadn": in working from his rough draft to his finished essay, Thoreau reduced the number of literary allusions and moral abstractions, presenting his account instead as a combination wilderness guidebook and adventure narrative. While Thoreau does retain certain literary allusions and quotations, especially at the climactic points of his narrative, he deleted from his first draft quotations from Donne, the *Iliad*, and Fletcher's *The Faithful Shepherdess*.[12] At the same time, Thoreau added to his first draft specific information on the names of the lakes, falls, and streams along their route and the intervening distances, "for the benefit of future tourists."[13] "I am particular to give the names of the settlers and distances," he explains, "since every log hut in these woods is a public house, and such information is of no little consequence to those who may have occasion to travel this way" (MW 18).[14] Thoreau also inserted into his first draft numerous remarks that underscore his attentiveness to those readers whose interest in the northern wilderness was merely vicarious. After a lyrical and minute description of their camp at midnight, for example, Thoreau explains, "I have been thus particular in order to convey some idea of a night in the woods" (41); and, after detailing their route along the waterways, Thoreau writes, "I will describe particularly how we got over some of these portages and rapids, in order that the reader may get an idea of the boatman's life" (47). In general, Thoreau's revisions throughout the essay create a more informal and practical relationship between author and reader.

Thoreau went to the Maine woods for much the same reason he went to the Walden woods, "to front only the essential facts of life" and to explore man's fundamental relationship to nature. But because "Ktaadn" recounts an actual journey to a nearly uncharted wilderness rather than the inward exploration of *Walden*'s "home-cosmography," the essay is less overtly metaphysical and more fully aligned with popular interests and issues of the day. Katahdin represents the pristine wilderness, and by juxtaposing the signs he discovers along his route of civilization's progress with the looming symbol of primal natural force toward which he is headed, Thoreau not only gives his narrative a sense of coherence and heightened drama but makes "Ktaadn" a provocative contribution to the discourse on nature and our national destiny that so deeply engaged the American imagination.

Thoreau's essay begins with a straightforward, literal statement of his itinerary, which nevertheless also introduces the principle thematic tension between civilization and nature. The opening sentence, while announcing the "backwoods" as his destination, is notable chiefly for its abundant images of civilized society: he tells us that he traveled to Bangor "by way of railroad and steamboat"; that he was "to accompany a relative . . . engaged in lumber trade in Bangor"—that is, in the business of converting natural resources into commodities; and that their immediate business was to look into a real estate transaction for his cousin. His opening thus constitutes a tacit admission of his own complicity in this world of technology, commerce, and property. He goes on to make it clear, however, that his aim is to travel outside of this world; his excursion only really begins when he is "five miles beyond the last log hut" (3). Thoreau further explains that he chose the more difficult approach to Mount Katahdin because by the easier route "you see much less of the wilderness, none of the glorious river and lake scenery, and have no experience of the batteau and the boatman's life" (3).

Thoreau notes that Katahdin was first ascended by white men in 1804, and he cites three accounts of subsequent ascents with which he was familiar: those of J. W. Bailey in 1836, Dr. Charles T. Jackson (Emerson's brother-in-law) in 1837, and "two young men from Boston" (Edward Everett Hale and William Francis Channing) in 1845. "Besides these," he writes, "very few, even among backwoodsmen and hunters, have ever climbed it, and it will be a long time before the tide of fashionable travel sets that way" (4).[15] Thoreau did not exaggerate the primitiveness of the landscape, but he did deliberately dramatize it here, for interest in such landscape was becoming quite fashionable. Of the three accounts of Katahdin Thoreau cites, the first two were scientific, but the most recent (Hale and Channing's trip was made just a year before Thoreau's) described a romantic excursion for scenery and adventure, like Thoreau's own, and in contrast to Thoreau's prediction, Hale had forecast: "I think it will not be ten years before all this country will be the resort of pleasure travellers in summer. I am sure I hope so."[16] Like Thoreau's, Hale's forecast is also somewhat exaggerated but not entirely incorrect: several excursions to Katahdin were made in the years immediately following Thoreau's. Before he finished writing "Ktaadn," Thoreau read accounts of an 1847 botanical expedition to the mountain; several ascents were made by the Reverend Marcus Keep, beginning in 1846 (the same summer as Thoreau's excursion), and Keep actively sought to make the mountains more accessible for pleasure trips. In 1849 Keep led a party of men and women to the summit, but the laurels for being the first woman on the mountaintop went to author Elizabeth Oakes Smith and her female companion N. C. Morman, who preceded the Keep party to the summit by less than two weeks. In 1855, Thomas Wentworth Higginson also ascended the mountain in a mixed party and wrote an anonymous account of their journey told from the point of view of one of the women. By the mid 1850s, Katahdin had become a favorite subject for Frederick Edwin Church, who was just emerging as the leading landscape painter of the day. His companion on an 1856 excursion, the writer Theodore Winthrop, wrote a popular account of their journey, and Church brought several of his fellow landscape painters to Katahdin over the next few decades.[17]

The romantic interest in the wilderness that characterizes Thoreau's opening point of view had been taking an increasingly strong hold of the American imagination since the early years of the nineteenth century; in their pristine landscape, Americans discovered the expression of divinity unobscured by man, and thus they converted the lack of civilization and history into a supreme virtue, the characteristic that most clearly distinguished America from the Old World and seemed to sanctify the national destiny. As Thoreau's opening paragraphs suggest, however, this romantic interest in the wilderness *as* wilderness was threatened by the commercial and utilitarian exploitation of the landscape, which was proceeding more energetically than ever before.

Just thirteen years before "Ktaadn" was published, Alexis de Tocqueville charged in *Democracy in America*,

> [Americans] are insensible to the wonders of inanimate nature and they may be said not to perceive the mighty forests that surround them till they fall beneath the hatchet. Their eyes are fixed upon another sight: the American people views its own march across these wilds, draining swamps, turning the course of rivers, peopling solitudes, and subduing nature. This magnificent image of themselves does not meet the gaze of the Americans at intervals only; it may be said to haunt every one of them in his least as well as in his most important actions and to be always flitting before his mind.[18]

Tocqueville exaggerated the Americans' insensitivity to the landscape, but certainly the attraction of the utilitarian view, which regarded the wilderness as valuable only to the extent that it could be *transformed* into the materials for building and advancing civilization, remained strong. An article entitled "Scenery and Resources of Maine," printed in the *American [Whig] Review* shortly before Thoreau's trip to Maine, confirms Tocqueville's assessment. While nodding to the beauty of the landscape, the author chiefly promoted the region's opportunities for settlement and commercial exploitation: "Tracts that will, one day, bloom in cultivated fertility, and be enlivened by the arts of civilization, are still hidden beneath the deep shadows of the wilderness."[19] Charles T. Jackson, too, in his 1837 geological survey of Maine, understood that, in suggesting the *value* of the data he had gathered on this government-sponsored expedition, he must address the utilitarian prospects for settling and exploiting the region: the timber, soil quality, and mineral resources, he concludes, make the region "a most valuable territory, possessing every advantage required by settlers," and he goes on to provide a detailed guide to mining iron from the land there.[20] J. K. Laski's newspaper account of Dr. Aaron Young's 1847 botanical expedition to Katahdin—aimed at a popular audience—is much freer in emphasizing the romantic grandeur of the scenery and the glories of God to be experienced in the mountain wilderness, yet he too feels compelled to conclude his account by imagining the public's question "What is the use of this survey—what is the *use* of the study of Botany?" and answering that the study of nature is "of the first importance to the State—and as of the highest utility to mankind."[21] And the Reverend Marcus Keep, while principally celebrating Katahdin as a source of recreation and inspiration, also defends himself by explaining, "I have an object of something more than romantic interest, and hope to develop facts of some utility to the citizens of Maine in giving some account of my rambles in the wilderness."[22] Keep's particular project was to market the mountain cranberries of Katahdin. As these various remarks suggest, the rise of both utilitarian and romantic interests in the wilderness resulted in a profound and increasingly tense ambivalence toward the fate of that wilderness; the tension between nature and civilization, which had been apparent from the very first settlements in the New World, was no longer a question merely of whether man *would* succeed in conquering the wilderness but whether he *should* do so.

This is the issue Thoreau introduces in "Ktaadn" when, at the beginning of his excursion, he describes the lumber mills at the Penobscot Falls. He describes how "the once green tree . . . becomes lumber merely"; and while his account is seasoned with good-humored puns, he beseeches his reader:

> Think how stood the white-pine tree on the shore of Chesuncook, its branches soughing with the four winds, and every individual needle trembling in the sunlight—think how it stands with it now—sold, perchance to the New England Friction Match Company! There were in 1837 . . . two hundred and fifty saw mills on the Penobscot and its tributaries. . . . and they sawed two hundred millions of feet of boards annually. . . . The mission of men there seems to be, like so many busy demons, to drive the forest all out of the country, from every solitary beaver swamp, and mountain side, as soon as possible. (MW 5)

The tremendous force and industriousness of the commercial interests here command attention, but Thoreau's own antimaterialistic bias is clearly revealed by the contrast between his attentive and sympathetic description of the individual pine and his merely numerical report of the work of the sawmills. By calling the loggers "busy demons" rather than "busy bees," he converts their industriousness from a virtue to a vice.

Thoreau's plea on behalf of the pine tree was far from original: the contrasting images of evergreen and ax had become, by 1848, immediately recognizable icons in the American imagination, evoking fundamental questions about our national identity and destiny. James Fenimore Cooper had immortalized the images in his sketch from *The Pioneers* (1823) of the logger Billy Kirby chopping down "one of the most noble" trees of the forest, and "from that moment the sounds of the ax were ceaseless."[23] Thomas Cole had emerged in the 1820s as America's leading landscape painter with such paintings as *The Woodchopper, Lake Featherstonhaugh* (1826), and for the rest of his career he continued to work with the image of the solitary woodchopper confronting the pristine wilderness. When John James Audubon lamented, in the pages of his extremely popular *Ornithological Biography* (1832), the fact that "the dense and lofty summits of the forest . . . [once] almost unmolested by the axe of the settler. . . . are fast disappearing under the axe by day, and the fire by night," he cautiously reserved judgment, saying, "Whether these changes are for the better or worse, I shall not pretend to say."[24] In fact, both views found frequent popular expression. The romantic defense of the forests against the incursions of man is expressed, for example, in Thomas Cole's 1841 poem "The Lament of the Forest," in which he has the forest sing, "Then all was harmony and peace; but MAN / Arose . . . / He the destroyer . . . / . . . the axe unresting smote / Our reverend ranks."[25] This same view is reiterated by Lydia Sigourney, in a chapter from her 1845 *Scenes in My Native Land* entitled "Fallen Forests," which opens with this poetic lament:

> Man's warfare on the trees is terrible.
> He lifts his rude hut in the wilderness,
> And lo! The loftiest trunks, that age on age
> Were nurtured to nobility, and bore
> Their summer coronets so gloriously,
> Fall with a thunder-sound, to rise no more.[26]

But the contrasting view is expressed in John Greenleaf Whittier's 1845 poem "The Lumbermen." Whittier's poem, one of his "Songs of Labor," describes the same region Thoreau now traveled—the "Swift and strong Penobscot . . . / Where, through clouds, are glimpses given / Of Katahdin's sides." Here, the lumberers can abjure the village church, for in the wilderness they discover "the old, majestic temple" of Nature, where, "Through each branch-enwoven skylight, / Speaks He in the breeze, / As of old beneath the twilight / Of lost Eden's trees!" And yet, without any apparent sense of irony, Whittier celebrates the lumberers' work, enjoining them to "Strike then, comrades! Trade is waiting / On our rugged toil"—a toil that is justified by the vision of women and children by the hearth at home and of "the age to come," in which the lumberman will give way to "smiths" and "farmers," and the virgin forests to "waving wheat and golden maize-ears."[27]

The tension merely latent in these poems had been articulated more fully in Thomas Cole's "Essay on American Scenery," which gave voice to the national ambivalence toward the wilderness. On the one hand, Cole suggested that

> although an enlightened and increasing people have broken in upon this solitude [of primaeval forests], and with activity and power wrought changes that seem magical, yet the most distinctive, and perhaps the most impressive, characteristic of American scenery is its wildness. . . . and there are those who regret that with the improvements of cultivation the sublimity of the wilderness should pass away: for those scenes of solitude from which the hand of nature has never been lifted, affect the mind with a more deep toned emotion than aught which the hand of man has touched. Amid them the consequent associations are of God the creator—they are his undefiled works, and the mind is cast into the contemplation of eternal things.

Yet, in spite of having identified pristine nature with God and nation, Cole ultimately supports the forces of progress and concedes the necessary sacrifice of the wilderness. For all the power of uncultivated nature, Cole wrote, "the cultivated . . . is still more important to man in his social capacity," and "in looking over the yet uncultivated scene, the mind's eye may see far into futurity. Where the wolf roams, the plough shall glisten; on the gray crag shall rise temple and tower—mighty deeds shall be done in the now pathless wilderness; and poets yet unborn shall sanctify the soil."[28]

The future envisioned by both Cole and Whittier appropriates through picturesque description the utilitarian view of the landscape into their paeans to "the sublimity of the wilderness." While these positions were fundamentally at odds, Cole's final vision here of *poets* sanctifying the soil suggests one means by which Americans might come to terms with the conflict: by preserving the *images* of pristine nature, *art* might compensate for the loss of the actual wilderness. This sense of the artist's role was reiterated in the *Literary World*'s review of the paintings on exhibit at the National Academy in 1847—a review that also reiterates the archetypal symbols of the ax and the evergreen:

> We wish it were in our power to impress it upon the minds of our landscape painters, particularly, that they have a high and sacred mission to perform; and woe betide them or their members if they neglect it. The axe of civilization is busy with our old forests, and artisan ingenuity is fast sweeping away the relics of our national infancy. What were once the wild and picturesque haunts of the Red Man . . . are becoming the abodes of commerce and the seats of manufactures. . . . and even the primordial hills, once bristling with shaggy pine and hemlock, like old Titans as they were, are being shorn of their locks . . . and made to figure in the shape of deal boards and rafters for unsightly structures . . . Yankee enterprise has little sympathy with the picturesque, and it behooves our artists to rescue from its grasp the little that is left, before it is for ever too late. This is their mission.[29]

By designating the poets and artists as the recorders and preservers of images of the passing wilderness, these writers implicitly concede a fundamental separation between the moral/aesthetic sphere and the social sphere, between private good and public good, and thus they are able to sidestep any ultimate challenge to the validity of Yankee enterprise. To domesticate the wilderness is to *enact*, in historical time, the national destiny. Moral and aesthetic responses to nature are outside of the historical and public spheres, however, and exist in the private and ahistorical sphere where we *contemplate* nature's "eternal things." Cole can celebrate "the mighty deeds [that] shall be done in the now pathless wilderness" at the same time he insists that that very wilderness "affect[s] the mind with a more deep toned emotion than aught which the hand of man has touched" because *art* can preserve those scenes for private inspiration without impeding the advance of our public destiny.

In "Ktaadn," however, Thoreau is not interested merely in the impressions nature makes on a securely civilized, genteel sensibility, but in examining how we live in relation to nature. Thus he is not interested merely in capturing the picturesque view, but in asking how our lives ought to be modified to conform to the values nature teaches. By refusing to distinguish among the moral, aesthetic, and social spheres as readily as did most of his contemporaries, Thoreau is also prompted to penetrate further into the question of whether subduing the wilderness indeed constitutes genuine progress; and if so, whether there are nevertheless aspects of nature that should not or cannot be appropriated for those ends.

In the popular romanticism of his contemporaries, to appreciate the wilderness was, in effect, to appropriate it in the service of genteel culture rather than to step outside of and so assess that culture. Moreover, the record of fresh impressions was the stuff reputations were made of. Asher Durand advised aspiring artists in an 1855 series of "Letters on Landscape Painting," "Go not abroad then in search of material . . . while the virgin charms of our native land have claims on your deepest affections," for America's "untrodden wilds, yet spared from the pollutions of civilization, afford a guarantee for a reputation of originality that you may elsewhere long seek and find not."[30] When Thoreau wrote "Ktaadn," the Maine wilderness was only beginning to be recognized as a promising area for exploitation—both by commercial interests and by the romantic artists of the day. In his 1845 account of Katahdin, Edward Everett Hale commented that "it surprised me to think that here was such natural scenery utterly unheard of among the picturesque hunters." Thoreau's subject was thus particularly well chosen, and it is not surprising that in the decade following the publication of "Ktaadn" the Maine wilderness became an increasingly popular subject for American writers and artists.

Yet while "Ktaadn" benefited from, and must be seen in the context of, this romantic vogue for the natural landscape, his essay can be distinguished from those of most of his romantic contemporaries, both thematically and stylistically. Thoreau's straightforward account involved the deliberate rejection of the urbane, erudite style and persona of the genteel familiar essay. These had been helpful in his earlier efforts to popularize his ideas but were ill suited for capturing his engagement with the true wilderness. Thoreau's most literary contemporaries, on the other hand, tended to adopt an exaggerated urbanity, since for them the wilderness was largely a vehicle for expressing their refined sensibilities.[31] Ironically, this stance tended to prevent them from getting beyond the most conventional responses to picturesque scenes, characters, or incidents. James Russell Lowell's 1853 sketch "A Moosehead Journal," for example, uses the uncultivated landscape merely as a backdrop against which he brings his own highly cultivated persona into sharp relief; Lowell concludes his essay by reminding his reader that what he promised to write was "*my* journal, with a little nature, a little human nature, and a great deal of *I* in it, which last ingredient I take to be the true spirit of this species of writing; all the rest being so much water for tender throats which cannot take it *neat*."[32] Theodore Winthrop's more ambitious essay "Life in the Open Air—Katahdin and the Penobscot," which recounts his 1856 excursion with Frederic Church, treats the wilderness more earnestly than had Lowell, but when he is not providing conventional descriptions of picturesque scenes, Winthrop too seems to feel that the backwoods are interesting only to the extent that they provide material for his wit in puns, anecdotes, and character sketches. Both authors are particularly anxious that in their accounts of the wilderness they not be mistaken for rustic provincials themselves, and both call exaggerated attention to their cosmopolitan standards of taste and judgment. Lowell's essay, written in the form of a letter "addressed to the Edelmann Storg at the Bagni di Lucca," begins: "I have seen many lakes, ranging from that of Virgil's Cumean, to that of Scott's Caledonian Lady, but Moosehead, within two days of me, had never enjoyed the profit of being mirrored in my retina. At the sound of the name, no reminiscential atoms (according to Kenelm Digby's Theory of Association—as good as any), stirred and marshalled themselves in my brain."[33] Winthrop's description of the same lake, though not so extravagant in its wit, is strikingly similar in its fundamental condescension toward nature, and especially toward the American landscape. "Moosehead Lake is a little bigger than Lago di Guardi, and therefore, according to our American standard, rather more important. It is not very grand, not very picturesque, but considerably better than no lake."[34]

By contrast, Thoreau travels very light into the Maine woods, leaving behind as much intellectual baggage as he can afford to do without. Thoreau's essay has its share of wit and humor, but it is a down-to-earth, native humor, akin to the tall tale, through which he captures rather than obscures the flavor of the region. He describes his encounter with a small trader in Molunkus, for example: "I saw him standing in his shop-door—his shop was so small, that, if a traveller should make demonstrations of entering in, *he* would have to go out by the back way, and confer with his customer through a window . . . I should have gone in, for I felt a real impulse to trade, if I had not stopped to consider what would become of him" (MW 13). Later, when the travelers are surprised to discover a handbill advertising a Boston clothing store posted on a pine tree in the wilderness, Thoreau comments: "This should be recorded among the advantages of this mode of advertising, that so, possibly, even the bears and wolves, moose, deer, otter and beaver, not to mention the Indian, may learn where they can fit themselves according to the latest fashion, or, at least, recover some of their own lost garments" (50).

If Thoreau was, in truth, less cosmopolitan than Lowell or Winthrop (though certainly no less erudite), he knew how to make his provincialism a virtue, and the unobstructed clarity and vividness of his descriptions make "Ktaadn" the best nineteenth-century account of the region and one of Thoreau's most entertaining and readable pieces. Even Thoreau's conventional set piece on the white pine and the lumber mills is notably more vivid and engaging, with its description of the pine's "every individual needle trembling in the sunlight," than Winthrop's entertaining but heavy-handed treatment of the same theme, in which the lumbering operation is described as a military campaign against the forest regent "Pinus I." Even in their very descriptions of the wilderness, writers like Lowell and Winthrop reveal their absolute commitment to the social sphere and the progress of civilization. For Thoreau, as he stated explicitly in *Walden*, this was not a foregone conclusion.

Not that Thoreau was entirely opposed to the forces of civilization, either. Thoreau's sympathy for the forest pine in the face of the "demon" lumberers is balanced by his admiration for the bateau manufactory he visits in Oldtown, and throughout his account Thoreau seems to be assessing the virtues of both civilization and nature, balancing one against the other. Between Oldtown and Katahdin, which mark the boundaries of his narrative and represent the poles of civilization and nature, there lies a middle ground that he must traverse, where he can examine the relationship between man and nature as if along a graduated scale of relative ascendancy of one over the other.

Traveling through the settled regions, Thoreau juxtaposes images of civilization's inroads with images of nature's resistance. The "straight and well made" Houlton military road, for example, would seem to be an emblem of the imposition of civilization and order upon the chaos of the wilderness; but Thoreau wryly adds that, as they traveled along it, "everywhere we saw signs of the great freshet—this house standing awry, and that where it was not founded, but where it was found, at any rate, the next day" (7). Analogously, Thoreau gives an amusing account of the buzz of politicking he encounters in Passadumkeag, exposing the ineffectuality of the political state when he observes that the propensity for naming places along the road, "in the midst of the unnamed and unincorporated wilderness, was to make a distinction without a difference" (8). On the other hand, when he observes a large orchard of apple trees, he notes that they bore "all natural fruit, and comparatively worthless for want of a grafter. . . . It would be a good speculation, as well as a favor conferred on the settlers, for a Massachusetts boy to go down there with a trunk full of choice scions, and his grafting apparatus in the spring" (8). It should be remembered that Thoreau went to Katahdin while living at Walden Pond, where his "half-cultivated" bean field represented a transcendentalist's adaptation of Jefferson's agrarian idealism. Thus, while Thoreau deplored the destruction and exploitation of nature, he did not strictly oppose the intervention of man upon nature—on the contrary, he desired that man adapt to nature, and so be naturalized himself. Thus, paralleling his remarks in the "Economy" chapter of *Walden*, Thoreau here asserts that any emigrant who can afford the few dollars' fare to this region may "be as rich as he pleases," for "land virtually costs nothing, and houses only the labor of building, and he may begin life as Adam did" (14).

This passage, with its Adamic allusion uniting nature, God, and national destiny, made for a fitting conclusion to the first installment of "Ktaadn" as it appeared in the *Union Magazine*. The next installment, titled "Life in the Wilderness," brings the travelers one step farther from the civilized world. "Leaping over a fence," he writes, "we began to follow an obscure trail up the northern bank of the Penobscot." The fence is a symbolic as well as an actual boundary, on the other side of which "there was now no road further, the river being the only highway, and but half a dozen log huts confined to its banks, to be met with for thirty miles; on either hand, and beyond, was a wholly uninhabited wilderness, stretching to Canada. . . . This was what you might call a bran new country; the only roads were of Nature's making, and the few houses were camps" (16). This fascination with the boundaries between civilization and nature is characteristic of Thoreau's writing but is by no means unique to him; two of the three previous accounts of Katahdin that Thoreau cited in his essay similarly note such transitions from one realm to the other. In his largely scientific report of 1837, for example, J. W. Bailey writes, "Crossing the Mattawamkeag by the fine bridge built at the expense of the United States, and bidding farewell to civilization, we plunged into the woods by a blind path, (if path it might be called,) which was scarcely passable, although we were on foot, it was so obstructed by fallen trees, tangled roots, bushes and mudholes."[35] Crossing the bridge here parallels Thoreau's leaping over the fence, but the differences between the two accounts are as striking as their similarities, for Bailey regards nature in its primitive state as merely an obstacle to be overcome and subdued. Edward Everett Hale, on the other hand, shares Thoreau's romantic eagerness for crossing the border between civilization and nature. He begins his account of his hike to Katahdin by noting, "You will see that we made a descending climax in the arrangements of civilization till we got to the end of it, and perhaps a particle farther,—but never beyond hail of it" (here, he puns on his own name, perhaps in order to reveal to the cognoscenti the author's identity); when he observes the "framed prints from the New York Mirror round the wall" of the first inn along his route, he comments with good-natured disappointment "Still civilization." In his 1847 "Notes of an Excursion to Mount Katahdin," George Thurber similarly observes of Hunt's farm, "This is the limit of civilization in this direction, and the point from which loggers and explorers date their departure into the forest."[36] In Thoreau's more complex account, such observations of various imagined boundaries between civilization and nature act as a principal structuring device of his narrative.

In crossing the fence into the roadless forest Thoreau does not actually enter the "uninhabited wilderness," which still lies "beyond" the sparsely populated banks of the waterways, and he is as interested in the backwoods life of the people here as he is in nature itself. He carefully notes each house along the way—for the benefit, as he says, of future travelers, but also to note the shifting relationship between civilization and nature here. He provides detailed descriptions of the construction of the backwoods farmhouses and of the loggers' rude log huts; he describes the kinds of food and drink popular or available; and he takes particular interest in noting what kinds of reading material are available in these wilderness regions. The printed word is not only a fit emblem of civilization's presence, but it seems quite literally to be the most potent link between the backwoods dweller and the rest of humanity. The newspapers the travelers distributed at one stop proved to be "really an important item in our outfit, and, at times, the only currency that would circulate" (MW 17). When they spend that night at George McCauslin's farm, Thoreau again takes note of the available reading matter: "There was the Wandering Jew, cheap edition, and fine print, The Criminal Calendar, and Parish's Geography, and flash novels two or three. Under the pressure of circumstances, we read a little in these. With such aid, the press is not so feeble an engine after all" (25). And when they subsequently reach a logging camp on the Penobscot, Thoreau again details the titles of the miscellaneous reading material he discovers, finding it "well thumbed and soiled" (34). (J. W. Bailey had similarly observed in his account, "I was much pleased by discovering at this [loggers'] cabin—the very out-post of civilization in this direction—a well-thumbed copy of Scott's Heart of Mid Lothian. 'There's fame for you!'")[37]

The McCauslin farm struck Thoreau as a model of backwoods life, and when the Indian guides from Oldtown failed to meet the travelers here as they had arranged (one of whom, Louis Neptune, Thoreau knew to have guided the Jackson expedition in 1837), they persuade McCauslin himself to join them as their guide (McCauslin and his brother had been guides for the Bailey expedition of 1836).[38] They then hike four miles to McCauslin's nearest neighbor, Thomas Fowler, whom they enlist as their second boatman and guide. McCauslin and Fowler represent to Thoreau the apparently harmonious integration of civilization and nature. "Fowler was just completing a new log hut," Thoreau explains and notes that "he had begun to paper his house with spruce bark, turned inside out, which had a good effect, and was in keeping with the circumstances" (MW 27). In his enthusiasm for this naturalized life Thoreau celebrates the spruce beer Fowler serves them, "clear and thin, but strong and stringent as the cedar sap. It was as if we sucked at the very teats of Nature's pine-clad bosom in these parts. . . . a lumberer's drink which would acclimate and naturalize a man at once" (27–28). When Fowler points out a "sacred" bald eagle's nest, Thoreau discovers another emblem of naturalization: "There were these two houses only there, his low hut, and the eagles' airy cartload of fagots" (28). The complementary images of Fowler's rude log hut and the eagles' aerie suggests the breakdown of the opposition between man and nature; and, as the national bird, the bald eagle is a particularly appropriate counterpart to Fowler himself, whose naturalized life Thoreau would also like to make a national symbol.

These emblems of harmony between man and nature are undercut, however, when the travelers stop at the elder Fowler's house, two miles farther up the Millinocket, in order to procure a sturdy bateau. Thoreau is careful to note that this is the last permanent house and that Fowler is the region's oldest inhabitant, but here, at this next significant boundary between civilization and nature, Thoreau provides a rather graphic description of the loss of eighteen of the Fowlers' sheep to wolves. He also notes that "there were steel traps by the door of various sizes, for wolves, otter, and bears, with large claws instead of teeth, to catch in their sinews" (30). This image, and not that of the complementary abodes of woodsman and eagle, becomes their omen of departure into the wilderness as they launch their bateau on the waters of the Penobscot "and commence our voyage in good earnest" (30, 31).

"Life in the wilderness" turns out to demand alertness, a shrewd intelligence, and endurance as the men struggle to negotiate the waterways. Thoreau describes their first experience of being poled up the rapids in the bateau by their skilled guides: "We shot up the rapids like a salmon, the water rushing and roaring around, so that only a practised eye could distinguish a safe course, or tell what was deep water and what rocks, frequently grazing the latter on one or both sides, with a hundred as narrow escapes as ever the Argo had in passing through the Symplegades" (32). Thoreau concedes, "I, who had had some experience in boating, had never experienced any half so exhilarating before." Because Thoreau undoubtedly understood that the popular appeal of wilderness accounts lay in the description not only of the exotic and unfamiliar but of just such incidents of adventure, he passed up few opportunities to emphasize them. His analogy to the voyage of the *Argo* through the treacherous floating islands is one of the literary allusions Thoreau did not drop from his first draft (J2: 308), because its primary effect is to call attention not to the narrator's erudition but to the heroic dimensions of their journey. Later in the essay Thoreau heightens the sense of danger on the rapids by describing the rocks as "lying in wait like so many alligators," eager to crush their poles "and jerk them from your hands, before you have stolen an effectual shove against their palates" (49). "Ktaadn" is indeed Thoreau's most exciting narrative (significantly more so than either of his subsequent accounts of the Maine wilderness), even while he tends to fall back upon rather conventional imagery to underscore the elements of danger and adventure. It is not surprising to find, for example, that in *Life in the Open Air* Theodore Winthrop uses both the allusion to the Symplegades and the crocodilian simile in describing the Penobscot rapids.[39] To portray the wilderness as both exotic and dangerous perhaps ran counter to Thoreau's transcendentalist imagination, which was more inclined to represent nature as familiar and domestic, but it certainly brought Thoreau into line with the prevailing vogue for adventures into the uncultivated landscape.

Throughout his account of their progress up the Penobscot waterways, Thoreau plays off the various tensions between the forces of nature and civilization. Thoreau had progressively marked off the last settlement and the last *permanent* habitation along their route, and now, at the end of the second installment of his essay, he identifies the logging camp toward which they had been heading as "the last human habitation of any kind in this direction"; yet this passage is strikingly similar to that with which he introduced this installment—their crossing the fence into the "bran new country." At both points Thoreau creates the impression that he is about to leave the last outpost of civilization and enter the virgin wilderness. On the one hand, this keeps the reader, as well as Thoreau, looking ahead, anticipating the truly novel experiences in store; on the other hand, it introduces an element of disappointment and consequently of skepticism, since each *apparent* entrance into the true wilderness turns out to be something less than that, and nature in its pristine state remains elusive, continually withdrawing before them as they advance.

The third installment, titled "Boating on the Lakes," begins with another evocation of just such unspoiled nature as he has been seeking. Breaking camp under a full moon on the banks of North Twin Lake, Thoreau discovers,

> There was the smoke of no log-hut nor camp of any kind to greet us, still less was any lover of nature or musing traveller watching our batteau from the distant hills; not even the Indian hunter was there, for he rarely climbs them, but hugs the river like ourselves. No face welcomed us but the fine fantastic sprays of free and happy evergreen trees, waving one above another in their ancient home. (36)

Thoreau is exhilarated by this scene, described in a series of negatives through which he casts off the layers of civilization to reveal the "ancient home" of primitive nature. Yet Thoreau concedes that commerce had actually preceded him to these shores: "In fact the most valuable white pine timber, even about this lake, had been culled out, [though] this would never have been suspected by the voyager" (36).[40] Thoreau tries to retrieve the impression of the landscape as pristine and exotic when, passing their landmark at the head of North Twin Lake, he imagines it was "as if by the watery links of rivers and of lakes we were about to float over unmeasured zones of earth, bound on unimaginable adventures" (38). And, describing their camp that night, he writes, "The glassy smoothness of the sleeping lake, laving the shores of a new world, with the dark, fantastic rocks rising here and there from its surface, made a scene not easily described. It has left such an impression of stern yet gentle wildness on my memory as will not soon be effaced" (40). Yet at the entrance to Ambejijis Lake the next morning they discover the traces of a thriving logging industry. Thoreau notes that "it was always startling to discover so plain a trail of civilized man there," and his imagination again turns to the forceful symbols of man's presence that he discovers: "It was easy to see, that driving logs must be an exciting as well as arduous and dangerous business," and he fancifully imagines the logger subduing the wilderness with the aid of "his faithful dogs, Thaw, and Rain, and Freshet, and Wind" (42).

Negotiating their way through the wilderness becomes increasingly difficult, however, and Thoreau says he "could not sufficiently admire the skill and coolness" with which his guides poled their bateau up rapids and falls (49).[41] In these detailed descriptions of their efforts, which provide some of the liveliest adventures of the essay, Thoreau pits man against nature, and their success is hard-won, tentative, and limited; they do not achieve mastery over nature so much as they are compelled to adapt to it. After a difficult ascent of Aboljacarmegus Falls, the voyagers discover further evidence of the lumber industry in some huge logs, which turn out to carry the marks of their own party members. But these logs were now immovable, "piled up high and dry on the rocks on either hand, the relics probably of a jam which had taken place here in the Great Freshet in the spring. Many of these would have to wait for another great freshet, perchance, if they lasted so long, before they could be got off" (52).[42] Earlier Thoreau had portrayed the logger as the master of nature, who had merely to "whistle" for his "faithful dogs, Thaw, and Rain, and Freshet, and Wind" in order to send his immense pile of logs "scrambling down the country . . . toward the Orono Mills" (42); here, the logger has no such authority over the elements: as if with a will of its own, the great freshet alone will determine when, if ever, the logger will bring the results of his labor to market. Thus this scene is not an occasion for celebrating the force of commerce; rather, recognizing man's subordination to nature here, Thoreau discovers in this scene a symbol of his own, very different ambitions and his own subjection to forces beyond his control: "Methinks that must be where all my property lies, cast up on the rocks on some distant and unexplored stream, and waiting for an unheard-of freshet to fetch it down. O make haste, ye gods, with your winds and rains, and start the jam before it rots!" (52–53). This is one of the few passages in "Ktaadn" in which Thoreau exercises his more habitual transcendentalist imagination, converting facts into emblems of his spiritual life. As in so many of his apostrophes to the gods, Thoreau pleads for the fulfillment of his special destiny—for the arrival of his spiritual "property," his inspiration, which he hopes might be crafted in the "mills" of his own imagination—and so too be brought to market.

In the fourth installment, entitled "The Ascent of Ktaadn," Thoreau at last reaches the goal of his journey and the climax of his narrative. The segment begins, however, with an extended description of fishing at their campsite that functions as an important counterpoint to his experience of nature on the mountain. There, nature will appear grim, inhospitable and threatening; but here Thoreau experiences nature at its most beautiful, hospitable, and generous. As the fish "fell upon our bait, and one after another were landed amidst the bushes," Thoreau experiences a moment of transcendent beauty, a glimpse of that primal state of nature he had been seeking:

> While yet alive, before their tints had faded, [the fish] glistened like the fairest flowers, the product of primitive rivers; and he could hardly trust his senses, as he stood over them, that these jewels should have swum away in that Aboljacknagesic water for so long, so many dark ages;—these bright fluviatile flowers, seen of Indians only, made beautiful, the Lord only knows why, to swim there! I could understand better, for this, the truth of mythology, the fables of Proteus, and all those beautiful sea-monsters,—how all history, indeed, put to a terrestrial use, is mere history; but put to a celestial, is mythology always. (54)

The transforming perception here is of the almost painful beauty of nature totally distinct from its merely material, utilitarian, and commercial value. What strikes this perception home for Thoreau is his recognition that these "jewels," these "fluviatile flowers," possessed a perfect and self-contained beauty for uncounted ages before they were ever seen by white men's eyes. If his remarks seem rather crudely to discount the human sensibility of the Indians, it is nevertheless clear that his intention is to evoke an image of the almost mystical beauty of nature in its primitive and pristine state, independent of man, and complete in itself. The highest destiny of the primitive wilderness lies outside of history, is fufilled in its very existence, and does not await or depend upon its transformation by man in the service of progress and civilization. Man is not and cannot be master of this aspect of nature; he is, at best, a privileged witness to it.

It is not surprising that Thoreau's perception of this transcendent beauty should come while he is fishing; for as early as the "Natural History of Massachusetts" and again in "A Winter Walk," as well as in both of his drafted but as yet unpublished books, Thoreau treated fishing as a symbol of the integration of man in nature. In each of these works, Thoreau is careful to distinguish between the higher ends of fishing and the merely material ends. Thoreau makes a similar distinction in "Ktaadn" when his perception of the "celestial" uses of the fish—in their perfect, gemlike beauty—is interrupted by the "terrestrial" demands of his companions: "But there is the rough voice of Uncle George, who commands at the frying pan, to send over what you've got, and then you may stay till morning" (54).

The perception of the mythic, transcendent dimension of nature is almost tragically ephemeral, as man's "terrestrial" life intrudes upon it, commanding the mastery of nature and its consequent reduction to mere commodity; yet this is a redemptive vision nevertheless. Thoreau joins his companions in eating the fish they have caught, but this satisfies only his physical hunger, and he still longs for that "celestial" nature which the fish had disclosed to him. Thus, he explains:

> In the night I dreamed of trout-fishing; and, when at length I awoke, it seemed a fable, that this painted fish swam there so near my couch, and rose to our hooks the last evening—and I doubted if I had not dreamed it all. So I arose before dawn to test its truth, while my companions were still sleeping. There stood Ktaadn with distinct and cloudless outline in the moonlight; and the rippling of the rapids was the only sound to break the stillness. Standing on the shore, I once more cast my line into the stream, and found the dream to be real, and the fable true. The speckled trout and silvery roach, like flying fish, sped swiftly through the moonlight air, describing bright arcs on the dark side of Ktaadn, until moonlight, now fading into daylight, brought satiety to my mind, and the minds of my companions, who had joined me. (55)

Significantly, it is not merely fishing but fishing in the moonlight that provides the occasion here (as well as in the "Natural History" and *Walden*) for the semimystical experience in which dream and reality become one. Thoreau seems to share Hawthorne's sense that in the moonlight one may discover "a neutral territory, somewhere between the real world and fairy-land, where the Actual and the Imaginary may meet, and each imbue itself with the nature of the other."[43] It is thus tempting to see in the "bright arcs" described by the glistening fish, as they sail through the moonlight, the image of a nocturnal rainbow, which, like the rainbow that appeared to Noah after the Flood, stands as a visible sign of the covenant between man and God. Throughout his account, Thoreau has reminded his readers of the great flood of the previous spring that had upset houses, destroyed dams, and left huge logs high and dry upon the rocks; witnessing this, Thoreau called upon the gods to discover to him his own spiritual property, which he imagined "cast up on rocks on some distant and unexplored stream." Now, on just such a distant and unexplored stream, Thoreau experiences a vision of transcendent beauty in which the terrestrial and the celestial become one, uniting history and myth, reality and dream, truth and fable; and this vision culminates in the image of a nocturnal rainbow, consecrating his vision and bringing him now a sense of *spiritual* satiety.

Even on the most literal level, it is clear that this idyllic interlude fulfills Thoreau's desire to discover nature in its pristine state and that it thus constitutes the climax of at least one strand of his narrative. Critical discussions of "Ktaadn" have focused too exclusively on Thoreau's disturbing confrontation with raw matter on the summit of the mountain, neglecting this complementary and crucial perception of nature's "celestial" state. Throughout the narrative Thoreau has juxtaposed the hostile and the hospitable sides of nature, so it is not simply, as some critics have suggested, that before his ascent Thoreau indulges in a naively romantic view of nature which he is afterward unable to sustain.[44] His perception of the mountain's grim terror is, after all, as much a product of his romantic imagination as is his perception of transcendent beauty at the trout stream. Significantly, Thoreau emphasizes the fact that both experiences occur in the unviolated wilderness, unaltered by the long reach of civilization; both are confrontations with nature in its primal state, independent of and superior to human history, in which Thoreau experiences what Emerson had called "an original relation with the universe."

Nevertheless, the trout fishing episode is only the penultimate and not the ultimate stage in their excursion, and it is clearly subordinated in the narrative to the obvious climax, Thoreau's powerful account of Katahdin itself. Thoreau initiates his account of this final leg of their outward journey by noting, as they leave their camp in the morning, that their guide "had never been any nearer the mountain than this, and there was not the slightest trace of man to guide us further in this direction" (56). This comment takes its place in the sequence of observations Thoreau has made throughout the journey, measuring just how far they had traveled away from civilization into the uncharted wilderness, and so denoting another boundary traversed. Here, if anywhere, Thoreau will encounter a wilderness destined to remain pristine and unappropriated, and Thoreau's description of Katahdin seen from a bare ridge underscores both the novelty of their experience and the sense that this mountain indeed represents the terminus to their quest for absolute wilderness: "Ktaadn presented a different aspect from any mountain I have seen, there being a greater proportion of naked rock, rising abruptly from the forest; and we looked up at this blue barrier as if it were some fragment of a wall which anciently bounded the earth in that direction" (56–57). Thoreau's description combines accurate reporting and suggestive allusiveness. On the one hand, Thoreau's impression of the mountain only confirms what he had already learned from Dr. Jackson's geological survey, that Katahdin was indeed "the most abrupt granite mountain in New England."[45] On the other hand, Thoreau's description of the mountain as the fragment of some ancient wall recalls that which Milton's Satan saw in his first glimpse of Eden: in "a steep wilderness" thick with trees, "Yet higher than their tops / The verdurous wall of Paradise up sprung" (bk. 4, 132–43). When Thoreau begins his ascent, his identification with Milton's Satan will become explicit.

Ironically, Thoreau's ascent of Katahdin results in the contraction rather than the expansion of his vision. The woods are so dense that they hike for the entire morning without a view of the summit; "buried in the woods," and contending with dense underbrush, Thoreau calls it "the worst kind of travelling" (MW 59). As Thoreau pushes ahead of his companions to climb the mountain alone, the landscape seems to bear down and close in upon him, and rather than expanding with spiritual inspiration he seems to diminish in size as he proceeds: he climbs along the bed of a mountain stream, "pulling myself up by the side of perpendicular falls of twenty or thirty feet . . . ascending by huge steps, as it were, a giant's stairway, down which a river flowed. . . . seemingly not diminishing in breadth as I advanced; but still it came rushing and roaring down, with a copious tide, over and amidst masses of bare rock" (60). Here and throughout the ascent Thoreau's imagery emphasizes his own insignificance, and he seems to exploit all the conventions of the romantic sublime as he expresses his awe and terror in the face of the mountain's vastness.

While many critics have insistently characterized Thoreau's account of the mountain as a record of his confrontation with the "reality" of nature as opposed to his earlier "romanticism" or "mythologizing" of it,[46] it is actually at this point in the essay that Thoreau is his most literary and allusive, *insisting*—as he had not previously—that we acknowledge the mythological dimension of his actions. His route, he writes, was "scarcely less arduous than Satan's anciently through Chaos." He finds himself "scrambling on all fours over the tops of ancient black spruce-trees" that he describes as being as "old as the flood." He even "walked some good rods erect over the tops of these trees," beneath which was "a dark and cavernous region," and again he explicitly compares his route to Satan's through Chaos, quoting, "—nigh founder'd, on he fares, / Treading the crude consistence, half on foot, / Half flying" (60–61). Unlike Satan, however, Thoreau does not reach Eden, but a landscape which parodies that other Eden, the pastoral Arcadia: "Having slumped, scrambled, rolled, bounced, and walked, by turns, over this scraggy country, I arrived upon a side-hill, or rather side-mountain, where rocks, gray, silent rocks, were the flocks and herds that pastured, chewing a rocky cud at sunset. They looked at me with hard gray eyes, without a bleat or low"

(61). While Thoreau ironically undermines the pastoral vision of nature here, his elaborately literary treatment of the landscape makes it clear that its very intractableness stimulates his imagination.

The mixed emotions of terror and awe, of being at once overwhelmed and exhilarated by the immensity and power of the scene, increase in intensity through each stage of Thoreau's account of the mountain. This first brief climb comes to a halt when Thoreau reaches the skirt of a cloud, and he returns to the cramped, makeshift camp his companions have set up in his absence. His description of their rather uncomfortable accommodations makes it clear, though, that his preliminary encounter with Katahdin has whetted rather than stifled his romantic sensibility. He describes the scenery of their camp at night as "savage and dreary," and "wildly rough," but his imagination eagerly embraces these qualities: "It was, perhaps, even a more grand and desolate place for a night's lodging than the summit would have been, being in the neighborhood of those wild trees, and of the torrent" (62). The conjunction of the terms "grand and desolate" epitomizes the emotional tenor of the sublime. Only when he finds himself truly shaken by his encounter with this grandeur and desolation, however, will his experience of the sublime be complete. As of yet, nature has not overwhelmed him but only provoked his fancy.

The next morning Thoreau retraces his ascent in the company of others, though he soon pushes ahead of his companions so that once again he climbs alone. And again he evokes the image of Milton's Chaos, that primeval mass of warring elements as yet uninformed by the harmonizing spirit of divinity: "The mountain seemed a vast aggregation of loose rocks, as if sometime it had rained rocks. . . . They were the raw materials of a planet dropped from an unseen quarry, which the vast chemistry of nature would anon work up, or work down, into the smiling and verdant plains and valleys of earth. This was an undone extremity of the globe" (MW 63). This sense of having penetrated to the very source of creation is part of the conventional rhetoric of the romantic sublime, and Thoreau exploits it further when, finding himself "deep within the hostile ranks of clouds" upon a summit ridge, he describes the scene as "a cloud-factory,—these were the cloud-works, and the wind turned them off done from the cool, bare rocks" (64). Thoreau's figurative language conveys the heightened tension in his confrontation with this alien landscape: it expresses both the elemental power of this creative force that threatens to overwhelm him and also his resistance to that force through images of human creation and mastery of the elements—the quarry, the chemistry laboratory, the factory, the kitchen. But these ironic comparisons of great things to small give way to mythic imagery, "of Atlas, Vulcan, the Cyclops, and Prometheus." Thoreau is able to sustain a verbal mastery over the scene only by shifting from the first person to an impersonal third person, as he acknowledges the overpowering force and mystery of elemental nature.

> It was vast, Titanic, and such as man never inhabits. Some part of the beholder, even some vital part, seems to escape through the loose grating of his ribs as he ascends. . . . Vast, Titanic, inhuman Nature has got him at disadvantage, caught him alone, and pilfers him of some of his divine faculty. She does not smile on him as in the plains. She seems to say sternly, why came ye here before your time? This ground is not prepared for you. Is it not enough that I smile in the valleys? . . . Why seek me where I have not called thee, and thus complain because you find me but a stepmother? Shouldst thou freeze or starve, or shudder thy life away, here is no shrine, nor altar, nor any access to my ear. (64)

Seeking the boundary between nature and civilization, Thoreau has come upon that even more elemental boundary between spirit and matter, and he discovers that nature uninformed by spirit is chaotic, alien, hostile. Raw matter claims only the kinship of a "stepmother": Thoreau implies that his true "mother" is that Nature wedded to Spirit which resides in the plains below. Yet Thoreau does not mean merely to retreat to those plains. Challenged by this stepmother Nature to explain why he violates this alien territory, Thoreau answers by quoting the reply of Milton's Satan to a similar challenge:

> "Chaos and Ancient Night, I come no spy
> With purpose to explore or to disturb
> The secrets of your realm, but * * *
> * * * * * * * as my way
> Lies through your spacious empire up to light." (64)

The chaos Thoreau envisions atop Katahdin confirms the spirit by confronting his imagination with the absence of spirit. That is, by experiencing the momentary dissipation of spirit he reconfirms its existence, both in himself and in creation.

As the intensity of the experience subsides, Thoreau reasserts his mastery of the scene through reiteration and generalization: "The tops of mountains are among the unfinished parts of the globe, whither it is a slight insult to the gods to climb and pry into their secrets, and try their effect on our humanity. Only daring and insolent men, perchance, go there. . . . Pomola is always angry with those who climb to the summit of Ktaadn" (65). Rhetorically, this summary seems to conclude the episode, and at this point Thoreau abruptly abandons his subjective response to the mountain in order to interject Dr. Jackson's estimates of the mountain's elevation. These measurements implicitly assert man's mastery over nature, but such claims for mastery are belied by Thoreau's personal experience of "vast, Titanic, inhuman Nature," which "has got [the beholder] at a disadvantage." Thoreau did not actually even reach the summit, and it is hard to tell whether his citation of Dr. Jackson is essentially evasive or ironic.[47] Significantly, Thoreau did not include this passage until he revised his essay for publication; he may have seen this addition as bringing his narrative into line with the national myth of subduing the wilderness.

If Jackson's account represents the mastery of science, Thoreau next suggests the mastery of commerce over nature. Descending the mountain to join his companions, Thoreau finds them gathering mountain cranberries, and, in another passage added only when he revised his first draft, he comments, "When the country is settled and roads are made, these cranberries will perhaps become an article of commerce" (66). Again, it is hard to know what to make of such a remark, which appears only two paragraphs after he has imagined "inhuman Nature" telling him, "This ground is not prepared for you," but it is very likely that when Thoreau added this, he was aware of Marcus Keep's proposals to trade in Katahdin's mountain cranberries.[48] We might again take Thoreau's remark as essentially ironic, intended now to expose the false complacency of such a narrowly utilitarian view of nature, but this seems oversubtle. More likely, it merely reflects an effort on Thoreau's part to bring his essay into line with other published accounts of Katahdin, even though there remains a disturbing disjunction between these remarks and Thoreau's powerful description of the unappropriable mountaintop. For the moment, Thoreau defers addressing the most disturbing questions raised by his confrontation with Katahdin, but he will therefore be forced to confront his experience again before his journey is over.

Having rejoined his companions, just below the layer of clouds, Thoreau now has a clear view of the mountain prospect he was denied higher up: "There it was, the State of Maine, which we had seen on the map, but not much like that" (66). Here Thoreau echoes his earlier description of the view from Mount Wachusett: "There lay Massachusetts, spread out before us in its length and breadth, like a map." Verbally so similar, these passages actually express contrasting impressions. In "Wachusett" the landscape *does* appear "like a map," and Thoreau goes on to describe his vision of man's westward migration across the land to fulfill his destiny; in "Ktaadn," Thoreau observes that the landscape is in fact "*not* much like" the map of the state, and he goes on to celebrate what at least appears to be the virgin wilderness (though he now knows that in fact this is not quite the case): "Immeasurable forest for the sun to shine on . . . No clearing, no house. It did not look as if a solitary traveller had cut so much as a walking-stick there" (66).

Thoreau's description of this panoramic view conforms to the conventional and expected climax of such mountain excursions, and it is perhaps inevitable that his rhetoric closely resembles that of the comparable descriptions in several of the contemporary accounts of Katahdin; but Thoreau drew directly upon at least one of these when composing this section of the essay. He had already completed his rough draft of "Ktaadn" when his sister Sophia sent him J. K. Laski's sketch of "Dr. Young's Botanical Expedition to Mount Katahdin," which had been printed in the *Bangor Courier* in September 1847.[49] Thoreau subsequently doubled the length of his paragraph describing the mountain view (all of the passages quoted above were among the additions), and in doing so he was strongly influenced by Laski's report. While Thoreau had noted in his journal draft the "countless lakes" to be seen from the mountain, for example, he added in the revision the observation that Moosehead Lake lay "like a gleaming silver platter at the end of the table" (66); Laski had described the lakes as "glowing like burnished silver in the noontide effulgence."[50] Thoreau also added for the published version the remark that "the forest looked like a firm grass sward," echoing Laski's observation that "the tallest trees were like grass in the distance."[51] While these are highly conventional similes (Thoreau's additions also bear a strong resemblance at various points to other available accounts), Thoreau goes on to quote Laski directly, saying that "the effect of these lakes in its midst has been well compared by one who has since visited the same spot, to that of a 'mirror broken into a thousand fragments, and wildly scattered over the grass, reflecting the full blaze of the sun'" (66).

Laski's sketch may well have been only one of several contemporary accounts Thoreau drew upon in expanding this paragraph; in either case, however, Thoreau seems to have felt compelled to provide a conventional panoramic description as a concession to popular tastes and expectations. Thoreau ends the paragraph by observing, "We had to console ourselves with the reflection that this view was probably as good as that from the peak, as far as it went, and what were a mountain without its attendant clouds and mists? Like ourselves, neither Bailey nor Jackson had obtained a clear view from the summit" (67). Actually, by the time Thoreau wrote his final draft of the essay, he knew that the Young botanical expedition had had a beautifully clear and unobstructed summit view, but that was really beside the point; in his journal draft Thoreau had added that he "preferred" the mountain "in its every day dress" of clouds and mists (J2: 341). Thoreau knew, moreover, that it was up in the mountain clouds, and not here, that he had a true perception of the unappropriated and unappropriable aspect of nature, and that his account of that experience provided an even more powerful climax to his excursion than an unobstructed summit view could have. His reminder that his predecessors too had been denied a summit view also reminds us of how brilliant a *literary* achievement his account is; a comparison with other accounts of climbing Katahdin when it was obscured by clouds reveals how Thoreau both took his cue from these predecessors and far surpassed them, discovering his most powerful material in an experience that, for others, had been deemed a disappointment and a failure.

Although Thoreau knew that to those who had climbed Katahdin after his own ascent the mountain had appeared benign, he was following an already well-established tradition in portraying Katahdin as severe, imposing, and inhospitable: each of the earlier accounts Thoreau cited (as well as many of the several accounts that appeared in the following decades) emphasized the mountain's formidable granite abruptness; each described the pervasive bank of clouds on the summit; and each rehearsed some version of the Pomola legend that Thoreau used so effectively. Only Thoreau, however, fully saw how to make literary capital of such conditions. J. W. Bailey, for example, stopped six hundred feet short of the summit, explaining, "Had the day been fine there would have been more inducement to proceed; but we were enveloped in clouds, drenched with rain, and there was no prospect of the weather becoming such as to enable us to enjoy that view from the summit which is the principal inducement to reach it."[52] Even more instructive is Theodore Winthrop's 1856 account, for Winthrop knew the whole range of the vocabulary of the sublime, both of "Mountain Gloom" and "Mountain Glory."[53] Winthrop is the advocate par excellence of what Thomas Weiskel has called the "imperialist" aspects of the romantic sublime, which involve "a kind of spiritual capitalism, enjoining a pursuit of the infinite of the private self."[54] Winthrop distinguishes between the "lover of largeness and scope" and the "lover of variety": the former is attracted to the view *from* the mountain, the latter to the view *of* the mountain. He acknowledges the appeal of the panoramic mountain view: "It is a wide view, and a proud thing for a man six feet or less high, to feel that he himself, standing on something he himself has climbed, and having Katahdin under his feet as a mere convenience, can see all Maine. It does not make Maine less, but the spectator more, and that is a useful moral result."[55] But Winthrop himself is a "lover of variety" and so hopes to discover this form of the sublime in Katahdin. Yet when he discovers that the mountain is enshrouded by clouds and obscured from view, he can only offer a description of what he *wished* he had found:

> We lost . . . the view of the mountain itself. All the bleak, lonely, barren ancient waste of the bare summit was shrouded in cold fog. The impressive gray ruin and Titanic havoc of a granite mountain-top, the heaped boulders, the crumbling crags, . . . the downright plunge of precipices, all the savageness of harsh rock, . . . all this was hidden, except when the mist . . . opened whimsically and delusively . . . and gave us vistas into the upper desolation. . . . Besides what our eyes lost, our minds lost, unless they had imagination enough to create it, the sentiment of triumph and valiant energy that the man of body and soul feels

> upon the windy heights, the highest, whence he looks far and wide, like a master of realms, and knows that the world is his; and they lost the sentiment of solemn joy that a man of soul recognizes as one of the surest intimations of immortality, stirring within him, whenever he is in the unearthly regions, the higher world.[56]

There are obviously close parallels between Thoreau's description of Katahdin and Winthrop's description of what he wishes he had seen there—the vocabulary of the sublime was necessarily highly conventional; but there is an even more crucial and revealing difference, for Thoreau's description of being overmastered by raw nature is an overt and deliberate undercutting of the "imperialist" thrust of Winthrop's notion of the sublime, whether in the panoramic vista or the "Titanic havoc" of the mountain itself. If Thoreau casts himself as the insolent rebel-hero, it is not because he has appropriated the infinitude of nature, but because nature has remained essentially alien and unappropriable. Winthrop's notion of the sublime is actually more typically transcendental, more Emersonian—and more like Thoreau's mountain vision in "A Walk to Wachusett"—whereas in "Ktaadn" Thoreau articulates a sense of the sublime in which the observer is dwarfed and overwhelmed in the face of the awesome terror of the infinite.

If this version of the sublime is not typically Thoreauvian (and it is not, as the modern critics' difficulty with "Ktaadn" makes clear), it nevertheless enables Thoreau to accomplish several desirable ends in the essay. On a literary level, it enables him to make a powerful narrative climax out of an experience that would otherwise be a failure, as Winthrop's is when he decides to pierce the bank of clouds and attempt the summit:

> We turned from sunshine and Cosmos into fog and Chaos. We made ourselves quite miserable for naught. We clambered up into Nowhere, into a great, white, ghostly void. We saw nothing there but the rough surfaces we trod. . . . Up we went,—nothing but granite and gray dimness. Where we arrived we knew not. . . . When we had thus reached the height of our folly and made nothing by it, we addressed ourselves to the descent, no wiser for our pains.[57]

Winthrop concludes petulantly, "We wasted our time."[58] Thoreau, on the other hand, understood precisely how to make something of "nothing but granite and gray dimness," and whatever the metaphysical implications of his essay, no reader should feel disappointed with Thoreau's treatment of his ascent, which is a literary tour de force.

Moreover, Thoreau's encounter with nature on the mountaintop carries significant thematic weight as well. Clearly, transcendentalism implied a kind of metaphysical imperialism: Emerson wrote in *Nature*, "Every rational creature has all nature for his dowry or estate. It is his, if he will. . . . In proportion to the energy of his thought and will, he takes up the world into himself."[59] In these terms, Thoreau's experience must be regarded as a failure of the imagination. But because Thoreau has been, throughout the essay, deeply ambivalent about the relation between man and nature and skeptical about man's appropriation of nature, there is an obvious sense of satisfaction and, ironically, of triumph, in the discovery that elemental nature *cannot* be appropriated. At the highest level, our relation to nature is one of *mystery* rather than *mastery*.

Thoreau concludes the fourth installment of "Ktaadn" with a straightforward and lively account of the party's descent to the open land, but the fifth part, entitled "The Return Journey," begins with Thoreau's reexperiencing the sense of nature's unappropriability he had had on the mountain: "Perhaps I most fully realized that this was primeval, untamed, and forever untameable *Nature*, or whatever else men call it, while coming down this part of the mountain" (MW 69–70). They were passing over the "Burnt Lands," which he describes as "exceedingly wild and desolate." Trying now to come to terms with "pure Nature . . . thus vast, and drear, and inhuman," he repeats the language of his mountaintop account, which in turn generates the repeated experience of awe and alienation before nature:

> Nature was here something savage and awful, though beautiful. I looked with awe at the ground I trod on. . . . This was that Earth of which we have heard, made out of Chaos and Old Night. Here was no man's garden, but the unhandselled globe. . . . Man was not to be associated with it. It was Matter, vast, terrific,— not his Mother Earth that we have heard of, not for him to tread on, or be buried in,—no, it were being too familiar even to let his bones lie there— the home this of Necessity and Fate. There was there felt the presence of a force not bound to be kind to man. (70)

Up to this point, Thoreau reiterates almost exactly the sense of nature he had felt near the summit. There, however, he had abruptly turned away from the experience and adopted a conventional but unsatisfactory stance toward nature; here, he follows through on the unavoidable implications of his perception. Thus the metaphysical climax of the essay, which had been deferred at the narrative climax, is now brought to completion. Contemplating the vision of "some hard matter in its home," he writes,

> I stand in awe of my body, this matter to which I am bound has become so strange to me. I fear not spirits, ghosts, of which I am one,—*that* my body might,—but I fear bodies, I tremble to meet them. What is this Titan that has possession of me? Talk of mysteries!—Think of our life in nature,—daily to be shown matter, to come in contact with it,—rocks, trees, wind on our cheeks! the *solid* earth! the *actual* world! the *common sense! Contact! Contact! Who* are we? *Where* are we? (71)

Here, the sense of awe and radical alienation Thoreau had felt in the face of the elemental wilderness landscape is now transferred to his *own* materiality, the "Titan" that possesses him, the "pure Nature" he *inhabits*. This transference of his sense of alienation from the mountain wilderness to his own body enables Thoreau, not to reconcile this duality of spirit and matter, but to appropriate and internalize the sublime mystery of that duality into his own nature. This is, indeed, not the typically Emersonian moment of transcendence, but Thoreau's account conforms almost exactly to the three phases of the "dynamical" sublime, as defined by Thomas Weiskel in *The Romantic Sublime*. Weiskel describes this as a process of internalization wherein "the 'unattainability' of the object with respect to the mind would be duplicated as an inner structure, so that in the sublime moment the mind would discover or posit an undefinable (ungraspable) domain within." The first phase of the sublime moment consists of the habitual relation of mind and object, in which "no discrepancy or dissonance interrupts representation, the smooth correspondence of inner and outer." This phase is represented by both Thoreau's initial ascent of Katahdin, where the boulders appear as "flocks and herds," and his initial impression of the "Burnt Lands," which at first appear to him as like "a natural pasture" that he crosses "familiarly" (MW 70). In the second phase, "the habitual relation of mind and object suddenly breaks down. Surprise or astonishment is the affective correlation, and there is an immediate intuition of a disconcerting disproportion between inner and outer." This corresponds to the moment on Katahdin when Thoreau suddenly finds himself "alone" and "pilfered" of his divine faculty, and to the moment here when he suddenly looks "with awe at the ground I trod on." In the third, or "reactive" phase of the sublime moment, which Thoreau experiences *only* now as he crosses the "Burnt Lands," "the mind recovers the balance of outer and inner by constituting a fresh relation between itself and the object such that the very indeterminacy which erupted in phase two is taken as symbolizing the mind's relation to a transcendent order." This is precisely what Thoreau does when he transfers his sense of awe from the earth to "my own body." "The function of the sublime moment," Weiskel explains, "is to expose the cheat or subruption by which an object in nature invites awe and to redirect the awe to the subject himself."[60] At first, Thoreau's sense of alienation from his body is perhaps even more profound and terrifying than his alienation from nature on the mountain, for he feels himself "possessed" by this alien Titan, matter. His sense of his "true" self is of pure spirit—what he calls his "vital part" and his "divine faculty" on the mountain and which here leads him to claim, "I fear not spirits, ghosts, of which I am one." The primitive wilderness had shocked him into a sense that "man was not to be associated with. . . . Matter, vast, terrific"; but in the very recognition that *he* contains this duality, his fear gives way to awe before the "mysteries" of "*our* life *in* nature." The sublime moment is not the apprehension of his spiritual nature but of his life in "the *actual* world," the mystery of our "*common sense*" through which we can experience such things as the "wind on our cheeks." Again, Thoreau's experiences imply that our fundamental relation to nature must be one of mystery rather than mastery.

Thoreau does not resolve the duality; as Weiskel notes, "In the sublime moment, dualism is legitimated and intensified" even as it is internalized. But the internalization allows him to reorient himself in relation to outward nature. Thoreau does this quite literally by announcing, after this climactic passage, "Ere long we recognized some rocks and other features in the landscape which we had purposely impressed on our memories" (MW 71).

The remainder of the account returns to the straightforward, descriptive narrative that characterizes the earlier sections of the essay. He gives a fine, lively account of their headlong descent down the rapids of the Penobscot, and he celebrates without any apparent ambivalence their mastery of the elements here. He is delighted with the boatmen's cool resourcefulness, and in his exhilaration he suggests that "there was really danger of [the rapids'] losing their sublimity in losing their power to harm us" (75). Thoreau brings the excursion toward its close on a note of triumphant and stimulating adventure. His buoyancy is still infectious, and contemporary readers must have delighted in his account. Given Thoreau's climactic encounters with "pure Nature," this jocularity may seem to ring false, but Thoreau is able to give himself over to this feeling because he realizes, on the one hand, how superior nature ultimately is to man's actions, and on the other hand, he has rediscovered the fact of our inescapable life *in* nature, so that the distinction between mastery and submission is not as clear as it might seem, and might more appropriately be called naturalization.

Nature remains, as it has appeared throughout, both hostile *and* genial, terrible *and* beautiful, the symbol of spirit *and* "Matter, vast, terrific." Thoreau does not resolve the duality; he embraces it and absorbs it. In his brief epilogue to the account he therefore characterizes the wilderness as "grim and wild" and "stern and savage," on the one hand, and as possessing an "inexpressible tenderness" on the other; it is both "blissful, innocent Nature" and a "howling wilderness" (80–83), and he celebrates it all. When Thoreau felt himself radically alienated from nature, he had said, "Man was not to be associated with it. It was . . . not for him to tread on, or be buried in" (70); but having recognized the mystery of his own dual life in nature, he can now conclude by explicitly reversing his earlier declaration: "What a place to live," he now writes, "what a place to die and be buried in! There certainly men would live forever, and laugh at death and the grave" (81). This Whitmanesque conclusion is possible because he has discovered in his own being "some star's surface, some hard matter in its home."

"Ktaadn" was from the beginning the literal and external counterpart to

Walden's metaphorical and metaphysical search for "the essential facts of life." Appropriately, then, the conclusion of "Ktaadn" is an almost exact counterpart of *Walden*'s call for *inward* exploration. There he urges his reader to "be a Columbus to whole new continents and worlds within you, opening new channels, not of trade, but of thought" (*Walden* 321); here he urges the exploration of the *actual* American landscape: "I am reminded by my journey how exceedingly new this country still is. . . . If Columbus was the first to discover the islands, Americus Vespucius, and Cabot, and the Puritans, and we their descendants, have discovered only the shores of America" (MW 81). America's rapacious expansionism, he suggests, is misguided: "We have advanced by leaps to the Pacific, and left many a lesser Oregon and California unexplored behind us"; just sixty miles above the busy Atlantic port of Bangor, Thoreau has discovered that "the country is virtually unmapped and unexplored, and there still waves the virgin forest of the New World" (83). This call for a literal "home-cosmography" was certainly more comprehensible and more palatable to the readers of the *Union Magazine* than *Walden*'s metaphysics would be, but the differences between the two excursions are more apparent than real, for in both Thoreau discovered his own nature.

Eager for "Ktaadn" to make an impression on the reading public, Thoreau was anxious and easily frustrated over the *Union Magazine*'s handling of the essay. At the end of August, when Thoreau sent George Thatcher a copy of the third installment of "Ktaadn," he complained that the editor "had bargained, as I thought, to send me many copies for distribution, but I have received none." Then he worried that, as Greeley had repeatedly told him, his narrative was too long for the magazines: he called it "that everlasting mountain story" and conceded that "it should have been printed all together in some large newspaper—and then it would have gone down at one dose by its very gravity" (Corr 229). Already worried about his essay's reception, Thoreau was particularly upset when he discovered printers' errors. Bayard Taylor later recalled that when the compositor had trouble deciphering Thoreau's writing and printed "scows" for "aeons" in the last installment, "the monthly number had not been published many days before Mr. Greeley received a letter from Thoreau, hot with rage and indignation," and that the error "long rankled in Thoreau's memory."[61]

Nevertheless, "Ktaadn" was clearly Thoreau's most successful venture to date in the literary marketplace, and one that seemed to promise an increasingly successful professional career. At the end of October, Greeley wrote to Thoreau that he was to receive seventy-five dollars for "your glorious account of 'Ktaadn and the Maine Woods,'" and so, "as I don't choose to *exploiter* you at such a rate, I shall insist on inclosing you $25 more in this letter, which will still leave me $25 to pay various charges and labors I have incurred" (Corr 231–32). Thoreau was doing a variety of odd jobs that fall to earn his living, so the money was certainly welcome.

Moreover, "Ktaadn" proved that Thoreau could produce works capable of winning genuine and broad popularity without compromising his literary integrity. Greeley's *Tribune* was unstinting in its praise for the essay. Reviewing the *Union Magazine* for October, Greeley wrote, "Henry D. Thoreau takes us to the top of Ktaadn where he finds—not sermons, but the most delightfully descriptive fancies in stones. We can think of nothing in this style which surpasses it—one feels as if the air of the topmost rock were sweeping around him, as he reads. This article is the pearl of the number."[62] Greeley followed this by printing long extracts from "Ktaadn" in the *Tribune* for November 17 and 18. In his introductory note to the first set of extracts, Greeley wrote that Thoreau's sketches "are quite superior to any descriptions of wild-woods life that we have seen for several years. There is all the freshness and odor of the pine-forests about them, and the language flows with as clear and sparkling a stream as the mountain rapids down which the author whirled in his canoe."[63] Significantly, but not surprisingly, Greeley's second set of extracts includes not only the dramatic description of Katahdin's summit, but also the powerful "Contact! Contact!" account of his descent—as controversial as this passage is for modern Thoreau scholars, Greeley knew this was exactly the kind of dramatic encounter with the sublime wilderness that readers were seeking. Greeley ends his extracts by quoting what he calls Thoreau's "splendid conclusion—as fine a piece of unrhymed poetry as we have ever read."[64] Even after the last installment was printed, Greeley persisted in his praise: reviewing the next month's issue of the *Union Magazine*, he wrote that while there was still worthy material to be found there, "we miss Mr. Thoreau's pine-scented pages."[65] In January of 1849, the juvenile magazine *The Student* reprinted part of the *Tribune* extracts under the title "The Backwoods of Maine."[66] At the other end of the intellectual spectrum, Emerson too celebrated "Ktaadn," writing in his journal for October 1848, "We have not had since ten years a pamphlet which I have saved to bind! and here at last is Bushnell's; and now Henry Thoreau's Ascent of Katahdin" (JMN 11: 20). Indeed, Thoreau's account quickly became a classic of the literature of Katahdin and the Maine woods, and subsequent accounts almost all reflect its influence.[67] Ironically, the same October that Emerson celebrated Thoreau's essay in his journal, Putnam's published James Russell Lowell's *A Fable for Critics*, in which Thoreau was chided for being a paltry imitator of Emerson. But "Ktaadn," which was just then concluding in the *Union Magazine*, belied Lowell's estimate and revealed Thoreau as a writer with his own voice and an independent energy.

PART IV

Practical and Popular Influence

Chapter 7

"ONLY AS IT SERVES AS AN ADVERTISEMENT OF ME": LECTURING ON WALDEN, LOOKING FOR A PUBLISHER

In the winter of 1848–1849, Thoreau again must have felt his professional ambitions were about to be realized. This was by far his most successful lecture season to date: he lectured more often, in more places, and earned more money than ever before. His lectures were not universally admired, but they were sufficiently controversial to attract attention and did find some ardent admirers. Thoreau was being noticed, albeit on a moderate scale, and he now actually found himself solicited not only for further lecture engagements but also for written contributions to periodicals. These successes undoubtedly bolstered Thoreau's confidence as he again sought a publisher for his two book manuscripts, on which he centered his deepest ambitions. And even when it became apparent that he would have to settle for less than ideal terms of publication, Thoreau clearly felt he had some basis for thinking that these works would establish his literary reputation. As it turned out, by the end of the year 1849, Thoreau had to confront a failure far more profound than that of his New York venture, a failure that immeasurably altered the shape of his career. The failure of *A Week on the Concord and Merrimack Rivers* was not simply a matter of public hostility or indifference to the literary value of this first book; the history of *A Week*'s composition and Thoreau's efforts to get it published (and his decisions *not* to write or publish other material) is, in terms of the *business* of writing, a record full of erroneous assumptions, poor judgments, and missed opportunities. Moreover, the failure of *A Week* was only the most tangible manifestation of a more far-reaching and complex failure in Thoreau's relation with the literary marketplace. That failure becomes all the more poignant when we recognize both that Thoreau genuinely wanted to succeed there and that, had he been more astute and more accommodating to the nature of that marketplace, he might have achieved a greater degree of success without sacrificing the integrity of the writing itself.

There were three principal outlets available to the writer—the lecture, the periodical, and the book—and there was a logical sequence from one to the next, in terms of both the creative process and the marketplace. During his first year at Walden Pond Thoreau had written in his journal:

> From all points of the compass from the earth beneath and the heavens above have come these inspirations and been entered duly in such order as they came in the Journal. Thereafter when the time arrived they were winnowed into Lectures—and again in due time from Lectures into Essays—And at last they stand like the cubes of Pythagoras firmly on either basis—like statues on their pedestals—but the statues rarely take hold of hands—There is only such connexion and series as is attainable in the galleries. And this affects their immediate practical & popular influence. (J2: 205–6)[1]

The problem he raises at the end of this passage, of the disconnectedness of his essays, is the one he faced when trying to organize his first book, and I shall return to this issue in the following chapter. But the point to be noted here is Thoreau's more general sense of the composition process, in which the progression from journal to lecture to essay (to book) represented a move from private "inspirations" to "practical and popular influence." The difficulty for Thoreau lay in his sense of the "due time" that determined the progress of the sequence. Thoreau seems to imply that some private inspiration, some sense of naturalness, or ripeness, determined "when the time arrived" to work up his journal entries into lectures or his lectures into essays. That is, even as he worked outward toward public influence and popularity, he listened only to some inner voice to tell him when each step should be taken. The literary marketplace reinforced the advantages of working from lecture to essay to book, since each step advertised the next and multiplied the opportunities for commercial profit; but it observed a different timepiece, had its own inviolable seasons, and urged a sense of the "due time" that was different from Thoreau's.

Ever since he first moved to Walden Pond, Thoreau had invested his greatest energy and his highest hopes in writing a book and getting it into print. Perhaps as a result of his frustration with the magazines in New York, he never took full advantage of the opportunities for periodical publication even when Greeley offered them. Yet Greeley, who was Thoreau's most reliable guide to the rhythms of the marketplace, kept urging Thoreau to send him short pieces for the magazines because he knew that the "due time" had not yet arrived for a book from Thoreau. When Greeley sent him payment for "Ktaadn" in October 1848, he summarized the advice he had been giving Thoreau for the previous two years: "You must write to the magazines in order to let the public know who and what you are. Ten years hence will do for publishing books" (Corr 232). Considering that Thoreau had been working with drafts of his books since 1845 and had been trying to get A *Week* published since 1847, another ten-year delay must have sounded absolutely intolerable to Thoreau; but Greeley was not really advising infinite patience—he was advising Thoreau to strike while the iron was hot. With "Ktaadn" before the public in the *Union Magazine* and advertised prominently in the *Tribune*, Thoreau would certainly have found (with Greeley's aid) a ready market in the periodical press for other accounts of America's natural landscape. Had Thoreau grasped, or accepted, the rhythms of the marketplace as Greeley tried to explain them, one might easily imagine Thoreau offering to undertake a series of essays on the mountains of New England, for example (in his journal and *A Week* he already had material that might have been the basis for sketches of the White Mountains, the Berkshires, and the Catskills); and had Thoreau shown any inclination or ability to produce shorter pieces, one might just as easily imagine Greeley even offering to underwrite these or other excursions. If such a hypothetical scenario is, in fact, not easily imaginable, this is not because there was no common ground between Thoreau and a popular reading audience—"Ktaadn" had fully demonstrated that there was; rather, it is a measure of the degree to which Thoreau failed to respond to the nature of the literary marketplace that mediated between author and audience.

Thoreau replied to Greeley's recommendation by announcing that he had in fact renewed his assault on the publishing companies with his two book manuscripts; Greeley therefore responded in turn by offering the best advice he could give under the circumstances. He told Thoreau to send him passages from his books to sell to the magazines (he suggested *Graham's* or the *Union*) and explained, "This will be the best kind of advertisement whether for a publisher or for readers. You may write with an angel's pen, yet your writings have no mercantile, money value till you are known and talked of as an author." To bolster his case, Greeley added, "Mr. Emerson would have been twice as much known and read if he had written for the magazines a little, just to let the common people know of his existence" (Corr 232). Perhaps when Thoreau read this letter he reflected that Emerson had, after all, established an enviable reputation without resorting to the magazines—still failing to recognize that however closely he followed Emerson's model, he could not enter the marketplace on the same footing as his mentor had. In any event, naive about the demands of the marketplace and anxious to get his books into print, Thoreau chose again to ignore Greeley's advice (this was a mistake he did not repeat when, five years later, Thoreau arranged for extracts from *Walden* to be printed in both the *Tribune* and *Sartain's Union Magazine* in advance of that book's publication).

Lecturing was, of course, another important means of advertisement, and while Thoreau seems stubborn or obtuse in his failure to write for the magazines as Greeley advised, he clearly saw in Emerson's example that he might use the lecture platform to generate interest in the works he was preparing to publish. Emerson, who perhaps more than any other American demonstrated that a major literary reputation could be built upon the lecture platform, wrote to James Freeman Clarke on October 16, 1848, urging him to enlist Thoreau for a Boston lecture: "There is good and better wine in Concord than any you know however and Henry Thoreau has an admirable lecture which he read to our Lyceum which I think your audience would prize as a quite new cordial" (EmL 4: 190). While Clarke did not take up Emerson's suggestion, the 1848–1849 lyceum season nevertheless proved to be something of a breakthrough for Thoreau. A week after Emerson wrote to Clarke, Thoreau received a letter from Hawthorne inviting him, on behalf of the Salem Lyceum, "to deliver a lecture before that Institution," and informing him that "the stated fee for Lectures is $20" (Corr 230–31). This proved to be the first of nine lectures Thoreau is known to have delivered that season, five of which were engagements outside of Concord, and for at least three of which he was paid (in addition, Thoreau had to decline an invitation for a paying engagement in Bangor). Further, his lectures were reviewed quite regularly, and often at considerable length, in the local papers.

All of the lectures he read this season were drawn from his *Walden* manuscript, and had that book been published shortly, as he hoped it would be (and as, in fact, it might have been), this series of lectures and the attendant publicity might have substantially enhanced public interest in *Walden*. As it turned out, the advertising value of this season would be lost by the time *Walden* was published—though the book undoubtedly benefited from having been tried out repeatedly on lecture audiences.

Thoreau's lecture in Salem, on November 22, was on the subject of "Student Life in New England, its economy," and his performance seems to have elicited a generally favorable response. The lecture was reviewed at some length in the *Salem Observer* for November 25. Although the reviewer begins by commenting on Thoreau's extraordinary resemblance to Emerson (not only in "thought, style & delivery," but in "tone of voice" and even "in personal appearance"), he ultimately credits Thoreau with a degree of originality others did not always find. "The close likeness between the two would almost justify a charge of plagiarism, were it not that Mr. Thoreau's lecture furnished ample proof of being a native product, by affording all the charm of an original." Interestingly, the reviewer remembers that Thoreau's experiment in economy had been described in the letter Greeley printed in the *Tribune* the previous spring as "A Lesson for Young Poets." Of the current lecture he writes,

> This was done in an admirable manner, in a strain of exquisite humor, with a strong under current of delicate satire against the follies of the times. Then there were interspersed observations, speculations, and suggestions . . . sufficiently queer to keep the audience in almost constant mirth, and sufficiently wise and new to afford many good practical hints and precepts. The performance has created "quite a sensation" amongst the Lyceum goers.[2]

The response is particularly interesting in that it reveals so clearly just what the public's expectations were: it demanded originality and either humor or utility, or both.[3] In this case, Thoreau's lecture was sufficiently successful with his audience that he was invited to deliver another lecture in Salem later that season, though he was not always so well received.

The review in the *Salem Observer* evaluates Thoreau strictly as a moralist and as an economist; Sophia Hawthorne, however (like her husband), found Thoreau most interesting and original as a nature writer, and she provides us with a very different impression of this lecture. On the day of Thoreau's second Salem lecture, she wrote to her sister,

> This evening Mr. Thoreau is going to lecture, and will stay with us [as he had on the occasion of his first lecture, also]. His lecture before was so enchanting; such a revelation of nature in all its exquisite details of wood-thrushes, squirrels, sunshine, mists and shadows, fresh, vernal odors, pine-tree ocean melodies, that my ear rang with music, and I seemed to have been wandering through copse and dingle!

In fact, Sophia had been so impressed by this lecture that it altered her entire conception of the man: "Mr. Thoreau has risen above all his arrogance of manner, and is as gentle, simple, ruddy and meek as all geniuses should be; and now his great blue eyes fairly outshine and put into shade a nose which I once thought must make him uncomely forever."[4]

The success of Thoreau's initial lecture resulted not only in the second engagement in Salem, but also in an invitation from the Gloucester Lyceum to repeat his lecture there, which he did on December 20. The review that appeared in the *Gloucester Telegraph* on December 23 was distinctly unfavorable, however, and the reviewer's objections illuminate the dangers of Thoreau's complex and ironic rhetoric. In his discussion of "Economy," Thoreau cleverly uses the pragmatic and utilitarian principles he assumes are held by his audience in order to undermine the narrow materialism he sees governing their lives; but if the audience fails to appreciate Thoreau's irony, his use of hyperbole and paradox appear to be nonsense—as is the case with this reviewer, who reports,

> The lecturer gave a very strange account of the state of affairs at Concord. In the shops and offices were large numbers of human beings suffering tortures to which those of the Bramins [*sic*] are mere pastimes. We cannot say whether this was in jest or in earnest. If a joke, it was a most excruciating one—if true, the attention of the Home Missionary Society should be directed to that quarter forthwith.[5]

It is probably safe to credit this reviewer with recognizing that Thoreau's account of Concord was "in jest," but he understood only enough to see that it was a joke he did not quite get (it is obvious that the reviewer himself was no master of irony). The review goes on to make it clear, however, that at least a substantial part of the lyceum audience did appreciate Thoreau's ironic wit and wisdom. Undoubtedly, this irritated the reviewer all the more, and his comments suggest that he came away as peeved with his neighbors for enjoying the lecture as he was with Thoreau for delivering it:

> The lecturer spoke at considerable length of society, men, manners, travelling, clothing, etc., often "bringing down the house" by his quaint remarks. Now and then there was a hard hit at the vices and follies of mankind, which "told" with considerable effect. . . .
>
> We believe that concerning this lecture there are various opinions in the community. With all deference to the sagacity of those who can see a great deal where there is little to be seen—hear much where there is hardly anything to be heard—perceive a wonderful depth of meaning where in fact nothing is really meant, we would take the liberty of expressing the opinion that a certain ingredient to a good lecture was, in some instances, wanting.

Three days after this review appeared, Thoreau wrote to his cousin George Thatcher, "I hear that the Gloucester paper has me in print again, and the Republican—whatever they may say is not to the purpose only as it serves as an advertisement of me. There are very few whose opinion I value" (Corr 234). Whether or not Thoreau's indifference was a mere pose, he was certainly correct in recognizing that, positive or negative, such notices served to make his name known. And by the end of the lecture season, Greeley would show how such conflicting opinions as were implied in the Gloucester review were not merely a matter of indifference but could in fact be carefully exploited to generate further publicity for Thoreau and his book.

On January 3, 1849, Thoreau lectured at the Concord Lyceum, delivering "White Beans and Walden Pond." Since he had read an early version of his introductory Walden lecture to his Concord neighbors in 1847, he could now offer them the latest installment in his account of his life at the pond. Thoreau was not paid for lecturing in Concord, however, and there would be an interval of nearly two months before his next lecture (nine lectures in a season was a small number, after all, even while it represents a substantial increase in Thoreau's popularity as a lecturer). In the meantime, he was busy trying to come to terms with Ticknor & Co. for the publication of his two books. Ticknor & Co. was unwilling to publish both books at its own risk but wrote to Thoreau on February 8: "If however you feel inclined we will publish 'Walden or Life in the Woods' on our own acc, say one Thousand copies, allowing for 10 pr.ct. copyright on the Retail Price on all that are sold. The style of printing & binding to be like Emerson's Essays" (Corr 236). This was clearly Thoreau's best offer to date, and a good offer by any standards for a first book, but Thoreau was not willing to let *A Week* go unpublished and so inquired further about the terms under which they *would* publish it. Buoyed by their offer for *Walden*, Thoreau was cautiously optimistic about coming to terms with Ticknor & Co. On February 16, he wrote to George Thatcher that he had been engaged to lecture in Portland in late March and asked if Thatcher could arrange for a lecture in Bangor as well at that time; he added that he hoped to extend this trip to travel up the Chesuncook River, but that he might be constrained by publishing arrangements: "The fact is I am once more making a bargain with the Publishers Ticknor & Co., who talk of printing a book for me, and if we come to terms I *may* then be confined here correcting proofs—or at most I should have but a few days to spare" (Corr 237). The same day on which Thoreau wrote to his cousin, Ticknor's sent Thoreau their offer: they would print A *Week*, but only at Thoreau's expense. For an edition of one thousand copies, 448 pages each, "on good paper" and bound "in our style fine cloth," they estimated a cost of $501.24. They noted that "the book can be condensed & of course cost less," and added, "As you would not perhaps, care to bind more than 1/2 the Edn at once,—you would need to send $450.—to print 1000 cps. & bind 1/2 of the same" (Corr 238).

This put Thoreau in a dilemma. Ticknor & Co. was an extremely attractive publisher. Largely due to the efforts of the junior partner James T. Fields, Ticknor & Co. was at this time establishing itself as the preeminent publisher of belles lettres in America (thus winning back to Boston some of the prestige as a publishing center it had steadily been losing to New York). Oliver Wendell Holmes, John Greenleaf Whittier, and Henry Wadsworth Longfellow were already part of the Ticknor stable of authors, and Hawthorne would be the next major addition. Yet Thoreau was neither able nor willing to put up $450 in advance to publish A *Week*, and he was also unwilling to let Ticknor & Co. publish *Walden* first, even though they would do so on their account.

Thoreau had not quite given up on Ticknor & Co. when Hawthorne wrote him on February 19 to arrange for Thoreau's second Salem lecture. "Mr. Alcott delighted my wife and me, the other evening," Hawthorne added, "by announcing that you had a book in prep. I rejoice at it, and nothing doubt of such success as will be worth having. Should your manuscripts all be in the printer's hands, I suppose you can reclaim one of them, for a single evening's use, . . . or perhaps that Indian lecture, which you mentioned to me, is in a state of forwardness. Either that or a continuation of the Walden experiment (or, indeed, anything else,) will be acceptable" (Corr 238–39). Thoreau replied the next day: "I am glad to know of your interest in my book, for I have thought of you as a reader while writing it. My MSS. are not even yet in the hands of the printer, but I am doing my best to make him take them into his hands. In any case the MSS which he will begin with is not that from which I shall read."[6]

As his last comment makes clear, Thoreau was adamant about publishing A *Week* first. The version of *Walden* Thoreau was discussing with publishers in 1849 was of course not the same book Thoreau would eventually publish in 1854, and he most likely felt even at this point that the manuscript needed much more work than did that of *A Week*, which had undergone prolonged and thorough revisions.[7] Nevertheless, *Walden* was obviously close enough to completion in his own mind that he was approaching publishers with it. His insistence on printing *A Week* first, then, seems to have been based more on personal, psychological considerations than on practical ones. Practically speaking, of course, profits from an edition of *Walden* published on Ticknor's account might well have underwritten the publishing costs of *A Week* or, if it were indeed profitable, have persuaded Ticknor & Co. to take it, too, on their account. Instead, Thoreau rejected Ticknor's terms not only for *A Week* but for *Walden* as well. Thus, shortly after writing to Hawthorne he once more approached James Munroe & Co., with whom he had unsuccessfully negotiated for the publication of *A Week* two years earlier.

In the meantime, Thoreau continued to draw exclusively upon his *Walden* manuscript for his lectures this season. He returned to Salem on February 28, where he lectured on "student life, its aims and employments," a sequel to his earlier lecture. This second lecture was also reviewed in the *Salem Observer*, and the reviewer explained that whereas Thoreau's "first lecture was upon the economy of [his life in the woods]; this was upon its object and some of its enjoyments"[8] (the first lecture drew upon the "Economy" chapter of *Walden*, the second upon "Where I Lived, and What I Lived For," as well as upon the "Reading" and "Sounds" chapters). This second lecture elicited even more sharply divided opinions than the first and forced the distinction between those who could respond to his transcendental idealism and those who could not:

> The diversity of opinion is quite amusing. Some persons are unwilling to speak of his lecture as any better than "Tom-foolery and nonsense," while others think they perceived, beneath the outward sense of his remarks, something wise and valuable. It is undoubtedly true that Mr. Thoreau's style is rather too allegorical for a popular audience. He "peoples the solitudes" of the woods too profusely, and gives voices to their "dim aisles" not recognized by the larger part of common ears.

This reviewer (unlike the *Gloucester Telegraph*'s) was both perceptive and, at least to a degree, responsive to Thoreau's themes, yet he makes it abundantly clear that Thoreau was most readily accepted when he dealt with conventional material. The parts of his lecture "generally admitted to be excellent" were his "well-considered defense of classical literature, in connection with some common sense remarks upon books; and also some ingenious speculations suggested by the inroads of railroad enterprise upon the quiet and seclusion of Walden Pond." When his remarks were grounded in "common sense," he was admired; when he gave expression to voices "not recognized by the larger part of common ears," he was not. In addition to revealing Thoreau's divided audience, this reviewer astutely remarks that Thoreau's language itself interfered with the popularity of his lectures. If his language was not strictly "allegorical," it is true that his puns, paradoxes, ironies, and extended metaphors would present a challenge even to sympathetic auditors, let alone to a "popular audience," and this reviewer was only the first of several in Thoreau's career to suggest that he might be better read than heard: "In regard to Mr. Thoreau, we are glad to hear that he is about issuing a book which will contain these lectures and will enable us perhaps to judge better of their merit." This concluding remark also demonstrates how directly lecturing could serve as advertising for the book Thoreau still thought would be published soon—and Thoreau made another twenty dollars for this lecture besides.

On March 6, Thoreau lectured at the Lincoln Lyceum, apparently repeating the lecture he had read in Concord, "White Beans and Walden Pond." Here, as elsewhere, some of his auditors were undoubtedly mystified by Thoreau's transcendental "nonsense," but others were intrigued. James Lorin Chapin, a Lincoln native and regular lecture-goer, described this "curious lecture" in his diary:

> He had a strange mixture of sense and folly of poetry and halting prose, of science and fable, of physics and ethics. He touched on the pond the woods, the road, the cars, the church bells, the distant roar of cannon, the sound of martial music, and the conversation of travellers on the highway, and more fully on the morals of hoing beans. I was very much interested with the lecture, perhaps not so much with the logic and beauty of the subject as the novelty of the style.[9]

Ten days after the Lincoln lecture, Thoreau wrote again to George Thatcher, informing him that "I am now receiving the proof sheets of my book from the printers, so that without inconvenience I cannot make you a visit at present" (Corr 240–41). Thoreau did not explain to his cousin that his negotiations with Ticknor & Co. had fallen through, and that it was James Munroe & Co. who would be publishing *A Week*. As when Thoreau first approached them with the manuscript, Munroe & Co. still would publish *A Week* only at Thoreau's risk, but they did not insist that he put up the money in advance; costs could be taken out of expected sales, as long as Thoreau agreed to reimburse them for any expenses not met by sales, and *Walden* was to be published following *A Week*. The deferment of payment for printing *A Week* was the concession that persuaded Thoreau to agree to Munroe's terms. It was a shortsighted decision, and one Thoreau came to regret, but at the moment he worked through the proof sheets with excited anticipation.

Busily preparing one book for press, Thoreau persisted in lecturing exclusively from his *other* manuscript, ironically generating public interest in a book he refused to publish at this point. George Thatcher had already persuaded the Bangor Lyceum of Thoreau's desirability for one lecture, and they had hoped to pay him twenty-five dollars "if their funds will hold out";[10] but because he was busy with his book, Thoreau now replied, "I thank you heartily for your exertions in my behalf with the Bangor Lyceum—but unless I should hear that they want *two* lectures to be read in *one* week or nearer together, I shall have to decline coming, this time" (Corr 240–41). The Bangor Lyceum was apparently unable or unwilling to engage him for two lectures, so Thoreau's only lecture in Maine this season was the one he delivered in Portland on March 21, for which he was paid twenty-five dollars.[11] The following announcement appeared in Portland's *Eastern Argus* that morning: "The 18th LYCEUM LECTURE will be delivered this evening, by Henry D. Thoreau, Esq., of Concord, Mass. Subject—'HOME'—*Sweet home, or domestic economy.* A correspondent of the Boston Traveller, writing from Salem, says of this lecture—'*It was a delectable compound of oddity, wit and ne-plus ultraism.*' It will be worth hearing."[12] Thoreau's audience must have been surprised by the lecture he delivered—clearly his introductory lecture on the "economy" of his life at Walden Pond—but they were not disappointed. On March 23, the *Eastern Argus* reported,

> The lecture on Wednesday evening was by H. D. Thoreau, Esq., of Concord, Mass. The subject was announced in the papers as "Home, or domestic economy"; but the real topic was "MYSELF-I." The lecture was unique, original, comical, and high-falutin. It kept the audience wide awake, and most pleasantly excited for nearly two hours. It was like the dashing out of a comet that had broken loose from its orbit—hitting here and there, a gentle rap at this folly, and a severe one at that—but all in good nature.[13]

If this review is short on detail, it is nevertheless long on enthusiasm, and Portland was neither starved for lectures nor indiscriminate in its praise. Greeley lectured there on the Monday following Thoreau's performance, and Emerson lectured there two days later. In its review of Greeley's lecture (on the "American Congress"—Greeley having just served as a representative), the *Eastern Argus* notes that Greeley "called out the largest audience probably that ever assembled in Exchange Hall" in spite of wet and gloomy weather that evening, but he left them disappointed: he treated his subject superficially, and "of the delivery of the lecture we cannot speak in unqualified praise. We presume we shall tell Mr. Greeley no new thing when we say that his rhetorical powers are not of the highest grade, and that there is space for improvement."[14] Emerson's performance was more successful, for it was a novelty and was treated as one: "Our citizens have been anxious to hear a transcendental lecture from RALPH WALDO EMERSON," the *Eastern Argus* reviewer explained, and "their desire was fully met." Yet even Emerson elicited less enthusiasm from the local press than Thoreau had: Emerson's lecture on "*the Laws of Mind and Mental inspiration*" was "a cluster of admirable proverbs, rather than a compact argument. It fascinated and electrified, but did not convince."[15]

Greeley must have heard reports of Thoreau's recent success in Portland when he was there, and—overlooking his own cool reception[16]—generously printed a notice in the *Tribune* for April 2 that began,

> Henry D. Thoreau of Concord, Mass. has recently been lecturing on "Life in the Woods" in Portland and elsewhere. There is not a young man in the land—and very few old ones—who would not profit by an attentive hearing of that lecture. Mr. Thoreau is a young student, who has imbibed (or rather refused to stifle) the idea that a man's soul is better worth living for than his body.

Since Thoreau was nearly thirty-two years old (it had been almost twelve years since his graduation from Harvard), he could not fairly be characterized as a "young student" any longer; yet such a characterization does reflect the fact that, as a man of letters, Thoreau was still perceived as a novice who had not yet reached maturity. Moreover, the characterization is consistent with the thrust of the *Tribune* notice, which echoes the praise for the frugal scholar that Greeley had expressed nearly a year earlier when he printed Thoreau's "A Lesson for Young Poets." Greeley provides some detailed figures on the nature of Thoreau's Walden life (erroneously stating that "he has lived in this way for four years") and concludes by suggesting that "if all our young men would but hear this lecture, we think some among them would feel less strongly impelled either to come to New-York or go to California."[17]

The potential publicity value of even a brief note like this was incalculable, for not only did the *Tribune* have an extraordinarily large and widespread readership of its own, but its items were also frequently reprinted in other newspapers and magazines across the country. One of the many ironies involved in Thoreau's professional career is that it took this notice in the *Tribune* to arouse Thoreau's local press on his behalf. Greeley's notice was reprinted in Concord's *Yeoman's Gazette* under the title "Our Townsman—Mr. Thoreau." The local editor included an introductory note in which he took obvious delight in being able to correct the *Tribune*'s error regarding the duration of Thoreau's Walden experiment and added his own praise for this native son: "Mr. Thoreau lived upon the banks of our beautiful Walden Pond for two years, where he wrote some of the most interesting and instructive lectures we have ever heard. . . . He is a gentleman of rare attainments, and now has one or two works in press which all who have heard him lecture are anxious to see."[18]

It was not only the Concord press that picked up Greeley's notice, however. The most immediate response was in the form of a letter to the editor of the *Tribune*, which Greeley printed, along with his reply, on April 7, 1849, under the title "How to Live—Mr. Thoreau's Example." The correspondent, "Timothy Thorough," writes, "Having always found in the *Tribune* a friend of sociability and neighborly helping-each-other-along, I felt a little surprised at seeing such a performance held up as an example for the young men of this country." Not trusting his own reading, Mr. Thorough explains that he consulted his wife, who concluded in no uncertain terms

> that the young man is either a whimsy, or else a good-for-nothing, selfish, crab-like sort of chap, who tries to shirk the duties whose hearty and honest discharge is the only thing that in her view entitles a man to be regarded as a good example. She declares that nobody has a right to live for himself alone, away from the interests, the affections, and the suffering of his kind. Such a way of going on, she says, is not living, but a cold and snailish kind of existence, which, as she maintains, is both infernal and infernally stupid.[19]

The correspondent's apparently assumed name, his self-dramatization, and the comic irony all suggest that this may have been a literary contrivance; "Timothy Thorough" and his wife are stock characters—the good-natured but ineffectual and browbeaten husband and his shrewish wife, in the tradition of Irving's Rip and Dame Van Winkle. The subtext of this set piece is that Mr. Thorough really envies the freedom and independence of his alter ego Mr. Thoreau. Mrs. Thorough, recognizing how Thoreau's experiment threatens to subvert her authority—and that of woman's domestic sphere generally—hurls abuse at Thoreau (and indirectly at her husband, should he take any notions from him) in the name of sociability, in order to quash any incipient domestic rebellion. The vehemence of Mrs. Thorough's scorn has the ironic effect of encouraging a closer consideration of Thoreau's proposals, if they promise respite from such viragoes.

In his reply, Greeley initially enters into the comic banter and (apparently overlooking the appropriateness of the correspondent's signature) suggests that he was misnamed "and that he must have been changed at nurse for another boy whose true name was Shallow." For the most part, however, Greeley plays it straight, claiming in earnest that "nobody has proposed or suggested that it becomes everybody to go off into the woods . . . and live hermit-like," but defending Thoreau in terms again essentially identical to those of his 1848 column on Thoreau's "Lesson for Young Poets"—that the "large class of young men who aspire to Mental Culture" would be well-advised to learn from Thoreau to "preserve their proper independence without starving their souls."

Greeley consciously exploited this controversy in order to generate further publicity for Thoreau, and the issue was indeed picked up by other major papers. Under the title "Solitude Seeking," Philadelphia's *North American and U.S. Gazette* for April 11, 1849, reprinted Greeley's original notice of Thoreau's lecture but went on to repudiate at length the antisocial nature of Thoreau's life. The *North American*'s column was in turn reprinted in an edited (and somewhat mangled) version in the Washington, D.C., *Daily National Intelligencer* for April 19, 1849.[20] Greeley's original *Tribune* editorial was also reprinted in the *Saturday Evening Post* for April 14, under the title "A Young Philosopher,"[21] and again, under the title "Life in the Woods," in the *Youth's Companion* for July 19.[22] While these last items repeat and so implicitly share Greeley's favorable opinion of Thoreau's experiment, Kenneth W. Cameron has described the *North American*'s editorial and its reprint in the *National Intelligencer* as "damning" and "embarrassing" national publicity for Thoreau that, he suggests, may have had a severely damaging effect on Thoreau's career;[23] but certainly Thoreau knew his lectures were controversial—they were intended to be so, to provoke his neighbors, wake them up. Challenging the status quo, he could neither have expected nor desired that his proposals would win only benevolent nods and smiles, and even Thoreau recognized (in response to the review of his Gloucester lecture) that "whatever they may say is not to the purpose only as it serves as an advertisement of me." For both the prophet and the professional, controversy would be far more effective than bland approval. Concerning authors' recognition of the professional advantages of controversy, one thinks not only of the entire career of Poe, whose deliberate outrages were perhaps ultimately masochistic, but also of Hawthorne, who, when he learned that *The Scarlet Letter* was attacked in the *Church Review*, wrote to his publisher, "I think it essential to my success as an author, to have some bitter enemies."[24] There is also, of course, the later but more famous example of Samuel Clemens, who, upon learning that *Huckleberry Finn* had been banned by the Concord Public Library, reacted gleefully, "That will sell 25,000 copies for us sure!"[25] It is less to the point that the press was occasionally taking issue with Thoreau than that Thoreau, by not publishing the account of his Walden experiment, lost the advantage of having it discussed in papers across the country.

Thoreau did not lecture again after his March 21 reading in Portland until April 20. During this hiatus he was largely occupied with reading the proofs of A *Week*. Also in the midst of the *Tribune* debate over his Walden experiment, Elizabeth Peabody wrote to Thoreau requesting his lecture "Resistance to Civil Government" for her new journal, *Aesthetic Papers*. On April 5, Thoreau replied to Peabody that although he was extremely busy preparing his book for publication, he would send her his essay before the end of the following week. He added significantly in a postscript, "I offer the paper to your *first volume* only" (Corr 242). Thoreau's essay appeared in what turned out to be the *only* volume of *Aesthetic Papers*, published on May 14, 1849.

In the meantime, Thoreau's friend and disciple H.G.O. Blake invited him to lecture in Worcester, and Thoreau concluded this lyceum season with a series of three lectures there: on April 20 he read his introductory lecture on the "economy" of his Walden experiment; on April 27 he read its sequel on the "object and enjoyments" of his Walden sojourn; and on May 3 he read his lecture "White Beans and Walden Pond." These lectures were reported in some detail in the Worcester papers, the *Palladium* and the *Spy*; the reviews are generally unfavorable and reiterate the charge that he imitated Emerson, but they also concede some notable strengths in Thoreau's performances, and, as in Salem and Gloucester, the reviews make it clear that at least some of his auditors were favorably impressed. The *Palladium* review of Thoreau's first lecture details the fiscal economy of Thoreau's experiment, but the reviewer refuses to be taken in by the "Sylvan philosopher":

> Such philosophers illustrate the absurdities the human mind is capable of. What would a forest of them be good for? Nothing but curiosities for people to look after, as they pay their shilling to see a menagerie. They are watches without any pointers; their springs and wheels are well adjusted, and perform good service; but nobody is the wiser for it, as they do not tell the time of day. They are a train of car wheels; they run well and in good time, but can carry no passengers or luggage. A wheelbarrow, with an Irishman for its vitals, renders the world a far better service.[26]

The reviewer's choice of metaphors here could not have been more telling. To the hard-nosed Yankee materialist, the question of usefulness was paramount, and from this point of view the transcendentalist seemed like a watch that could not "tell the time of day." The transcendentalist himself, of course, felt he was an instrument—a "dial," in fact—that measured a higher, absolute time, and Emerson had pleaded on behalf of those "superior chronometers" in "The Transcendentalist." From Thoreau's point of view, his lectures were indeed utilitarian and could "render the world a far better service" than an Irishman and a wheelbarrow. And at least part of his Worcester audience appreciated Thoreau: the *Palladium* reviewer conceded that others found the lecture "to have been witty, sarcastic and amusing."

This response is confirmed by the reviewer for the *Spy* who, although he missed Thoreau's first lecture, reports in his review of the second that "the commendations we heard of [the first] assure us that it would have been a source of enjoyment to us."[27] Unfortunately, he adds, "those commendations had possibly led us to expect too much, and we are free to say, that in hearing the second lecture, we were disappointed." He complains that Thoreau gave "a better *imitation* of Emerson than we should have thought possible, even with two year's [*sic*] seclusion to practice in." Still, he saw flashes of originality in Thoreau that showed promise, even though the reviewer does not count himself among the transcendentalist sympathizers. The *Palladium* review of the second lecture also notes that Thoreau reflected Emerson's image, but the keynote of this review is Thoreau's eccentricity, and the reviewer seems unsure whether Thoreau is to be more admired or ridiculed: his lecture was "a mingled web of sage conclusions and puerility—wit and egotistical effusions—bright scintillations and narrow criticisms and low comparisons. He has a natural poetic temperament, with a more than ordinary sensibility to the myriad of nature's manifestations." In spite of his Emersonianism and his eccentricity, the reviewer allows that "the lecturer says many things that not only amuse the hour, but will not be easily forgotten."[28]

For Thoreau's third lecture, on his Walden bean field, he was still able, according to Walter Harding, to draw "an audience of about a hundred,"[29] but a correspondent to the Worcester *Spy* complained that Thoreau's bean field was "barren to my apprehension of witty product." He, too, charged Thoreau with mimicking Emerson (and Carlyle) and felt that after three lectures Thoreau's novelty was wearing off. But his elaborately affected criticism of Thoreau's lectures is actually directed ironically at Thoreau's auditors and critics even more than at Thoreau himself. He advises Thoreau that the public

> gather not before you to be instructed but to be amused; they come not to hear corroborating voice, urging them to penetrate to the reality of things; they want no new or better philosophy; but they are willing to have their sluggish intellects stirred up as with a long pole by some novelty. But look to it that there is novelty. . . . Therefore, Mr. Thoreau, I henceforward warn you to quit the arena while the novelty is on. . . . Thoreau, how dared you seem to think like Emerson, how could you draw similar inferences, inspirations from your intercourse with Nature, to those of Emerson. Does Nature mean the same thing to any two persons? Impossible! We, the Worcester sofa lolling literati think that she would be more original.[30]

If these Worcester reviews make it clear that Thoreau's lectures did not meet with universal approval, they also demonstrate that his lectures provoked strong reactions. Thoreau was indeed an eccentric—the very premise of his Walden experiment was his assuming an *eccentric* stance in relation to society, and he adopted an appropriate persona. A lecture on a half-cultivated bean field was indeed a novelty; in spite of the repeated charges that Thoreau merely imitated Emerson, Emerson never lectured on any topic that so deliberately affronted and challenged the expectations of lecture audiences as Thoreau's Walden lectures did (Emerson had lectured in Worcester in March, for example, on "Mind and Manners of the 19th Century" [EmL 4: 135n]). And at least some auditors were delighted: H.G.O. Blake eventually cultivated a small but extremely loyal circle of admirers for Thoreau in Worcester, where he lectured more or less regularly for the rest of his life. Indeed, in spite of the mixed reviews Thoreau received throughout this lecture season, he seems clearly to have found at least some admirers and interested listeners almost everywhere he spoke. The Portland Lyceum was sufficiently impressed, for example, to extend Thoreau a warm, almost effusive invitation to lecture there again during the 1850–1851 lecture season (Corr 267). The very number and length of the reviews suggest how provocative his performances were: if they sometimes provoked scorn and laughter, they also provoked curiosity and, more often than not, a grudging admiration even among those who could not muster unrestrained enthusiasm. Always, it seems, they provoked controversy, and given the nature of Thoreau's literary ambitions, he must have found this satisfying. The reviews did not constitute damning national publicity for Thoreau; they created an audience for his writing—but especially for the book he chose *not* to publish at this time.

At the end of the 1848–1849 lecture season, then, Thoreau must have once again felt fairly optimistic about his professional prospects. But the publication in May of both "Resistance to Civil Government" and A *Week*, the latter of which he undoubtedly envisioned as establishing his literary reputation, instead marked the collapse of those prospects. The creative momentum of the previous year ground to a halt.

Elizabeth Peabody's *Aesthetic Papers* was, like the *Dial*, conceived of as a forum for a wide range of diverse and even conflicting expressions of the "new views." Both Parke Godwin's Fourierist manifesto "Organization" and Stephen H. Perkins's essay "The Abuse of Representative Government," for instance, stand in particular opposition to Thoreau's essay. Also included among the twelve principal essays and six poems of this collection were Emerson's lecture "War" and Hawthorne's sketch "Main Street," which Peabody knew would guarantee her journal a certain amount of attention and respect. While perhaps only a few contributions are individually memorable, the volume as a whole was a provocative debut.

When the volume appeared on May 14, 1849, however, it received relatively little notice, and in the responses it did elicit, Thoreau's contribution was most often either ignored or damned. The *Boston Daily Evening Transcript* printed a cursory but polite notice on May 15 and included Thoreau's name in its list of the contributors but did not actually review the volume.[31] The *Boston Post* looked more closely at the contents in its May 17 review, but it did not care for what it found there. The pieces "by Dwight, Emerson and Hawthorne are well written," the reviewer conceded, "but are uninteresting—that by Perkins is weak—that by Thoreau is crazy." The reviewer found "nothing of real value" in the volume and concluded, "We cannot think it will hit the taste of many even in this city, renowned or notorious as it is for the birth or growth of all sorts of quiddities in literature, politics, morals and religion."[32]

The *Salem Gazette* wrote warmly of the volume in its brief review on May 18 and commented that the "diversity of subjects . . . and the manner of treating them, are strikingly contrasted with the uniformity of style and thought so often observable in our Reviews";[33] but the reviewer was really interested almost exclusively in the two pieces of particular local interest—Hawthorne's "Main Street," which he praises at length, and the essay on the "Vegetation about Salem." The reviewer confesses, in fact, that he had read only about half the other essays, briefly citing the contributions of Emerson, Reed, Peabody, Dwight, and Ward. Thoreau's essay is not mentioned.

The review in the *Boston Daily Traveller* on May 22 was uncharacteristically generous toward Thoreau's essay without quite approving of it. The reviewer was enthusiastic about Peabody's project generally and admired this first number. The variety of matter commanded the readers' tolerance of particular ideas expressed, he argued;

> besides, everything is said in so good a spirit, that one cannot say that he dislikes that which is least consonant with his own notions. An article, for instance, which goes so radically against our government as a government, and against all governments, is so pleasant and frank in manner, and so obviously honest in sentiment—and we must say, is intermixed with so many truths withal—that the most rigid advocate of civil government cannot be either offended or alarmed by it.[34]

Other reviewers could not muster a similar enthusiasm. The most influential—that is, the most widely circulated—review to appear was George Ripley's in the *New York Tribune* for May 31. It was an ostensibly positive review, but even his praise was damning:

> We have a characteristic Boston publication, which both on account of the nature of its subjects, and the names of its writers, will receive a cordial greeting from those who read less for pleasant amusement than for mental suggestion and excitement. It displays scarcely a single quality of the popular magazine or review, but nevertheless it will make its way to a large circle that will appreciate its merits and delight in its influence. It is addressed expressly, though not professedly, to readers of thought and intelligence, and in spite of the merely practical, commercial, money-getting character which is so often charged upon the American people, there is no country in the world where books of this stamp which rely for circulation entirely on their substantial worth, meet with a more general perusal or a heartier recognition.[35]

Ripley's assessment was perceptive and accurate in everything but its characterization of American readers and this volume's reception—and one suspects he knew as much. Even more than the *Dial* had been, *Aesthetic Papers* was a coterie journal incapable of attracting a new audience in any significant numbers. Ripley's cautious and almost humorously equivocal praise for the individual contributions could not have helped: the contributions of Peabody herself, he says, "will attract attention"; Emerson's essay "may be taken as a pleasing specimen of the peculiar style of that intensely individual thinker"; and the poetry demonstrates "that the subtle, shadowy reflective, and deeply earnest race of the 'Dial' poets is not altogether extinct in Massachusetts." His only emphatic and unambiguous praise was reserved for John Sullivan Dwight's essay "Music" and for Hawthorne's "Main Street." Significantly, he did not even name Thoreau's essay.

The *Boston Courier*'s review of June 19 did take up Thoreau's essay, but only to condemn it. Ironically, this review was the result of James Russell Lowell's intervention on behalf of Peabody's journal. Lowell, who was then a frequent contributor to the *Courier*, knew that its editor Samuel Kettel would treat *Aesthetic Papers* harshly; he therefore asked Thomas W. Parsons—poet, translator of Dante, and mutual friend of Lowell and Kettell—to help. Parsons's reply confirmed Lowell's suspicions: Kettell, he said, could write "savagely and scurrilously" when aroused; "he contemns the kind of literature exemplified by this book, and I fear that it would have been an unfriendly office to give it to him with a *carte blanche* to say at random what he thought." To avoid this, Parsons offered to write a review himself, though he was not without his own reservations about the volume: "I cannot write a *puff* and you must not ask me to. But if you give me the permission I will say what I candidly think of this affair." Hawthorne's sketch "has charmed me into a semi good nature with the publication," and he knew that he could "honestly say something favourable" about Emerson's lecture as well; thus, he told Lowell, "if I may qualify my notice with some dispraise I shall be happy to try and write a brief comment that may help the *sale* of the brochure." Parsons did not care at all for the poetry, but the chief target of his "dispraise" was indicated in his final comment to Lowell on the volume: "I think that Mr. Thoreau has got into better company than he deserves and doubt if there is much in him."[36] In the review that subsequently appeared in the *Boston Courier*, Parsons calls *Aesthetic Papers* "a pleasant pamphlet to carry up into the country and read under the elm trees. It contains many things to admire—some to smile at—and a few that to plain understanding will appear absurd." Not surprisingly, he singles out Emerson and Hawthorne for praise, and calls "Main Street" "the most charming thing in the book." On the other hand, he says, "We must dismiss Mr. Thoreau, with an earnest prayer that he may become a better subject in time, or else take a trip to France, and preach his doctrine of '*Resistance to Civil Government*' to the red republicans."[37]

The *Literary World* had printed a favorably disposed advance notice of *Aesthetic Papers* on March 31,[38] but when it finally got around to reviewing the actual volume, on September 29, the reviewer responded peevishly to the entire project. He rejected Peabody's definition of "aesthetic," and he could not agree that the various and often contradictory views offered in the volume "coalesce[d] in a region above strife," as Peabody had envisioned in her "Prospectus"—a point that he illustrates by contrasting Perkins's essay "The Abuse of Representative Government," of which he approves, with Thoreau's essay, which he condemns.

> He has carried out his theory in his own case, and been shut up in prison for refusing to pay his "poll-tax." He appeals to the New Testament, even; by which he means, of course, that part of it which may be made to coincide with his own opinions, and not those ugly precepts about the paying of tribute, and submission to the powers that be. This article is about as fit in a volume of "Æsthetic Papers" as would be "the voyage of Gulliver."[39]

Thoreau's essay did receive one particularly favorable notice, in the London periodical *People's Review*. Sophia Dobson Collet reviewed "Resistance to Civil Government" together with *A Week on the Concord and Merrimack Rivers* and praised both works highly. She particularly appreciated the political commitment of "Resistance" as a counter to the transcendentalists' tendency to abandon politics. Pleased with the "manly tone" of Thoreau's lecture, she included a two-paragraph extract.[40] Much closer to home, Longfellow also found Thoreau's essay admirable. In his diary for June 29, 1849, he wrote, "In the evening F. read me Emerson's lecture on 'War,' in Miss Peabody's Æsthetic Papers, a very clever periodical. Also Thoreau's account of his one night in Concord jail. Both extremely good."[41] Neither the foreign review nor the private diary, however, could do much practical good, and the response of the general public seems to have been more accurately captured by reviews such as the *Boston Courier*'s and the *Literary World*'s.

That only one issue of *Aesthetic Papers* was ever published is further explained by the fact that Peabody did not plan it as a regularly issued periodical. As she explained in the "Prospectus," subsequent volumes would be printed only when two criteria were met: first, "a number should appear whenever a sufficient quantity of valuable matter shall have accumulated to fill 256 pages. This will in no case happen more than three times a year; perhaps not oftener than once a year"; second, readers were to subscribe to only one number in advance, so that "whoever is so far pleased with the current number as to desire another is requested to send an order to that effect to the Editor. . . . When a sufficient number of orders are given to pay for the publication, including compensation to the authors, a new number will be printed."[42]

Peabody may have conceived her plan in the wake of the hard economic lesson learned with the *Dial*, but she was nevertheless strikingly naive in her hopes that there would ever be enough subscriptions to pay for subsequent issues. Thoreau probably approved in principle of Peabody's plan to publish only when sufficient material of merit was accumulated and only when the public had demonstrated sufficient interest in having it—his earlier critique of the *Massachusetts Quarterly Review* and of the proposal for a transatlantic successor implied as much; but at the same time he had suggested that the commercial magazines made such a plan both superfluous and impracticable. It is no wonder, then, that Thoreau had made his essay available to Peabody for the "*first volume* only." Thoreau did not want his lecture committed indefinitely to some subsequent volume that he well knew might never reach print, and his suspicions were borne out. Several reviews explained the publishing arrangement and so urged interested parties to write to the editor, but Peabody's journal seems to have attracted only fifty subscribers,[43] and so its first volume was also its last.

However, the failure of *Aesthetic Papers* to find an audience ironically meant that the neglect or scorn to which Thoreau's own contribution was subjected would not really damage his career significantly. Certainly Thoreau's night in jail and his ideas on the duties of resistance to the state were important in his intellectual career; he alluded to this episode in both *A Week* and *Walden*, and the essay itself is perhaps Thoreau's most eloquent, thoughtful, and carefully considered political statement. Yet in terms of his professional career, it constitutes only a kind of aside; he had not even used it as a lecture that season, and he worked it up for publication on short notice only by the happenstance of Peabody's request. His real energies and ambitions were concentrated overwhelmingly on *A Week*. The hostility or neglect shown "Resistance to Civil Government" thus takes on significance only when considered in conjunction with—or as an ominous foreshadowing of—the reception of his first book, which immediately followed the publication of *Aesthetic Papers*.

A Week on the Concord and Merrimack Rivers was officially published by James Munroe & Co. of Boston on May 30, 1849, though the book had actually been printed by May 26, when Thoreau went to Boston to pick up his author's copies. He left instructions to have a copy sent to H.G.O. Blake (which Munroe did not follow until two months later [Corr 247]), and he eagerly returned to Concord with the others. Yet after what amounted to two years of off-and-on negotiations for the publication of *A Week*, the arrangement Thoreau finally settled for virtually doomed the book to failure; certainly he had passed up better opportunities.

Emerson, too, published his books with Munroe & Co., and at his own expense, and this undoubtedly encouraged Thoreau to think he might succeed this way as well. The difference between Emerson's and Thoreau's positions was enormous, however, and thus the same terms that could be profitable for one were disastrous for the other; moreover, even Emerson did not always recognize the best offer when it presented itself. Emerson's own rationale for his publication arrangements is most fully articulated in a letter of 1846 to his brother, in which he explains his rejection of an offer for his poems from Appleton & Co. in favor of Munroe:

> It is best for me to keep the property of my own book as I have usually done and only employ them as publishers. I have usually found that in that way, I received at last only a little less than 33 per cent on the retail price of the book or if I cheapen the book to trade say 30 or 25 per cent. There is no risk in doing so, for my books uniformly pay for themselves, and this book of poems is much more sure of an easy sale than its foregoers. The objection to this course is, that the bookseller will not press the sale of the book at a distance which he prefers to sell at his own counter and monopolize the retail commission, which is larger. But if the book is good, the distant trader will have to send for it, & then it will go to him at trade prices. If I publish it myself, as I incline to, I shall have to employ, I suppose, my old agents here [Munroe & Co.]; as I can more easily work with them, & can know if they do me any wrong; but at a distance I cannot work so well, nor know if I am fairly treated. (EmL 3: 350–51)[44]

Emerson's reasoning here is not flawed exactly; the most popular writers did indeed make more money by owning their own plates and paying the publisher a commission for printing (in this Emerson is following the example of Irving, Cooper, and Longfellow), and Emerson understood that his works were sufficiently popular that he need not worry about making up the initial expense of the plates, paper, printing, and binding. Nevertheless, Emerson's attitude is also naive and essentially provincial. Whereas he recognizes that publishers are not inclined to push books "at a distance" under this arrangement, he understands this only in terms of the per copy commission to the printer; this in fact was probably the way provincial publishers like Munroe viewed the situation, but the more ambitious and successful houses of New York and Philadelphia willingly sacrificed retail commissions for high volume and wide distribution. This, in turn, served the author by encouraging large editions and active, widespread distribution and advertising. Emerson was largely oblivious to this growing and complex network of publication, distribution, and advertisement, naively thinking only in terms of increased sales "if the book is good."

Because of his consistent popularity, Emerson could indeed rely on profiting by hiring Munroe as printer merely, but his naïveté made him a poor advisor to his less popular peers and protégés. The limits of Emerson's and Thoreau's business sense become even clearer if we look at the 1844 negotiations for Fuller's *Summer on the Lakes*. Emerson acted as Fuller's agent, and he presented her with offers from Little & Brown and from James Munroe & Co. Little & Brown offered to publish it at their own expense, with no risk to the author, who would receive 10 percent of the retail sales *after* expenses were met (EmL 3: 246, 248). James Munroe & Co. offered Fuller half the profits on sales to booksellers (who bought at a 20 percent discount off the retail price); but the offer of half profits also involved the risk of taking half the losses, so she would only begin to show a profit after sales had recouped expenses (as with Little & Brown), and, further, in the event of poor sales, she risked losing up to half the costs—which, for an edition of one thousand, amounted to $359.90 (EmL 3: 248–50). When the two offers were compared, it turned out that *if* the entire edition of one thousand sold, Fuller would make $103.38 through Munroe & Co. and "only $100" through Little & Brown (EmL 3: 249n, 250). The advantages of "half profits" were illusory, then, unless the book went into multiple editions, and involved far greater risk. Yet Emerson was optimistic that "enough of the book is sure to sell to pay the costs," and he considered the only advantage of Little & Brown to be their "greater power in N.Y." He thus told Fuller that she could accept either offer, "but if left to myself shall perhaps at last be found at Munroe's, it is so much easier to me to go there" (EmL 3: 249–50). It was "easier" for Emerson only in the sense that he already had a working relation with Munroe (and not even a very good one, for Munroe was often lax in keeping their account with him current);[45] physically, the offices of Little & Brown were practically next door to those of Munroe & Co. on Boston's Washington Street, popularly known as "publishers' row."

At this point in the discussion between Emerson and Fuller, the even more naive Thoreau stepped in: Emerson reported to Fuller that "Henry Thoreau has been showing me triumphantly how much cheaper & every way wiser it would be to publish the book ourselves paying the booksellers only a simple commission for vending it & conducting personally the correspondence with distant booksellers;—but such heroisms are not for me this spring" (EmL 3: 250). Fuller, who seems to have best understood the publishing business (or the prospects of her own book), decided to accept Little & Brown's offer—as Emerson and Thoreau would not have. Emerson duly reported back to Fuller that he had told Brown, "It is your pleasure to make a somewhat less lucrative bargain with him for the sake of securing his best correspondence at South & West, etc." (EmL 3: 251). Fuller's decision turned out to be an especially wise one, since *Summer on the Lakes* actually sold poorly.[46] Fuller thus spared herself the added humiliation and hardship, which Thoreau was eventually to face, of having to earn the money to pay for the printing of a book that did not sell.

If Emerson was not prepared to publish Fuller's book himself, he was nevertheless sufficiently confident in the potential sales of his friends' works that he repeatedly urged them to risk their own capital; thus he not only urged Fuller to take such a risk with *Summer on the Lakes* but told Thoreau at the end of 1847, even after learning that no one would publish *A Week* except at Thoreau's own risk, that he "should print it at once, nor do I think you would incur any risk in doing so that you cannot well afford. It is very certain to have readers" (Corr 195). Thoreau resisted in 1847, but in 1849—his own naïveté reinforced by both Emerson's example and his advice—he took the risk of publishing on his own account. Under such terms, a book by a virtually unknown writer was by no means "certain to have readers," whatever its merits. To save money, Munroe initially (and ultimately) bound only 550 copies of the edition of 1,000, and the company made only the most cursory gestures toward promotion and distribution: prepublication notices appeared in the *Literary World* and several Boston papers, but Munroe never advertised Thoreau's book;[47] New York, Philadelphia, and London publishers were identified as the outlying distributors, but since none of the parties had a vested interest in the book and Munroe had no real influence outside Boston, this meant very little. Thus the two elements most crucial for the success of a book published by the author were lacking—an established reputation and a large, widely distributed edition.

Even when publishing on its own account, Munroe & Co. did not serve its authors well. Hawthorne's experience with Munroe & Co. is a case in point. Hawthorne had contracted with them late in 1841 to publish an expanded, two-volume edition of *Twice-Told Tales*. The contract called for "one edition not exceeding fifteen hundred copies," paying Hawthorne a royalty of 10 percent on the retail price of $2.25 for the set, on the whole number of copies published. In fact, the edition was probably only one thousand copies of the set, and Hawthorne would not collect any royalties until publishing expenses had been met.[48] Munroe issued *Twice-Told Tales* in December, 1841 (dated 1842). When Hawthorne wrote to Munroe in October of 1842 for an account of sales, he learned that "they had not been sufficient to pay the expenses." A year later, he had still received no royalty payments and asked his friend George S. Hillard to inquire at Munroe's. "Surely the book was puffed enough to meet with a sale," he complained; "What the devil is the matter?"[49] Indeed, Hawthorne's book had been "puffed" widely and favorably;[50] the problem was, to a large extent, with Munroe. Munroe was a conservative and provincial publisher who largely clung to the old methods of the local bookseller-printers even while the larger and more aggressive publishing houses were rendering such practices obsolete and ineffective. As Emerson understood, publishers like Munroe wanted to minimize their investment by keeping editions small and to maximize their profits by emphasizing retail sales at their own counter rather than wholesale distribution to other booksellers. Hawthorne's connections and growing reputation among the literati could not counteract obstacles created by Munroe & Co. in spite of their vested interest in the work. By May of 1844, six hundred sets of *Twice-Told Tales* remained unsold; Hawthorne's friend from the *Democratic Review*, John O'Sullivan, proposed to buy the unsold copies from Munroe, have them "furbished up anew into a fresh Edition . . . so as to be sold off through the superior facilities of our New York publishing houses. In this way," O'Sullivan explained to Munroe, "even if nothing may perhaps be made upon it, all parties will get smoothly out of the scrape, the Edition sold off, and the market will no longer be blocked up against the issue of another enlarged one, in a form better adapted to the new system of publication which has grown up since the date of the present one." O'Sullivan was clearly, if tactfully, insulting Munroe here, charging him with failing to keep up with current publishing practices and implicitly blaming him for the poor sales of *Twice-Told Tales*. But the insult was the only satisfaction to be had here. Hawthorne was reluctant to agree to this "humbug of a new edition," especially when he learned that it would cost $275 to buy the remaining volumes from Munroe, and thus that he "could not make anything" even if all six hundred sets were eventually sold. In his frustration, Hawthorne could only "wish that the devil had the books—for I suppose he is a member of the 'Trade.'"[51] Hawthorne succeeded in the marketplace (and revised his view of the "Trade") only when he published his *Mosses* in Wiley & Putnam's American Library and took full advantage of their larger and multiple printings, wide distribution, heavy advertising, and lower retail prices (eventually Hawthorne was even better served by Ticknor & Fields). It is no wonder that in 1846 Hawthorne regarded Emerson as provincial in his attitude toward publication and urged him to look to New York.

Publishing with Munroe & Co. had been both frustrating and unprofitable for Hawthorne; Thoreau, publishing on his own account a volume with inherently less popular appeal than Hawthorne's, could hardly expect his book to be anything but a failure. Thoreau had not been able to find a publisher to take A *Week* on their account, but since he was ultimately willing to take the responsibility for its publication, he would undoubtedly have been better off with either of the New York houses he had contacted in 1847 (Wiley & Putnam and Harper's) or now with Ticknor & Co., even if they would not take it on their account as they would *Walden*, since Ticknor & Co. not only kept up with "the new system of publication" but in fact was now emerging as the pacesetter, in advance of the New York houses, in publishing and promoting belles lettres. It is true that Thoreau could not on his own easily raise the capital required by these other publishers, but it is quite likely that, had he been so inclined, he could have found backers or raised a subscription among his friends and supporters—Emerson had, in the past, helped both Ellery Channing and Alcott in this way, and Thoreau had often enough accepted Emerson's backing in the past as well; moreover, Thoreau also had acquired a handful of loyal followers in Worcester he might have called upon. Turning to friends for financial backing would have been painful to the defiantly self-reliant Thoreau, however, and especially to underwrite A *Week*, since, just as his life at Walden had been an attempt to establish his personal independence, so the book that he wrote there was to be his bid for literary independence. Thoreau squatted on Emerson's land and borrowed an ax, but perhaps he was unwilling to accept the irony of publishing A *Week* at the expense of friends or acquaintances.

None of these alternatives would guarantee success, of course, but they almost certainly would have contained the extent of *A Week*'s failure more successfully than did his arrangement with Munroe. As it turned out, the book's poor sales led Munroe to back out of its agreement, announced in the back pages of *A Week*, that *Walden* "will soon be published." While the five-year delay in the publication of his next book enabled Thoreau to transform it into an American classic, the fate of *A Week* embittered Thoreau toward the "Trade." Ironically, Thoreau's bid for literary independence left him in debt to Munroe & Co.—a debt he was not able to pay off until 1853. Nevertheless, for better or worse, Thoreau's book was now launched upon the public.

Chapter 8

"FLOWING TO HIGHER LEVELS": *A WEEK ON THE CONCORD AND MERRIMACK RIVERS*

A *WEEK* had undergone significant revision and expansion since Thoreau had last tried to find a publisher for it. He had set it aside by November of 1847, when he told Emerson no one would publish it, and when he wrote Cabot in March asking whether the *Massachusetts Quarterly Review* paid for articles, he indicated that he had still not returned to the manuscript; but by May he told Greeley, "My book is swelling under my hands" (Corr 225). He incorporated into the "Wednesday" chapter of A *Week* the "Friendship" lecture he had written during the winter (although he never read the lecture publicly, the admiration expressed for it by intimates such as Alcott must have encouraged Thoreau to include it in his book).[1] Sometime after H.G.O. Blake wrote to Thoreau in March of 1848 praising the *Dial* essay on Persius, Thoreau inserted that essay in the "Thursday" chapter. During this period Thoreau also added a critique of Christianity to "Sunday," commentary on Hindu scriptures to "Monday," further episodes from local history and a critique of Goethe to "Thursday," and a variety of miscellaneous journal entries. Thoreau made deletions as well during this period, but the total length of the book increased considerably.[2]

Like all of Thoreau's earlier excursions and nature essays (including the "Natural History of Massachusetts" and his *Walden* manuscript), A *Week* is held together by the narrative structure of a journey away from society into nature and back again; and like the "Natural History" and "A Winter Walk" (and *Walden*), it is a mosaic of fragmentary observations taken from throughout his journals. But as the book approached its final shape, it strained the conventions and form of the travel narrative almost to the breaking point.[3] In 1847 Emerson had commented on A *Week* to Evert Duyckinck: "The narrative of the little voyage, though faithful, is a very slender thread for such big beads & ingots as are strung on it"; in 1849, this was truer still, and the narrative thread was made to sustain an even heavier burden.

Ironically, the longer A *Week* went unpublished, the more Thoreau seems to have regarded his book as a repository for all his writing that was *not* marketable in the magazines. In some respects, then, Thoreau became increasingly self-indulgent in his revisions of A *Week*, but he also thought that by incorporating these individually unmarketable compositions into his book he might eventually be able to bring them before a popular audience. When, during the early stages of *A Week*'s composition, Thoreau recorded in his journal his process of working from inspiration to lecture to essay, he noted the problem of going further: "And at last they stand . . . like statues on their pedestals—but the statues rarely take hold of hands—There is only such connexion and series as is attainable in galleries. And this affects their immediate practical & popular influence" (J2: 205–6). In *A Week* Thoreau wanted to take his thoughts out of the "galleries" into which he had inscribed them as discrete essays and lectures, connecting them by making them appear to be speculations prompted by his actual experience on the river journey. They would appear as the fruits of a receptive mind responding to nature as it is encountered, meandering as desultorily as the rivers themselves but equally expressive of inviolable and universal laws.

It is thus one of the several ironies of *A Week* that its composition was in effect an elaborate, ten-year process in which Thoreau first selected and distilled the raw material of his journals into lectures and essays, and then reconstituted these into a book that employed elaborate artifice to create the *impression* of its being a journal. This irony informs the whole of *A Week* but is perhaps manifest most clearly in a passage in the final chapter, "Friday":

> We confess that we feel a disposition commonly to concentrate sweets, and accumulate pleasures, but the poet may be presumed always to speak as a traveller, who leads us through a varied scenery, from one eminence to another, and it is, perhaps, more pleasing, after all, to meet with a fine thought in its natural setting. Surely fate has enshrined it in these circumstances for some end. Nature strews her nuts and flowers broadcast, and never collects them in heaps. This was the soil it grew in, and this the hour it bloomed in; if sun, wind and rain came here to cherish and expand the flower, shall we not come here to pluck it? (*Week* 374)

These thoughts were originally recorded by Thoreau in his journal for February, 1841, when (after "The Service" had been rejected by Fuller) he was questioning the legitimacy of his mosaic method of composition and acknowledging the integrity and authority of the journal form. The journal passage, in which he was clearly referring to his own practices, began, "When I select one here and another there and strive to join sundered thoughts, I make but a partial heap after all" (Jl: 253). Thoreau subsequently revised and depersonalized the passage for inclusion in his lecture and essay on the poets Homer, Ossian, and Chaucer. There, it was made to serve (less compellingly than in the original journal) as an excuse for Chaucer's lack of taste and polish, and he introduces the passage by explaining, "If we have to wander through many dull and prosaic passages in

Chaucer, we have at least the satisfaction of knowing that it is not an artificial dullness, but too easily matched by many passages in life, and it is, perhaps, more pleasing after all, to meet with a fine thought in its natural setting" (EEM 170). Thoreau slightly revised this essay once more, for inclusion in A *Week*, but here the essay was broken up and integrated into his meditations on the river: the "Homer" fragment is included in "Sunday" (*Week* 71–95); the "Ossian" and "Chaucer" segments are both included in "Friday" but are separated by a narrative interlude of considerable length. Thus while this particular passage on the "natural setting" of thoughts retains as its immediate context Thoreau's commentary on Chaucer, it also recovers much of the original journal entry's personal reference and so functions as a reflexive commentary upon the *apparent*—but not *actual*—design of A *Week*. Thoreau's actual method of composition was in fact the opposite of that described here—A *Week* is certainly Thoreau's most elaborate and complex mosaic of "sundered thoughts"—yet this passage ironically seems more apt, more richly resonant, in A *Week* than in either of its earlier contexts. Here the simile comparing the poet to the traveler seems to be a natural and obvious reference to the writing of A *Week* itself; and the defense of leaving thoughts in their natural setting seems both to justify the frequent digressions from the narrative account and to reinforce the illusion that the river trip was in fact the natural setting of these thoughts.

This illusion is created and sustained throughout A *Week* by Thoreau's crafting associational links between observed phenomena on the river and the subject of his digressions, as well as by explicit transitional phrases—often addressed directly to the reader—that introduce digressions and return us to the travel narrative proper. In "Saturday," for example, the sight of a solitary fisherman on the shore leads through a brief sequence of associations to his whimsical essay on the character of Concord's fishes; Thoreau then brings us back to the excursion by announcing, "That was a long pull from Ball's Hill to Carlisle Bridge" (39), thus creating the impression that these were the thoughts that actually occupied his imagination during that interval of the journey. In "Tuesday," the brothers wake to a dense fog, which reminds Thoreau of the sea of clouds he once saw from the summit of Saddleback Mountain in the Berkshires. "As we cannot distinguish objects through this dense fog," he says, "let me tell this story more at length" (180), thus introducing a long account of that excursion, at the end of which he says, "But now we must make haste back before the fog disperses to the blithe Merrimack water" (190). His transitions are not equally strong or effective. In "Wednesday," Thoreau introduces the longest single digression of the book—his "Friendship" lecture —simply by saying, "While we float here, far from that tributary stream on whose banks our friends and kindred dwell, our thoughts, like the stars, come out of their horizon still" (259); and he returns to the narrative by relocating us on the journey—"Having rowed five or six miles above Amoskeag before sunset" (289). Thoreau strained rather painfully to integrate some of his works, such as his *Dial* piece on Anacreon, which he inserts into "Tuesday" by saying that they rested on an island "where the weary voyageur could read the journal of some other sailor, whose bark had plowed, perchance, more famous and classic seas. At the tables of the gods, after feasting follow music and song; we will recline now under these island trees, and for our minstrel call on ANACREON" (225). He makes the transition back to the narrative by observing, "Late in the afternoon, for we had lingered long on the island, we raised our sail for the first time" (231).

While the artifice of such transitions is transparent, the point is that Thoreau invariably made some gesture, however strained, toward creating the sense of connectedness and naturalness—the "connexion and series"—that he felt his books needed and which "affects their immediate practical & popular influence." Moreover, Thoreau establishes a pattern in the narrative, whereby each day has its natural rhythms, alternating between activity and meditation, and each day includes a midday "nooning"—a time to rest from the morning's exertions and an occasion to indulge at some length in reflections on a topic or topics that tend loosely to govern all the meditations for that day.

While A *Week* is an astonishing miscellany of Thoreau's thoughts and writings on a wide variety of topics, they are indeed held together by a complex web of associations, and Thoreau returns to and develops related topics as the days progress; but the result is a structure as much like Whitman's "Song of Myself," with its recurring images, motifs, and themes, as it is like a travelogue of a linear excursion across the actual landscape. The mosaic of A *Week* creates the illusion of its being a journal of private inspirations left in their natural setting of an excursion through the actual, outward landscape. But through the elaborate artifice with which he linked the "truths" gleaned from ten years of writing to the "facts" of a two-week excursion (itself artificially compressed into the days of a single week), Thoreau forged what might more accurately be called a mythic narrative. While the narrative structure of A *Week* is determined by the river journey, the thematic structure and rhythm of the book are created by Thoreau's regular alternations between the personal and the universal, the temporal and the eternal, the historic and the mythic, the actual and the ideal—alternations in which the latter term is constantly breaking free from the former. Throughout A *Week* Thoreau therefore implicitly instructs his readers that the book is not quite what it appears to be—that it aims higher and must therefore be read differently from a book that aspires to convey merely the personal, temporal, and historical aspects of experience. Consequently, there is an ongoing tension in A *Week* between Thoreau's exploitation of the travelogue's conventions and his simultaneous attempt to undermine all the particular and personal aspects of the account—the aspects that constitute the raison d'être of travel literature. That is, Thoreau's complex sense of the relation between his professional and prophetic ambitions leads him simultaneously to construct and deconstruct the narrative thread of A *Week*. Universal truths are made manifest by particular facts and individual experience, but they are not contained by them, and A *Week* is therefore a book that ultimately turns on itself, achieving its ends by undermining its means—not only an excursion that undermines the value of travel but finally a book in which language itself must give way to a higher silence.

Thoreau's brief introductory chapter, "Concord River," is the most unified and apparently conventional chapter of the book, containing no extended digressions and narrated in the voice of the familiar essayist; yet Thoreau also establishes the pattern that informs the entire narrative, in which the surface attention to the personal and the historical is undermined and gives way to the universal and the mythic. In the opening paragraph, Thoreau seems cheerfully to adopt the role of local historian—or, more precisely, of the romantic travel writer who filters the dry facts of the historian through his more genial sensibility and regards them with a certain bemused detachment. In either case, he begins by locating the scene in history, and he furthermore implies that "history" is the narrative of the inevitable advance of Western civilization, that it begins, therefore, at the point when the white farmer supplants the Indian hunter:

> The Musketaquid, or Grass-ground River, though probably as old as the Nile or Euphrates, did not begin to have a place in civilized history, until the fame of its grassy meadows and its fish attracted settlers out of England in 1635, when it received the other but kindred name of Concord from the first plantation on its banks, which appears to have been commenced in a spirit of peace and harmony.

Yet Thoreau immediately undermines this conventional historical perspective by asserting nature's indifference to such changes: "It will be Grass-ground River as long as grass grows and water runs here; it will be Concord River only while men lead peaceable lives on its banks. To an extinct race it was grass-ground, where they hunted and fished, and it is still perennial grass-ground to Concord farmers, who own the Great Meadows, and get the hay from year to year" (5). By framing the date of the English settlement between observations on the enduring *pre*historical and *post*historical character of the "grass-ground" river, Thoreau reduces "civilized history" to an inconsequential interlude in the eternal and timeless rhythms of nature.

The surface of Thoreau's narrative remains insistently focused on the local, the particular, the historical: he goes on to quote from Lemuel Shattuck's history of Concord, which carefully traces the course of the river through various Massachusetts townships; yet there is a sly irony—both comic and cosmic—when Thoreau says of Shattuck's book, "for I love to quote so good authority" (5), for Thoreau has already undermined the authority of the narrowly historical perspective that presumes to define nature by reference to transient human communities. All the place names, which Thoreau seems to take such pleasure in repeating, get us no closer to an understanding of the essential character of the place, with respect to which the particulars of time and place are matters of indifference. Thoreau makes the point explicit when he asserts, "As yesterday and the historical ages are past, as the work of to-day is present, so some flitting perspectives, and demi-experiences of the life that is in nature are, in time, veritably future, or rather outside to time, perennial, young, divine, in the wind and rain which never die" (8).

Indeed, *A Week* is profoundly concerned with time, and with the relation between experience in and outside of time. Here, and throughout *A Week*, Thoreau simultaneously plays the roles of historian and antihistorian. The narrative thread of *A Week* is presented as a conventional travelogue in time, in which the author presents us with a detailed account of his progress across the landscape: he provides sometimes minutely detailed descriptions of the scenery; he charts his route with geographic precision, identifying each village, each tributary, each lock; he observes local commerce and agriculture. We know just where he is and at what time of day. Moreover, he enriches that account for us by pointing out all the appropriate historical associations. On each day of the excursion Thoreau recalls incidents from colonial history associated with the local landscape: here John Elliot had preached to the Indians (80); here Jonathan Tyng stubbornly defended his land during King Philip's War (110–12); here was the site of Lovewell's famous fight against the Indians (119–22); here Farwell was the only survivor of an Indian ambush (166–68); here the Mohawks drove out the Penacooks (220–21); and here Hannah Dustan made her desperate and murderous escape from her Indian captors (320–24). For these and other accounts, Thoreau relies heavily on local histories and gazetteers, often quoting them directly at considerable length.

As I discussed in chapter 3, in relation to "A Walk to Wachusett," historical anecdotes based on association of place were a staple of romantic travel literature; and many of the episodes Thoreau recounts here were thus familiar to the popular audience he hoped to address in *A Week*. Timothy Dwight's classic *Travels in New-England and New-York* included extended accounts of both Lovewell's Fight and the Dustan captivity, for example; and in November of 1849 (just a few months after *A Week* was published) the magazine *Youth's Companion* narrated the story behind the popular ballad "Lovewell's Fight," which Thoreau also quoted at length.[4] Such anecdotes did more than lend color and romance to accounts of the landscape; they constituted the most popular form of literary nationalism, forging a national identity out of a historical narrative that begins with the arrival of the white man and charts the progress of civilization in the New World. Thoreau's historical anecdotes therefore provided a conventional form of entertainment and instruction, full of high adventure in the service of nationalism, both reinforcing a popular sense of national history and lending a conventional sense of narrative coherence to A *Week* itself. It is true that Thoreau's accounts tend to be more sympathetic to the plight of the Indians and more ironic in his treatment of the whites than versions such as Dwight's, but the romantic and heroic Indian was also a popular literary type; and Thoreau does not overtly challenge either the heroic character of the whites (claiming, "We have need to be as sturdy pioneers still as Miles Standish, or Church, or Lovewell" [120]) or the conventional sense of the progress of civilization they ushered in:

> It is a rapid story the historian will have to put together. Miantonimo,—Winthrop,—Webster. Soon he comes from Mount Hope to Bunker Hill, from bearskins, parched corn, bows and arrows, to tiled roofs, wheat fields, guns and swords. Pawtucket and Wamesit, where the Indians resorted in the fishing season, are now Lowell, the city of spindles and Manchester of America, which sends its cotton cloth round the globe. (82–83)

In searching out antiquities and exploring associations of a place, the travel writer affirms and embellishes the historian's narrative, and together they give Americans both a past and a measure of our progress from it, thereby celebrating our future as well. The travel writer therefore not only charts his progress spatially, across the landscape, but also reconstructs our collective progress temporally, by marking the signs of the historian's narrative.

Similarly, the basic structure of Thoreau's book, in which chapters correspond to the days of the week, suggests that Thoreau is committed to the historian's sense of linear, sequential progress of time. Yet in a variety of ways, the linear progress of the narrative—both spatial and temporal—is interrupted, cracked open, or undercut, and Thoreau as antihistorian explores phenomena that elude the historian altogether and absorb or transcend the story in which Miantonimo gives way to Webster. "There are," Thoreau cryptically asserts, "secret articles in our treaties with the gods, of more importance than all the rest, which the historian can never know" (125).[5]

The most conventional way in which the historical narrative is undercut is Thoreau's use of the principles of association to relate the American landscape he observes to classic analogues—just as he had in "A Walk to Wachusett." As in that essay, such associations are employed explicitly or implicitly in the interest of literary nationalism, as are the anecdotes of local history, though the two impulses imply conflicting visions. The Concord River evokes the Xanthus and Scamander, and Thoreau asserts, "I trust that

I may be allowed to associate our muddy but much abused Concord river with the most famous in history" (12). The harbors of Chelmsford and Dracut along the Merrimack "lay as smooth and fairy-like as the Lido, or Syracuse, or Rhodes, in our imagination" (80). Of the farms along the banks above Tyngsboro he says, "All that is told of mankind, of the inhabitants of the Upper Nile, and the Sunderbunds, and Timbuctoo, and the Orinoko, was experience here. Every race and class of men was represented" (123). The Concord cattle show is analogous to "the ancient festivals, games, and processions of the Greeks and Etruscans" (337). The point of such associations is to refute any charges of American inferiority and to demonstrate that "there are no more quiet Tempes, or more poetic and Arcadian lives, than may be lived in these New England dwellings" (234). But the further implication of such universalizing is to undercut the myth of historical progress that Thoreau-as-historian has been narrating. Moreover, the idea of spatial as well as temporal "progress" is also undercut as a consequence. If the implication of historical associations is that we are drawn to travel to places where particular noble or romantic incidents took place, the result of the more broadly imagined associations is, as Thoreau realized in "A Walk to Wachusett," the discovery that "man's life is rounded with the same few facts, the same simple relations everywhere, and it is vain to travel to find it new" (W 5: 137). Similarly, he observes in A *Week* that the New England farmers "had no need to travel to be as wise as Solomon in all his glory, so similar are the lives of men in all countries" (*Week* 215); and he further declares, "Go where we will, we discover infinite change in particulars only, not in generals" (124).

In neither "A Walk to Wachusett" nor A *Week* is the excursion really undermined by such classic associations, for even if one will not see new things by traveling, one may come to see things anew—may, in fact, come to discover the universality of experience expressed by those analogies. In "A Walk to Wachusett," Thoreau had concentrated almost exclusively on this response to the American landscape, eschewing for the most part both the celebration of local history and the celebration of the sublime *pre*historical wilderness landscape (as in "Ktaadn"). In A *Week,* however, Thoreau exploits all three responses, and while each is enlisted in the name of literary nationalism, there is a tension among them that tends to deconstruct the surface narrative in a way we do not find in either "A Walk to Wachusett" or "Ktaadn."

We find Thoreau exploring the nationalistic implications of the prehistoric, natural landscape, for example, when the brothers reach Amoskeag Falls, in "Wednesday." Thoreau makes note of the thriving industry and in particular of the canal and artificial falls of the Manchester Manufacturing Company here, but he is much more interested in the natural phenomenon of the numerous "pot-holes" found at the falls, formed by centuries of erosion. A natural curiosity in themselves, these potholes are brought into the service of his larger themes as he reflects on their nature and significance: "The periods of Hindoo and Chinese history, though they reach back to the time when the race of mortals is confounded with the race of gods, are as nothing compared with the periods which these stones have inscribed. . . . They teach us lessons, these dumb workers; verily there are 'sermons in stones, and books in the running streams'" (248).

Like the vast geological ages of the "Grass-ground River," these potholes dwarf the span of civilized history by comparison, and Thoreau goes on to suggest that "these, and such as these, must be our antiquities, for lack of human vestiges" (249). Thoreau takes up here the conventional response of Americans to the apparent barrenness of the New World compared with the rich historical and cultural associations of the old. He begins defensively and concedes that nature is indeed dignified by "the fact that Romans once inhabited her" (249); but he goes on to assert that "our own country furnishes antiquities as ancient and durable, and as useful, as any," which the poet, at least, is able to decipher. He provides a rather lengthy catalog of our natural antiquities—"the lichen on the rocks," the rivers and winds, "the first faint sounds of spring, older than the summer of Athenian glory," "the red-maple and birchen leaves, old runes which are not yet deciphered; catkins, pine-cones, vines, oak-leaves, and acorns; the very things themselves, and not their forms in stone,—so much the more ancient and venerable" (250–51). Thoreau's impassioned climax to this commentary is his explicit declaration of literary nationalism and, more specifically, a defense and explanation of his own motives for writing a travel book about his native region:

> What though the traveller tell us of the ruins of Egypt, are we so sick or idle, that we must sacrifice our America and to-day to some man's ill-remembered and indolent story? Carnac and Luxor are but names, or if their skeletons remain, still more desert sand, and at length a wave of the Mediterranean sea, are needed to wash away the filth that attaches to their grandeur. Carnac! Carnac! here is Carnac for me. I behold the columns of a larger and purer temple. (251–52)

But if the pinecone and the acorn are more venerable and ancient artifacts than Athenian ruins, then it is not just ancient history and foreign travel but also colonial history and local travel that are rendered superfluous. Through nature, America is presented not as a place where history is *enacted* but as a place where it may be *transcended* entirely. Thus, while Thoreau's narrative is shaped and propelled in part by his diligent reconstruction of civilized history along the banks of the Concord and Merrimack rivers, that history is subsumed by the timeless reality of nature.

As Thoreau's narrative develops, the history of civilization becomes increasingly suspect, and Thoreau implies that our national destiny—indeed, our salvation—lies not in subduing and appropriating nature but in naturalizing our own lives. History itself—the record of the linear advance of time—becomes inherently tragic in *A Week*, and we can be redeemed from that tragic narrative only through integration with the natural world, which affords us "flitting perspectives . . . outside to time, . . . in the wind and rain which never die."

Perhaps *A Week*'s most complex treatment of these competing perspectives is in Thoreau's version of the Hannah Dustan story, in "Thursday." In his earlier accounts of Indian-white relations, Thoreau had been sympathetic to the Indians' fate but did not deviate significantly from the conventional treatment of such episodes as part of the heroic advance of civilization in the New World. Here, however, Thoreau not only explores the moral ambiguity of Mrs. Dustan's taking the scalps of ten of her captors during her escape but treats the mutual corruption of Indians and whites in terms of his ongoing concern with time and history in general. Hannah Dustan's home had been burned to the ground and "she had seen her infant's brains dashed out against an apple-tree" by the Indians; Hannah Dustan, in turn, effects her escape by adopting the Indians' methods, not only killing her captors with their own tomahawks but returning to take their scalps, "fearing that her story would not be believed" (321, 322). While the Indian's fall from innocence seems to be incited by the white man's invasion of his wilderness home, the white man's fall is in turn enacted by his adopting the methods of the Indian. The image of the apple tree at the center of this episode evokes the original Fall in Eden and suggests that Thoreau is interested in issues larger even than our national history and identity.

Thoreau recreates these events in the past tense, but he then complicates the issue of his relation to them by shifting dramatically into the present tense: "Early this morning this deed was performed, and now, perchance, these tired women and this boy, their clothes stained with blood, and their minds racked with alternate resolution and fear, are making a hasty meal of parched corn and moose-meat, while their canoe glides under these pine roots" (322). Their bloodstained clothes suggest the fall from innocence involved in supplanting the Indians; yet ironically their actions are indistinguishable from those of Indians—not only their scalping, but their meal of parched corn and moose meat and their appropriation of the Indians' canoe. But these actions are not sufficient to naturalize the white race in this new world, for their fear keeps them alienated from nature. Thoreau imagines all the wildlife around them as they descend the river, "but they do not observe these things, or they speedily forget them. . . . On either side, the primeval forest stretches away uninterrupted to Canada or to the 'South

Sea;' to the white man a drear and howling wilderness, but to the Indian a home, adapted to his nature, and cheerful as the smile of the Great Spirit" (322–23).

The tragedy of the white race, as represented by the Dustan narrative, is that while they supplanted the Indians in the New World, they failed to become naturalized in it—they appropriated the Indian's land, food, and canoe, but still they saw only a "howling wilderness" and not a "home." Thoreau's shift to the present tense for this part of the narrative not only heightens the dramatic tension but also makes this moment *present* to Thoreau—not an irrevocable and thus tragic fact of history, but an ever-present moment of mythic time. Our redemption is in our naturalization; by calling attention to the *temporal* as well as spatial coincidence of his journey with Hannah Dustan's, Thoreau can recover that critical moment and redeem it by effecting that naturalization. Thus, having established a close identification with Hannah Dustan by using the present tense, he now appropriates the moment and distances himself from her actions:

> While we loiter here this autumn evening, looking for a spot retired enough, where we shall quietly rest to-night, they thus, in that chilly March evening, one hundred and forty-two years before us . . . have already glided out of sight, not to camp, as we shall, at night, but . . . onward to the settlements, it may be, even to old John Lovewell's house on Salmon Brook to-night. (323)

Separated by 142 years, their actions nevertheless both take place "to-night." That is, both actions stand both in and out of historical time. Whereas Hannah Dustan's fearful return to the settlements (even, perhaps, to the home of the hero of Indian battles) is an archetypal reenactment of man's original flight from the Garden and his alienation from nature, Thoreau's search for a campsite *in* nature is an emblem of his efforts to recover that lost innocence and return to the garden.

Whatever promise of redemption Thoreau envisions in the naturalized life, however (and such a vision informs the whole of A *Week*, not just this interlude), he is still oppressed by the consciousness of man's fallen state. He thus concludes the narration of the Dustan episode by reporting,

> According to the historian, they escaped as by a miracle all roving bands of Indians, and reached their homes in safety, with their trophies. . . . The family of Hannah Dustan all assembled alive once more, except the infant whose brains were dashed out against the apple-tree, and there have been many who in later times have lived to say that they had eaten of the fruit of that apple-tree.

Thoreau's conclusion is deeply ironic, however, for while their escape may be legitimate "according to the historian," it is more doubtful from Thoreau's perspective "outside to time." They reached their homes with their trophies, but the bloodstained apple tree stands as an emblem of the Fall, and subsequent generations have continued to eat of its fruit.

As an epilogue to the anecdote, Thoreau appends a brief meditation on the subjective perception of time, which brings together some of the themes implicit in the digression. "This seems a long while ago," he says of the Dustan captivity, "and yet it happened since Milton wrote his Paradise Lost. But its antiquity is not the less for that, for we do not regulate our historical time by the English standard" (324). The allusion to *Paradise Lost* is more significant as an assertion of his theme of the Fall of Man than as a merely historical touchstone. He then recounts the genealogy of humankind "from Adam and Eve at one leap sheer down to the deluge, and then through the ancient monarchies . . . down through Odin and Christ—to America. It is a wearisome while.—And yet the lives of but sixty old women . . . strung together, are sufficient to reach over the whole ground" (325). The course of history after the Fall is both infinitely long and also negligible; the fact of the Fall throws us into historical time but also renders the passage of that time insignificant—that is, without meaning, because our redemption cannot come through *historical* progress. Earlier in A *Week*, Thoreau had noted the "rapid story the historian will have to tell" to trace the progress from the aboriginal settlements to the mills of Lowell, seemingly in celebration of the great progress of civilization; here, however, that rapid story is but a "wearisome while," and history itself offers no hope.

Redemption may come through the naturalization of our lives, however, for in such a state we are afforded perspectives outside of time. Significantly, then, the "Thursday" chapter in which the Dustan episode is narrated ends with the brothers' sense of being *at home* in nature, as Hannah Dustan had not been. As the night advances, they even forget that they "lay on the bank of the Merrimack, and not in our chamber at home." And the sounds they hear in the wind and water are perceived as the domestic sounds of "a great haste and preparation throughout Nature, as for a distinguished visitor" (333), so that the brothers drift off to sleep imagining wood spirits sweeping the forest aisles, boiling pots, sewing a new carpet for the earth and new draperies for the trees.

The final chapter, "Friday," then includes Thoreau's most explicit claims for the redemptive force of the naturalized life. The "distinguished visitor" they had anticipated the previous night turns out to be autumn (though technically the season would not change for another week), which reintroduces the theme of time to the narrative. While the autumnal mood of "Friday" enables Thoreau to develop the elegiac strand of A *Week*, as a tribute to John, autumn is not primarily associated here with loss, decay, and diminution, as we might expect, but with its other set of connotations: ripeness, fruition, freshness, and fecundity. It is, in effect, the counterpart of *Walden*'s "Spring." Though he describes the times of man as "these degenerate days," the sound of the river, with "a freshness of autumn," is an effective stay against despair; in the autumnal dawn the brothers arise to find their boat "all cool and dripping with dew," their tracks "still fresh in the wet sand," and the shore itself "so coolly fresh and shining with dew" (334–35). The redundant imagery of the cool, fresh morning dew suggests a kind of baptism into a new life, so when Thoreau declares they could see by all these signs that "the Fall had commenced," it is a celebratory proclamation, comparable to the declaration of "Spring" that "Walden was dead and is alive again" (*Walden* 311), and implying that the "fall" of *nature* can redeem the Fall of *Man*, if man will only naturalize his life. Throughout the chapter, Thoreau returns to his theme of life in nature, and looking at the Merrimack skies he explains their redemptive power in a passage echoing his early remarks on "perspectives outside to time": "Sometimes we see objects as through a thin haze, in their eternal relations. . . . If we see the reality of things, of what moment is the superficial and apparent longer? . . . While I sit here listening to the waves . . . I am absolved from all obligation to the past" (*Week* 359).

Just as Thoreau's celebration of natural facts and a life in nature undercuts the historical narrative sustained in *A Week*, so too does his rhetorical trick of beginning each chapter/day with imagery evoking a mythic, prehistoric dawn: Thoreau implies that to experience the world most fully and to recover our *natural* innocence, we must step outside of history—even our own—and regard each day as the day of Creation itself, not as a step in the relentlessly cumulative sequence of days in postlapsarian history. "Sunday" (their first morning on the river) begins with a description of the dense morning fog giving way to reveal a dawn "with more of the auroral rosy and white than of the yellow light in it, as if it dated from earlier than the fall of man, and still preserved a heathenish integrity" (43). As in *Walden*, dawn has special symbolic significance: it is the "waking moment" when the infinite and the finite merge. To emerge from the fog into the morning light is to emerge into consciousness, into the waking moment in time and place when one finds oneself anew, but with the lingering memory of the infinite from which one has come. It is a continual rebirth, and the symbol of new life and new beginning. When the two brothers begin this day's journey by giving names to all the islands they pass, then, Thoreau is suggesting the symbolic reenactment of Adam's giving names to all the creatures in Eden. "Monday" too opens with the brothers awaking to a prelapsarian dawn: "When the first light dawned on the earth, and the birds awoke, and the brave river was heard rippling confidently seaward, and the nimble early rising wind rustled the oak leaves about our tent, all men, having reinforced their bodies and their souls with sleep, and cast aside doubt and fear, were invited to unattempted adventures" (117).

As on the previous day, Monday's journey also begins with rowing through the morning fog, but it is on the next morning, "Tuesday," that the fog and the dawn become the subject of a full-scale meditation. As I noted earlier, the fog on the river reminds Thoreau of his having seen "the day break from the top of Saddleback Mountain in Massachusetts, above the clouds" (180), and he inserts an extended account of that excursion. After spending the night on the mountain's summit, Thoreau awakens, and, he writes, "as the light increased I discovered around me an ocean of mist, which . . . shut out every vestige of the earth, while I was left floating on this fragment of the wreck of a world, on my carved plank in cloud land" (188). Thoreau not only awakens to a prelapsarian dawn, as he had on the river, but undergoes a symbolic resurrection, for during the night he had symbolically entombed himself, "encased . . . completely in boards, managing even to put a board on top of me, with a large stone on it, to keep it down" (186). Now, in the dawning light, this ocean of clouds appears as "the new world into which I had risen in the night, the new terra firma perchance of my future life. . . . It was such a country as we might see in dreams, with all the delights of paradise" (188). Unlike his mountain vision in "A Walk to Wachusett"—which had illuminated the world below, revealing "Massachusetts, spread out before us in its length and breadth"—here "there was not a crevice left through which the trivial places we name Massachusetts, or Vermont, or New York, could be seen" (188). But unlike "Ktaadn," too, where the sea of clouds *obscured* his vision, threatened to overwhelm him, and confronted him with his own material existence, here the cloudscape *is* his vision, imaging a life of *pure* spirit:

> As there was wanting the symbol, so there was not the substance of impurity, no spot nor stain. It was a favor for which to be forever silent to be shown this vision. The earth beneath had become such a flitting thing of lights and shadows as the clouds had been before. It was not merely veiled to me, but it had passed away like the phantom of a shadow. . . . As I had climbed above storm and cloud, so by successive days' journeys I might reach the region of eternal day beyond the tapering shadow of the earth. (188–89)

This vision of an "eternal day" is clearly so significant, so transforming, that it renders merely ironic both the temporal sequence of the narrative frame of *A Week* and the historical sensibility which governs at least one thematic strand of the book. Moreover, this mountain vision is but one of several epiphanic, visionary moments recounted in *A Week*, each of which similarly undercuts the travelogue narrative.

Thoreau had hinted that such visionary moments were the true object of his journey when he contrasted historical time with those "flitting perspectives . . . outside to time, perennial, young, divine" (8). His first account of such an experience occurs at the end of "Monday," as the brothers, listening to the baying of dogs and other night sounds, drop off to sleep. Hearing "some tyro beating a drum incessantly," Thoreau writes, "These simple sounds related us to the stars" (173). As we have seen, Thoreau had long associated his special destiny with the stars, and here the perception suddenly gives way to a genuinely mystical experience, a moment of transcendence:

> I stop my habitual thinking, as if the plow had suddenly run deeper in its furrow through the crust of the world. How can I go on, who have just stepped over such a bottomless skylight in the bog of my life. Suddenly old Time winked at me,—Ah you know me, you rogue,—and news had come that IT was well. That ancient universe is in such capital health, I think undoubtedly it will never die. . . .
>
> Then idle Time ran gadding by
> and left me with Eternity alone;
>
> . . . .
>
> I see, smell, taste, hear, feel, that everlasting Something to which we are allied, at once our maker, our abode, our destiny, our very Selves; the one historic truth, the most remarkable fact which can become the distinct and uninvited subject of our thought, the actual glory of the universe. (173–74)

This epiphanic moment is both complemented and paralleled by the vision atop Saddleback: one occurs at midnight, the other at dawn; one is primarily aural and leads to extended reflections on celestial music, the other is emphatically visual; one employs imagery creating a *downward* orientation ("the plow had suddenly run deeper in its furrow through the crust of the world" as he "stepped over such a bottomless skylight in the bog of my life," revealing "how the foundations of the world are laid"), while the other emphasizes ascension—floating and climbing *above* the world to an "eternal day." At the heart of both, however, is the transcendence of time and the immediate apprehension of the eternal. Such moments, in which Thoreau pierces through the transitory and apprehends the eternal, constitute the fulfillment of the metaphysical quest of A *Week*. These *intuitions* both fulfill and validate all the *tuitions* of the river narrative, in which Thoreau has relentlessly sought out the signs of the universal in the particular, the permanent in the transient.

On the more private level at which A *Week* functions as an elegy for John, such moments also constitute his private consolation, and in glimpsing "the region of eternal day beyond the tapering shadow of the earth" Thoreau is granted a vision of eternal life both for and with his brother. (The fact that his ascent of Saddleback took place after John's death is effectively masked by its integration into "Tuesday" as a *recollected* experience.) Fittingly, then, a third account of the transcendence of time is recorded in his "Friendship" essay, inserted into the "Wednesday" chapter and devoted largely to commemorating John. In the midst of this essay he writes:

> There are passages of affection in our intercourse with mortal men and women, such as no prophecy has taught us to expect, which transcend our earthly life, and anticipate heaven for us. What is this Love that may come right into the middle of a prosaic Goffstown day, equal to any of the gods? that discovers a new world, fair and fresh and eternal, occupying the place of this old one, when to the common eye a dust has settled on the universe? which world cannot else be reached, and does not exist. (268)

The qualities of the experience he describes here link it to those moments of transforming intuitive perception described in "Monday" and "Tuesday." Though more generalized, and perhaps therefore lacking some of the intensity of the earlier passages, this too describes an unexpected and overwhelming moment of insight in which Thoreau is translated out of his normal relations with the world. Significantly, the catalyst for this epiphanic moment, however, is not some natural phenomenon (the nocturnal sounds or the mountaintop sunrise) but a perfectly realized moment in his human intercourse. Thoreau links this passage to the river narrative by describing this love as coming "right into the middle of a prosaic Goffstown day"—Goffstown being a town along their route that afternoon. Thus we are led to infer that Thoreau himself experienced this moment of transforming love here, on Wednesday, on the Merrimack River, and further, that the love he describes is that between him and John. Indeed, this digression is Thoreau's fullest and deepest tribute to his unnamed companion. Though he addresses all kinds of friendships here, the emotional climax of this essay is his tribute to John: "My Friend is not of some other race or family of men, but flesh of my flesh, bone of my bone. He is my real brother" (284).

While such epiphanic moments represent the metaphysical achievement of *A Week*, they ironically threaten to undermine the narrative thrust of the journey. As a travelogue, *A Week* threatens to come unraveled. Only because these moments of illumination are merely "flitting perspectives" does the narrative resume. There is no *further* objective to be reached; it is simply that one must inevitably return to the river of time. Thoreau is like the Puritan who must exercise his moral faculty as a preparation for grace, should it be bestowed upon him, but who can never *effect* grace by his own acts: on the river Thoreau constantly *seeks* signs of the eternal, but his moments of genuine transcendence are intuitions and cannot be effected by his will. The river excursion itself then seems increasingly to have no ultimate objective other than the continual exercise of his faculties in the intervals between moments of illumination. When he does experience these moments, he asks, on Monday night, "How can I go on," and on Tuesday says that his vision was "a favor for which to be forever silent." Increasingly, then, *A Week* becomes a book that consumes itself, undermining the sufficiency of either travel or language itself.

Significantly, the Saddleback vision is not even part of the river journey but an interpolated account of a separate excursion. Thus, not only do the metaphysical implications of his vision undermine the rationale for the excursion, but the narrated incidents themselves undercut A *Week*'s coherence as a travelogue. This becomes clearer when we consider the importance of the Saddleback episode in relation to the calculated *in*significance of their ascent of Agiocochoook (Mount Washington), the *actual* object of their 1839 journey.

"Thursday" posed the greatest structural difficulties for Thoreau, since it actually includes an entire week within this chapter of a day and so compresses their pedestrian tour (through Hooksett to Concord, New Hampshire, and on to Agiocochook) into little more than notes on their itinerary. These pages still include numerous moral and metaphysical reflections, as well as his interpolated "Persius" essay, but because of the larger structure he has imposed on his book, he necessarily minimizes the sense of time's passage. Thoreau compresses the bulk of their hike to Agiocochook into three relatively short paragraphs, disposing of the incidents of the week with the remark, "Suns rose and set and found us still on the dank forest path which meanders up the Pemigewasset" (313). The actual ascent of the mountain is given only a single paragraph:

> We at length crossed on prostrate trees over the Amonoosuck, and breathed the free air of the Unappropriated Land. Thus . . . we had traced up the river to which our native stream is a tributary, until from Merrimack it became the Pemigewasset that leaped by our side, and when we had passed its fountain-head, the Wild Amonoosuck, . . . guiding us toward its distant source among the mountains, and at length, without its guidance, we were enabled to reach the summit of AGIOCOCHOOK. (314)

There is no description of the mountain prospect, no account of a transforming mountaintop vision—no further comment at all. In a book where Thoreau has indulged at length in meditations on apparently trivial or incidental episodes, distilling from them any symbolic meaning they might yield, the deliberateness with which this episode is rendered insignificant is striking—especially in a chapter given over largely to contemplating the nature and meaning of frontiers. This passage is full of richly suggestive elements that Thoreau uncharacteristically chooses not to exploit: the act of crossing over into the "Unappropriated Land" (so evocative of "Ktaadn" 's thematic concerns) would seem to invite some explicit contrast with his earlier assertion of the passing of the frontier and perhaps a meditation on the nature of true wilderness; Thoreau seems to take some pains here to point out that their route traced the Merrimack back to its source, more or less, but whereas previously in A *Week* Thoreau had let hardly any opportunity pass to elaborate on the symbolic and metaphorical implications of the river, he again ignores the various metaphorical possibilities now offered (by contrast, his essays "Herald of Freedom," "Resistance to Civil Government," and that on Thomas Carlyle had all employed the figurative image of a stream's fountainhead to develop his themes).

Thoreau's decision not to describe Agiocochook at all is remarkable for reasons both internal and external to his text. Thoreau's contemporaries were surely surprised by his patent disregard for the fact that the White Mountains generally, and Mount Washington in particular, had, since the 1820s, become one of the most popular natural attractions of New England, drawing hordes of tourists annually, as well as almost all the notable painters and writers of the day.[6] This very popularity undoubtedly drew Thoreau there in 1839: when he first began his record of that excursion, he described it as "our White Mountain expedition" (J1: 124); he duly recorded the inns he stayed at (Thornton's Inn on the way there, Thomas Crawford's more famous inn on his return); he noted where "the scenery commences" and visited the region's most popular sites—the "Stone Flume," the "Basin," and the "Old Man of the Mountain" in Franconia Notch (J1: 136–37). Yet when he finally determined on a shape for *A Week*, he deleted virtually all of this; instead, he reached outside the events of the 1839 excursion entirely for his lengthy account of his ascent of Saddleback, making that episode one of the spiritual climaxes of the book. It is not, then, a matter of *A Week*'s being about rivers rather than mountains; instead, Thoreau seems to be deliberately frustrating our expectation of a narrative climax here:[7] *A Week* consciously refuses to grant a sense that there is any particular object to be reached in this journey, any point at which to *arrive*. And in doing so, Thoreau seems to make manifest what he had been hinting at all along—that *A Week* is in effect an antitravel travelogue, in which the transcendent imagination undermines the rationale for actual travel. Like all of Thoreau's excursions, *A Week* has an out-and-back structure; but in "A Walk to Wachusett" and "Ktaadn," for example, Thoreau made it clear from the outset that there was some specific point *out there* toward which he was journeying; and he made it clear that arriving at that point was the climax of the narrative. "Ktaadn," especially, demonstrates Thoreau's mastery of such a narrative structure when he chooses to employ it, and that narrative drives relentlessly toward its goal even while it lingers over the route. In *A Week*, on the other hand, Thoreau does not present the voyage either as an excursion to the mountain (though he and John regarded it as such in 1839) or as a quest for the river's source—though he might easily have done so; on the contrary, he announced in "Concord River" merely that he had "resolved to launch myself on its bosom, and float whither it would bear me" (*Week* 13). And when he does reach the terminus of his voyage, Thoreau not only fails to create a narrative climax here, he virtually shows us that he has chosen not to do so.

It is, in fact, difficult to say just what the terminus of the voyage is in A *Week*. At the beginning of "Thursday," Thoreau announces that they had reached "the limit of our voyage," by which he presumably means their *river* voyage, since he immediately proceeds to state that they went on by foot. But the brothers do not appear to travel by river at all on Thursday—they break camp and hike up the riverbank—which means that the terminus of the river voyage had actually been reached on Wednesday evening, though this went unremarked then, and indeed there was nothing remarkable about the end of that day's travel. Thursday morning's announcement that they had reached the limit of their voyage is thus rendered merely ironic, for it turns out that nothing in their experience is limited by that fact. If we go on to look for a terminal point to their pedestrian tour, we also find only meaningless or false landmarks. When the brothers pass through Concord, New Hampshire, Thoreau says, "This would have been the proper place to conclude our voyage, uniting Concord with Concord by these meandering rivers" (303), but they do not conclude it here—their river travel stops short of it and their walking tour goes beyond it. This brings us back to the summit of Agiocochook, which is of course the *actual* limit of their voyage, but Thoreau refuses to grant that any special value. He does not even say they actually arrived at the summit but uses the passive voice to say they "were enabled to reach" it. This is perhaps an overrefinement of the point, since we are clearly to infer that they did reach it, but Thoreau's sentence structure does render the *act* of reaching the summit insignificant and vague. Moreover, this paragraph does not end the chapter but occurs midway through "Thursday," the remainder of which proceeds with the return voyage. The effect, then, is to change the shape of the narrative from the linear to-and-from structure of "Ktaadn" to a continuous, circular voyage, in which they do not arrive anywhere until they arrive *home*. Thoreau had perhaps subtly implied this in his remarks on Concord, New Hampshire, for his excursion does unite Concord with Concord, but it has only been, as he wrote in *Walden*, "great-circle sailing" (*Walden* 320) at last. Having declared that the true frontiers are "wherever a man *fronts* a fact" (*Week* 304), Thoreau remains as good as his word and will not allow us to mistake them again for any place in the actual landscape. *Walden* of course carries the implications of this theme to their logical conclusion, being an excursion (still retaining an out-and-back structure) in which Thoreau does not *go* anywhere but builds himself a home.

The peculiarity of Thoreau's inclusion of the Saddleback episode, while minimizing Agiocochook, is thus a shrewd part of his antitravel strategy. Lawrence Buell has written that "it is saddening to think that the Greylock [Saddleback] experience is not a 'real' event in A *Week*, but an analogue from the 'past,'" and that "it is ironic that the moment of intensest ecstasy does not take place during the week itself."[8] This is indeed ironic, but the irony is deliberate, I believe, and is aimed at conventional travel narratives. If we take Thoreau's metaphysical reflections seriously, then the Saddleback episode is not "saddening" but the triumph of his philosophy, in which, as Whitman expressed it, "time avails not, space avails not." Monday night's epiphany made that point clear and so already undermined any further travel *toward* some point. Thoreau's ironic displacement of the mountain vision from *this* journey's ascent of a mountain in "Thursday" to a recollected ascent in "Tuesday" thus becomes his shrewd way of insisting on the legitimacy of his vision. The Saddleback episode is not "past" (even in the sense that Buell means it, acknowledging that it actually took place after the river trip) but is "really" *present*—in the same sense that John is "really" present to Thoreau ten years after their voyage, seven years after his death.

By the time Thoreau wrote A *Week*, he had pretty fully mastered the conventions of popular travel literature and had generally stayed within those bounds in "A Walk to Wachusett" and "Ktaadn." A *Week* was a far more ambitious work, however, and Thoreau loaded his narrative with an almost crushing burden of meditative digressions and essays. Aware of how much strain he was placing on the genre within which he was writing, Thoreau devoted much of A *Week* to reflexive commentaries on the true or proper aim of literature, on what to read and how to read. These were questions Thoreau would address in *Walden*'s chapter "Reading" as well, and though in A *Week* Thoreau's commentaries are more miscellaneous and distributed among digressions throughout the book, in both works his observations reflect upon Thoreau's own books and so function implicitly as guides, warnings, and instructions to his readers. In A *Week* especially, Thoreau's commentaries on literature seem to instruct the reader not to expect this to be a conventional travelogue.

In "Sunday," for example, Thoreau celebrates the fable and the myth as literary forms capable of capturing the universal aspects of nature, and in so doing he illuminates his own ambitions in A *Week*. Of mythology he writes, "To some extent, mythology is only the most ancient history and biography. So far from being false or fabulous in the common sense, it contains only enduring and essential truth, the I and you, the here and there, the now and then, being omitted" (*Week* 60). Unlike modern writers who "collect only the raw materials of biography and history," "the poet is he who can write some pure mythology today without the aid of posterity" (60). Thoreau had learned, through experiments like "The Service," the dangers of omitting entirely "the I and you, the here and there, the now and then," so he includes all of these in A *Week* but then goes on to dissolve them, as it were, revealing the "enduring and essential truth" they express but cannot contain.

These comments on fable and myth are subsequently picked up in the extended "nooning" meditation for that day on the subject of primitive literature. Here he embeds further self-reflexive comments that effectively instruct his readers on the proper way to read A *Week*: "Certainly, we do not need to be soothed and entertained always like children. He who resorts to the easy novel, because he is languid, does no better than if he took a nap. . . . Books . . . such as an idle man cannot read, and a timid one would not be entertained by, which even make us dangerous to existing institutions,—such call I good books" (96). Having just delivered a sermon attacking the church, Thoreau must have recognized that these remarks constituted an explanation and defense of his own licenses in A *Week* and his deliberate violation of the proprieties of a romantic travelogue. And as for his treatment of natural history in A *Week*, Thoreau writes,

> Books of natural history aim commonly to be hasty schedules, or inventories of God's property, by some clerk. They do not in the least teach the divine view of nature, but the popular view, or rather the popular method of studying nature. . . . A book should contain pure discoveries, glimpses of *terra firma*, though by ship-wrecked mariners, and not the art of navigation by those who have never been out of sight of land. (97–98)

Implicitly, Thoreau is letting his reader know why he is not writing a merely literal account of his journey—why he is not writing what Hawthorne had earlier recommended in order to approach the popular mind, "a book of simple observation of nature, somewhat in the vein of White's *History of Selborne*." His book is, instead, to be a book of *true* exploration and must therefore go beyond matter to spirit. Thus he added what amounted to an explanation of the true nature of this river voyage and a defense of his method in A *Week*. He had originally written this in his journal for 1840, as I have shown earlier, apparently in defense of the abstractions in "The Service," but it took on new meaning as an explanation of this book:

> We hear it complained of some works of genius, that they have fine thoughts but are irregular and have no flow. . . . We should consider that the flow of thought is more like a tidal wave than a prone river, and is the result of a celestial influence, not of any declivity in its channel. . . . The reader who expects to float down stream for the whole voyage, may well complain of nauseating swells and choppings of the sea when his frail shorecraft gets amidst the billows of the ocean stream, which flows as much to sun and moon as lesser streams to it. But if we would appreciate the flow that is in these books, we must expect to feel it rise from the page like an exhalation, and wash away our critical brains like burr millstones, flowing to higher levels above and behind ourselves. There is many a book which ripples on like a freshet, and flows as glibly as a mill stream sucking under a causeway. . . . But the most rapid trot is no flow after all,—and thither, reader, you and I, at least, will not follow. (102–3)

Thoreau recognized that because he presented his narrative as a travel excursion, his readers might not be prepared for the lengthy and abstract digressions, and they might indeed "complain of nauseating swells"; but he was writing something other than a merely popular narrative, and so he gave his reader due and pointed warning.

In his remarks on literature in "Monday," Thoreau is even more explicit about the self-reflexive nature of his comments: "This pledge of sanity cannot be spared in a book," he says, "that it sometimes pleasantly reflect upon itself" (147). With the reader thus alerted, he says, explicitly of the Vishnu Sarma, but implicitly of A *Week*, "The story and fabulous portion of this book winds loosely from sentence to sentence as so many oases in a desert, and is as indistinct as a camel's track between Mourzouk and Darfour. It is a comment upon the flow and freshet of modern books" (147). In this self-reflexive remark Thoreau acknowledges the slenderness of A *Week*'s own narrative thread, and his shift in metaphors—from camel tracks to freshets—both recalls the remarks on the "flow" of books inserted in "Sunday" and underscores the applicability of his remarks to his own river journey. "The reader leaps from sentence to sentence," he adds, "as from one stepping stone to another, while the stream of the story rushes past unregarded" (147). Turning to the Bhagavad-Gita, Thoreau summarizes his conception of great works: "It is the characteristic of great poems that they will yield of their sense in due proportion to the hasty and the deliberate reader. To the practical they will be common sense, and to the wise wisdom; as either the traveller may wet his lips, or an army may fill its water casks at a full stream" (147). The Concord and Merrimack rivers of Thoreau's book were full streams. For the hasty and practical reader, Thoreau offered an entertaining travel narrative through the New England landscape, presenting fine descriptions of the indigenous flora and fauna and providing informational accounts of the history and legends of the region; for the deliberate, wise reader he offered his profounder meditations on nature and the spirit. The problem with A *Week* was that it did not simply offer a text that yielded both superficial and profound meanings, both literal and symbolic: too often it merely juxtaposed the superficial with the profound, alternating between the literal and the abstract, and so giving his reader no real choice in how to use the book. The "nauseating swells" of this stream, as it rose to "higher levels," perhaps made it impossible for the hasty reader to "wet his lips" here without getting a larger dose than he bargained for or cared for.

Thoreau's description in "Tuesday" of Alexander Henry's account of fur trading in Canada "as a sort of classic among books of American travel" (218) provides another occasion for some commentary on his own aims in A *Week*, for he also aspires to write a classic book of American travel. Thoreau admires Henry's naturalness and lack of pretension, his good sense, and the fact that "he does not exaggerate, but writes for the information of his readers, for science and for history." These, in fact, are qualities not easily found in A *Week*, but Thoreau wrenches Henry's account into conformity with his own aims when he concludes, "What is most interesting and valuable in it, however, is not the materials for the history of Pontiac, or Braddock, or the North West, which it furnishes; not the *annals* of the country, but the natural facts, or *perennials*, which are ever without date. When out of history the truth shall be extracted, it will have shed its dates like withered leaves" (219). Invariably, Thoreau reminds his readers that he is trying to release the universal, the mythic, and the eternal from the particular, the historical, and the temporal phenomena he observes on his excursion.

Thoreau's self-revelatory reflections on poetry and genius in "Friday" again manifest a striking tension between his obvious efforts to create a coherent and integrated narrative for the sake of "immediate practical and popular influence" and his simultaneous defense of great art's superiority to such concerns. Thus he warns the genius against "succumb[ing] and conform[ing] to the ways of the world. Genius is the worst of lumber, if the poet would float upon the breeze of popularity" (339–40). In this pastiche of epigrammatic assertions on genius, the constant note is his representation of the poet as heroically resisting the temptation to seek immediate popular influence and remaining faithful to his inspiration. These are old ideas for Thoreau, and his mosaic sometimes results in contradictions: for example, he writes here that "great prose, of equal elevation, commands our respect more than great verse, since it implies a more permanent and level height," but in "Sunday" he had included his assertion that "the loftiest written wisdom is either rhymed, or in some way musically measured,—is, in form as well as substance, poetry" (91). Although individual remarks must thus be regarded cautiously, the overall effect of this and similar digressions is to create a kind of apologia for A *Week* itself, implying that while Thoreau is willing to accommodate his readers to make this book fluent, they must in turn accommodate him and respect the integrity of his poetic inspiration, which will not fall readily into popular and conventional literary forms. "The breath with which the poet utters his verse must be that by which he lives," Thoreau proclaims (342).

Later that day, when the brothers pass through the locks from the Merrimack back to the Concord, their encounter with the locksman, a "lover of higher mathematics," becomes the occasion for a digression on the relation of mathematics and science to his aesthetic and moral vision. Asserting that most men are unable to perceive the moral aspect of scientific facts or the scientific aspect of moral facts, he adds, "Aristotle defined art to be . . . *the principle of the work without the wood*; but most men prefer to have some of the wood along with the principle; they demand that the truth be clothed in flesh and blood and the warm colors of life. They prefer the partial statement because it fits and measures them and their commodities best" (361–62). Thoreau's citation of Aristotle's idealistic definition of art here gains added resonance when we discern its relation to two other passages in A *Week*. Thoreau first referred to this definition at the beginning of "Saturday," when he described the construction of their boat: they had looked to fish and birds for the principle of their amphibious craft, but they had only "partially obeyed" these hints. "However," Thoreau writes, "as art is all of a ship but the wood, and yet the wood alone will rudely serve the purpose of a ship, so our boat being of wood, gladly availed itself of the old law that the heavier shall float the lighter, and though a dull water fowl, proved a sufficient buoy for our purpose" (16). Thoreau's book itself is analogous to the boat as Thoreau's *craft*, the *vehicle* of his thoughts; and though both book and boat are only dull and imperfect manifestations of the *ideas* informing them, they seem sufficient to his purpose, and Thoreau launches both crafts with some optimism. However, as Thoreau draws toward the conclusion of his parallel excursions—the actual river voyage and his interior exploration—he seems to be increasingly concerned about the sufficiency of his literary craft, at least. Thus, he had observed earlier this day that "genius is the worst of lumber, if the poet would float upon the breeze of popularity," for genius, with its eye fixed upon the ideal, is impatient with the merely actual facts of experience (and language) that are nevertheless the chief attraction to the popular mind. Now Thoreau returns again to Aristotle's definition to clarify further his sense of his own work and his audience. This passage is particularly interesting because at first the preference of "most men" for "the wood" as well as the "principle" seems reasonable and appropriate, adding "the warm colors of life"; but their preference is then shown to be *at the expense of the principle*, and the wood alone—which is but an imperfect manifestation of the ideal, a "partial statement" only—becomes an obstacle to the principle rather than its vehicle. Thoreau seems to anticipate readers who regard his work merely as "wood," providing information and entertainment only, and who regard him as merely a writer and not as a prophet. There is an element of resentment and defensiveness here, as if Thoreau feared his book would be misread; but it is also a kind of final instruction to his readers and thus suggests that he was still hopeful of success—hopeful that his readers might be shown the proper way to read his book. Thoreau provides the groundwork of concrete and literal observation because he recognizes the value of a fact, and its value is that it may flower into a truth, not merely in its usefulness as commodity. Thus he goes on to explain,

> My friends mistake when they communicate facts to me with so much pains. Their presence, even their exaggerations and loose statements, are equally good facts for me. I have no respect for facts even except when I would use them, and

> for the most part I am independent of those which I hear, and can afford to be inaccurate, or, in other words, to substitute more present and pressing facts in their place.
>
> The poet uses the results of science and philosophy, and generalizes their widest deductions. (363)

In "Monday" Thoreau had said of great poems that "to the practical they will be common sense, and to the wise wisdom," and he seemed to be offering his own book, therefore, to both the hasty and the deliberate reader. Now at the end of his book, however, Thoreau seems more irritable, more anxious that he will be misunderstood. He chides the reader who cannot distinguish between "common" and "uncommon" sense:

> What is called common sense is excellent in its department, and as invaluable as the virtue of conformity in the army and navy,—for there must be subordination,—but uncommon sense, that sense which is common only to the wisest, is as much more excellent as it is rare. Some aspire to excellence in the subordinate department, and may God speed them. (387)

Though overtly generous here, Thoreau is clearly ironic in his characterization of those who perfect only the subordinate sense, and in wishing them "God speed" he seems to be dismissing those readers who will not understand his aims in A *Week*.

Except for a brief description of their landing again at Concord, A *Week* concludes with a meditation on silence. This digression was drawn from a composition recorded in his journal for December 1838, and there is thus a nice irony in his completing the circuit in this mosaic excursion with one of his earliest compositions. In the context of A *Week*, the significance of this meditation is double-edged. His overt tone is one of confidence that he has brought off his task as prophet: silence is the fruit of his exploration, the wisdom of "uncommon sense." Just as matter is but the manifestation of spirit in time and place, so sound is but the temporal manifestation of the eternal harmony of the universe. "Silence is audible to all men, at all times, and in all places. She is when we hear inwardly, sound when we hear outwardly. Creation has not displaced her, but is her visible frame-work and foil. All sounds are her servants and purveyors, proclaiming not only that their mistress is, but is a rare mistress, and earnestly to be sought after" (391).

If Thoreau has succeeded in bringing the reader to his "uncommon senses" and to "hear inwardly," the silence at the end is a triumphant one, the point to which he had been bringing his reader all along. Thus Thoreau ends by reminding the reader that his discourse itself, like the natural facts he has been describing, is not an end but a means, a "visible frame-work." "A good book," he explains, "is the plectrum with which our else silent lyres are struck. We not unfrequently refer the interest which belongs to our own unwritten sequel, to the written and comparatively lifeless body of the work. Of all books this sequel is the most indispensable part" (392–93). Significantly, Thoreau focuses here not on the creation of the book but on its effect on the lives of readers—the indispensable sequel is the silent resonance of his words in their lives. Like the autumn in which summer thoughts are allowed to subside and ripen, this silence represents the true fruits of his labor, and he ends his book by turning to the reader to take up the burden; that is, he seems to be saying, like Whitman at the end of "Song of Myself," "I stop somewhere waiting for you."

Nevertheless, this emphasis on the reader also exposes Thoreau's vulnerability. The overt tone of confidence is tempered: the seams of the narrative have sometimes opened up to reveal Thoreau's suspicion that the prophet will fail in the marketplace, that his readers will not read him rightly. As in the "Natural History," silence is an emblem of universal wholeness that is contrasted to the necessarily partial "din" of discourse. But the prophet, who might prefer to "speak" through the cosmic silences of the spirit, is forced to use the din of discourse for a public that can only hear audible words. Thus there is a poignancy to the final meditation on silence here that suggests, if not the anticipation of failure, at least the recognition that his voice is imperfect, inadequate to the task. "It were vain for me to endeavor to interpret the Silence. She cannot be done in English" (*Week* 393). His silence is, then, at least for the moment, also the resignation of his prophetic role. "Nevertheless," he concludes, "we will go on, like those Chinese cliff swallows, feathering our nests with froth, which may one day be bread of life to such as dwell by the seashore" (393). And so he promises that he will resume the prophet's mantle.

. . .

A *Week* is a strange and ambitious book, both exhilarating and irritating in its efforts to forge a link between the visions of a prophet and the polite narrative of a genteel traveler. Thoreau knew, or thought he knew, the reading public well enough to realize that they would not attend to his transcendental vision alone. As he acknowledged in a coda to his attack on Christianity in "Sunday," "If I should ask the minister of Middlesex to let me speak in his pulpit on a Sunday he would object, because I do not pray as he does, or because I am not ordained" (76). Though Thoreau asks, "What under the sun are these things?" he knows that he had always lacked the public sanction to speak as a prophet, and so he availed himself of a Sunday morning, under the sun on the Concord River, to deliver his sermons in the guise of a travelogue.

It is perhaps not surprising that the public would reject A *Week*, finding, as Hawthorne had anticipated in his 1845 letter to Evert Duyckinck, that Thoreau burdened his narrative with too much metaphysics to attract a popular audience. But the reasons for A *Week*'s failure are somewhat more complex than this, for mediating between the writer and his potential audience is the cumbersome and often obscure machinery of the marketplace. Thoreau's friends generally admired the book. Alcott optimistically and naively predicted, "It seems likely to become a popular book with our people here, winning at once the reader's fancy and his heart, inspiring a natural piety for nature and natural things, as surprising as it is refreshing."[9] Thoreau's friend H.G.O. Blake also expressed his "hearty appreciation" of the book (Corr 251), and Thomas Wentworth Higginson, who eventually became one of Thoreau's most influential champions, was another early admirer of A *Week*.[10]

Thoreau's book won at least some admiration from more distant quarters as well. With Emerson's help, Thoreau had sent out seventy-five copies of A *Week* to potential reviewers and notable literary figures in England and America. The most enthusiastic response came in a letter to Thoreau from James Anthony Froude, the English historian and Carlyle's biographer. "When I think of what you are," Froude wrote, "—of what you have *done* as well as of what you have written, I have a right to tell you that there is no man living upon this earth at present, whose friendship or whose notice I value more than yours" (Corr 248).[11]

Froude's extraordinarily enthusiastic response must have been gratifying, but personal reactions would have little impact on actual sales, and the book first needed to be publicized so that it would reach the attention of the general public not privileged to receive review copies and personal notes of recommendation. The energetic distribution of copies by Thoreau and Emerson helped somewhat to counteract Munroe & Company's lack of commitment—though this was now of course at Thoreau's expense—and A *Week* actually received fairly adequate attention from reviewers. Most reviewers found the book worthy of at least some praise, and while many objected to Thoreau's attacks on Christianity and his pantheism, few were entirely hostile, and some were quite clearly enthusiastic about it.

The first notice of the book, that in the *New York Evening Post* for June 8, 1849, was brief, but generous and tolerant of its "German"—i.e., transcendentalist—inclinations:

> It is a record of wanderings and meditations on the banks of the two streams of eastern Massachusetts, which, although not rich in the elements of picturesque scenery, have yet their gentler and quieter beauties. The author is apparently a man of a contemplative turn of mind, deeply imbued with German reading, so much so as to have given his reflections a German cast, but not unversed in other literature. He conducts his readers through a maze of reflections of a

> most desultory nature, often as agreeable as they are quaint, and sometimes running into a certain mysticism through which we do not always find it so easy to follow him. Sometimes he makes excursions to Greece, giving us fragments of the old Greek poets, in prose translations, the best, by the way, in our opinion; and sometimes his own thoughts involuntarily express themselves in verse.[12]

More prominent was the review that appeared in the *New York Tribune* on June 13, 1849. Though largely taken up by extracts, it covered nearly two full columns on the front page—the kind of notice generally accorded only the most popular writers by the *Tribune*. The reviewer found it an admirable and original book and, significantly, was apparently undisturbed by its long digressions; but he took Thoreau harshly to task for his criticism of Christianity:

> A really new book—a fresh and original, thoughtful work—is sadly rare in this age of omniferous publication. Mr. Thoreau's, if not entirely this, is very near it. Its observations of Nature are as genial as Nature herself. . . . His reflections are always striking, often profoundly truthful, and his scholastic treasures, though a little too ostentatiously displayed, are such as the best instructed reader will enjoy and thank him for. His philosophy, which is the Pantheistic egotism vaguely characterized as Transcendental, does *not* delight us. It seems secondhand, imitative, often exaggerated—a bad specimen of a dubious and dangerous school.

After further charging Thoreau with a "misplaced Pantheistic attack on the Christian Faith," which he finds "revolting alike to good sense and good taste," the reviewer ends by balancing "our admiration of his book and our reprehension of its Pantheism" and offers to let Thoreau reply to the charge in the pages of the *Tribune*.[13]

Thoreau might have taken advantage of the offer to turn controversy into publicity, but he did not respond. His book, he felt, spoke for itself, and he would not descend to engage in debate with those who could not forgo a narrow creed for the sake of a larger faith. Nevertheless, the controversy had begun, without his assistance, and another newspaper review replied to the *Tribune*'s charges with a warmly sympathetic defense of *A Week*. The reviewer begins by employing a strategy Greeley had taken earlier in advertising Thoreau's Walden lectures—offering Thoreau's exploration of local regions as a "*prophylactic* of the California fever." And far from being disturbed by the book's digressiveness, the reviewer writes, "It is worth while to read it, if only to see how rich the lives of some men may be. The grain of gold has been drawn out into its miles of shining wire, and yet has not been attenuated." Then, comparing *A Week* to another popular phenomenon, the reviewer says, "With more fidelity and artistic skill than Champney or Banvard, Mr. Thoreau paints his river panorama, and in the pauses of his unrolling scrolls, he will tell you tales of his former wanderings, and unfold the pages of his genius and graceful criticisms." Banvard's panorama of the Mississippi had drawn record crowds, attracted widespread attention, and earned immense amounts of money in its New England tour that year, so the reviewer's comparison not only calls attention to the similar subject matter and form of Thoreau's excursion but also implies its potential to attract a popular audience. Only after lavishing this praise upon Thoreau's book does the reviewer take up the *Tribune*'s criticism of its pantheism. While he concedes that there is "something . . . objectionable in the religious philosophy of the book," he does not find this a serious impediment. First, he argues, "the peculiar speculations of the author stand by themselves. They may be absolutely skipped." "Moreover," he adds, "if read never so carefully, we cannot conceive of their doing harm. . . . We should no more fear the 'dangerous tendencies of this book' to propagate Pantheism than that the image of the Goddess of Liberty on our coin, would tend to revive her Pagan worship."[14]

Notice of *A Week* appeared in the *Liberator* on June 15. Thoreau was presumably on good terms with the journal, having written an enthusiastic report of Wendell Phillips's antislavery speech at the Concord Lyceum in 1845 for the *Liberator*; and Thoreau's whole family was active in the antislavery movement (a long obituary tribute to his sister Helen appeared in the *Liberator* the following week). The reviewer was thus favorably disposed. Significantly, however, the Thoreau this reviewer has most obviously in mind is the Thoreau of the Walden experiment. He implies, in fact, that Thoreau is still at the pond—probably a consequence of Thoreau's Walden lectures of the season just past, and demonstrating again that these lectures had created a potential market for the book Thoreau chose not to publish at this time. After confessing to a more hurried reading of *A Week* than desirable, the reviewer writes:

> For its amiable author, we have much respect. His mode of life is *sui generis*—all alone by himself in the woods of Concord, an enthusiastic child and lover of Nature, in spirit an occupant of an ideal world, and with an eye of genius "in a fine-phrenzy rolling"—and this production of his is equally peculiar. We have spent many years "on the Merrimack River," our dear, native stream; but this was "long, long ago." We shall accept this invitation of Mr. Thoreau to pass "a week" with him on the same river, and, making that the starting-point from which to ascend to "cloud-land," we shall accompany him on the wings of imagination as far as we can sustain such a flight. Of our entertainment and success, we may report hereafter.
>
> The numerous admirers of Carlyle and Emerson will read this book with a relish; for Mr. T. writes in their vein, and to some extent in their dialect, and is

> a match for them in felicitous conceits and amusing quaintnesses; yet he is not a servile imitator—only an admirer, by affinity and kindred one of a trinity, having his own sphere in which to move, and his own mission to consummate.[15]

The review concludes with an extract, taken from Thoreau's reflections at the Dunstable graveyard. Favorable reviews also appeared in the July number of *Holden's Dollar Magazine* and in the *New Hampshire Patriot*, of Concord, New Hampshire, on July 26. The *Dollar Magazine* did not give it a full-scale review, but under the heading of "Deferred Books" it gave A *Week* a highly laudatory paragraph, calling it "a rare work in American literature," and also defusing the nagging charges that Thoreau was but a second-rate imitator of Emerson by saying that, for all their similarities of philosophy and love of nature, they are quite unlike in "style and habits of thought." "We advise our readers to procure [A *Week*]," the paragraph concludes; "it is full of fine thoughts and pleasant descriptions of Nature."[16] The *New Hampshire Patriot* was also indifferent to the book's pantheism, saying only that while they do not endorse it, they "will let it stand or fall by itself." Perhaps favorably biased by the book's treatment of the local environs, the *Patriot* reviewer called it "a remarkable volume and its author a remarkable man." He, too, found the digressions satisfying, describing Thoreau as alternately turning "his mental eye inward . . . to read the mysterious page of his own soul" and then "looking upon objects around which meet his senses, he reads lessons of wisdom. The thread of his narrative is very simple, but upon it he has strung pearls"; "on closing the book we find ourselves in love with the author, satisfied with ourselves and at peace with the world."[17]

The *North American Review* for July listed A *Week* under "New Publications Received" but never reviewed it.[18] In August, the *Knickerbocker Magazine*'s "Editor's Table" blithely reported,

> We propose, by-and-by, to follow Mr. Henry D. Thoreau down the Merrimack, even from Squam, Newfound Lake, Winnepisiogee, White-Mountains, Smith's-and-Baker's, Mad Rivers, Nashua, Souhegan, Pitcataquoag, Suncook, Soncook, and Contookook; but we haven't leisure for the jaunt just now. Meantime, let us commend "A *Week on the Concord and Merrimack Rivers*," for which we are indebted to the publishers, Mssrs. James Monroe [*sic*] and Company, to the attention of our readers.[19]

It is noteworthy that this editor assumed such an excursion would naturally treat the most popular sights in the region—the White Mountains and Lake Winnipesaukee, especially. Perhaps disappointed in the matter, perhaps never finding enough leisure to read it, the editor in any case never reviewed A *Week* in the magazine.

The review in *Godey's Lady's Book* was potentially valuable in terms of the large audience the magazine reached, but its brief notice of A *Week* did not appear until September, and then the editor thought it was the work of Whittier. Still, *Godey's* praised "this clever and interesting work," describing it as "just the book to read in the idleness of summer, when wishing to enjoy the pleasures of journeying, without the inconvenience which the actual packing up and going off in hot steamboats and dusty cars occasion."[20] Though, given this judgment, it is unlikely that the reviewer read the book very carefully, the review is interesting in that it reveals exactly the public's expectations of a genteel travel narrative and suggests that Thoreau indeed succeeded in giving his book, on the surface at least, a recognizable form which appealed to the popular mind.

Evert Duyckinck, who had been offered the book in 1847, presented a more thorough critical reading in his two-page review of *A Week* in the *Literary World* for September 22, 1849 (Duyckinck had returned to the editorship of the magazine in 1848, and the *Literary World* was still looked to for high-quality literary criticism). He praised Thoreau as both an observer of nature and a scholar, and said, "We have read his book backwards, if he is not kind and humane." Having allowed Thoreau this much, however, he went on to complain that

> when this writer, so just, observant, and considerate, approaches what civilized men are accustomed to hold the most sacred of all, he can express himself in a flippant style which he would disdain to employ towards a muscle [*sic*] or a tadpole. . . . We are not so rash or uninformed in the ways of the world as to presume to give counsel to a transcendentalist, so we offer no advice; but we may remark as a curious matter of speculation to be solved in the future—the probability or improbability of Mr. Thoreau's ever approaching nearer to the common sense or common wisdom of mankind.[21]

Duyckinck was aware of the radical implications of Thoreau's book but refused to accept what amounted to Thoreau's prophetic message—that the partial and institutional views which "civilized men are accustomed to hold the most sacred of all" were indeed less sacred than the intimations of eternal laws manifest in "a muscle or a tadpole." He seems particularly offended by Thoreau's tone, for the orthodox institutions of civilization were not a subject to be treated in a "flippant style"; Duyckinck's jibe at Thoreau's inability to approach "common sense" is his indignant rebuttal to Thoreau's own contemptuous treatment of those who "aspire to excellence in [this] subordinate department" and his seemingly perverse privileging of the "uncommon sense." Yet the overall tenor of Duyckinck's perceptive review is favorable, and it is a testament to Thoreau's success that Duyckinck could find so much to praise in a book whose central thesis he rejected. In fact, when Duyckinck wrote his own "Ascent of Mount Saddleback," printed in the *Literary World* in 1851, he paid more gracious, if bemused, tribute to Thoreau's book:

> Mr. Thoreau in his Week on the Concord and Merrimack Rivers, a book filled with minute and delicate observations of nature, describes his experiences on this mountain. He ascended it alone by a path of his own; with characteristic love of nature drank the moisture from the horse tracks in the pathway; slept on the ground with his head to the fire, and recommends a board for a covering with a stone on the top of it to increase its warmth. He saw in the morning a vast sea of mist touching the foot of the Observatory, from whence arose islands, where stretched promontories and other phenomena of cloud land. "It was a favor," says he, "for which to be forever silent to be shown this vision." We, too, had our vision.[22]

A few other, brief reviews continued to appear in the American press. The *Universalist Quarterly* found some things to admire but roundly condemned the book's "lack of healthy moral discrimination, with contempt for the things commonly esteemed holy, with reflections which must shock every pious Christian."[23] The *Pictorial National Library* briefly described the excursion in neutral terms but noted that Thoreau's "primitive habits of living" had "attracted some attention in the vicinity of Concord," again suggesting some familiarity with Thoreau's Walden lectures.[24] By late October 1849, a few reviews began to appear in the English press as well. Thoreau and Emerson had sent complimentary copies to some of their English acquaintances, and Munroe listed John Chapman, Ltd., as their English distributor—though they could not actually have sent more than a few copies. The most favorable English review was that by Sophia Dobson Collett in London's *People's Review,* in which she had also reviewed Thoreau's "Resistance to Civil Government." Regarding A *Week,* she praises his simultaneous attentiveness to detail and his ability to grasp "the peculiar spirit of a landscape." "But Mr. Thoreau has a gift beyond this," she adds. "Every object seen is, with him, an element in a higher vision. The infinity of meaning that dwells in everything existent, is visible to him. . . . And these thoughts fall from him not as moral lessons, tacked on, fringe-like, but as the natural hints which ever arise in those souls to whom nothing is profane. . . . To such souls, Life and Thought continually inter-act." Undisturbed by the book's digressions, she in fact calls them an "additional element of interest . . . essays not unworthy to stand beside those of Emerson himself." She singles out for particular praise those on "Eastern Literature, on Christianity, on Poetry, and especially the exquisite Essay of Friendship, [which] would of themselves make the book valuable."[25]

The more influential *Westminster Review* offered more tempered praise in its number for January 1850 but called A *Week* an "exceedingly pleasant narrative" and the author "one whom we could gladly journey with, amid the scenery described in the volume." Though the reviewer demurs at the "rather long-winded disquisitions upon religion, literature, and other matters—sometimes naturally arising from the incidents of the voyage, sometimes lugged in apparently without rhyme or reason," he points out that such matter "may be skipped by those who don't like it, while such as prefer this kind of reading to the narrative portions, may revel in it to their heart's content; and so may each class of readers find something to suit them in these pages."[26] Apparently the reviewer accepted Thoreau's definition of great poetry.

Reviews in the *London Athenaeum* and the *Spectator* were considerably less favorable and did not recommend the book. The *Athenaeum* charged that Thoreau was not really interested in the rivers and that the book would "be better described as a series of essays on love, poetry, religion—and so on." Moreover, the reviewer called its matter poor and its manner "the worst offshoots of Carlyle and Emerson: all Mr. Thoreau's best things are spoilt in the utterance." He concedes that Thoreau has the makings of an original thinker and that "he has things to say which might command a larger audience. But imitations of an imitation! The world is too old and the prophets are too many for such things to have a chance of a public hearing in these days."[27] The *Spectator* said only that the book was "rather flat and not of a kind to interest."[28] Since copies of *A Week* were so rare in England, however, the quality of the reviews there was more or less irrelevant to *A Week*'s immediate prospects. This was in fact only slightly less true back home.

Thoreau's friends were slow in giving a public evaluation of the book. On June 1, immediately after *A Week* was published, Theodore Parker invited Emerson to review it for the *Massachusetts Quarterly Review* at the end of the month, but Emerson replied on June 11,

> I am not the man to write the Notice of Thoreau's book. I am of the same clan & parish. You must give it to a good foreigner. E. P. Whipple has good literary insulation and is a superior critic. Will he not try his hand on this? If not he, will not Starr King? If not the one or the other, why not send it to the New Yorkers, to Henry James, Parke Godwin, or C. Dana? The book has rare claims & we must have an American claim & ensign marked on it before it goes abroad for English opinions.
>
> I see from your note that you have not opened it, but you must & will. (EmL 4: 151)

Emerson's refusal to write the review is somewhat surprising, for he had encouraged Thoreau to publish the book at his own risk and knew the importance of getting it noticed. There is some validity in his plea that he was "of the same clan & parish" and that it should therefore be reviewed by "a good foreigner," but Emerson had not hesitated earlier to write a review of Channing's poems, and surely he recognized that if the book needed a favorable American review, no one was better suited to write it than himself. Parker's offer to Emerson was in fact a generous one, for Emerson was fully aware of Parker's frequently expressed scorn for what he regarded as Emerson's entourage of poor imitators—Thoreau, Channing, and Alcott. To turn down the opportunity was to commit the book knowingly into the hands of, if not the enemy, at least one who was biased against Thoreau.

Parker actually found A *Week* to be a valuable book, and it gave him a new respect for Thoreau, but he still regarded him essentially as an imitator of Emerson. On July 15, Parker replied to Emerson:

> I had read the greater part of Thoreau's Book when I wrote you. It is full of beautiful things, some of them are evidently remembered from you, some of them I only suspect of being yours from their family likeness; but some are undoubtedly original. I think the book is to be judged by its original part, & not by its imitations, the descriptions of natural objects are certainly uncommonly fine, there is a good deal of sauciness, & a good deal of affectation in the book, the latter seems to me to come from his trying to be R. W. Emerson, & not being contented with his own mother's son. Still I think the book has great merits. It surpasses my expectations in some particulars, & makes me like the man better than I did before, & I have long liked him very well. I have written to ask Lowell to write a notice of it—if he will not—I like Dana the best of those you name. (EmL 4: 151)

The prospect of assigning the review to Lowell should perhaps have been sufficient cause for alarm, for Lowell had amply demonstrated in A *Fable for Critics* (1848) that he shared Parker's condescending view of Thoreau and Channing as facile imitators of Emerson. Though it must have been clear that the *Massachusetts Quarterly*'s review of A *Week* would not be the wholehearted seal of approval Emerson had hoped for, he remained apart from the matter. Moreover, Lowell was slow in writing the review. It did not appear in the *Massachusetts Quarterly* until the December number, and this in itself was damaging—Thoreau had recognized as early as September that the book would not sell. Lowell's lengthy review actually turned out to be the most positive commentary he ever wrote on Thoreau, though he had his reservations. It is a rather self-indulgent composition—Thoreau and his book are not mentioned until the fourth page of the eleven-page review. But the point of his prologue is to lament the passing away of the poetic sensibility among travelers, who are now mere fact finders, and so he welcomes Thoreau, whom he describes as "both a wise man and a poet."[29] Lowell is entirely pleased with Thoreau the nature writer, and especially with his treatment of fish and fishing. "We know nothing more thoroughly charming than his description of twilight at the river's bottom," he says, and he quotes from such passages at length. Not surprisingly, these are the passages of A *Week* most similar to Lowell's own style in his familiar essays and nature sketches, and Lowell knows a master when he sees one (Thomas Wentworth Higginson later recorded that when Lowell heard Thoreau compared to Izaak Walton, he replied, "There is room for three or four Waltons in Thoreau").[30]

Lowell was fully aware of the transcendentalist aesthetic that privileged private discourse—what Emerson had called "the literature of the portfolio" in his defense of Channing's poetry—but there is considerable irony in his characterization of Thoreau's book as a product of this aesthetic:

> The great charm of Mr. Thoreau's book seems to be, that its being a book at all is a happy fortuity. The door of the portfolio-cage has been left open, and the thoughts have flown out of themselves. The paper and types are only accidents. The page is confidential like a diary. . . . It has been written with no uncomfortable sense of a public looking over the shoulder.

Less ambiguous, however, is Lowell's judgment of the interpolated digressions.

> We come upon them like snags, jolting us headforemost out of our places as we are rowing placidly up stream or drifting down. . . . We could forgive them all, especially that on Books, and that on Friendship. . . . we could welcome them all, were they put by themselves at the end of the book. But as it is, they are out of proportion and out of place, and mar our Merrimacking dreadfully. We were bid to a river-party, not to be preached at.

Of all the reviewers of *A Week*, Lowell was the most critical of the digressions as irrelevant. Thoreau had intended to engage the general reader by embedding his philosophical and critical discourses in a romantic narrative, but Lowell felt misled. Himself an extremely popular writer of familiar essays and travel sketches, Lowell upheld what Lawrence Buell calls the "tacit convention of levity" in the popular romantic excursions[31]—a convention that Thoreau clearly violated. Thus, while Duyckinck had condemned Thoreau for the levity with which he treated "serious" topics, Lowell condemned him for treating serious topics at all. Thoreau regarded the excursion as the appropriate structure for his discourse, for it was itself symbolic of the kind of spiritual exploration that interested him; he thus attempted to raise the genre of travel narrative to a higher level. Lowell felt, however, that by prophesying, Thoreau was violating rather than exploring the possibilities of the genre's conventions. Certainly there were grounds for Lowell's complaint, but it is significant that he did not object to Thoreau's preaching per se, but to his preaching in the context of what he assumed to be an idyllic and light travel narrative. That is, his criticism was an aesthetic one and had its basis in Lowell's sense of the conventions of the romantic excursion.

Since most of the other reviewers seemed relatively undisturbed by the miscellaneous and philosophical digressions in *A Week*, it would seem that Lowell's criticism was based less on established conventions than on his own attempts to formalize the conventions of an inherently miscellaneous genre that was currently undergoing numerous transitions under the influence of romanticism. Lowell shared the view of the mainstream essayists and critics that writing should above all entertain—his own review exemplified this principle; and this put him in direct opposition to Thoreau, who regarded humor as transient, Scripture as enduring (though A *Week* does display ample wit and humor in places). Scornful of what he considered to be the pretentiousness and affectation of transcendental seriousness, Lowell reacted: "'Give me a sentence,' prays Mr. Thoreau bravely, 'which no intelligence can understand!'—and we think that the kind gods have nodded." Yet Lowell also conceded, "But it seems ungrateful to find fault with a book which has given us so much pleasure."

The reviews of A *Week* were on the whole, then, favorable. Various reservations were expressed, but there was no clear consensus on these, and reviewers recognized in Thoreau a distinct and original talent. Yet the book was a resounding and absolute failure in terms of sales, and it is inadequate to lay the blame entirely on the public's inability to appreciate it. Thoreau had indeed made heavy demands on his readers and offended some of them with his unorthodoxy—that the book did not achieve a substantial degree of popularity is hardly surprising; but Thoreau was writing within the broad boundaries of a popular genre,[32] and the reviews certainly suggest a far more favorable and tolerant response than is reflected by actual sales.

It is, I think, safe to assume that had Munroe & Co.—or any other publisher—published A *Week* at its own expense, more copies would have been sold. In January of 1851, Alcott recorded in his journal, "I went with [Thoreau] to his publisher, Munroe & Co., and learned that only about two hundred of an edition of a thousand copies were sold."[33] Seventy-five copies had been given away by Thoreau, but with no stake in distributing copies themselves, Munroe had made the book virtually inaccessible to the public unless they applied for it directly. For a book like A *Week* such circumstances made failure virtually inevitable. Alcott, the quixotic optimist, had added to his journal entry, "But author and book can well afford to wait"; Thoreau, however, had already given up any hope of paying for publication costs through sales, and Alcott noted that he had taken up surveying to cover his debt.

One of the first repercussions of the book's failure was the estrangement of Thoreau and Emerson. In September of 1849, Thoreau wrote in his journal, "I had a friend, I wrote a book, I asked my friend's criticism, I never got but praise for what was good in it—my friend became estranged from me and then I got blame for all that was bad,—& so I got at last the criticism which I wanted" (J3: 26).

Though the two remained close to each other in many respects, a new reserve entered their relationship that was never entirely dispelled. Yet Thoreau never really dismissed A *Week* as "bad," nor did he abandon hopes for its ultimate success. By June of 1851 he was detached enough from the initial publication of the book to record in his journal, "I thought that one peculiarity of my 'Week' was its *hypaethral* character—to use an epithet applied to those Egyptian temples which are open to the heavens above, *under the ether*" (J3: 279).[34]

Thoreau came to recognize that Munroe & Co. had not *published* his book; they had merely *printed* it. On October 27, 1853, he recorded in his journal:

> For a year or two past, my *publisher*, falsely so called, has been writing from time to time to ask what disposition should be made of the copies of "A Week on the Concord and Merrimack Rivers" still on hand, and at last suggesting that he had use for the room they occupied in his cellar. So I had them all sent to me here, and they have arrived to-day by express, filling the man's wagon,—706 copies out of an edition of 1000 which I bought of Munroe four years ago and have been ever since paying for, and have not quite paid for yet. The wares are sent to me at last, and I have an opportunity to examine my purchase. They are something more substantial than fame, as my back knows, which has borne them up two flights of stairs to a place similiar to that to which they trace their origin. Of the remaining two hundred and ninety and odd, seventy-five were given away, the rest sold. I have now a library of nearly nine hundred volumes, over seven hundred of which I wrote myself. (JV: 459)

Thoreau's ability to find humor in the situation is impressive. In a characteristic effort to convert his failure into success, he added, "Indeed, I believe that this result is more inspiring and better for me than if a thousand had bought my wares. It affects my privacy less and leaves me freer" (JV: 460). But it did not leave him freer, and it was not until a month later, on November 28, 1853, that Thoreau could record in his journal that he had finally paid off his debt to Munroe at a total cost of $290 (JV: 521). Nor was Thoreau truly satisfied with the privacy he had bought, since it was achieved at the expense of his immediate hopes for making his mark in the wider literary arena. Though the failure of A *Week* had forced him to postpone the publication of *Walden* for five years and made him increasingly suspicious of publishers, Thoreau did not end his efforts to make his writings public. Not until the astute and aggressive firm of Ticknor & Fields published *Walden* at their own expense, however, in 1854, did Thoreau find a publisher with whom he was satisfied.

Between 1853 and the time of his death, then, Thoreau was forced to become his own agent for A *Week*, selling copies in response to occasional requests from a growing number of admirers. As Thoreau explained to one such admirer, Calvin Greene, in a letter of January 18, 1856, "The 'Week' had so poor a publisher that it is quite uncertain whether you will find it in any shop. I am not sure but authors must turn booksellers themselves. The price is $1.25. If you care enough for it to send me that sum by mail (stamps will do for change) I will forward you the copy by the same conveyance" (Corr 406).[35]

Thoreau had at last won literary independence of a sort with his book, but it had been at a tremendous price. If Thoreau's early career was marked by a series of failures—with Fuller on the *Dial*, with the magazines in New York, and with his auditors in the lyceum—the failure of *A Week* was the most severe of all. It was Thoreau's most ambitious work, in many respects an even more ambitious work than *Walden*. Thoreau had, to a considerable extent, staked his career on his first book, and when it failed, his sense of his professional life changed. Yet each of his failures had ironically brought him a greater understanding of his audience—about how to reach them and about the extent to which he could hope to reach them. With the failure of *A Week*, Thoreau had to come to terms with the realization that he was not to achieve widespread "practical and popular influence"—that he would not be a prophet to all the world.

Chapter 9

"SOME INTERIOR SHOOT": THOREAU'S CAREER AFTER 1850

THE FAILURE of *A Week* delayed the publication of *Walden* for five years, during which time it was considerably revised and expanded. One of Thoreau's additions—made in 1852, when he first returned to the manuscript—was an anecdote about an Indian who had industriously woven baskets only to find that no one wanted to buy them.[1] Clearly thinking of *A Week*, Thoreau compares the Indian's experience to his own:

> He had not discovered that it was necessary for him to make it worth the other's while to buy them, or at least make him think that it was so, or to make something else which it would be worth his while to buy. I too had woven a kind of basket of a delicate texture, but I had not made it worth any one's while to buy them. Yet not the less, in my case, did I think it worth my while to weave them, and instead of studying how to make it worth men's while to buy my baskets, I studied rather how to avoid the necessity of selling them. The life which men praise and regard as successful is but one kind. Why should we exaggerate any one kind at the expense of the others? (*Walden* 19)

In the context of *Walden*, this anecdote functions as a parable explaining and justifying his experiment in self-reliance at the pond; it explicitly raises questions about success that are implicit throughout the opening chapters' ironic use of the language of commerce, and it contributes to Thoreau's challenge to narrowly materialistic and utilitarian values. If, as a parable about the need for self-reliance, this anecdote belongs naturally in "Economy," however, it is nevertheless both anachronistic and untrue as an allegory of his experience with *A Week*.

First of all, the Walden years of course antedated the publication of *A Week*, so it is obviously not literally true that the failure of that book led either to his experiment in subsistence farming or to his implied withdrawal from the literary marketplace while there (since Thoreau had suffered an analogous failure in the marketplace of New York before going to the pond, his parable might be taken as referring to that experience, of course; but in that case it is not clear what the delicate "basket" he had woven refers to). More difficult to account for is his claim that "instead of studying how to make it worth men's while to buy my baskets, I studied rather how to avoid the necessity of selling them," for this was not true either before or after the failure of *A Week*. If his simplified life at the pond had alleviated the immediate need to market his writing, he nevertheless "studied" how to market his wares more successfully while at the pond: he enlisted Greeley as an agent, succeeded in selling commercially viable works to two popular periodicals, and, immediately after leaving Walden, worked vigorously to find a publisher for the book he had written there—being particularly interested in a cheap format for wide sales.

Nor is it true that Thoreau withdrew from the literary marketplace after the failure of *A Week*, though this may at first seem to be the case. It is true that after the publication of *A Week* Thoreau set aside his *Walden* manuscript and did not publish anything at all for three years; he took up land surveying and odd-jobbing to support himself and turned his attention more fully to the private writing of his journal. After 1850, Thoreau wrote much longer and more regular entries and stopped his earlier practice of cutting out journal pages as he composed works for publication. By leaving his journals intact he indeed accorded them an integrity and status they had not previously had. Taking this point to an extreme, Perry Miller has argued that after 1850 the journals take on a "self-intoxicated . . . character," which he explains in terms of Thoreau's commercial failures:

> Had Thoreau ever become a "successful" writer . . . he might then have journalized with the public in mind. But the failure of the *Week* in 1849, the seemingly hopeless fate of *Walden* thereafter, and then the dull thud with which it did fall in 1854—these circumstances decreed that for him the Journal would become not a means to an end, not a storage room for items subsequently to be displayed, but an end in itself. It became *the* work.[2]

Several scholars have recently echoed Miller's judgment,[3] and certainly they are correct in suggesting that the failure of *A Week* led Thoreau to reaffirm the value of his private inspiration, regardless of public influence, and also to reconsider the literary value of the journal form. We find Thoreau addressing both of these points in his journal for the winter of 1851–1852, for example. In an entry for December 25, 1851, he wrote:

> Do not speak for other men; speak for yourself. . . . Though you should only speak to one kindred mind in all time, though you should not speak to one, but only utter aloud, that you may more completely realize and live the idea which contains the reason of your life, . . . speak—though your thought presupposes the non-existence of your hearers—thoughts that transcend life and death. What though mortal ears are not fitted to hear absolute truth! (JIII: 157–58)

And on January 27, 1852, he wrote:

> I do not know but thoughts written down thus in a journal might be printed in the same form to greater advantage—than if the related ones were brought together into separate essays. They are now allied to life—& are seen by the

> reader not to be far fetched—It is more simple—less artful—I feel that in the other case I should have no proper frame for my sketches. . . . Whether the flower looks better in the nosegay than in the meadow where it grew and we had to get our feet wet to get it! (JIII: 239; cf. J1: 578)

Together, these passages may seem to confirm the implication of Thoreau's Indian basket anecdote, that he studied "how to avoid the necessity of selling" his works by turning inward to his private writing; but this is not quite what these passages actually imply, nor is it what his outward literary activity confirms. In the first passage, though Thoreau exhorts himself to speak only for himself, it is only with great reluctance that he relinquishes an audience, hoping for "at least one kindred mind in all time." His ultimate ambition is still that of the poet-prophet, and this necessarily means his primary commitment is to the "absolute truth" and not to an audience; but his self-exhortation bespeaks his underlying public ambitions and his implicit hope that his words will *not* fall on deaf ears. The second passage even more clearly reveals his public ambitions, even as it reasserts the value of the journal, for it is an a priori assumption in this passage that his thoughts will be printed for an audience; the only questions he raises have to do with how best to convey his thoughts to that audience—whether the journal or the mosaic composition "looks better," which shows his thoughts off to "better advantage," and how they will be "seen by the reader."

Both of these passages, in fact, closely echo journal entries of a decade earlier and represent but one side of Thoreau's habitual private debate about his role as a writer. The first passage here returns to the stance of the journal entry of March 24, 1842, in which Thoreau had admonished himself that great writers "do not write down to others, but make their own taste and judgment their audience. . . . It is enough if I please myself with writing" (J1: 388); the second passage here reworks again that 1841 journal entry on leaving his thoughts in their natural soil (his journal) which he had incorporated into both "Ancient Poets" and A *Week*. As he had a decade earlier, Thoreau in 1852 also vacillated from such arguments for the integrity of private writing to acknowledgments of the legitimate demands upon the professional writer. On February 6, 1852—shortly after these journal entries and roughly at the time he incorporated the anecdote of the Indian baskets into *Walden*—Thoreau conceded in the pages of his journal, "Who will not confess that the necessity to get money has helped to ripen some of his schemes?" (JIII: 282).

In spite of the implications of the Indian basket passage, in the years following the publication of A *Week* Thoreau was actively engaged in public literary performances (and, significantly, he continued to employ his mosaic method for public compositions). Though Thoreau did not publish anything between 1849 and 1852, when he inserted the Indian basket anecdote into his *Walden* manuscript, he had been busily working up new material for lectures and, eventually, for publication. Moreover, the principal material he worked up was not the "absolute truth" of his private intuitions but accounts of his excursions to Cape Cod and Canada—material that he knew, from his success with "Ktaadn," was more likely to appeal to a broad popular audience. Thoreau had gone to Cape Cod with Ellery Channing in October, 1849 (just as the failure of *A Week* was becoming apparent), and though he was normally a slow writer he completed two lectures on his excursion in time for the lyceum season just getting under way. They succeeded so well in Concord that Emerson was able to arrange for Thoreau to repeat one for the South Danvers Lyceum; Emerson wrote to Thoreau of his conversation with the lyceum director: "I told him there were two lectures to describe Cape Cod, which interested him and his friends. . . . I hope it will not quite discredit my negotiation if I confess that they heard with joy that Concord people laughed till they cried, when it was read to them. . . . They will pay your expenses and $10.00" (Corr 255). Thoreau returned to Cape Cod for more material during the summer and delivered his new lectures during the 1850–1851 season, speaking at several of the Massachusetts lyceums and making a return trip to Portland, Maine, where he was again received enthusiastically.[4] Thoreau's excursion to Montreal and Quebec was made in September 1850 (again in the company of Channing), and he used this for lectures during the 1851–1852 lyceum season.

Thoreau continued to prepare and deliver lectures on more abstract, transcendental themes during this period—during the 1850–1851 season he gave his earliest lecture version of "Walking, or the Wild," and the next season he tried out some *Walden* material again—but he recognized that these were not likely to succeed with a popular audience, and he read them knowing full well that he was overstepping the general public's limits of tolerance. For the most part, he anticipated the failure of these pieces as lectures and was in fact reluctant or unwilling to read them to certain audiences; they seem to have been intended for a more select group of auditors rather than for general consumption. On April 2, 1852, for example, Thoreau responded to Thomas Wentworth Higginson's invitation to lecture in Boston by saying,

> I do not see that I can refuse to read another lecture, but what makes me hesitate is the fear that I have not another available which will *entertain* a large audience, though I have thoughts to offer which I think will be quite as worthy of their attention. However I will try, for the prospect of earning a few dollars is alluring. As far as I can foresee, my subject would be Reality rather transcendentally treated. It lies still in Walden or Life in the Woods. (Corr 278–79)

The next day Thoreau wrote a note to Higginson reluctantly confirming his acceptance of the invitation: "I certainly do not feel prepared to offer myself as a lecturer to the Boston public, and hardly know whether more to dread a small audience or a large one. Nevertheless I will repress this squeamishness, and propose no alterations in your arrangements" (Corr 280). In contrast, Thoreau wrote to his friend Marston Watson of Plymouth on December 31, 1852, declining to lecture there at that time because, having already read from "Economy" and on "Walking, or the Wild" to Watson's group the previous season, he now had no more material transcendental *enough* for Watson's select gatherings:

> I would be glad to visit Plymouth again, but at present I have nothing to read which is not severely heathenish, or at least secular,—which the dictionary defines as "relating to affairs of the present world, not holy,"—though not necessarily unholy. . . . Don't think I say this to get off; no, no! It will not do to read such things to hungry ears. "If they ask for bread, will you give them a stone?" When I have something of the right kind, depend upon it I will let you know. (Corr 290–91)[5]

The failure of *A Week* had left its mark on Thoreau; he could never again be so innocently hopeful in his expectations of the public, and so he increasingly saw himself as addressing two, more or less distinct audiences. But he had not withdrawn from the marketplace, and, not surprisingly, therefore, it was his travel pieces, and not his abstract moral essays, that he sought to publish. Ironically, it was in 1852, just when he was adding the Indian basket anecdote to *Walden*, that Thoreau escalated his assault on the literary marketplace, making a more concerted effort to sell his wares than he had since the publication of *A Week*.

The impetus for again taking the step from the lyceum platform to the periodical press came from Greeley. In February 1852, Thoreau had asked Greeley to help arrange for Thoreau's participation in a lecture series, and Greeley replied,

> The People's course is full for the season; and even if it were not, your name would probably not pass; because it is not merely necessary that each lecturer should continue *well* the course, but that he shall be *known* as the very man beforehand. Whatever draws less than fifteen hundred hearers damages the finances of the movement, so low is the admission, and so large the expense. But, Thoreau, you are a better speaker than many, but a far better writer still. Do you wish to swap any of your "wood-notes wild" for dollars? If yea, and you will sell me some articles, shorter, if you please, than the former, I will try to coin them for you. (Corr 276–77)

Thoreau promptly sent Greeley his "Canadian Journey" and two short sketches that he had written for inclusion in the *Walden* manuscript. Greeley was unhappy with the length (as well as the quality) of the Canadian excursion and had difficulty placing it—at the end of June he reported, "I have had only bad luck with your manuscript. Two magazines have refused it on the grounds of its length" (Corr 282)—but he sold the two sketches fairly quickly to *Sartain's Union Magazine* of Philadelphia, which promised Thoreau three dollars per page (Corr 278). "The Iron Horse" appeared in the July number, and "A Poet Buys a Farm" appeared in August, both of which Greeley duly applauded in the *Tribune*'s notice of "New Publications."[6] Shortly thereafter, Thoreau sold "A Canadian Journey" to his friend George William Curtis, now an editor of the new *Putnam's Magazine*, to whom he then sent his essays on Cape Cod. Thoreau was not studying "how to avoid the necessity of selling" his work; on the contrary, he was studying this art assiduously—for by now he knew he would have to pay Munroe for the costs of printing A *Week*. For the moment this looked like the most commercially successful period of Thoreau's career with the periodical press.

The moment did not last. Typical of Thoreau's bad luck, *Sartain's* folded shortly after his sketches were printed, and once again he was never paid (Corr 290, 294). Thoreau was equally responsible for the collapse of this latest assault on the commercial press, however. *Putnam's* began printing "A Canadian Journey" in the issue of January 1853, but Thoreau withdrew his manuscript after only three of the five intended monthly installments were published. As he explained in a letter to his friend Blake,

> I do not wonder that you do not like my Canada story. It concerns me but little, and probably is not worth the time it took to tell it. . . . It has come to an end at any rate, they will print no more, but return me my mss. when it is but little more than half done—as well as another I had sent them, because the editor Curtis requires the liberty to omit heresies without consulting me—a privilege California is not rich enough to bid for. (Corr 299)

"A Canadian Journey" is moderately engaging and thoroughly researched, though thematically and metaphysically it is perhaps Thoreau's least successful and most superficial excursion essay. Thoreau's excursion to Canada involved him, more than any of his other travels, in the commercial tourist industry—from his cheap railway fare that obliged him to return within ten days, to the crowded and poorly timed steamer trip from Montreal to Quebec, to the obligatory attractions on the tour which he visited. Nevertheless, precisely because Thoreau thought of himself as accommodating the marketplace in his travel pieces, and most particularly in this Canadian excursion, he was tremendously sensitive whenever that marketplace imposed on him further. He would go so far but no further. Withdrawing his manuscript was a brave, if rather perverse, gesture on Thoreau's part. Curtis, who remained a gentleman and even a friend throughout his dealings with Thoreau, paid him seventy-nine dollars for the three printed installments, but this was just enough to pay back, "principal & interest," the seventy-five dollars Thoreau had borrowed from Greeley the previous July, so Thoreau was still no closer to paying off his debt to Munroe (Corr 295). Greeley was unhappy that Thoreau had cut off publication of the Canadian excursion, explaining to Thoreau that it now could not be sold anywhere, but Thoreau could only say, "I am sorry that my manuscript should be so mangled, insignificant as it is, but I do not know how I could have helped it fairly, since I was born to be a pantheist—if that be the name of me, and I do the deeds of one" (Corr 294). Not only did Thoreau lose the additional payments for "A Canadian Journey," but now the publication of "Cape Cod" was postponed as well. Thus it was only by his land surveying and odd-jobbing that he was able to pay off his debt to Munroe & Co. by November 1853.

Thoreau's anecdote of the Indian baskets is belied by his actual efforts to enter the literary marketplace, both before and after the publication of *A Week*. Thoreau was invariably frustrated by these efforts, however, and the anecdote does express the heightened sensitivity, skepticism, and hostility he felt toward the marketplace after the failure of *A Week*, even as he refused to withdraw from it.

Much of this attitude was of course present well before *A Week*. It was after his failure in New York that Thoreau moved to the pond, and the pre-*Week* version of *Walden* is essentially a reaction to *this* failure. More than any of his other works, the early chapters of *Walden* speak to the question of the prophet's relation to the marketplace, and these chapters were all but complete by 1849. Yet in spite of Thoreau's biting satire on materialism and his emphasis on self-reliance, this pre-*Week* version of *Walden* proposes an Emersonian correspondence between material and spiritual economy—a correspondence that he subsequently came to doubt. Thoreau (and Emerson) had early discovered that the language of commerce provided useful tropes for their spiritual endeavors, and "Economy" is but Thoreau's most extended and brilliant exploitation of this relationship, in which he urges us to apply to our moral estate the sound principles that we have learned with our material estate. In the pre-*Week* version of *Walden* Thoreau treats his own failures in the literary marketplace with self-deprecating humor and irony as he learns how to succeed at his chosen business. He describes himself as having been a "reporter to a journal, of no very wide circulation, whose editor has never yet seen fit to print the bulk of my contributions, and, as is too common with writers, I got only my labor for my pains." He was a "self-appointed inspector" of the Concord landscape who "went on thus for a long time . . . faithfully minding my business, till it became more and more evident that my townsmen would not after all admit me into the list of town officers, nor make my place a sinecure with a moderate allowance" (*Walden* 18). Rather than attacking the market economy at this point, Thoreau explains that his response was to go into business for himself: "I determined to go into business at once, and not wait to acquire the usual capital, using such slender means as I had already got." The skills he needs for his venture are "a little common sense, a little enterprise and business talent." Thoreau goes on then to epitomize the correspondence between material and spiritual commerce in his brilliant paragraph on the "strict business habits" required for conducting trade with the "Celestial Empire" (19–21).

Stylistically, this is perhaps Thoreau at his best. More than in *A Week* he fulfills his own prescriptions for good writing: it has the density and artfulness of the "*double entendre* . . . for the alert reader," which he had found absent in Carlyle; and so it indeed has the characteristics of those great poems which he described in *A Week* as offering "their sense in due proportion to the hasty and deliberate reader." Thus, in *Walden* as well as *A Week*, Thoreau instructs his readers on how to read his books. In "Reading" he warns us that to read great books "we must laboriously seek the meaning of each word and line, conjecturing a larger sense than common use permits" (100). In both *A Week* and the early version of *Walden*, then, Thoreau already conceived of two classes of readers—a lesson he had early learned in the marketplace; yet up to this point Thoreau felt that he might effectively speak to both the hasty and the alert reader—that he could therefore address them simultaneously, offering a kind of truth to each and perhaps elevating the one to the status of the other. After the failure of *A Week*, however, Thoreau's skepticism intensified to the point at which he could no longer regard either the obtuse reader or the marketplace itself with equanimity. Thoreau's anecdote of the Indian basket was thus inserted into the middle of the "Economy" passage on his own business—between his ironic self-portrait as the inspector of snowstorms without sinecure and his instructions on trade with the Celestial Empire. Only superficially does the anecdote conform to this context, however, for it actually implies a complete rejection of and withdrawal from the marketplace altogether, which contradicts the controlling metaphor of private enterprise and threatens to undermine the very premise of "Economy."

Another late addition to "Economy" underscores this shift in attitude. Toward the end of the chapter, Thoreau returns to the subject of his past efforts to earn a living—this time without metaphors, but still rather vaguely. In the early versions of the passage he explains that his present experiment provided the greatest freedom; that he had tried schoolteaching "and found that my expenses were . . . out of proportion, to my income"; that he had tried trade, "but I found that it would take ten years to get under way in that, and that then I should probably be on my way to the devil"; and so he concluded that,

> As I preferred some things to others, and especially valued my freedom, as I could fare hard and yet succeed well, I did not wish to spend my time in earning rich carpets or other fine furniture, or delicate cookery, or a house in the Grecian or the Gothic style just yet. If there are any to whom it is no interruption to acquire these things, and who know how to use them when acquired, I relinquish to them the pursuit. (*Walden* 69–70)

Although Thoreau's comment that trade would most likely lead him to the devil clearly expresses his bias, this passage is nevertheless very deliberately open-minded and genial toward commerce and the marketplace generally; he leaves it to others to pursue material comforts, but he does not preclude the possibility that even he may *yet* devote his time to such pursuits. In a revision of 1853–1854, however, Thoreau interjected here a passage (from his 1851 journal) that concluded with a violent hostility toward trade quite inconsistent with the larger context:

> When formerly I was looking about to see what I could do for a living, some sad experience in conforming to the wishes of friends being fresh in my mind to tax my ingenuity, I thought often and seriously of picking huckleberries; that surely I could do, and its small profits might suffice. . . . While my acquaintances went unhesitatingly into trade or the professions, I contemplated this occupation as most like theirs; ranging the hills all summer . . . so, to keep the flocks of Admetus. . . . But I have since learned that trade curses everything it handles; and though you trade in messages from heaven, the whole curse of trade attaches to the business. (*Walden* 69–70)[7]

It is difficult to identify precisely the oblique autobiographical references in this passage. The "sad experience in conforming to the wishes of friends," for example, could refer to his New York sojourn in 1843 as easily as to his publishing *A Week* at his own expense—both were undertaken at Emerson's urging, and both put Thoreau in debt. But the 1851 date of the original journal entry suggests the latter incident as the more likely occasion, as does his comment on business cursing even "trade in messages from heaven," since that was essentially how he regarded his "hypaethral" first book.[8] In any case, this anecdote functions, like that of the Indian baskets, as a kind of private parable of his disillusionment with his professional literary efforts. These added passages do not merely sharpen the tone of *Walden*, however; they contradict the central metaphor governing "Economy," for his assertion that business curses even "trade in messages from heaven" would seem to proscribe Thoreau's even attempting to market this account of his own trade with the Celestial Empire on the shores of Walden Pond.

Thoreau reiterated and extended the huckleberry anecdote's attack on the marketplace in another addition of 1853–1854, this one inserted at the beginning of the chapter entitled "The Ponds." In the earlier version, Thoreau simply mentions that he would occasionally make a supper of huckleberries and blueberries and then goes on to discuss his fishing excursions and the local ponds; the mention of the berries is incidental, merely marking a transition away from his discussion of the village. In his late revisions of the manuscript, however, he made this passing reference to huckleberries the occasion of another bitter digression.

> The fruits do not yield their true flavor to the purchaser of them, nor to him who raises them for the market. . . . A huckleberry never reaches Boston; they have not been known there since they grew on her three hills. The ambrosial and essential part of the fruit is lost with the bloom which is rubbed off in the market cart, and they become mere provender. As long as Eternal Justice reigns, not one innocent huckleberry can be transported thither from the country's hills. (173)[9]

Even more virulent is Thoreau's attack in this chapter on the farmer Flint, of Flint's Pond, "who would carry the landscape, who would carry his God, to market, if he could get anything for him; who goes to market *for* his god as it is . . . whose fruits are not ripe for him till they are turned to dollars" (196). While large portions of "The Ponds" and all of the subsequent chapters were also composed during the period between 1852 and 1854, it is nevertheless noteworthy that virtually all of his outbursts against the marketplace were composed during this period and not before 1849.

Thoreau's disillusionment with the marketplace was accompanied by a corresponding disillusionment with his prospective audience, a suspicion confirmed by the failure of *A Week* that they would not be able to "conjecture a larger sense than common use permits." Thoreau's satire on his neighbors was certainly sharp enough even in the earliest accounts of his life at the pond, and since his relation with his audience is principally established in those opening chapters composed before 1849, there is not a dramatic shift in tone in the subsequent revisions; nevertheless, his diminished expectations do seem to be reflected in some of his late additions. Even in the first version of *Walden*, of course, Thoreau deliberately employed double entendres, paradoxes, and elaborate metaphors, which were intended to make demands upon the reader's imagination and which Thoreau recognized might elude his superficial readers; thus he instructed his readers on how to read his book, and, in "Economy," he explained, "You will pardon some obscurities, for there are more secrets in my trade than in most men's, and yet not voluntarily kept, but inseparable from its very nature. I would gladly tell all that I know about it, and never paint 'No Admittance' on my gate" (17). Here, as in *A Week*, Thoreau approaches his reader with a kind of cautious optimism that his apologies and genial explanations might suffice; his tone is eminently civil. By the time he composed the "Conclusion," however (all of which was written between 1852 and 1854), his tone grew more peevish. Although the chapter as a whole, like "Spring," expresses a buoyant transcendental optimism, when he returns to the subject of his book's obscurities he becomes grim:

> It is a ridiculous demand which England and America make, that you shall speak so that they can understand you. . . . As if Nature could support but one order of understandings, could not sustain birds as well as quadrupeds, flying as well as creeping things, and *hush* and *who*, which Bright can understand, were the best English. As if there were safety in stupidity alone. (324)[10]

Thoreau's point is not new, but we can detect here a tone of frustration, even desperation, that was not present in his earlier explanation of his obscurities. Thus it is with a kind of defiance rather than civility that he echoes the earlier remark, now asserting, "I do not suppose that I have attained to obscurity, but I should be proud if no more fatal fault were found with my pages on this score than was found with the Walden ice" (325). Whereas he had earlier insisted that his secrets were not voluntarily kept, he now seems to be willfully withholding them from an obtuse public, and his earlier deference gives way here to a barely restrained contempt.

The ultimate irony of Thoreau's interpolated anecdote about how he studied to avoid selling his wares and about the curse of trade is that *Walden* proved to be Thoreau's most successful venture in the literary marketplace. Although hindsight suggests that both Thoreau and his publisher might have done even more on behalf of the book, *Walden* was in every respect handled more effectively than A *Week*, and the greater initial success of *Walden* (if not its ultimate critical reputation) surely had as much to do with the more successful marketing practices employed as with its inherent literary merits. Business, it turned out, did not curse his trade in messages from heaven when he indeed employed a little common sense and sound business practices.

In the narrowest commercial sense, of course, even *Walden* was probably not quite a success; it was merely not a failure. Thoreau earned only a few hundred dollars from sales, and there was no second printing until the year of his death. But in the larger context of his professional career, *Walden* was more important than sales alone imply. The publication of *Walden*—and by this I mean not merely the printed text but the attendant publication notices and reviews as well—did not make Thoreau a popular writer, but it did give him an established reputation.

Thoreau was now associated with the firm of Ticknor & Fields, New England's most astute and aggressive publishing house and, by 1850, America's most prestigious publisher of belles lettres. James T. Fields had attracted and retained the loyalty of America's best writers (including Whittier, Holmes, Longfellow, Hawthorne, and, later, Emerson) by paying them generously and treating them with consideration. Thoreau signed a contract with them for *Walden* on March 16, 1854, on terms that were surprisingly favorable to him.[11] Thoreau retained the copyright, and Ticknor and Fields held the sole printing rights for five years; the first edition consisted of two thousand copies, bound with Ticknor & Fields's simple but distinguished embossed covers, and sold for one dollar per copy. Thoreau was to receive a royalty of 15 percent of retail on all copies sold—a level reserved for their "first class authors," rather than the more standard 10 percent.[12] Accounts were to be paid twice a year, and Thoreau would receive twenty-five copies of his book free of charge. In contrast with *A Week*, then, the publisher rather than the author assumed the entire risk for *Walden*. The inflated royalty offered to Thoreau is especially remarkable in light of the utter failure of *A Week*, but Fields probably understood that that failure had been Munroe's and not the book's; he knew how to promote books aggressively and so could offer Thoreau a high royalty, even though he lacked an established reputation, as a vote of confidence—in both Thoreau's talent and his own.

The book was ready to print by May, but the actual publication was delayed until August. Part of this delay was caused by the efforts of Fields and others to secure an English as well as an American copyright for *Walden*, which required that the book first be printed in England. Emerson wrote to his London agent, Richard Bentley, on March 20, praising *Walden* and offering it to Bentley for publication. Bentley apparently asked to see some sheets, and on June 7, Fields himself left for England with proof sheets of the book, hoping to sell the copyright there, but he became seasick and left the ship at Halifax, Nova Scotia, to return home. Fields subsequently wrote to Bentley on July 2, acknowledging Emerson's earlier proposition, and offering him the copyright for one hundred dollars. He then sent a copy of *Walden* to his agent in England, urging him to sell it to some London publisher—preferably Bentley—"for the most you can obtain." He compared the book to Emerson's writings and said, "Walden is no common book & is sure to succeed."[13] The book did not find an English publisher, in spite of these efforts, but this was more likely a result of disputes over the copyright law than of negative appraisals of Thoreau's book. The policy of granting English copyrights to foreign authors as long as the book was first published in England was based on a judgment of the Queen's Bench; but the Court of Exchequer disagreed, and in an 1854 appeal of the ruling, the House of Lords sided with the Court of Exchequer. English publishers were thus naturally reluctant to pay for copyright privileges that were no longer recognized by British law. Emerson learned of this in August and so noted, "Bad for Thoreau, bad for me, yet I wish it may drive us to granting foreign copyright which would no doubt restore this Eng. privilege" (EmL 4: 459). But international copyright laws were not passed until the end of the century, and *Walden* remained unpublished in England for thirty years.

Fields's efforts to promote the book at home were, in any case, more important than those abroad. Fields sent review copies to individuals a month before publication; he placed prepublication advertisements in numerous newspapers, including the *Boston Transcript*, the *New York Evening Post*, and the *New York Tribune*; and each of these papers also puffed the book in additional prepublication notices, which included extracts from the advance sheets Fields had sent.[14] Because Fields energetically distributed review copies, and because of his firm's influence and reputation, once *Walden* was officially published, it was reviewed far more widely, more prominently, and at greater length than A *Week* had been. *Graham's*, the *Knickerbocker*, the *Southern Literary Messenger*, and the *North American Review*—none of which had reviewed his first book—now reviewed *Walden*; and although the *North American* dismissed it curtly, *Graham's* gave it three pages, and *Putnam's* gave it five. It was praised highly in the *Christian Register* (by T. Starr King) and in the *National Anti-Slavery Standard*, in J. S. Dwight's *Journal of Music*, and in the *National Era*. It was reviewed, at least sometimes enthusiastically, in a wide range of daily and weekly papers in New York, Philadelphia, and throughout New England, as well as in Louisville, Columbus (Ohio), Richmond, and (thanks to Elizabeth Stoddard's regular column, "Our Lady Correspondent") as far afield as the *Alta California*.[15]

In addition to Fields's efforts on behalf of *Walden*, Thoreau's reputation received a boost from several other quarters. Greeley, of course, needed no urging from Fields to promote Thoreau. In March of 1854 he had written to Thoreau urging him "to collect and arrange your 'Miscellanies' and send them to me." He asked for "Ktaadn," "Carlyle," "A Winter Walk," "A Canadian Journey," and anything new, promising to try to find a publisher to "bring them out at his own risk, and (I hope) to your ultimate profit" (Corr 323). When he learned *Walden* was about to be published, he suggested deferring the "Miscellanies," so as not to glut the market, and selling them later to Ticknor & Fields. In the meantime, he promised to announce *Walden "at once"* (Corr 324). He printed long excerpts in a prepublication notice in the *Daily Tribune* of July 29, which he repeated in the *Semi-Weekly* and *Weekly Tribune* editions of the following week.

In a more general way, Thoreau's reputation was enhanced by timely references to him in other publications. In May of 1854, Thoreau received a request from Charles Scribner for biographical and bibliographical information to be included in the forthcoming *Cyclopedia of American Literature*, to be edited by Evert and George Duyckinck. The aim of the volume, the letter stated, was to provide "notices of the Lives and Writings of all American authors of importance" (Corr 326). Thoreau had not been deemed important enough to merit inclusion in any of Griswold's anthologies, but now he was included in the Scribner volume, published in 1855, in the wake of

Walden's publication.[16] Equally timely were the references to Thoreau in George William Curtis's essay on Emerson in the 1854 *Homes of American Authors*. "If every quiet country town in New England," he wrote, "had a son who, with a lore like Selborne's and an eye like Buffon's, had watched and studied its landscape and history, and then published the result, as Thoreau has done, in a book as redolent of genuine and perceptive sympathy with nature as a clover-field of honey, New England would seem as poetic and beautiful as Greece."[17] Curtis's is an amusing and engaging sketch, in a popular volume that, like the Duyckinck *Cyclopedia*, was aimed at a broad audience. While these references probably had little or no effect on actual sales, they contributed significantly to the establishment of Thoreau's general reputation as an American author of merit.

Thoreau's reputation, if not his income, was similarly enhanced by the efforts of both Greeley and Hawthorne in England. Greeley, in England during the summer of 1855, wrote to Thoreau instructing him to send a review copy of *Walden* to the *Westminster Review*, since he felt there was "a small class in England who ought to know what you have written" (Corr 380). As a result, a highly complimentary review written by George Eliot was printed in the *Westminster* for January 1856. Hawthorne, in Liverpool as American consul, had Ticknor & Fields (his own publishers) send him copies of both of Thoreau's books to give to interested English friends.[18]

None of these efforts by his publisher and friends succeeded in making *Walden* a best-seller, but initial sales were in fact quite strong, in marked contrast to A *Week*. Ticknor & Fields's promotional work garnered 402 orders by the day of publication and another 164 by the end of the first week. After five weeks, 689 copies had been sold, and although sales tapered off, at the end of the first six months after publication, only 600 copies remained of the edition of 2,000.[19] Even if we subtracted distribution copies, Thoreau must have been paid approximately $200—a modest profit after all, but more than he had earned for any single composition previously, and infinitely preferable to his debt to Munroe. Sales fell off after that, however, and at the end of the next six-month accounting period only 344 more copies had been sold, for which he was paid $51.60 (Corr 387). The remainder of the edition did not sell out until 1859.

Thoreau feigned indifference to the fate of his book—he conspicuously avoided any mention of it in his letter to H.G.O. Blake on the day before its publication, and his sole journal entry for August 9, 1854, consists of "'Walden' published. Elder-berries. Waxwork yellowing" (JVI: 429). The *absence* of his usual lengthy descriptions of the Concord landscape this day, however, eloquently bespeaks his genuine anxiety about the fate of his book. Emerson reported to George Bradford on August 28, "All American kind are delighted with 'Walden' as far as they have dared say, The little pond sinks in these very days as tremulous at its human fame. . . . We account Henry the undoubted King of all American lions. He is walking up & down Concord, firm-looking, but in a tremble of great expectation" (EmL 4: 459–60).

Although he did not achieve instant fame with *Walden*, Thoreau did begin to receive appreciative letters from various readers. Almost immediately upon the book's publication, Thoreau received an enthusiastic letter from Daniel Ricketson, of New Bedford, one more to be added to the list of his lifelong disciples (Ricketson had first learned of Thoreau's book from the *Tribune*'s prepublication notice). From farther afield, Thoreau received a letter in French from the Abbé Adrien Rouquette of Louisiana, praising *Walden* (JVII: 71; Corr 349). At the beginning of 1856 he received a letter from Calvin Greene of Michigan who, having admired *Walden*, was trying to locate a copy of *A Week*. (It is a further testament to Ticknor & Fields's advertising and distribution that Thoreau reached admirers in Louisiana and Michigan.) Thoreau acknowledged how gratified he was by such interest in his work and, in response to Greene's inquiry about the reception of *Walden*, he wrote, "It has found an audience of excellent character, and quite numerous, some 2000 copies having been dispersed"; typically, however, he added, "I should consider it a greater success to interest one wise and earnest soul, than a million unwise & frivolous" (Corr 406–7; cf. 425–26). Still later that year Thoreau began a correspondence with another admirer, a Providence, Rhode Island, banker, B. B. Wiley, who, having read *Walden*, had already—surprisingly—managed to obtain a copy of *A Week* from another Providence banker (Corr 431–32). Wiley subsequently made contact with Thoreau's Worcester circle of admirers. Thoreau found another lasting admirer in Thomas Cholmondeley, an Englishman who came to Concord in 1854 to meet Emerson but who discovered Thoreau instead.

Thoreau relished the modest reputation he had achieved with *Walden*, and in spite of the contempt he continued to feel toward both the apparatus of the marketplace and the mass of readers, he continued to pursue his career as both professional lecturer and writer. In September of 1854 he informed Blake that, having already arranged to lecture in Plymouth and Philadelphia, he hoped to put together a lecture tour to the West, "*if they shall want me*" (Corr 339). This was a typically cautious qualifier, but he was sufficiently optimistic that he told Blake he would be too busy to join him on a proposed excursion. By November Thoreau had been invited to lecture in Akron, Ohio (for a proposed payment of fifty dollars), and apparently in Canada as well, but he was unable to secure enough engagements to make the western tour worthwhile, and so he did not go at all (Corr 347, 352). Instead, he lectured throughout New England that season, delivering some of his most transcendental lectures—"Moonlight," "The Wild," and "Getting a Living."

The last of these (later titled "What Shall It Profit?" and finally published as "Life without Principle") was essentially a distillation of his theme in "Economy," examining the true business of one's life and attacking the marketplace with the same acerbity that informed his late revisions of *Walden*. As the lecture underwent revisions between 1854 and 1860, Thoreau incorporated commentary attacking the negative influence of the marketplace on the lecturer and writer in particular; yet ironically this became the lecture Thoreau delivered most frequently—a fact that captures his profound ambivalence toward his role.

Though Thoreau never became a commercially popular lecturer, lecturing in fact became an increasingly important part of his professional career. First of all, it kept him from becoming the recluse he was often accused of being (and which he was often tempted to become). Thoreau did not compromise much; he did not pander to popular tastes, and he frequently burst out, both in public and in private, in fierce invectives against the stupidity and inadequacies of lecture audiences. But this, too, was a kind of interaction with the public—far more valuable, in the long run, than merely condescending to entertain them—and it helped Thoreau clarify those ideas which he felt *needed* to be raised before the public. That is, lecturing helped Thoreau shape his identity as both a prophet and an artist. The lecture platform served as a testing ground, a place for Thoreau to listen to his own words and to see how an audience responded to them. As Thomas Wentworth Higginson noted in an essay on "American Audiences," "The Lyceum gave to the literary man, especially, not only a different form of reaching the public, but a readier test of his own powers. He must face the people, eye to eye."[20] Face to face with his audience, Thoreau discovered the language, form, and tone necessary to transform his journal's private hymns to the gods into the art of public discourse.

The work Thoreau composed after the failure of *A Week* falls into four general categories: his travel pieces (on Cape Cod, Canada, and the Maine woods), which he regarded as potentially the most popular material, and thus the most suitable to be worked up for the literary magazines; his nature sketches ("Autumnal Tints," "Moonlight," "Wild Apples," "Huckleberries"), which provided a wealth of detailed observation and were written in a familiar tone, but which he did not prepare for magazine publication until he was on his deathbed (perhaps because they remained works in progress, perhaps because he saw them as part of a larger, emerging project, or perhaps because he suspected that he treated his subjects too transcendentally for a broad popular audience); his abstract moral essays ("Walking," "The Wild," "What Shall It Profit?"), which distilled the essence of his transcendentalist faith into pithy aphorisms and extended metaphors, and which, while among his favorite pieces, were therefore less suitable for the periodical press; and, finally, the biting political lectures written in reaction to specific political actions that provoked him—his incarceration for nonpayment of taxes, the arrest of the fugitive slave Anthony Burns, and the arrest and execution of John Brown. Much more than the commercial press, the lecture platform allowed Thoreau the freedom of his entire repertoire, but because Thoreau was so deeply ambivalent about whether, and how, and to what extent he ought to accommodate his audience, he was extremely sensitive to their expectations and responses.

There is no denying, of course, that some of Thoreau's lectures were more or less straightforward attacks on the commonly held values of the community. If Thoreau had anything to say, it was because he did not share those values, and he had no illusions that he was speaking for the community as it was. Neither Thoreau nor Emerson had as his aim mere popular success; the transcendentalists, by nature, fell outside the sphere of popular literature insofar as they aimed to reform rather than give voice to popular values, so their sense of purpose and their standards of success were necessarily different. In discussing the popular lecturers of the period, Carl Bode writes, "When Starr King was asked what he lectured for he answered 'FAME—Fifty And My Expenses.' . . . Oliver Wendell Holmes remarked to Herman Melville and some others that 'a lecturer was a literary strumpet, subject for a greater than whore's fee to prostitute himself.'"[21] Thoreau felt this even more keenly. But if a monetary response was less important to him than to the popular writers and lecturers of the day, a moral and intellectual response was more important: he wished to move the public, not prostitute himself to it. Thoreau therefore grew suspicious of both himself and the public when he felt he was merely an entertainer, or when he felt he was being asked to lecture on what the public wanted to hear rather than on what he had to say. He was willing to write out his inspirations in a form that could engage and even entertain the public, but once that was done, he expected the public to make a comparable effort to adopt his perspective. Thus Thoreau was angered when the public refused to return the accommodation he felt he had already made toward them. In December of 1854, Thoreau wrote in his journal:

> After lecturing twice this winter I feel that I am in danger of cheapening myself by trying to become a successful lecturer, *i.e.*, to interest my audiences. I am disappointed to find that most that I am and value myself for is lost, or worse than lost, on my audience. I fail to get even the attention of the mass. I should suit them better if I suited myself less. . . . You cannot interest them except as you are like them and sympathize with them. I would rather that my audience come to me than I should go to them, and so they be sifted; *i.e.*, I would rather write books than lectures. . . . To read to a promiscuous audience who are at your mercy the fine thoughts you solaced yourself with far away is as violent as to fatten geese by cramming, and in this case they do not get fatter. (JVII: 79)[22]

The public's demand to be entertained and their refusal or inability to reciprocate his gestures toward them became recurring themes in Thoreau's journal, and he became ever more recalcitrant and uncompromising. In February of 1855 (having recently read "What Shall It Profit" at the Concord Lyceum) he wrote,

> Many will complain of my lectures that they are transcendental. "Can't understand them." . . . A criticism true enough, it may be, from their point of view. But the fact is, the earnest lecturer can speak only to his like, and the adapting of himself to his audience is a mere compliment which he pays them. If you wish to know how I think, you must endeavor to put yourself in my place. If you wish me to speak as if I were you, that is another affair. (JVII: 197)

As his audiences continued to demonstrate their unwillingness to put themselves in his place (and, perhaps, as he felt increasingly secure about the small but intensely loyal following he had won), he came increasingly to see his public failures as a sign of private success. In December of 1856 he wrote to his friend Blake, "I never triumph so as when I have the least success in my neighbor's eyes. . . . I could lecture on dry oak leaves: I could, but who could hear me. If I were to try it on any large audience, I fear it would be no gain to them, and a positive loss to me. I should have behaved rudely toward my rustling friends" (Corr 461).[23]

Thoreau did, in fact, lecture on "dry oak leaves" in the late composition "Autumnal Tints," which he read to audiences several times in 1859 and as the last lecture of his career on December 11, 1860. The lecture was "transcendental" at heart, but it is significant that Thoreau attempted to present his vision through an entertaining and informative familiar essay on commonplace phenomena, particularly close to the hearts of his fellow New Englanders.

Thoreau's ironic view of success *through* failure—triumphing privately while failing outwardly—must not be misinterpreted. Typical of Thoreauvian paradox, this is a complex attitude. It was, to a certain extent, simply a defensive pose on Thoreau's part, an act of self-justification. Yet in spite of his protests, Thoreau did not withdraw into private life. On the contrary, he lectured as long as his health permitted, and he spent his last year, aware of his imminent death, preparing as many essays as he could for publication and arranging for second editions of his two books. Nor does his letter to Blake imply an indifference to public response. Rather, it suggests the extent to which he genuinely desired to engage his audience. Thoreau's mature works everywhere exhibit his awareness of audience, and nowhere more clearly than in the challenges he issued to them. In claiming to succeed through failure, Thoreau was still judging his works in terms of their public reception, even though he characteristically inverted conventional expectations. On the one hand, Thoreau's attitude expresses what might be called a "will to failure" in the popular and commercial sphere, and there is an inevitable logic in this stance for the moral reformer who resisted the ways of the world. Yet there is also a double-edged irony in his claim to triumph most when his neighbors think he has failed: one side is a benign, self-directed irony—the self-deprecatory pose he assumed in *Walden* when he described his career as surveyor of snowstorms, and which actually has the rhetorical aim of ingratiating himself with his audience by seeing himself from *their* perspective; the other side, however, in which the irony is aimed at his audience, is more sinister, for Thoreau implies that there may be an element of dissimulation in his writing, a significance deliberately withheld, so that his triumph is in his *keeping it from* them.

For the most part, however, lecturing taught Thoreau the need for the *mutual* involvement of the speaker and the hearer. Although he frequently resorted to the high ground of claiming that the writer must speak only for himself, must "speak—though your thought presupposes the non-existence of your hearers—thoughts that transcend life and death," Thoreau in fact regarded it as essential to engage in a dialectical relationship with his audience, and he believed that the lecture, especially, was the joint creation of speaker and hearer. He eventually generated a strikingly modern sense of audience involvement dramatically at odds with his assertions of the artist's necessary aloofness. In a long journal entry for March 3, 1859, Thoreau wrote:

> Talk about reading!—a good reader! It depends on how he is heard. There may be elocution and pronunciation (recitation, say) to satiety, but there can be no good reading unless there is good hearing also. It takes two at least for this game, as for love, and they must cooperate. The lecturer will read best those parts of his lecture which are best heard.

He goes on to compare the public lecture to a team rolling hogsheads up an inclined plane, one pushing, one pulling:

> The first man was the lecturer, the last was the audience. It is the duty of the lecturer to team his hogshead of sweets to the depot, or Lyceum, place the horse, arrange the ropes, and shove; it is the duty of the audience to take hold of the ropes and pull with all their might. . . . If it is pronounced good, it is partly to the credit of the hearers; if bad, it is partly their fault. . . . The lecturer, therefore, desires of his audience a long pull, a strong pull, and all pull together. (JXII: 9–11)

Only when he repeatedly found his audience unwilling or unable to take their part, then, did he resort to invective or dissimulation. Thus he complained in his journal for November 1859, "It is no compliment to be invited to lecture before the rich Institutes and Lyceums. . . . The audiences do not want to hear any prophets; they do not wish to be stimulated and instructed, but entertained" (JIX: 327). Thoreau's frustration with such audiences is apparent in his response to a lyceum manager's invitation to lecture in Buffalo, New York, in 1860:

> I shall be happy to read to your association three lectures on the evenings named, but the question is about their character. They will not be scientific in the common, nor, perhaps, in any sense. They will be such as you might infer from reading my books. . . . they will be *transcendental*, that is, to the mass of hearers, probably *moonshine*. Do you think that will do? Or does your audience prefer lamplight, or total darkness these nights? I dare say, however, that they would interest those who are most interested in what is called nature. (Corr 584)

Although it was in lecturing that Thoreau became most acutely aware of the mutual dependence of author and audience, the particular demands his works made upon the public rendered them ultimately better suited to the printed page than the lecture platform. In his best writing, there is a density and subtlety, a concentration of "double entendres" and a play with the language, that made it difficult for listeners to follow. Thoreau's friend Daniel Ricketson wrote that "his thoughts were often too subtle to be readily interpreted,"[24] and apparently the lecture audiences agreed. Yet through his experiences in the literary marketplace he also realized that only his most easily accessible and least controversial pieces would meet with the approval of publishers and editors. He thus approached the periodical press only with a great deal of caution and suspicion after *Walden* and reacted even more sensitively than to lecture audiences when further constraints were imposed upon him.

Thoreau had withdrawn the truly innocuous "Canadian Journey" from *Putnam's* in 1853 when Curtis wanted to edit out some pantheistic remarks. In 1855, Curtis belatedly began printing Thoreau's vastly superior "Cape Cod" sketches, but again a controversy arose over apparently heretical statements. Thoreau was at first accommodating, but when further disagreements arose, over payment and copyright as well as Thoreau's tone, he again withdrew his manuscript before all the installments had been printed.[25]

While he and Curtis remained cordial and goodwilled throughout their negotiations, Thoreau reacted far more violently when James Russell Lowell took licenses with Thoreau's texts. As editor of the newly established *Atlantic Monthly*, Lowell solicited from Thoreau in 1858 an account of some of his Maine woods experiences, which had been the basis of several of Thoreau's lectures. Thoreau complied by sending him the account of his 1853 excursion to the Maine woods. "Chesuncook" was published in three installments, June through August 1858. But on June 22, having noted the omission of a line about a pine tree, Thoreau wrote his now-famous letter to Lowell:

> When I received the proof of that portion of my story printed in the July number . . . I was surprised to find that the sentence—"It is as immortal as I am, and perchance will go to as high a heaven, there to tower over me still." . . . was, in a very mean and cowardly manner, omitted. I hardly need to say that this is a liberty which I will not permit to be taken with my MS. The editor has, in this case, no more right to omit a sentiment than to insert one, or put words into my mouth. I do not ask anybody to adopt my opinions, but I do expect that when they ask for them to print, they will print them, or obtain my consent to their alteration or omission. . . . I feel this treatment to be an insult, though not intended as such, for it is to presume that I can be hired to suppress my opinions. . . .
>
> I am not willing to be associated in any way, unnecessarily, with parties who will confess themselves so bigoted & timid as this implies. I could excuse a man who was afraid of an uplifted fist, but if one habitually manifests fear at the utterance of a sincere thought, I must think his life is a kind of nightmare continued in broad daylight. . . . Is this the avowed character of the Atlantic Monthly? I should like an early reply. (Corr 515–16)

Thoreau seems to have gotten no reply at all, though he continued to badger Lowell for the payment he was due—"for thirty-three pages at six dollars a page—$198.00" (Corr 521).[26] Presumably he was paid, and he thereafter refused to have anything to do with the *Atlantic Monthly* until James T. Fields had replaced Lowell as editor. Thus, in spite of Thoreau's attempts to accommodate a popular audience, he could not accommodate conservative editorial policies. As a result, not one of his major travel books, on the Maine woods, Canada, and Cape Cod, was published in its entirety during Thoreau's lifetime.

Thoreau's disillusionment with the marketplace is probably expressed most explicitly in "Life without Principle," published by Fields in the *Atlantic Monthly* shortly after Thoreau's death. "If you would get money as a writer or lecturer, you must be popular, which is to go down perpendicularly. Those services which the community will most readily pay for it is most disagreeable to render" (RP 158). There is a nice irony in this, for when Fields first approached Thoreau about printing his lectures in the *Atlantic*, Thoreau's first question was "What will you give me for them?" (Corr 635). Moreover, with Fields in place as both editor of the *Atlantic* and publisher of Thoreau's book, Thoreau finally found himself in a highly desirable position in the literary marketplace.

Though "Life without Principle" expresses fundamental Thoreauvian ideas, it is not his best essay; nor should it be the final word on his attitude toward the marketplace. It is a string of aphorisms, loosely bound by the interplay between secular and spiritual business, in which Thoreau vents his various frustrations. More fully representative of his powers as a mature writer is "Wild Apples," another late lecture, which Thoreau also prepared for publication in the *Atlantic Monthly* in the months before his death. Like "Autumnal Tints" and "Huckleberries," it is an essay on nature, transcendentally treated. Of particular interest is the way in which "Wild Apples," without abandoning the prophet's mission, concedes the power of an unenlightened audience to thwart that mission. The essay implicitly acknowledges two classes of readers, both the "hasty and the deliberate readers" he had described in A *Week*. But "Wild Apples" reflects Thoreau's deeper skepticism regarding the public's ability, or willingness, to respond to his message; therefore, not only is it densely symbolic, but it also involves the element of dissimulation implied in his remark to Blake that he triumphs most when he fails in his neighbor's eyes—implied also in his *Walden* anecdote of the Indian baskets, in which he explains that the Indian had not discovered "that it was necessary for him to make it worth the other's while to buy them, *or at least make him think that it was so*, or to make something else" (*Walden* 19; emphasis mine). Though Thoreau claimed to have withdrawn from the marketplace entirely, in fact what he learned to do in his subtlest compositions was to make his audience *think* it was worth their while to purchase his wares. The apparent modesty of "Wild Apples" is a calculated and richly subversive rhetorical stance. Though many of its themes look back to A *Week* and *Walden*, its transcendentalism remains relatively unobtrusive. The essay deserves careful study if for no other reason than to dispel the impression that Thoreau's last years were ones of failure and decay, for what seems at first to be a slight, whimsical piece is actually a highly crafted personal autobiography, a national biography, and an American jeremiad.[27]

"Wild Apples" was first presented as a lecture in February 1860; a somewhat revised version was published in the *Atlantic Monthly* in November 1862. Walter Harding characterizes the piece as Thoreau's "most successful 'familiar essay,' a delightful blending of wit and wisdom, filled with whimsical humor and facetious catalogs of imaginary species of the fruit."[28] Indeed, from the beginning "Wild Apples" has been appreciated as one of Thoreau's better nature essays—careful and precise though never strictly scientific. Yet the deliberate reader will soon discover that the essay's information and entertaining observations also carry a finely wrought symbolic significance.

The complexity of Thoreau's rhetorical task is signaled in the opening section of the essay, "The History of the Apple Tree." "It is remarkable," he begins, "how closely the history of the apple tree is connected with that of man" (W 5: 290). He goes on to cite evidence of prehistoric links between man and the apple tree and then to catalog allusions to the apple in the ancient literature of the Hebrews, Greeks, Romans, and Scandinavians. Thoreau's catalog is a conventional familiar essay introduction that itself has a somewhat complex rhetorical function. On one hand, it provides an opportunity for the author to display his erudition and to dignify his choice of topics by aligning it (and himself) with some established tradition. Yet these claims for the subject's importance must, in turn, be made somewhat facetiously; thus the author displays his cleverness and sets the proper tone for the familiar essay: the topic is, he implies, relatively trivial but worthy of the reader's casual attention in a moment of leisure, for it will prove to be both entertaining and informative.

In "Wild Apples," however, Thoreau goes beyond this convention and suggests that the history of the apple tree is a metaphor for the history of man himself. In a journal entry of February 15, 1860 (just after his lyceum readings of "Wild Apples"), Thoreau alluded to the technique used to achieve his purpose:

> As in the expression of moral truths we admire any closeness to the physical fact which in all language is the symbol of the spiritual, so, finally, when natural objects are described, it is an advantage if words derived originally from nature, it is true, but which have been turned (*tropes*) from their primary signification to a moral sense, are used, i.e., if the object is personified. (JXIII: 145)

As he traces the history of the apple tree, then, Thoreau is both discussing natural history and preparing the reader for a discussion of human destiny—implicitly conflating the two. The apple tree, he says, is "the most civilized of all trees":

> It has been longer cultivated than any other, and so is more humanized; and who knows but, like the dog, it will at length be no longer traceable to its wild original? It migrates with man, like the dog and horse and cow: first, perchance, from Greece to Italy, thence to England, thence to America; and our Western emigrant is still marching steadily toward the setting sun with the seeds of the apple in his pocket, or perhaps a few young trees strapped to his load. (W 5: 292)

Like the apple, man's western migration contains his fate. As he had in several of his earlier works, Thoreau exploits the conventional myth of the progress of civilization from Greece to the New World, and he proceeds to justify the "manifest destiny" of the western migration by cataloging the beneficial effects of the apple's introduction to America upon indigenous insects, birds, quadrupeds, and even Indians. At the same time, Thoreau subtly inverts the conventional understanding of the "progress" of civilization: he implies that we are in danger of a kind of diminishment in losing the traces of our "wild original." And by portraying the apple as enhancing the environment because it has adapted to it, Thoreau introduces one of the central themes of the essay: his preference for the wild to the cultivated apple and, symbolically, his belief that man himself will fulfill his destiny not by exploiting the American landscape but by allowing it to naturalize him.

Thoreau goes on to provide his readers with detailed, lively descriptions of the apple tree's flower and fruit and a quite specific calendar of the stages of the apple's growth. The information, both entertaining and practical, also serves Thoreau's prophetic impulse. He writes of the apple tree generally, "The flowers of the apple are perhaps the most beautiful of any tree's, so copious and so delicious to both sight and scent," and he notes how, walking through an orchard, "you pass through a little region possessed by the fragrance of ripe apples, and thus enjoy them without price, and without robbing anybody" (294–95). The fragrance of apples appeals to "common sense," to "sight and scent," but the fragrance is also a symbol of the spiritual qualities inherent in all creation. Thus the orchard becomes the prelapsarian Garden and the apple a symbol, not of man's Fall, but of the possibility of renewed innocence.[29] As in both *A Week* and *Walden*, but without the more obvious pretensions of those books, Thoreau insists that in order to transform America into the Garden, we must cultivate what he called the "uncommon senses" so that we may perceive the paradise around us; in other words, we must acknowledge uses of nature higher than mere commodity in order to recover that place in which we may enjoy the fruit "without price and without robbing anybody." Making his point more explicit, Thoreau adds, "There is about all natural products a certain volatile and ethereal quality which represents their highest value, and which cannot be vulgarized, or bought and sold" (295). Significantly, Thoreau's discussion of the "ethereal" qualities of apples falls under his treatment of the cultivated rather than the wild apple, for Thoreau wants to stress that the true value of even the most marketable apple is not measured in such directly materialistic terms.

When Thoreau turns from the cultivated to the wild apple, he focuses his analogy between man and apple: "The apple emulates man's independence and enterprise. It is not simply carried, as I have said, but, like him, to some extent, it has migrated to this New World, and is even, here and there, making its way amid the aboriginal trees" (300–301).

On the level of the entertaining familiar essay, "man" is the subordinate component in the man-apple analogy: he is introduced for the sake of illustration, to enliven what might otherwise be a rather dry, purely scientific topic. For the "prophetic" moral essay, however, the wild apple is subordinate. Having been "turned," as Thoreau said, "from their primary signification to a moral sense," wild apples are only the apparent and not the actual subject of this discourse. As Thoreau noted in a journal entry for February 23, 1860, "A fact stated barely is dry. It must be the vehicle of some humanity in order to interest us. . . . Ultimately, the moral is all in all, and we do not mind if inferior truth is sacrificed to superior" (JXIII: 160). Thoreau risks little here as he celebrates the adaptation and naturalization of the apple in the New World; yet the "deliberate" reader will recognize that Thoreau's theme in "Wild Apples" is the same one he had stated so explicitly in A *Week*: "Men nowhere, east or west, live yet a *natural* life. . . . He needs not only to be spiritualized, but *naturalized*, on the soil of the earth" (*Week* 379).

In a brief digression on the indigenous crab apple, Thoreau begins to develop his apple tree symbolism with greater precision:

> Nevertheless, *our* wild apple is wild only like myself, perchance, who belongs not to the aboriginal race here, but have strayed into the woods from the cultivated stock. Wilder still . . . there grows elsewhere in this country a native and aboriginal crab-apple, *Maluscoronaria*, "whose nature has not yet been modified by cultivation." (W 5: 301)

Thoreau describes the native habitat, size, flower, and fruit of the indigenous apple, and he briefly narrates his own first sighting of the tree on his 1861 trip to Minnesota (material he added to the essay just prior to its publication). Then he makes his transition from the discussion of the crab apple to his next section on the wild apple by remarking of the crab, "But though these are indigenous, like the Indians, I doubt whether they are any hardier than those backwoodsmen among the apple trees, which, though descended from cultivated stocks, plant themselves in distant fields and forests, where the soil is favorable to them" (302). With this sentence, Thoreau fully establishes his metaphorical equation: the "cultivated stock" is the European settler in the civilized communities of the east; the wild apple is the European who, like himself or the backwoodsman, has reattached himself and adapted to the natural environment; and the indigenous crab apple is the native American Indian.

Looking back, then, we find that Thoreau's comments on the aboriginal tree are simultaneously applicable to the aboriginal American. He quotes from his authority Michaux, for example, "If, on being cultivated, it does not yield new and palatable varieties, it will at least be celebrated for the beauty of its flowers, and for the sweetness of its perfume" (301). Thoreau seems to have found Michaux's observations interesting not only for their literal meaning but because they captured his feelings about the Indian as well. Thoreau felt that the Indian probably could not and, in fact, should not be civilized, or "cultivated"; that his integrity and worth should be respected even though his age had passed; that the study of the Indian was essential to the inheritors of the New World even though he would not play a leading role in the destiny of America. In a journal entry for February 1859, Thoreau had criticized the historians' neglect of the Indian and proclaimed, "But even the indigenous animals are inexhaustibly interesting to us. How much more, then, the indigenous man of America!" (JXI: 437).

Thoreau's special interest was in the wild apple derived from cultivated stocks—in the white man who had learned to live independently in the New World—and so he turns to the wild apple, saying, "These are the ones whose story we have to tell" (W 5: 303). In the section headed "How the Wild Apple Grows," Thoreau's levels of signification multiply, and his language becomes increasingly dense. Thoreau's detailed account, based on careful observation of the actual growth of wild apple trees over a period of several years, is also an exemplary lesson in self-reliance, and, on another level still, a private record of his own experience. "I know of no trees," he writes, "which have more difficulties to contend with, and which more sturdily resist their foes" (302–3). Their chief foe, aside from "drought and other accidents," is the cow, "a fellow-emigrant from the old country," who browses on their shoots (303). The story of the wild apple's heroic triumph over the cattle is not only an example of Thoreau's nature writing at its finest but the story of his own triumph over his "fellow-emigrants." As early as his 1838 lecture "Society," and frequently thereafter, Thoreau had characterized the mass of men as "cattle," and the alert reader begins to suspect here that there is a sharper edge to Thoreau's essay than was at first apparent. As the wild apple is cut back by the cattle year after year, "it does not despair" but grows "more stout and scrubby, until it forms, not a tree as yet, but a little pyramidal, stiff, twiggy mass, almost as solid and impenetrable as a rock. . . . No wonder they are prompted to grow thorns at last, to defend themselves against such foes" (303–4).

> The cows continue to browse them thus for twenty years or more, keeping them down and compelling them to spread, until at last they are so broad that they become their own fence, when some interior shoot, which their foes cannot reach, darts upward with joy: for it has not forgotten its high calling, and bears its own peculiar fruit in triumph. (305)

Here Thoreau proclaims his own endurance and reveals the means that have enabled him to declare victory at last. For twenty years Thoreau himself had been "browsed" by superficial readers and kept down by a society of cattle who did not realize he had a richer fruit to bear. He, too, had been forced to surround his "interior shoot"—his private inspiration and ambition—with a protective and increasingly thorny fence of material both to satisfy and to fend off browsers. But, like the wild apple, Thoreau did not forget his high calling. The anecdote continues:

> Such are the tactics by which it finally defeats its bovine foes. Now, if you have watched the progress of a particular shrub, you will see that it is no longer a simple pyramid or cone, but that out of its apex there rises a sprig or two,

> growing more lustily perchance than an orchard-tree, since the plant now devotes the whole of its repressed energy to these upright parts. In a short time these become a small tree, an inverted pyramid resting on the apex of the other, so that the whole has now the form of a vast hour-glass. The spreading bottom, having served its purpose, finally disappears, and the generous tree permits the now harmless cows to come and stand in its shade. (305)

The reading public, Thoreau's "bovine foes," have shaped his own "wild" American self and the expression of that self in his writing. In typical Thoreauvian fashion, he has converted hardship and failure into the source of his ultimate triumph: the twenty years of browsing, which kept his growth scrubby and stunted and which seemed to force him to naturalize himself and adapt to the native soil (literally, on the shores of Walden Pond), were the source of the independence and endurance that permit a second growth which surpasses that of the "orchard-tree"—the genteel writer who satisfies cultivated tastes. In his triumph, the cows become harmless and the tree generous.

The anecdote represents the perfection of Thoreau's mature style and exemplifies the very tactics by which he outwits his "foes." Thoreau is careful up to this point not to insist too heavily on the symbolic import of the anecdote, which, on a strictly literal level remains both informative and entertaining—the two qualities the general public demanded. The autobiographical dimension of this section of the essay is always fully embedded in the straightforward, though carefully selected, nature description. But because the wild apple has further significance as an exemplary (as opposed to private) emblem of self-reliance, endurance, and native strength, Thoreau gradually brings this public level of symbolic meaning into higher relief. "Through what hardships it may attain to bear a sweet fruit! . . . Who knows but this chance wild fruit . . . may be the choicest of all its kind, and foreign potentates shall hear of it, and royal societies seek to propagate it" (306–7). On the autobiographical level, Thoreau is expressing his private hope that his own fruits—his writings—may one day be sought after as the choicest of their kind; but his desire is generalized and made exemplary:

> What a lesson to man! So are human beings, referred to the highest standard, the celestial fruit which they suggest and aspire to bear, browsed on by fate; and only the most persistent and strongest genius defends itself and prevails. . . . Poets and philosophers and statesmen thus spring up in the country pastures, and outlast the hosts of unoriginal men. (307)

Thoreau's account thus satisfies both the "hasty and the deliberate reader," yielding both common sense and wisdom. Further, in the published essay, Thoreau is careful to temper the merely personal references and to maintain a genial tone that emphasizes the observed phenomena or, as in this case, a socially acceptable moral that tends to enhance his identification with his audience. Yet in the original journal entry from which this anecdote was drawn, Thoreau's personal identification with the fate of the wild apple is clearer, as is his contempt for his "cultivated" contemporaries. There, Thoreau immediately made the analogy between the wild apple and "the rude, neglected genius from amid the country hills" in whom he clearly sees himself. His personal frustration, resentment, and hope are clear in his description of the tree/man, who

> grows broad and strong, and scraggy and thorny, hopelessly stunted, you would say, and not like a sleek orchard tree all whose forces are husbanded *and the precious early years not lost*, and when at first, within this rind and hedge, the man shoots up, you see the thorny scrub of his youth about him, and he walks like an hour-glass, aspiring above, it is true, *but held down and impeded by the rubbish of old difficulties overcome*, and you seem to see his sands running out. But at length, thanks to his rude culture, he attains to his full stature, and every vestige of the thorny hedge which clung to his youth disappears, and he bears golden crops of Porters or Baldwins, *whose fame will spread* through all orchards for generations to come, while *the thrifty orchard tree which was his competitor will, perchance, have long since ceased to bear its engrafted fruit and decayed.* (JXI: 269–70; emphasis mine)

This passage needed to undergo several important transformations before Thoreau could present it to the public, the most important of which was the suppression of the personal bias and the tone of frustration and anger that it brought on. For it is obvious here that Thoreau resents the loss of his "precious early years," while the cultivated orchard trees—those urbane writers who were his contemporaries and whom he explicitly characterizes here as his "competitors"—flourished. More than a hint of malice is betrayed in his strangely violent concluding image of their death and decay. The "competition" was, of course, for fame, and Thoreau's identification with the wild apple implies his belief that *his* victory would be over the long run, that his true audience would be the "generations to come." With this evidence of his submerged bitterness, it is all the more telling that Thoreau chose to face his readers with apparent benevolence rather than open scorn.

While Thoreau revised his material in order to achieve a lighter, more generous tone, he was also willing to manipulate and, to some extent, misrepresent the natural facts in order to make the material conform to his symbolic construct. Thoreau, who had begun recording his annual observations of local wild apple trees as early as 1850 (though without any clear sense of their metaphorical significance), noted in his 1853 entries that the apple scrubs were "first planted by the cows, then browsed by them and kept down stubborn and thorny for years. . . . You see the cow-dung everywhere now with a hundred little trees springing up in it. Thus the cows create their own shade and food" (JV: 179–80). It was not until his journal entries of

1857 that Thoreau fully grasped the particular symbolic application of his observations, and he then discovered that the actual symbiotic relation between cattle and wild apples did not suit his purpose. The cattle, the "browsers," needed to be more clearly represented as the enemy; the wild apple, as his image of both personal and exemplary self-sufficiency, needed to appear more independent and more "generous." In his studies of seeds (particularly in "The Succession of Forest Trees"), Thoreau naturally found it essential to point out the importance of birds and animals in transporting seeds. Here, however, he minimized the significance of that relationship. As he noted in a journal entry cited earlier, "Ultimately, the moral is all in all, and we do not mind if inferior truth is sacrificed to superior."

In the essay the superior truth would presumably be the exemplary character represented by the wild apple, but his willingness to shape his material to his needs also allowed Thoreau to have a private joke at the expense of the "browsers," his superficial readers. In a journal entry from 1853, he had complained that his contemporaries hired him as a surveyor but not as a lecturer: "All the while that they use only your humbler faculties, your higher unemployed faculties, like an invisible cimetar [*sic*], are cutting them in twain. Woe be to the generation that lets any higher faculty in its midst go unemployed! That is to deny God and know him not, and he, accordingly, will know not of them" (JVI: 21–22). Acknowledging two distinct classes of readers, Thoreau manipulated the language of "Wild Apples" in such a way that he was able to inflict private attacks, intended to cut "like an invisible cimetar," on the conventional readers who remained unable to perceive the prophet in their midst.

This multilayered prose is sustained, then, with varying degrees of intensity, throughout the essay. In the section entitled "The Fruit and Its Flavor," Thoreau advises the reader of the best times to pick the wild apples and defends their "more racy and wild American flavors" (W 5: 310). He suggests that they are best eaten outdoors, where the eater partakes of the environment that nourished them—and, implicitly, is himself naturalized too—but adds, "Of course no flavors are thrown away; they are intended for the taste that is up to them. Some apples have two distinct flavors, and perhaps one half of them must be eaten in the house, the other out-doors" (312). The observation is no mere flight of fancy—Thoreau even quotes a letter of 1782 to the Boston Academy to verify his assertion; but it is also a comment on his own writing and his readers—the eaters of his fruit. Thoreau's essay can accommodate whatever taste is up to it—either the hasty, practical reader or the deliberate, wise reader, and there are flavors for both. He adds, however, "So there is one *thought* for the field, another for the house. I would have my thoughts, like wild apples, to be food for walkers, and will not warrant them to be palatable if tasted in the house" (314).

The section entitled "The Last Gleaning" is a wonderfully written account of searching for the last of the windfall late in the year, full of fine, detailed observations. Since Thoreau has made the analogy clear between the flavor of wild apples and that of his "thoughts," however, we read this section simultaneously on a literal and a symbolic level, for it is a wry lesson on how to find not only those apples but those *thoughts* that "lie concealed" in "lurking places," "where they are covered by leaves [he is punning here, as he had on "browsers"], safe from cows which may have smelled them out" (318).

In the final section of the essay, "The 'Frozen-Thawed' Apple," Thoreau writes, "Those which a month ago were sour, crabbed, and quite unpalatable to the civilized taste, such at least as were frozen while sound, let a warmer sun come to thaw them,—for they are extremely sensitive to its rays,—are found to be filled with a rich, sweet cider" (319). Here we have literal observation, exemplary symbol, and personal symbol. Like the anecdote at the conclusion of *Walden* about the "beautiful bug" that emerged from an apple-tree table after sixty years "to enjoy its perfect summer at last," this is a fable of metamorphosis. It is a millennial vision of the triumph of the self-reliant and principled individual who endures to create a new world, and it is a symbol of Thoreau's faith in the ripening of his own works under the genial rays of future time.

But unlike *Walden*, "Wild Apples" concludes not in the optimistic tone of the visionary but in the castigating tone of the biblical jeremiad. The commercial failures of his most ambitious works had not entirely dispelled Thoreau's faith, but they had displaced it from his own to future generations. He issues a final warning: "The era of the Wild Apple will soon be past. It is a fruit which will probably become extinct in New England" (321). At first his tone is nostalgic, a lament for lost pleasures and opportunities. Thoreau fears that the wild apple, which in its very toughness and durability represented the fruits of democracy, available to even the humblest, will be replaced by the cultivated apple available only in the marketplace. "Now that they have grafted trees, and pay a price for them, they collect them into a plat by their houses, and fence them in,—and the end of it all will be that we shall be compelled to look for our apples in a barrel" (321). As the wild apple disappears, so does the naturalized man in whom Thoreau has placed his hopes for America. As he noted in a journal entry for November 26, 1860,

> Do not think that the fruits of New England are mean and insignificant, while those of some foreign land are noble and memorable. Our own, whatever they may be, are far more important to us than any others can be. They educate us, and fit us to live in New England. Better for us is the wild strawberry than the pineapple, the wild apple than the orange, the hazelnut or pignut than the cocoanut or almond, and not on account of their flavor merely, but the part they play in our education. (JXIV: 274)

Thoreau ends his essay with a stark vision, cautiously expressed not in his own words but in those of the book of Joel: "The vine is dried up, and the fig tree languishes; the pomegranate tree, the palm tree also, and the apple tree, even all the trees of the field, are withered: because joy is withered away from the sons of men" (W 5: 322). The passage is especially striking when we recognize it as the converse of his description, earlier in the essay, of the triumphant wild apple: "when some interior shoot, which their foes cannot reach, darts upward with joy: for it has not forgotten its high calling, and bears its own peculiar fruit in triumph."

In his book on Thoreau and his work, Richard Bridgman sees in the quotations that conclude "Wild Apples" another symptom of the "dark Thoreau" whose "imagination ever returned to . . . the dismal. . . . Hence Thoreau chose to conclude this sunnily realistic essay with a series of diatribes from the prophet Joel. . . . The apocalyptic violence of these quotations in context is astonishing. Their presence is explicable only by referring to Thoreau's constitutional pessimism."[30] Yet there are other explanations, more consistent with the skillful and deliberate crafting of this complex essay. Even for the reader who has regarded "Wild Apples" as a "sunnily realistic" familiar essay and nothing more, Thoreau's conclusion would seem neither inexplicable nor astonishing; rather, it would be regarded as another instance of the witty mock seriousness and hyperbole that Thoreau has provided throughout the essay, as an ironic elevation into the prophet's rage of the genteel essayist's civilized nostalgia for the passing of a simpler, rustic era. As such, the closing neatly rounds out the essay by complementing the opening catalog of classical and scriptural allusions to the fruit. In this respect, it is of utmost importance that the diatribe not come from the author's own mouth, for the quotation allows the "hasty" reader to regard the closing as no more than a final example of the author's erudition and wit. Still, the essay does end on a disconcerting dying fall, and the "deliberate" reader will recognize that the prophecy is indeed genuine and applicable. Bridgman is correct to note a deep-seated pessimism in the passage, but not when he implies that a pessimism crippling and uncontrollable mars an otherwise pleasant essay. Rather, that pessimism is the culmination of the genuinely prophetic vein running throughout the essay, a thorny, protective pessimism aimed at Thoreau's own audience but which he controls and uses to create his art and triumph at last.

Even though his lyceum readings of "Wild Apples" in February 1860 were apparently quite successful,[31] Thoreau nevertheless complained in the pages of his journal the following week,

> Always you have to contend with the stupidity of men. It is like a stiff soil, a hard-pan. If you go deeper than usual, you are sure to meet with a pan made harder even by the superficial cultivation. The stupid you have always with you.

> Men are more obedient at first to words than ideas. They mind names more than things. Read to them a lecture on "Education," naming that subject, and they will think that they have heard something important, but call it "Transcendentalism," and they will think it moonshine. Or halve your lecture, and put a psalm at the beginning and a prayer at the end of it and read it from a pulpit, and they will pronounce it good without thinking. (JXII: 145)

Assessing his audience thus harshly, Thoreau had devised a literary strategy sufficient to his purposes. He had never given up his desire for acclaim in the literary marketplace, but it had usually eluded him; nor had he ever lost the conviction of his calling to be a prophet to America. At the end of his career, he achieved a degree of success in both areas by having learned how to appeal to two audiences. Thoreau's late essays, including "Wild Apples," did find a measure of popular success both as lectures and in print in the *Atlantic Monthly*. It was largely because of these (and the posthumously published travel books on Maine and Cape Cod) that Thoreau's reputation as a nature writer was kept alive after his death. Thoreau was not without his small following of "deliberate" readers during his lifetime, but for the most part this audience—those responsive to his embedded prophetic vision—emerged slowly in the years after his death. Early and repeated failures had driven Thoreau to regard posterity as his ultimate audience even as he did his best to win over the popular audience of his day. Ultimately, it was this dual effort that provided the impetus for his finest art.

NOTES

Introduction

1. Perry Miller, *Consciousness in Concord* (Boston: Houghton Mifflin, 1958), 5.

2. H. Daniel Peck, *Thoreau's Morning Work: Memory and Perception in* A Week on the Concord and Merrimack Rivers, *the* Journal *and* Walden (New Haven: Yale University Press, 1990), x.

3. William Charvat, *Literary Publishing in America, 1790–1850* (Philadelphia: University of Pennsylvania Press, 1959), 7–8.

4. Michael T. Gilmore, *American Romanticism and the Marketplace* (Chicago: University of Chicago Press, 1985), 9–10.

Chapter 1
"That Public Ground between God and Conscience"

1. See the biographical sketches in Joel Myerson's *The New England Transcendentalists and the* Dial: *A History of the Magazine and Its Contributors* (Rutherford: Fairleigh Dickinson University Press, 1980), and Anne C. Rose, *Transcendentalism as a Social Movement, 1830–1850* (New Haven: Yale University Press, 1981), 6–7.

2. Andrews Norton, "The New School in Literature and Religion," *Boston Daily Advertiser*, August 27, 1838; rpt. in Perry Miller, *The Transcendentalists* (Cambridge: Harvard University Press, 1950), 195.

3. Miller, *The Transcendentalists*, 193 (comma within quotation deleted).

4. Rose, *Transcendentalism as a Social Movement, 1830–1850*, 85–90, 103n.

5. Henry Wadsworth Longfellow, *The Letters of Henry Wadsworth Longfellow*, ed. Andrew Hilen, 6 vols. (Cambridge: Harvard University Press, 1967–1982), 2: 268. The "tutor" to whom Longfellow refers was Charles Stearns Wheeler, who had been Thoreau's close friend at the Concord Academy and subsequently his roommate at Harvard.

6. Compare this, for example, to his description of his bean field in *Walden*: "Mine was, as it were, the connecting link between wild and cultivated fields" (158).

7. Walter Harding, *The Days of Henry Thoreau* (New York: Alfred A. Knopf, 1965), 84.

8. Frederick Henry Hedge, "Coleridge," *The Christian Examiner* 14 (March 1833): 109–29; rpt. in Miller, *The Transcendentalists*, 69.

9. George Ripley, "Introductory Notice," *Specimens of Foreign Standard Literature* (1838); rpt. in Miller, *The Transcendentalists*, 295.

10. Orestes Brownson, "Emerson," *Boston Quarterly Review* 2 (January 1839): 1–27; rpt. in Miller, *The Transcendentalists*, 433.

11. Quoted in Myerson, *The New England Transcendentalists and the* Dial, 38.

12. This does seem to be the case; see Fuller's description of the journal she envisioned, in a letter to W. H. Channing, MFL 2: 126.

13. Compare Fuller's definition to Thoreau's description of his journal in an entry for February 8, 1841: "My journal is that of me which would else spill over and run to waste . . . I must not live for it, but in it for the gods—They are my correspondent to whom daily I send off this sheet post-paid" (J1: 259). The critic's correspondent is the public, the journalist's is the gods; but in fact the process of recording private impressions is identical.

14. George Allen, "Reproductive Criticism," *New York Review* 2.3 (January 1838): 49–75.

15. In Thoreau's "Index rerum"; quoted by Linck Johnson, "Historical Introduction," *Week* 437.

16. Fuller's complete response is actually rather confusing, and she was perhaps confused herself about Emerson's request. She replied to Emerson's letter, "The Persius shall go into the first number. I am sure they ought to be glad of it! How beautiful, how appropriate is your motto. I should think you would always have a regard for Persius who has furnished you with it" (MFL 2: 133; April 25, 1840). Her first sentence seems clearly to refer to Thoreau's essay, in direct response to Emerson's request that it be included in the first number. But her subsequent remarks seem to refer to the "Notes from the Journal of a Scholar," which Emerson had compiled from the journal of his dead brother Charles and to which he had added an epigraph from Persius, *Satire I*, lines 38–40. Fuller does not distinguish clearly between Thoreau's composition and Charles Emerson's (both of which Emerson had sent to her on April 24), and her response seems to conflate the two. Both, in fact, were included in the first issue of the *Dial*.

17. James Freeman Clarke to Sarah Clarke, cited in Myerson, *The New England Transcendentalists and the* Dial, 50.

18. "Sympathy," *Boston Morning Post*, July 4, 1840, 1.

19. See Bernard Rosenthal, "*The Dial*, Transcendentalism, and Margaret Fuller," *English Language Notes* 8.1 (September 1970): 28–36, for a concise and persuasive, though unsympathetic, discussion of Fuller's control over the *Dial* from 1840 to 1842.

20. In fact, the journal passage from which he extracted the concluding sentences of "The Service" begins, "Let us not wait any longer, but step down from the mountains on to the plains of the earth" (J1: 155 [July 11, 1840]).

21. There are three instances of the imperative in the first section, none in the second, and twelve in the final section (including two quoted from Sir Thomas Browne). As Otto Jespersen points out, "The most important division of human utterances from a purely notional point of view" is between those "in which the speaker does not want directly to influence the will of the hearer" and those "which aim at influencing the will of the hearer . . . i.e., at making him do something." The sentences of Thoreau's first two sections, however blunt and assertive in their way, belong to the first class, while the tone of the third section is controlled by the use of sentences of the second class, the imperative. These, Jespersen explains, "may range from brutal commands through many intermediate steps (demands, injunctions, implorations, invitations) to the most modest and humble prayer (entreaty, supplication)" (Otto Jespersen, *A Modern English Grammar on Historical Principles*, vol. 4 [Copenhagen: Ejnar Munksgaard, 1949], 467–68).

22. In his edition of Emerson's letters, Ralph Rusk identifies this as part of the

latter of two sheets he tentatively dates "April 21? and 23? 1840." Thoreau scholars have uniformly accepted this dating and Rusk's assumption that Emerson is referring to Thoreau's "Persius" essay, but Rusk is certainly mistaken. While his dating of the letter's first sheet seems correct, internal and external evidence makes it clear that this second sheet is actually a continuation of a letter Emerson began on Tuesday, August 4, in which he reported that Thoreau "has left with me a piece of prose for you, which I will send now or presently. I am to read it first" (EmL 2: 322). Emerson set the letter aside and continued it on a new sheet—the one Rusk dates "April 23?" but actually sometime on the afternoon of August 5 or 6—beginning "Dialling still." In the interval, he had read Thoreau's essay and so returns to that, saying "I believe I shall roll up with this, Thoreau's paper. I read it through this morning." Emerson set the letter aside again, briefly, and concluded with the paragraph headed "Thursday Eve," meaning Thursday, August 6. Emerson's characterization of Thoreau's piece here clearly refers to "The Service" rather than "Persius." In a letter to Fuller that *is* dated April 23, Emerson tells her, "I have Thoreau's Persius rewritten Can you not put it in Number One It is a piece of character" (EmL 2: 290). It is inconceivable that Emerson would write another letter to Fuller on the same day characterizing it as he does in the passage in question. Moreover, if the sheet is redated to August 6, the other information contained there will be seen to follow logically upon that in the letter of August 4.

23. In Thoreau's "Index rerum"; quoted and dated by Johnson, "Historical Introduction," *Week* 440.

24. This journal entry underwent an interesting metamorphosis when Emerson revised it for inclusion in his "Introductory Lecture on the Times," first delivered in December 1841 and later printed in the *Dial* for July 1842. The particular man, Henry Thoreau, becomes a generalized and exemplary character, so that the potentially tragic situation of the individual man, described in the journal entry, becomes an omen of universal triumph in the lecture—the lone, exceptional man "predicts what shall be the general fulness" (*Dial* 3.1: 5).

25. Rufus W. Griswold, *Passages from the Correspondence and Other Papers of Rufus W. Griswold*, ed. W. M. Griswold (Cambridge, Mass.: W. M. Griswold, 1898), 98–99.

26. Entry in Emerson's account book for November 28, 1841; rpt. in Walter Harding, "Thoreau in Emerson's Account Book," *Thoreau Society Bulletin* 159 (Spring 1982): 1–3. The most thorough discussion of this project is Robert Sattelmeyer, "Thoreau's Projected Work on the English Poets," *Studies in the American Renaissance, 1980*, ed. Joel Myerson (Boston: Twayne, 1980), 239–57.

Chapter 2
"The Value of a Fact"

1. See Richard Lebeaux's chapter "Grief Responses," in *Young Man Thoreau* (Amherst: University of Massachusetts Press, 1977).

2. Ibid., 184.

3. Thoreau revised this entry for inclusion in his essay "A Walk to Wachusett," which I discuss in chapter 3.

4. The *Dial*'s publishers, Weeks & Jordan, had gone bankrupt and were in debt to the journal; Emerson discovered that it had only about three hundred subscribers, and that it yielded only around $750 per year, of which $700 went to meet expenses. Thus Fuller could not be paid the meager $200 she had been promised, and certainly no contributors could be paid (EmL 3: 36; Myerson, *The New England Transcendentalists and the* Dial, 73–74.)

5. Fuller had a different view of her own and his open-mindedness as editors. When she learned that Emerson would take over the *Dial*, she wrote to him: "The work cannot but change its character a good deal, but it will now be understood there is a change of director, too. The only way in which this is of importance to me is that I think you will sometimes reject pieces that I should not. For you have always had in view to make a good periodical and represent your own tastes, while I have had in view to let all kinds of people have freedom to say their say, for better, for worse" (MFL 3: 57–58; April 9, 1842).

6. Portions of the following discussion draw upon my essay "'The Value of a Fact': Thoreau and His Audience in the 'Natural History of Massachusetts'" and are reprinted by permission of the *Bucknell Review*, where it originally appeared in Vol. 28.1 (1983): 65–80.

7. Stephen E. Wicher and Robert E. Spiller, eds., *The Early Lectures of Ralph Waldo Emerson*, vol. 1, 1833–1836 (Cambridge: Harvard University Press, 1959), xvii.

8. Sherman Paul, *The Shores of America: Thoreau's Inward Exploration* (Urbana: University of Illinois Press, 1958; 1972), 103.

9. Ibid., 120.

10. This passage complements his later, more famous meditation on the universality of foliate structure when he observes the thawing banks of the railroad cut in the "Spring" chapter of *Walden*. On the source of Thoreau's theory of universal foliate structure in Goethe's *Italienishe Reise*, see Robert D. Richardson, Jr., *Henry Thoreau: A Life of the Mind* (Berkeley: University of California Press, 1986), 29–30, 119, 156–59.

11. Thoreau's statement was taken from one of his earliest journal entries, for December 16, 1837, and was quite possibly a direct response to *Nature*; by 1842, however, and in the context of the "Natural History," the remark becomes more complex. Fuller may have recalled Thoreau's aphorism when she wrote in *Summer on the Lakes, in 1843* (Boston: Little, Brown, 1844), "Every fact is a clod, from which may grow an amaranth or a palm" (132).

12. Francis Bowen, "Emerson's Nature," *Christian Examiner* 21 (January 1837): 377; rpt. in Miller, *The Transcendentalists*, 174.

13. Paul, *Shores*, 107. Paul's view is reasserted approvingly by Charles Anderson in "Thoreau and the *Dial*: The Apprentice Years," *Essays Mostly on Periodical Publishing in America: A Collection in Honor of Clarence Ghodes*, ed. James Woodress (Durham: Duke University Press, 1973), 92–120.

14. Emerson's appreciation of "Dolon" is partly explained by the consolation he found in it for the loss of his son Waldo; see JMN 7: 179. Fuller, who was a close friend of Newcomb's at the time, took a typically more critical view of the piece, finding the style excessive and obscure; see MFL 3: 78.

15. Emerson, "The Naturalist," *The Early Lectures of Ralph Waldo Emerson,* 1: 72, 76.

16. Amos Bronson Alcott, *The Letters of A. Bronson Alcott,* ed. Richard L. Herrnstandt (Ames: Iowa State University Press, 1969), 88.

17. Carl Bode, *Anatomy of American Popular Culture, 1840–61* (Berkeley: University of California Press, 1959), 211.

18. Nathaniel Hawthorne, "Footprints on the Sea-Shore," *Twice-told Tales,* vol. 9 of *The Centenary Edition of the Works of Nathaniel Hawthorne* (Columbus: Ohio State University Press, 1974), 451.

19. "Natural Science . . . Lessons of Town and Country," *Knickerbocker Magazine* 16.2 (August 1840): 91–101.

20. Noting that Thoreau's "Natural History" practically ignores the books he is nominally reviewing, John Hildebidle calls this "a peculiar way to evaluate even the dullest book" (*Thoreau: A Naturalist's Liberty* [Cambridge: Harvard University Press, 1983], 99). Other Thoreau scholars have expressed a similar view, but it ought to be pointed out that here, too, Thoreau is well within the bounds of convention, for it was not at all unusual for reviewers of the period to treat their texts not as objects of close scrutiny or judgment but as the occasion for expressing the reviewer's own thoughts on the given subject. In addition to the *Knickerbocker* review discussed here, another example of this kind of "review" dealing with works of natural history is "Study of Natural History," *North American Review* 89 (October 1835): 406–30, nominally a review of William Swainson, *A Preliminary Discourse on the Study of Natural History* (London, 1834).

21. H[enry]. T. Tuckerman, "The Poetry of Bryant," *Democratic Review* 16 (February 1845): 185–91. Lewis Gaylord Clarke, the conservative editor of the *Knickerbocker,* had made a similar distinction in his praise for Oliver Wendell Holmes's treatment of nature. Holmes's descriptions, he said, are beautiful "only because they are accurate"; he approached nature sensibly, "not as one who gazes largely over hills and vales, meadows and brooks, but as one who keenly hunts for gems among the waters and the sands—and who finds them too." Quoted in Perry Miller, *The Raven and the Whale: The War of Words and Wits in the Era of Poe and Melville* (1955; rpt. Westport, Conn.: Greenwood Press, 1973), 283.

22. Nathaniel Hawthorne, *The American Notebooks,* ed. Claude M. Simpson, vol. 8 of *The Centenary Edition of the Works of Nathaniel Hawthorne* (Columbus: Ohio State University Press, 1972), 355.

23. Nathaniel Hawthorne, *The Letters, 1813–1843,* ed. Thomas Woodson et al., vol. 15 of *The Centenary Edition of the Works of Nathaniel Hawthorne* (Columbus: Ohio State University Press, 1984), 656–57.

24. "Literary Notices: the *Dial,*" *New York Daily Tribune,* July 6, 1842, p. 1, col. 1.

25. Quoted in Joel Myerson, "Thoreau and the *Dial*: A Survey of the Contemporary Press," *Thoreau Journal Quarterly* 5.1 (January 1973): 5; and Myerson, *The New England Transcendentalists and the* Dial, 80.

26. "Editor's Table, 'The Dial,'" *Knickerbocker Magazine* 20.2 (August 1842): 198.

27. Quoted in Myerson, "Thoreau and the *Dial,*" 6.

28. Thomas Wentworth Higginson, "My Out-door Study," *Atlantic Monthly* 8 (September 1861): 306.

Chapter 3
"The Poet Active"

1. "Literary Notices: The *Dial*," *New York Daily Tribune*, October 11, 1842, 1.

2. Harding, *Days*, 117.

3. "Herbert's Translation from Æschylus," *North American Review* 69 (October 1849): 414. The other reference to Thoreau's translation appeared in "Mr. Herbert's Translations," *Boston Semi-Weekly Advertiser*, September 29, 1849, l; rpt. in Kenneth W. Cameron, *Transcendental Log* (Hartford: Transcendental Books, 1973), 45.

4. "Literary Notices: The *Dial*," *New York Daily Tribune*, January 17, 1843, 1.

5. In addition to the responses cited below, see those contemporary reviews—from both the religious and secular presses—listed or reprinted in Philip F. Gura and Joel Myerson, eds., *Critical Essays on American Transcendentalism* (Boston: G. K. Hall, 1982).

6. "Editor's Table, 'The Dial,'" *Knickerbocker Magazine* 16.2 (August 1840): 190.

7. "Editor's Table, 'The Dial,'" *Knickerbocker Magazine* 16.5 (November 1840): 451–52. The reviewer noted that one Boston paper ran a parody of Alcott entitled "Gastric Sayings."

8. "Editor's Table, 'The Dial,'" *Knickerbocker Magazine* 17.2 (February 1841): 171–74. See also the parody of transcendental language, "Quozziana," by "Moonshine Milkywater" [Samuel Kettell], *Brother Jonathan* 1 (March 26, 1842): 354; rpt. in Gura and Myerson, *Critical Essays*, 30–31.

9. William A. Jones, "Ralph Waldo Emerson," *Arcturus* 1.5 (April 1841): 279–80. Jones's essay was later reprinted in his series of "Unitarian Portraits" for the *Democratic Review* 2 (October 1844): 389–96.

10. *The Correspondence of Emerson and Carlyle*, ed. Joseph Slater (New York: Columbia University Press, 1964), 280.

11. See ibid., 287, 312–13.

12. Ibid., 328–29.

13. Frank Luther Mott, *A History of American Magazines, 1741–1850* (New York: Appleton & Co., 1930), 510.

14. Ibid., 510.

15. Edward Everett Hale, *Lowell and His Friends* (Boston, 1899), 83.

16. W[illiam] A. Jones, "Criticism in America," *Democratic Review* 15 (September 1844): 241.

17. Margaret Fuller, "American Literature; Its Position in the Present Time, and Prospects for the Future," *Papers on Literature and Art* (New York: Wiley & Putnam, 1846), 137–38.

18. Ibid., 138.

19. Jones, "Criticism in America," 246. For an even breezier view of magazine style, see "Magazine Literature," *Arcturus* 2.12 (November 1841): 342–44.

20. Edgar Allan Poe, *The Letters of Edgar Allan Poe*, ed. John Ward Ostrom, 2 vols. (Cambridge: Harvard University Press, 1948; enl. ed., New York: Gordion Press, 1966), 1: 168; see also 162, 164, 166.

21. Jones, "Criticism in America," 247.

22. Reviews of *Boston Miscellany* for April 1842, *Brother Jonathan* 1.15 (April 9, 1842): 409; and for September, 1842, *Brother Jonathan* 3.1 (September 3, 1842): 16;

"Literary Notices: the *Boston Miscellany,*" *New York Tribune,* December 16, 1842, 1; "Literary Notices," *Quarto Boston Notion, or Robert's Weekly Journal* 1.40 (July 9, 1842): 630.

23. The seminal study on picturesque tourism is Hans Huth, *Nature and the American: Three Centuries of Changing Attitudes* (Berkeley: University of California Press, 1957). Much recent scholarship on both American landscape painting and writing has built on Huth's foundation; particularly useful here has been Edward J. Nygren, with Bruce Robertson, *Views and Visions: American Landscape before 1830* (Washington, D.C.: The Corcoran Gallery, 1986). The most important successor of Huth is undoubtedly John F. Sears, *Sacred Places: American Tourist Attractions in the Nineteenth Century* (New York: Oxford University Press, 1989).

24. Richard Fuller's fragmentary account of their excursion is printed in the *Thoreau Society Bulletin* 121 (Fall 1972): 1–4.

25. See Hawthorne, *American Notebooks,* 259–61; George William Curtis, *Early Letters of George William Curtis to John S. Dwight,* ed. George Willis Cooke (New York: Harper's, 1898), 224–25.

26. Thomas Cole, "Essay on American Scenery," in *American Art 1700–1960: Sources and Documents,* ed. John W. McCoubrey (Englewood Cliffs, N.J.: Prentice-Hall, 1965), 98–110; the quotation appears on 99–100.

27. Sears, *Sacred Places,* 6–7.

28. Thoreau later revised the essay for inclusion in the posthumously published volume of excursions. I quote from the *Boston Miscellany* text, as best representing Thoreau's intentions in 1843, but I include cross-reference to W 5 where substantive differences between the texts occur. In general, Thoreau's later revisions temper a stridency and dogmatism apparent in the 1843 version, as when he changes "surely" to "it seemed to us," and similar revisions.

29. Lydia Sigourney, for example, begins each chapter of her *Scenes in My Native Land* (Boston: James Munroe & Co., 1845) with verses on the place described therein, and the title of Caroline Gilman's *The Poetry of Travelling in the United States* (New York: Samuel Coleman, 1838) captures the sense of the picturesque travelogue of the period (though it is in fact a less poetic account than many). The romantic traveler's persona is succinctly conveyed by the anecdote with which George William Curtis prefaces his more exotic travelogue, *Nile Notes of a Howadji* (New York: Harper & Bros., 1851):

> When the Persian poet Hafiz was asked by the philosopher Zenda what he was good for, he replied—
> "Of what use is a flower?"
> "A flower is good to smell," said the philosopher.
> "And I am good to smell it," said the poet.

30. Sigourney, *Scenes in My Native Land,* 30–31.

31. Sarah J. Hale, *Traits of American Life* (Philadelphia: Carey & Hart, 1835), 189–91.

32. Cole, "Essay on American Scenery," 101, 108.

33. Fuller, *Summer on the Lakes, in 1843,* 241.

34. Cole, "Essay on American Scenery," 108.

35. *Boston Morning Post,* January 2–19, 1842, 4.

36. *New York Tribune*, December 19, 23, and 24, 1842, 4.

37. "Literary Notices: The *Boston Miscellany*," *New York Daily Tribune*, December 16, 1842, 1.

38. Lidian Emerson, *Selected Letters of Lidian Jackson Emerson*, ed. Delores Bird Carpenter (Columbia: University of Missouri Press, 1987), 130.

39. Fuller, "American Literature," 126.

40. Harding, *Days*, 142.

41. Quoted in ibid., 143. The records of the Concord Lyceum are reprinted in Kenneth Walter Cameron, *The Massachusetts Lyceum during the American Renaissance* (Hartford: Transcendental Books, 1969), 148–50.

42. Wicher and Spiller, *The Early Lectures of Ralph Waldo Emerson* 1: 94. Paul also notes the connection between Thoreau's "Raleigh" lecture and Emerson's 1835 series of biographies, as a popular subject that Thoreau "probably hoped . . . would launch him as a lecturer." Paul goes on to suggest that "because Thoreau was not yet an excursionist, 'Raleigh' provided the only materials he could treat in a popular way" (*Shores*, 127). As I argued in chapter 2, however, the "Natural History" had already initiated Thoreau into the treatment of popular topics, and although Paul discusses "A Walk to Wachusett" as if it were a later composition, it had in fact already been published in the *Boston Miscellany* when "Raleigh" was delivered as a lecture. Paul is correct in noting the popularity of "lives" and the model provided by Emerson, but the emphasis should be on the variety rather than the paucity of popular forms with which Thoreau was experimenting at this time.

43. Reading through the records of the lyceums and newspaper accounts of lectures, one is struck by the frequency with which it is recorded that bad weather resulted in poor attendance or in lectures canceled altogether. At the nearby Lincoln, Massachusetts, Lyceum, for example, inclement weather resulted in the cancellation of lectures on both February 1 and February 15, 1843. See Cameron, *Massachusetts Lyceum*, 209 and passim.

44. Selected Letters of Lidian Jackson Emerson, 128.

45. Quoted in Harding, *Days*, 143.

46. It is difficult to discern precisely when Thoreau composed "Raleigh," but it is clear that the lecture version was written sometime after March 1842 and, of course, before February 8, 1843, when he read it. Miller mistakenly asserts that both "Raleigh" and "The Service" were written in the summer and fall of 1840 and that Thoreau submitted both of them to Fuller, who had rejected them both by January 1841 (*Consciousness in Concord*, 2: 52). While a few of the "Raleigh" passages were drawn from Thoreau's journal entries of August 1840 (included in the "Lost Journal" edited by Miller; cf. J1: 174–75), the bulk of the essay is drawn from journal entries of January and March 1842 (see J1: 358–60, 363, 376–77), a fact that Miller seems not to have recognized. Since Thoreau was still making journal entries on Raleigh after Emerson took over the editorship of the *Dial*, it is hardly credible that Thoreau submitted a version to Fuller or that she rejected one (as Miller points out, the manuscript was found among Emerson's papers [*Consciousness in Concord*, 2: 144]). I have found no reference to "Raleigh" in the writings of Thoreau, Emerson, or Fuller before January 1843. This suggests that "Raleigh" was composed during the same period as "Natural History" and "A Walk to Wachusett," and not at the time of "The Service."

47. Paul, *Shores*, 126.

CHAPTER 4
"NOW GOES OUR BRAVE YOUTH"

1. See J1: 403–29.

2. "Literary Notices: the *Dial*," *New York Daily Tribune*, April 11, 1843, 1.

3. For Thoreau's early translations of Anacreon see J1: 62, 65–66; on Emerson's request, see Corr 89.

4. Ralph Barton Perry, *The Thought and Character of William James*, 2 vols. (Boston: Little, Brown & Co., 1935), 1: 47–48.

5. H. H. Furness, ed., *Records of a Lifelong Friendship, 1807–1882: Ralph Waldo Emerson and William Henry Furness* (Boston and New York: Houghton Mifflin, 1910), 20–21.

6. Incorrectly dated February 16, 1843, in Corr (after Sanborn); see Kenneth Walter Cameron, *Companion to Thoreau's Correspondence* (Hartford: Transcendental Books, 1964), 225.

7. Hawthorne, *The American Notebooks*, 369 (April 7, 1843).

8. Longfellow, *Letters*, 2: 162.

9. Mott, *A History of American Magazines*, 375. See also Charvat, *Literary Publishing in America, 1790–1850*, 17–37; Charles A. Madison, *Book Publishing in America* (New York: McGraw-Hill, 1966), 14; John Tebbel, *A History of Book Publishing in the United States*, vol. 1, *The Creation of an Industry 1630–1865* (New York: Bowker, 1972), 203, 206.

10. Perry, *The Thought and Character of William James*, 1: 45.

11. See also Corr 110, 128, 133, and compare Emerson's similar lack of affinity for the associationists in New York, EmL 3: 18.

12. Longfellow, *Letters*, 2: 174n, 200–201. For a detailed discussion of magazine payments, and especially the *Knickerbocker*'s practices, see Mott, *A History of American Magazines*, 504–12.

13. Quoted in Algernon Tassin, *The Magazine in America* (New York: Dodd, Mead & Co., 1916), 107.

14. Mott, *A History of American Magazines*, 628.

15. Many of the best writers of the day did publish in the ladies' magazines because of the high pay and large circulation, but those magazines were nevertheless criticized as degrading to the profession of letters and the nation's image. While *Brother Jonathan* regularly praised the *Ladies' Companion*, the *New World* just as regularly condemned it; in a survey of "Our Magazine Literature" for the *New World* of March 11, 1843, Poe called the *Ladies' Companion* "a receptacle of nonsense from first to last, of picture nonsense, fashion nonsense, poetical nonsense, and prose nonsense" (303). An essay on "Literary Phenomena" in the *American Whig Review* for October 1846 similarly attacks "magazines illustrated with plates of the fashions and engravings, bad copies from the tawdry originals of the English annuals," and protests that "there are degrees of merit, steps on the intellectual ladder, quite out of sight of 'Graham' and 'Godey,' which it is believed the public may reach in safety" (4.4: 405–8).

16. Tebbel, *A History of Book Publishing in the United States*, 1: 209.

17. *New Mirror* (New York) 2.12 (December 23, 1843): 185.

18. Tebbel cites as an example the fact that in 1842, "both supplements and Harper's published Bulwer's *Zanoni* almost simultaneously, with the result that it

could be bought for six cents a copy. During the following year, short books were selling for six and a quarter cents; longer ones ranged from $.18 3/4 to $.37 1/2" (*A History of Book Publishing in the United States*, 1: 243.)

19. *New York Herald*, March 1843; quoted in Madison, *Book Publishing in America*, 25.

20. "Our Cheap Editions," *The New World* 4.23 (June 4, 1842): 366. See also "The Book Publishers and the New World Press," *New World* 6.16 (April 22, 1843): 476.

21. Eugene Exman, *The House of Harper: One Hundred and Fifty Years of Publishing* (New York: Harper & Row, 1967), 27. See also Tebell, *A History of Book Publishing in the United States*, 1: 243–45; Madison, *Book Publishing in America*, 23–26.

22. "Authors and Authorcraft," *Brother Jonathan* 1.11 (March 12, 1842): 296–97.

23. "What We Have to Say," *Brother Jonathan* 4.15 (April 15, 1843): 435.

24. Quoted in Tassin, *The Magazine in America*, 127.

25. Ibid., 143.

26. Sophia Hawthorne wrote in a letter of January 9, 1843, "The *Democratic Review* is so poor now that it can only offer twenty dollars for an article of what length soever, so that Mr. Hawthorne cannot well afford to give any but short stories to it; and besides it is so sadly dilatory about payment" (quoted in Mott, *A History of American Magazines*, 680n). The fact that commitments for payment to authors were unreliable enraged Hawthorne; he wrote to Horatio Bridge in March 1843 (shortly before Thoreau left for New York), "The system of slack payments in this country is most abominable, and ought of itself to bring upon us the destruction foretold by Father Miller. All do wrong alike, O'Sullivan is just as certain to disappoint me in money matters, as any pitiful little scoundrel among the booksellers. . . . The devil take such a system" (Hawthorne, *Letters, 1813–1843*, 681–82).

27. John Stafford, *The Literary Criticism of 'Young America': A Study of the Relationship of Politics and Literature, 1837–1850*, English Studies, no. 3 (Berkeley and Los Angeles: University of California Press, 1952), 5–7. Graham's circulation, by comparison, was 40,000 by 1842; *Godey*'s was 25,000 by 1840 and 40,000 by 1849; and the *Knickerbocker*'s was 5,000 in 1837 (Mott, *A History of American Magazines*, 552, 581, 607; see also 513–16).

28. Stafford, *Young America*, 117. See also Miller, *The Raven and the Whale*, and also Benjamin Spencer, *The Quest for Nationality: An American Literary Campaign* (Syracuse, N.Y.: Syracuse University Press, 1957).

29. "L" [Edgar Allen Poe], "Our Magazine Literature," *New World* 6 (March 11, 1843): 302.

30. J. A. Etzler, *The Paradise within the Reach of All Men . . . , in Two Parts*, 2d English ed. (London, 1842). The book was originally published in Pittsburgh, Pennsylvania, in 1833. See Joel Nydahl, ed., *The Collected Works of John Adolphus Etzler* (Delmar, N.Y.: Scholars' Facsimiles & Reprints, 1977), for a reprint of the 1833 text, and Nydahl's introduction for further information about Etzler and his book.

31. In a letter to his mother, August 6, Thoreau said he had submitted the piece "a month ago" (Corr 132); the next day, August 7, he wrote to Emerson that he had submitted it "six weeks ago" (Corr 133). Paul claims that Thoreau submitted the essay in May (*Shores*, 247), but this is highly unlikely, since, in addition to the evidence of these letters, Thoreau had reported to his mother on June 8 that he was still preparing his "bait."

32. "Paradise (to Be) Regained," *Democratic Review* 13 (November 1843): 449–63. References will be to the text in RP 19–47. Publication of the review was delayed until November because O'Sullivan wanted Thoreau to include a review of Etzler's second volume, which was to provide the plans for the machinery referred to in the first volume (see Corr 142). The second book, *The New World, or Mechanical System, to Perform the Labours of Man and Beast by Inanimate Powers That Cost Nothing, for Producing and Preparing the Substances of Life* (Philadelphia: C. F. Stollmeyer, 1841), could not be found, however, and Thoreau was not even sure it had actually been written. For Etzler's second book, see Nydahl, *The Collected Works of John Adolphus Etzler.*

33. For a useful summary of Thoreau's relation to the Fourierists in terms of economic thought, see Robin Linstromberg and James Balowe, "Thoreau and Etzler: Alternative Views of Economic Reform," *Midcontinent American Studies Journal* 11.1 (Spring 1970): 20–29; and Nydahl's introduction to *The Collected Works of John Adolphus Etzler.*

34. Thoreau revised Etzler's text extensively when quoting it. See Wendell Glick, "Thoreau's Use of His Sources," *New England Quarterly* 44 (1971): 101–9; and Glick's "Textual Introduction," RP 275–79.

35. In writing this parody, Thoreau may have had in mind not only Etzler's proposals but possibly also an editorial review of Emerson's 1842 lectures in New York, titled "Condition of Man and the Earth," printed in the *Tribune* for March 19, 1842 (rpt. in Cameron, *Transcendental Log,* 14). Probably written by Albert Brisbane, this review challenged Emerson's philosophy of individual moral reform and asked him if the aims of reform movements were not sufficiently worthy to rouse the transcendentalist philosopher to action; then, turning to his own visionary proposals, Brisbane continues:

> Man is the OVERSEER of the globe, . . . he should cultivate, embellish and beautify it. . . . The Earth is now in a frightful condition. . . . Besides the Deserts on the Earth's surface, which may be compared to ulcers on a human body, there are vast Swamps and Marshes, which send forth Miasmas, and scourge Mankind with other diseases, like Cholera, Plague, and Yellow Fever. Thus we see that the Human Race are collectively interested in a proper cultivation of the Globe. . . . Association and Attractive Industry, and a true Universal Policy would direct the Energies and Genius of Mankind to such great objects.

Thoreau's essay, then, is not merely a review of Etzler's book, but a rebuttal in the ongoing debate between the material and moral reformers.

36. Nydahl, *The Collected Works of John Adolphus Etzler,* 75. This passage is not quoted by Thoreau in his review.

37. [William A. Jones], "Horne's New Spirit of the Age," *Democratic Review* 15 (July, 1844): 62; see also Stafford, *Young America,* 56–57.

38. Thoreau, "The Landlord," *Democratic Review* 13 (October 1843): 427–30. References to this essay will be to the text in W 5: 153–62.

39. Harding, *Days,* 141; Harding and Michael Meyer, *New Thoreau Handbook* (New York: New York University Press, 1980), 36; Leo Marx, "Thoreau's Excursions," *Yale Review* 51 (Spring 1962): 367; and Charles Anderson, "Thoreau and the *Dial,*" 119. Sherman Paul was the first to examine the serious themes of "The Landlord,"

in "Thoreau's 'The Landlord': Sublimely Trivial for the Good of Men," *Journal of English and German Philology* 54 (October 1955): 587–90; this article was subsequently revised and incorporated into *Shores*. Paul sees the landlord as "the spheral man, the good man, the whole man" (*Shores*, 148). Joseph DeFalco develops this in terms of mythic and Hindu themes, in "'The Landlord': Thoreau's Emblematic Technique" (*ESQ* 56 [1969]: 23–32).

40. Marie Law Hamilton, *The English Familiar Essay in the Early Nineteenth Century* (Philadelphia, 1934; New York: Russell & Russell, 1965), 80.

41. Washington Irving, *The Sketchbook of Geoffrey Crayon, Gent.*, ed. Haskell Springer, vol. 8 of *The Complete Works of Washington Irving* (Boston: Twayne, 1978), 9–10.

42. Henry T. Tuckerman, *The Optimist* (New York: Putnam, 1850), n.p.

43. Henry T. Tuckerman, "Inns," *Putnam's* (June 1853); rpt. in *The Criterion; or The Test of Talk about Familiar Things* (New York: Hurd and Houghton, 1866), 4.

44. See my "Building America: Henry Thoreau and the American Home," *Prospects, A Journal of American Culture Studies* 11 (1987): 327–65.

45. Although Tuckerman's sketch "Inns" primarily indulges in nostalgia for the lost comforts of the great inns of merry old England, he too concludes, as he begins, with the suggestion of a higher moral import, calling inns the "landmarks of our precarious destiny, for we are but 'pilgrims and sojourners on the earth.' Jeremy Taylor compared human life to an inn, and Archbishop Leighton used to say he would prefer to die in one" (*The Criterion*, 42).

46. "American Magazines," *New World*, October 7, 1843, 426.

47. Harding, *Days*, 141.

48. For early journal entries used in the essay, see, for example, J1: 198, 210–12, 216, 238, 254–55 and 345; see J1: 439–41 (after August 23, 1842), for a fragment; and J1: 455 (April 27, 1843) for a relatively late entry incorporated into the essay.

49. Favorably reviewing an early number of the *Boston Miscellany*, *Brother Jonathan* added, "We trust [it] will live down the impression that a monthly cannot survive in Boston" (1.15 [April 9, 1842]: 409); but that impression proved correct. When Nathan Hale, Jr., quarreled with Bradbury and Soden and resigned the editorship of the *Miscellany*, Hale's friend James Russell Lowell began the *Pioneer* (in January 1843) to compete with it, but neither magazine survived, in spite of their high quality and the praise of reviewers—the *Pioneer* lasted only three issues and outlived the *Miscellany* by only one month. When the *Pioneer* folded, *Brother Jonathan* duly noted the end of "the only monthly left in Boston since the extinction of the Miscellany" (4.14 [April 8, 1843]: 409). The *Pioneer* had promised to pay contributors ten dollars, but when it folded, Lowell was eighteen hundred dollars in debt, and contributors found themselves in the same position regarding payment as Thoreau with the *Boston Miscellany*. Hawthorne, who contributed to both magazines (and most likely contacted the *Boston Miscellany* on Thoreau's behalf), wrote to Sophia upon learning of the *Pioneer* failure, "Not improbably we shall have to wait months for our money, if we get it at all. Nobody pays us" (*Letters, 1813–1843*, 678). On the *Pioneer*, see Mott, *A History of American Magazines*, 343–48, 718–20, 735–38; for a contemporary account of the split between the *Pioneer* and the *Miscellany*, see [Poe], "Our Magazine Literature," *New World* 6.10 (March 11, 1843): 303.

50. Myerson, *New England Transcendentalists and the* Dial, 93–94.

51. Emerson recorded similar observations in his journal; the cutting edge of his disapproval is clearer here, as in his concluding remark that "W.E.C. declares the piece is excellent: but it makes me nervous & wretched to read it, with all its merits" (JMN 9: 9).

52. Emerson cut "two pages or so" from the essay, according to Sanborn (see Corr 138). When Thoreau saw the essay in print, he wrote to Emerson, "I see that I was very blind to send you my manuscript in such a state, but I have a good second sight (?) at least" (Corr 145). When Thoreau revised the essay for inclusion in *Excursions*, he made a few substantive changes, but no new material was added and nothing was cut out, so we do not know what the material was that Emerson originally edited out.

53. See Hawthorne, *American Notebooks*, 379–82 (April 25, 1843), and "Buds and Bird Voices," *Mosses from an Old Manse*, vol. 10 of *The Centenary Edition of the Works of Nathaniel Hawthorne* (Columbus: Ohio State University Press, 1974), 155.

54. "Literary Notices, the *Dial*," *New York Daily Tribune*, October 27, 1843, 4. Extracts from "A Winter Walk" were also printed under the heading "Winter Scenery" in the *Weekly Tribune* for November 4, 1843.

55. "Editor's Table, 'The Dial,'" *Knickerbocker Magazine* 23.5 (November 1843): 486–87.

56. Thomas Wentworth Higginson, "Snow," *Atlantic Monthly* 9 (February 1862): 188–201; James Russell Lowell, "A Good Word for Winter" (1870), *The Works of James Russell Lowell* (Boston and New York: Houghton Mifflin, 1870; 1890), 3: 256–90. When Higginson's essay was published in the *Atlantic*, he wrote to James T. Fields, the editor, "'Snow' seems quite popular and Thoreau likes it, the only critic whom I should regard as really formidable on such a subject" (Higginson, *Letters and Journals of Thomas Wentworth Higginson, 1846–1906*, ed. Mary Thatcher Higginson [Boston: Houghton Mifflin, 1921], 114).

Chapter 5
"Favored by the Gods"

1. Emerson, "Chaucer," *The Early Lectures of Ralph Waldo Emerson*, 1: 273.

2. Frederick Schlegel, *Lectures on the History of Literature, Ancient and Modern*, 2 vols. (Philadelphia: Thomas Dobson and Sons, 1818), 1: 46. On Thoreau's reading, see Kenneth W. Cameron, "Books Thoreau Borrowed from Harvard College Library," *Emerson the Essayist* (Hartford: Transcendental Books, 1945; 1972), 2: 193. See also Robert Sattelmeyer, *Thoreau's Reading: A Study in Intellectual History with Bibliographical Catalogue* (Princeton: Princeton University Press, 1988).

3. In an entry for December 2, 1842, Emerson recorded in his account book, "Cash to H.D.T. for papers for Dial 10.00." The "papers" presumably refers to the "Ancient Poets" and to Thoreau's translations from Pindar, both of which Emerson published in the January *Dial*. Though Emerson had previously recorded paying Thoreau a few odd dollars for "expenses for the Dial," these were most likely reimbursements for money he had spent out of pocket as assistant to the editor, and no other record exists of payment "for papers." Perhaps Emerson felt it would help Thoreau preserve his dignity upon returning from New York if he treated him as a professional writer. See Harding, "Thoreau in Emerson's Account Book," 1–3.

4. "The Dial for January," *New York Daily Tribune*, January 25, 1844, p. 1, cols. 1–3.

5. Sattelmeyer argues correctly, I think, that Thoreau's work on the English poets (whatever the ultimate purpose) reflected "his own somewhat misguided appraisal of his literary vocation, and the deeply ambivalent effects of Emerson's patronage"; "so long as it lasted the work represented a continuation of Thoreau's status as a protégé and disciple of Emerson" ("Thoreau's Projected Work on the English Poets," 239, 253).

6. "Literary Notices: The *Dial*," *New York Daily Tribune*, April 27, 1944, p. 1, col. 1. In its review of the *Dial*'s previous number, the *Tribune* had said of the *Dial*'s writers, "They embody a loftier as well as serener thought than we find expressed elsewhere. The writers are destined to be felt by the next age if disregarded by the present" ("The Dial for January," *New York Tribune*, January 25, 1844, 1).

7. Letter of April 4, 1844; in Furness, *Records of a Lifelong Friendship*, 33.

8. Linck C. Johnson refers to this lecture briefly in *Thoreau's Complex Weave: The Writing of* A Week on the Concord and Merrimack Rivers *with the Text of the First Draft* (Charlottesville: University Press of Virginia, 1986), 91; he discusses it more fully in an unpublished lecture delivered before the Thoreau Society on July 10, 1987, and I am grateful to Professor Johnson for sharing with me the text of his lecture. Much of Thoreau's lecture was eventually incorporated into the draft essay printed as "Reform and Reformers" in RP, but unpublished during Thoreau's life.

9. Advertisements of Thoreau's lecture in the *Boston Courier*, *Boston Evening Mercantile Journal*, and *Boston Post* for March 8 and 9 are listed in Raymond Borst, *Henry David Thoreau: A Reference Guide, 1835–1899* (Boston: G. K. Hall, 1987), 3; the same advertisement also appears in the *Boston Daily Evening Transcript*, March 8, 2. The notices do not list a lecture title but announce "Henry D. Thoreau, of Concord" as the speaker and indicate that he would lecture both morning and evening, implying that the lecture was in two parts.

10. The exact date of this poem is somewhat difficult to ascertain. It was recorded in Thoreau's "Long Book" journal, filled largely with transcripts from earlier journals with original but undated entries interlined. The "Long Book" as a whole contains entries written between 1842 and 1846. "The Offer," a poem not recorded in any earlier notebooks, appears shortly after transcriptions of entries from J1 that are clearly after January 7, 1844 (J2: 89; cf. J1: 494–95) and just before the account of his visit to the Rice farm on his trip to the Berkshires, which could not have been recorded before August 1, 1844. The tone and matter of the poem, as well as what textual evidence exists, suggest that this was written during Thoreau's fallow period after the cessation of the *Dial*. The poem was later included in A *Week*.

11. Robert Sattelmeyer tentatively dates the "Long Book," in which Thoreau first pulled together material for A *Week*, to 1842 (J2: 449–51); Johnson, however, argues compellingly that while Thoreau's sequentially dated entries begin with 1842, the "Long Book" compilation itself did not begin until 1844 (*Thoreau's Complex Weave*, 267).

12. Though numerous corrections must be made in it, the starting point for information on titles, places, dates, and payments for Thoreau's lectures is Walter Harding, "A Checklist of Thoreau's Lectures," *Bulletin of the New York Public Library* 52

(February 1948): 78–87. See also Hubert Hoeltje, "Thoreau as Lecturer," *New England Quarterly* 19 (December 1946): 485–94. Some corrections and additions to these are available in Cameron, *The Massachusetts Lyceum*. Bradley P. Dean has also generously shared with me some of the fruits of his research on Thoreau as a lecturer. For background on the lyceum system, see Carl Bode, *The American Lyceum: Town Meeting of the Mind* (New York: Oxford University Press, 1956).

13. Thoreau's journal draft of the letter is in J2: 120–24. For the record of Phillips's appearances at the Concord Lyceum and the controversies they generated, see Cameron, *The Massachusetts Lyceum*, and Harding, *Days*, 175–76.

14. See Johnson's reconstruction of this first draft, in *Thoreau's Complex Weave*.

15. Ibid., 224–25, and "Historical Introduction," *Week* 455–56.

16. Alcott, "Diary for 1846," quoted in Johnson, *Thoreau's Complex Weave*, 225.

17. Griswold, *Passages from the Correspondence*, 207.

18. Ibid., 213.

19. Mott, *A History of American Magazines*, 552–53.

20. "The Magazines for April," *Boston Morning Post*, March 27, 1847, 1.

21. The notice is quoted below; see n. 26.

22. J. Lyndon Shanley, *The Making of* Walden, *with the Text of the First Version* (Chicago: University of Chicago Press, 1957), 105–6; see also F. B. Sanborn's transcript of the lecture, quoted in Harding, "The Influence of Thoreau's Lecturing upon His Writing," *Bulletin of the New York Public Library* 60 (February 1956): 74–80.

23. Quoted in Harding, *Days*, 187–88.

24. Griswold, *Passages from the Correspondence*, 212.

25. Johnson, *Thoreau's Complex Weave*, 227–32, and "Historical Introduction," *Week* 456–60.

26. "American Literary Intelligence," *Literary World* 1.8 (March 27, 1847): 185.

27. Nancy Simmons, "The 'Autobiographical Sketch' of James Elliot Cabot," *Harvard Library Bulletin* 30.2 (April 1982): 142–43.

28. Johnson, *Thoreau's Complex Weave*, 232; *Week* 460.

29. Hawthorne, *The Letters, 1843–1853*, ed. Thomas Woodson et al., vol. 16 of *The Centenary Edition of the Works of Nathaniel Hawthorne* (Columbus: Ohio State University Press, 1985), 89.

30. Quoted in "Historical Introduction," *Mosses from an Old Manse*, 512; cf. *Letters, 1843–1853*, 105–6.

31. Hawthorne, *Letters, 1843–1853*, 105–6.

32. At the end of 1845, Emerson had actually been incensed with Wiley & Putnam, charging them with pirating Carlyle's book on Cromwell, which Emerson was to have turned over to James Munroe & Co. for American publication. When Wiley & Putnam's explanation showed that the source of the misunderstanding was Carlyle's own carelessness, however, Emerson was placated and so willingly assisted with Wiley & Putnam's publication of Carlyle's next book. See EmL 3: 315–20.

33. In May 1847, Duyckinck was dismissed as editor of the Wiley & Putnam–backed journal, the *Literary World*. On Duyckinck's falling-out with Wiley & Putnam, see Miller, *The Raven and the Whale*, 186–202.

34. Furness, *Records of a Lifelong Friendship*, 60–61.

35. Ibid., 63, 64.

CHAPTER 6
"CONTACT! CONTACT!"

1. Alcott, *The Journals of Bronson Alcott*, ed. Odell Shepard (Boston: Little, Brown, 1938), 201.

2. "I asked Thoreau if it were not proof of our inefficiency that we had not yet attracted some fine soul, some maid from the farmer's hearth or youth from the farm or workshop, to our houses, and there found a proof undeniable of having a positive and real existence here in this world. . . . It is true that neither by Lyceum nor other manner has anything like real intercourse been had between ourselves and our townspeople. . . . It is the office of a great life that it shine abroad and educate all within its neighborhood. . . . [But] our dealing with men have an aspect ridiculous and to be made game of at the bank and bar-room." Alcott, *Journals*, 204–5 (March 14, 1848).

3. Cabot later recalled, "The 'Review' I think was unable to pay anything" (Simmons, "The 'Autobiographical Sketch,'" 143). When Parker was rather desperately attempting to retain Emerson's participation in the journal, he promised Emerson, "I will pay you $1. a page, and $2. or $3. if it is possible," but this was the exceptional offer, and certainly one he would not have extended to Thoreau (EmL 4: 113n).

4. "Pay of Authors," *The Literary World* 1.10 (April 10, 1847): 221.

5. John Tebbel, *The American Magazine: A Compact History* (New York: Hawthorn Books, 1969), 82. Tebbel quotes a letter from Graham of October 1848: "Had I not in an evil hour forgotten my own true interests and devoted that capital and industry to another business which should have been confined to the magazine, I should today have been under no necessity."

6. In his letter of April 17, Greeley said he enclosed twenty-five dollars for the essay, and he added, "Send me a line acknowledging the receipt of the money, and say if all is right between us" (Corr 218); but the letter of May 17 (Sanborn's date) implies that Greeley had not yet paid him the twenty-five dollars. Thoreau's reply of May 19 and Greeley's letter of May 25 seem to confirm this inference, but see n. 9, below, on Thoreau's May 21 claim to have received a total of one hundred dollars from Greeley.

7. "A Lesson for Young Poets," *New York Daily Tribune*, May 25, 1848.

8. In his historical introduction to J2, Sattelmeyer discusses Thoreau's fragmentary journal "I" of winter 1846–1847 to spring 1848, of which only sixteen leaves are extant: "The likelihood is that if any Journal was kept, it was spent so exclusively on literary material for A *Week* and *Walden* that it was consumed in the process. . . . Preparing two book-length manuscripts for the press (as he thought), as well as fair copy for 'Ktaadn' and 'Resistance to Civil Government' may well have prevented him from keeping a Journal regularly" in 1848 (J2: 465).

9. If the dating of Thoreau's correspondence with Greeley is correct, Thoreau seems here to have exaggerated the amount he had received from Greeley by at least twenty-five dollars, though Greeley would indeed shortly pay Thoreau that difference. See n. 6 above.

10. Mott, *A History of American Magazines*, 769–72.

11. "A Letter from Mr. Bayard Taylor," *New York Tribune*, August 28, 1875, 3.

12. See J2: 304, 332, 333, and the corresponding passages in MW 27–28, 55, 58.

13. See J2: 384–85; cf. MW 45–46. This was added as late as spring 1948.

14. Cf. J2: 295–96. Thoreau's essay originally appeared in the *Union Magazine* 4 (July–November 1848): 29–33, 73–79, 132–37, 177–82, 216–20. I discuss the essay as it appeared in the *Union Magazine,* including its division into five installments and without the additions and corrections Thoreau made for the inclusion of this essay in *The Maine Woods;* but because *The Maine Woods* is more accessible and because it corrects a number of obvious printer's errors in the 1848 text, I cite page references from the Princeton *Maine Woods* (MW).

15. Earlier ascents of Katahdin had also been made by British and American surveying parties in 1819, 1820, 1825, and 1833; the Reverend William Blake climbed Katahdin two weeks before the Bailey expedition in 1836. See Myron H. Avery, "The Monument Line Surveyers on Katahdin," *Appalachia* 21.10 (June 1928): 33–43; Reverend William Blake, "An Excursion to Mount Katahdin," *Maine Naturalist* 6.2 (June 1926): 71–73. Blake's account of an 1856 ascent of Katahdin is printed in the same number of the *Maine Naturalist,* 74–83.

16. [Edward Everett Hale], "Visit to Mount Katahdin," *Boston Daily Advertiser,* August 15, 1845, 2.

17. On the Dr. Young botanical expedition of 1847, see J. K. Laski, "Dr. Young's Botanical Expedition to Mount Katahdin," *Bangor Courier* (September 1847); rpt. in *Maine Naturalist* 6.2 (June 1927): 38–62; and George Thurber, M.D., "Notes of an Excursion to Mount Katahdin," *Providence Journal* (September 1847); rpt. in *Maine Naturalist* 6.4 (December 1926): 134–51. Marcus Keep published accounts of his excursions as "Mount Katahdn" [*sic*], *Bangor Democrat,* December 7, 1847, 1; and "Mount Katahdin—Again," *Bangor Democrat,* October 9, 16, and 23, 1849. The latter provides details of Elizabeth Oakes Smith's ascent. Higginson's essay was printed as "Going to Mount Katahdin" in *Putnam's Monthly Magazine* 8 (September 1856): 242–56. Winthrop's "Life in the Open Air" was published serially in the *Atlantic Monthly* of 1862 and collected in *Life in the Open Air and Other Papers* (Boston: Ticknor and Fields, 1863). An account of a later Church expedition to Katahdin, along with landscape painters Sanford R. Gifford, H. W. Robbins, and L. DeForest, is given by A. L. Holley in "Camps and Tramps about Ktaadn," *Scribner's Monthly* 16 (May 1878): 33–47.

18. Alexis de Tocqueville, *Democracy in America* (New York: Alfred Knopf, 1945), 2: 78.

19. Rev. C. W. Upham, "Scenery and Resources of Maine," *American Whig Review* 2.3 (September 1845): 264.

20. Charles T. Jackson, *Second Annual Report of the Geology of the Public Lands, Belonging to the States of Maine and Massachusetts* (Boston: Dutton & Wentworth, 1838), 44.

21. Laski, "Dr. Young's Botanical Expedition to Mount Katahdin," 61.

22. Keep, "Mount Katahdn," 1; see also Keep's 1849 "Mount Katahdin—Again."

23. James Fenimore Cooper, *The Pioneers* (Albany: SUNY Press, 1980), 190–91. Useful discussions of this iconography include Barbara Novak, *Nature and Culture: American Landscape Painting 1825–1875* (New York: Oxford University Press, 1980), and Roderick Nash, *Wilderness in the American Mind,* rev. ed. (New Haven: Yale University Press, 1973).

24. John James Audubon, *Ornithological Biography* (Philadelphia: E. L. Carey & A. Hart, 1832), 31–32.

25. Thomas Cole, "The Lament of the Forest," *Knickerbocker Magazine* 17.6 (June 1841): 516–19.

26. Sigourney, *Scenes in My Native Land*, 117.

27. John Greenleaf Whittier, "The Lumbermen," *The Poetical Works of Whittier*, Cambridge edition, ed. Hyatt Waggoner (Boston: Houghton Mifflin, 1975), 359–61.

28. Cole, "Essay on American Scenery," 98–110.

29. "Exhibition at the National Academy," *Literary World* 1.15 (May 15, 1847): 347–48.

30. Asher B. Durand, "Letters on Landscape Painting: Letter II," *The Crayon* 1 (1855): 34–35; quoted in Nash, *Wilderness and the American Mind*, 82.

31. See Nash, *Wilderness and the American Mind*, 60.

32. James Russell Lowell, "A Moosehead Journal, Addressed to the Edelmann Storg at the Bagni di Lucca," *Putnam's Monthly* 2.11 (November 1853): 457.

33. Ibid., 469.

34. Winthrop, *Life in the Open Air*, 54.

35. J. W. Bailey, "Account of Excursion to Mount Katahdin, in Maine," *American Journal of Science and Arts* 32.1 (1837): 22.

36. Thurber, "Notes of an Excursion to Mount Katahdin," 137.

37. Bailey, "Account of Excursion to Mount Katahdin, in Maine," 24.

38. See Charles E. Hamlin, "Routes to Ktaadn," *Appalachia* 2.4 (December 1881): 314. Bailey spelled his guides' name "McAstlin," and Hamlin corrects it to "McCausland."

39. Winthrop, *Life in the Open Air*, 68. In spite of the similar imagery, Withrop seems to have been unaware of Thoreau's essay. Rather, both writers draw upon conventional images of adventure and danger.

40. Commenting on the same phenomenon, Winthrop wrote, "Not all trees are worthy of the axe. Miles of lesser timber remains untouched. A Maine forest after a lumber-campaign is like France after a *coup d'Etat*: the *bourgeoisie* are prosperous as ever, but the great men are all gone" (*Life in the Open Air*, 21).

41. Compare this passage to Bailey's description: "We had many opportunities of admiring the skill and coolness with which our boatmen managed their batteau, and forced it up rapids which at first seemed impassable" ("Account of Excursion to Mount Katahdin, in Maine," 24).

42. Compare this to Laski's 1847 account (which Thoreau read while revising his essay and which he later quotes directly): "On these enormous rocks, high and dry, sometimes ten or fifteen feet above the water, were mill logs which had been cut five or six years ago. . . . There were nearly $10,000 worth in this river and . . . for every season since attempts were made to get them down; and it seemed to us a hopeless task" ("Dr. Young's Botanical Expedition to Mount Katahdin," 44).

43. Nathaniel Hawthorne, *The Scarlet Letter*, vol. I of *The Centenary Edition of the Works of Nathaniel Hawthorne* (Columbus: Ohio State University Press, 1962), 35–36. See also Thoreau's later journal entry, JX: 141 (October 29, 1857).

44. Many critics argue that Thoreau's Katahdin experience was negative, even traumatic, but the argument that Thoreau's naive romanticism was shattered by the

"reality" of his summit experience is developed most recently and most vigorously by William Howarth, *The Book of Concord: Thoreau's Life as a Writer* (New York: Viking, 1982), 135–36, and Richard Bridgman, *Dark Thoreau* (Lincoln: University of Nebraska Press, 1982), 189–202. Howarth says of the fishing episode that it "seems a deliberate exaggeration, the sort of mythologizing that will cease after his mountain climb," which he says shatters his "still untested vision" of romantic nature (135–36). Bridgman similarly argues that while Thoreau's "romanticism went deep," on the summit "the reality of it all overwhelmed him" (194, 201).

45. Jackson, *Second Annual Report*, 17.

46. See n. 44, above. Robert D. Richardson, Jr., discusses the mythic elements of this account in *Myth and Literature in the American Renaissance* (Bloomington: Indiana University Press, 1978), 105–16.

47. As Thoreau knew, even Dr. Jackson's measurements were no clear claim to victory over the wilderness, for Jackson had written in his report that their "barometers were so much injured by the rough usage . . . that they could no longer be relied upon"; and his Indian guide Louis Neptune "declared that Pomola was angry with us for presuming to measure the height of the mountain, and revenged himself upon us with this storm" (*Second Annual Report*, vi, 17).

48. Keep, "Mount Katahdn." While Thoreau never refers directly to Keep's account, he had alerted his Bangor relatives to his interest in Katahdin material. In October 1847 he had written to his sister Sophia, then staying with the Thatchers in Bangor, thanking her for sending accounts of the Young botanical expedition and adding that he hoped she would "save and send me the rest, and anything else you may meet with relating to the Maine Woods" (Corr 187). Almost certainly, then, Sophia or the Thatchers would have sent Keep's sketch, which appeared on the front page of the local newspaper, two months later.

49. Corr 187; see n. 42 above for another echo of Laski's account. It is possible that Thoreau also obtained Thurber's account of the Young expedition, printed in the *Providence Journal* in September 1847, which has some similar descriptive passages; and, as I discuss in n. 48, above, he seems to have known Keep's report as well. See n. 17 above for sources.

50. Laski, "Dr. Young's Botanical Expedition to Mount Katahdin," 52.

51. Ibid.

52. Bailey, "Account of Excursion to Mount Katahdin, in Maine," 30. When the Reverend William Blake later recalled his 1836 ascent of Katahdin, he similarly expressed his "sad disappointment" at being overtaken by a cold rain on the mountain; climbing to a high tableland, they "stood a few minutes, shivering, gazed wistfully into the thick mist, thought and said, 'Foolish to go further,' and then turned and retraced our steps down the mountain" ("An Excursion to Mount Katahdin," 71–72).

53. I allude here to the title of Marjorie Hope Nicolson's invaluable study, *Mountain Gloom and Mountain Glory: The Development of the Aesthetics of the Infinite* (Ithaca: Cornell University Press, 1959).

54. Thomas Weiskel, *The Romantic Sublime: Studies in the Structure and Psychology of Transcendence* (Baltimore: Johns Hopkins University Press, 1976), 6. See also Henry Sayre, "Surveying the Vast Profound: The Panoramic Landscape in American Consciousness," *Massachusetts Review* 24.4 (Winter 1983): 723–42.

55. Winthrop, *Life in the Open Air*, 102. Compare Bayard Taylor on the pleasures of such panoramic views: "There is also a lurking, flattering sense of power, which we feel. . . . We are elevated above the earth: other men and their concerns are below us. . . . We stand on the pinnacle of the earth, whereof we are lords, and above us there is nothing but God." *At Home and Abroad*, 2d ser. (New York: G. P. Putnam's, 1862), 360–61.

56. Winthrop, *Life in the Open Air*, 103–4.

57. Ibid., 104.

58. Ibid., 105. When the weather clears, Winthrop and Church witness a beautiful mountain sunset, which Winthrop describes at length in what is a fine example of romantic landscape description, and he concludes, "Such are the transcendent moments of Nature, unseen and disbelieved by the untaught. The poetic soul lays hold of every such tender pageant of beauty and keeps it forever" (105). See also the accounts of Laski and Thurber, cited above.

59. CW 1: 15; cf. "American Scholar": "So much only of life as I know by experience, so much of the wilderness have I vanquished and planted, or so far have I extended my being, my dominion" (CW 1: 59).

60. Weiskel, *The Romantic Sublime*, 6, 23–24, 46, 48.

61. Bayard Taylor, "A Letter from Mr. Bayard Taylor," *New York Tribune*, August 28, 1875, 3. Thoreau's letter to Greeley is not extant.

62. "New Publications," *New York Tribune*, September 20, 1848, 1.

63. "The Backwoods of Maine," *New York Tribune*, November 17, 1848, 1.

64. "The Backwoods of Maine," *New York Tribune*, November 18, 1848, 1.

65. "New Publications," *New York Tribune*, November 15, 1848, 1.

66. Cited in Harding, *Days*, 230.

67. After *The Maine Woods* was published in 1864, Thoreau's essay became a standard reference in accounts of the Maine wilderness. A few earlier accounts are worth noting here as well, however, to suggest the influence of the *Union Magazine*'s serialized version of "Ktaadn." Keep's 1849 account of Katahdin in the *Bangor Democrat* never mentions Thoreau by name but hints at Thoreau's influence in a number of intriguing ways. He begins by acknowledging how much attention the mountain has recently received, and the sermon he delivers to his companions on the summit, on the text "I am fearfully and wonderfully made," seems to be this ultraconservative minister's orthodox counterpart to Thoreau's more pantheistic exclamations of awe at his own body, "this matter to which I am bound." More concrete evidence of the influence of Thoreau's essay is found in the Reverend John Todd's sketch "Mount Katahdin," in his *Summer Gleanings: or Sketches and Incidents of a Pastor's Vacation* (Northampton: Hopkins, Bridgman & Co., 1852). Without acknowledging his appropriations, Todd closely echoes many passages from Thoreau's essay (including Thoreau's quotation from Laski's account), but most clearly when he writes, "Nature is here unfashioned by man, stern, savage, awful, but beautiful. The eye rests on no garden, cultivated field, lawn, pasture for flock, nor even a place to bury the dead. It is the home of matter. . . . it seems as if it must have rained rocks. . . . You can hardly command your thoughts, classify your impressions, or realize the scene before you. . . . Great cloud-maker!" (131). Thomas Wentworth Higginson, on the other hand, explicitly acknowledges Thoreau's account as a classic and refers to it frequently in his 1855 essay "Going to Mount Katahdin."

Chapter 7
"Only as It Serves as an Advertisement of Me"

1. Thoreau's allusion to "the cubes of Pythagoras" has baffled Thoreau scholars, but the difficulty is resolved when we recognize that in writing this journal entry Thoreau misremembered his source. In his Literary Notebook, he copied: "Hierocles said—'That the discourses of Socrates resembled cubes, because they remained firm wherever they might fall.'" See *Thoreau's Literary Notebook*, ed. Kenneth W. Cameron (Hartford: Transcendental Books, 1964), 42.

2. "Salem Lyceum," *Salem Observer*, November 25, 1848; rpt. in Cameron, *Transcendental Log*, 37.

3. Also particularly illuminating on lecture audiences' demand to be both entertained and informed is the "Editor's Easy Chair" column on the lecture system in *Harper's New Monthly Magazine* 8 (February 1854): 415–17.

4. Quoted in Rose Hawthorne Lathrop, *Memories of Hawthorne* (Boston: Houghton Mifflin, 1897), 92.

5. Quoted in Harding, *Days*, 237–38, as are the subsequent passages from the review.

6. Cameron, *Companion to Thoreau's Correspondence*, 184.

7. By 1849 Thoreau had completed three of what would ultimately be the seven versions of *Walden*; Thoreau would not revise the manuscript again until 1852, when it underwent extensive revisions and expansion. The seminal study of the *Walden* texts is Shanley's *The Making of* Walden; even more useful in many respects, however, is Ronald Clapper's unpublished dissertation, "The Development of *Walden*: A Genetic Text" (Ph.D., University of California, Los Angeles, 1967), which enables the reader to see the alterations in the manuscript through all seven versions.

8. Salem Observer, March 3, 1849; rpt. in Cameron, *Transcendental Log*, 37.

9. Quoted in Thomas Blanding, "Thoreau's Local Lectures in 1849 and 1850," *The Concord Saunterer* 17.3 (December 1984): 21–26. Chapin was a member of the Lincoln Lyceum's committee to procure lecturers that season; see the records of the Lincoln Lyceum in Cameron, *Massachusetts Lyceum*, 218 and passim.

10. Maria Thoreau [HDT's aunt], letter to "P——," quoted in Henry Seidel Canby, *Thoreau* (Boston: Beacon Press, 1939), 248.

11. Harding, in both his "Checklist" and *Days*, says Thoreau was paid twenty dollars for this lecture; Harding's source is the letter from his Aunt Maria (cited in n. 10, above), in which she writes that at Bangor "they give 25 dollars, and at Salem and Portland 20." But Thoreau wrote to George Thatcher on February 16 that Portland would "pay me $25.00" (Corr 236); moreover, when the Portland Lyceum invited Thoreau to lecture there again during the 1850–1851 lecture season, they also offered twenty-five dollars (Corr 267). In the face of this evidence, one must consider Maria Thoreau's report erroneous.

12. Eastern Argus (Portland, Maine), March 21, 1849, 2.

13. "The Lyceum," *Eastern Argus*, March 23, 1849, 2.

14. "Portland Lyceum," *Eastern Argus*, March 28, 1849, 2.

15. "Portland Lyceum," *Eastern Argus*, March 30, 1849, 2. The review continues with two amusing anecdotes of auditors' responses, so characteristic of reports on

Emerson's lectures that their genuineness is suspect: "A gentleman, in reply to our question of 'how he liked,' answered, 'very much—it was splendid—but—then I didn't understand a blasted word of it!' An intelligent young lady, who listened with rapt attention, and who was enthusiastic in her admiration afterwards, was asked what the subject was. She was struck dumb. Her yankee shrewdness could not aid her in even hazarding a *guess* at it. She knew it was beautiful; the melody of the speaker's voice, the harmony of his prose-poetry, and the pure and perfect construction of the language, fell upon her senses pleasantly—but, like exhilerating [*sic*] gas, the effect passed speedily away."

16. Greeley's trip to Maine must not have been a pleasant one. Enduring injury added to insult, Greeley lost twenty dollars in cash on his subsequent journey between Waterville and Bath; the item from the Bath paper was reported by the *Eastern Argus* on April 3, noting Greeley's rather pathetic offer of five dollars for the return of the remaining cash.

17. *New York Daily Tribune*, April 2, 1849, 2.

18. "Our Townsman—Mr. Thoreau," *Concord Yeoman's Gazette*; rpt. in Harding, *Days*, 239.

19. "How to Live—Mr. Thoreau's Example," *New York Tribune*, April 7, 1849, 3.

20. In reprinting the Philadelphia editorial, the *National Intelligencer* failed to set off Greeley's original column in quotation marks, with the result that Greeley's approval and the Philadelphia editor's criticism appear as the contradictory remarks of a single writer. Both columns are reproduced in Cameron, *Transcendental Log*, 43–45.

21. "A Young Philosopher," *Saturday Evening Post*, April 14, 1849, 2.

22. "Life in the Woods," *Youth's Companion*, July 19, 1849; rpt. in *Youth's Companion* [selections from the original magazine], ed. Lovell Thompson (Boston: Houghton Mifflin, 1954), 903–4.

23. Kenneth W. Cameron, "Damning National Publicity for Thoreau in 1849," *American Transcendental Quarterly* 2 (1969): 22–23.

24. Hawthorne, *Letters, 1843–53*, 398.

25. Walter Blair, *Mark Twain and Huck Finn* (Berkeley: University of California Press, 1960), 372.

26. Quoted in Hoeltje, "Thoreau as Lecturer," 489–90.

27. "Thoreau's Lectures," *Worcester Daily Spy*, May 3, 1849; rpt. in Kent P. Ljungquist, "Further Responses to Thoreau's Worcester Lectures and a Review of *Walden*," *Thoreau Society Bulletin* 177 (Fall 1986): 2–3. The *Spy* had also announced Thoreau's second lecture as "intellectual entertainment that should not be neglected" (*Daily Spy*, April 26; quoted in Harding, *Days*, 242).

28. "Lake Philosophy," *Worcester Palladium*, May 2, 1849; rpt. in Ljungquist, "Further Responses to Thoreau's Worcester Lectures," 2.

29. Harding, *Days*, 242.

30. *Worcester Spy*, May 9, 1849; rpt. in Ljungquist, "Further Responses to Thoreau's Worcester Lectures," 3–4.

31. "New Publications," *Boston Daily Evening Transcript*, May 15, 1849, 2.

32. "Aesthetic Papers," *Boston Post*, May 17, 1849, 1.

33. "Aesthetic Papers," *Salem Gazette*, May 18, 1849, 2.

34. "New Publications," *Boston Daily Traveller*, May 22, 1849, 1. The reviewer

goes on to list the contents of the volume, including "Resistance to Civil Government, by H. Thoreau," thus clearly identifying the article he had described.

35. "R." [George Ripley], Review of "Aesthetic Papers," *New York Tribune*, May 31, 1849, 1.

36. Zoltan Haraszti, "Letters of T. W. Parsons," *More Books: Bulletin of the Boston Public Library* 13 (October 1938): 357–58. On Samuel Kettel's contempt for the transcendentalists, see his biting parody of transcendental writing, "Quozziana," by "Moonshine Milkywater" [Kettel], *Brother Jonathan* 1 (March 26, 1842): 354; rpt. in Gura and Myerson, *Critical Essays*, 30–31.

37. [T. W. Parsons], Review of "Aesthetic Papers," *Boston Courier*, June 19, 1849, 2. In *Transcendental Log*, 50, Cameron includes an 1850 reprint of the *Courier*'s notice in another, unidentified paper (the *Courier* is identified as the source at the end of the column, but Cameron does not identify the paper in which it was reprinted, nor does he cite the original *Courier* notice). It is worth noting, however, that this review of *Aesthetic Papers* therefore appeared in more than one paper at the time.

38. "Publishers' Circular," *Literary World* 4.113 (March 31, 1849): 300.

39. "Aesthetic Papers," *Literary World* 4.139 (September 29, 1849): 269–71.

40. Sophia Dobson Collet, "Literature of American Individuality," *People's Review* (London), undated clipping in A. B. Alcott's Autobiographical Collections, Houghton Library; rpt. in *Thoreau Society Bulletin* 179 (Spring 1987): 4–5.

41. *Life of Henry Wadsworth Longfellow, with Extracts from His Journals and Correspondence*, ed. Samuel Longfellow, 2 vol. (London: Kegan Paul, Trench, 1886), 2: 142–43.

42. [Elizabeth Peabody], "Prospectus," *Aesthetic Papers* (Boston: The Editor, 1849; Gainesville, Fla.: Scholars Facsimiles & Reprints, 1957), iv.

43. George Willis Cooke, *An Historical and Biographical Introduction to Accompany the Dial*, 1: 193; rpt. as *Memorabilia of the Transcendentalists in New England*, ed. Kenneth W. Cameron (Hartford: Transcendental Books, 1973), 58.

44. See also EmL 3: 307–8, to Duyckinck, also explaining his preference to publish himself rather than take a royalty from Wiley & Putnam. He says he gets five to six thousand dollars for each edition of *Essays*, first series (the first edition was of fifteen hundred copies, the second of two thousand); "I print them at my own risk, & Munroe & Co have 30 per cent as their commission."

45. In January 1843, for example, Lidian wrote to Emerson, "Munroe of course had not sent his account. Did you really think he would? There is reason to be sure the balance is in your favor or it would have come." *Selected Letters of Lidian Jackson Emerson*, 121.

46. The first printing of *Summer on the Lakes* was published in June 1844 and sold for seventy-five cents. A second printing, including etchings by Sarah Clarke, was issued somewhat later and sold at a higher price. Fuller reported that nearly seven hundred copies had been sold by the following year, but by May of 1845 W. H. Graham was advertising the sale of four hundred copies, probably remaindered, in the *New York Tribune*. See Joel Myerson, *Margaret Fuller, A Descriptive Bibliography* (Pittsburgh: University of Pittsburgh Press, 1978), 9–13.

47. Prepublication notices of A *Week* appeared in the *Literary World* for May 19, 1849, in both the "Publishers' Circular" (440) and the "Boston Correspondent" col-

umns (436); similar notices appeared in Boston's *Daily Evening Transcript* for May 19 ("New Publications," 2), the *Daily Advertiser*, and the *Boston Post* for May 23 ("Literary Notices," 1). No advertisements for A *Week* appeared in any of the Boston papers; Munroe advertised its books in the *Literary World* very infrequently and on a small scale (in contrast with the very prominent and regular advertising done by the major publishing houses), and they did not list Thoreau's book at all in 1849. On the rising importance of advertising books, see "Where, When, and How to Advertise," *American Publishers' Circular and Literary Gazette* 2.12 (March 22, 1856): 1–2, which claims, "A book were almost as well not printed as not advertised" (it also notes that publishers are generally of the opinion that "the last pages of books are not very valuable for advertisements"; this is where Munroe advertised the forthcoming publication of *Walden*).

48. J. Donald Crowley, "Historical Commentary," and John Manning, "Bibliographical Information," *Twice-Told Tales*, 523–24, 552; Hawthorne, *Letters, 1843–1853*, 11.

49. Hawthorne, *Letters, 1813–1843*, 652; *Letters 1843–1853*, 11. See also Hawthorne's letter to Duyckinck, November 26, 1843: "At present, [my copyrights] are not worth a sixpence" (10).

50. "Historical Commentary," 527–30.

51. Hawthorne, *Letters, 1843–1853*, 35–36n, 41, 35.

Chapter 8
"Flowing to Higher Levels"

1. F. B. Sanborn, *Henry D. Thoreau* (Boston: Houghton Mifflin, 1882), 304.

2. Johnson, *Thoreau's Complex Weave*, 239–45.

3. The best discussion to date of A *Week* in the context of travel literature remains Lawrence Buell's, in *Literary Transcendentalism: Style and Vision in the American Renaissance* (Ithaca: Cornell University Press, 1973), 188–238. See, too, John A. Christie, *Thoreau as World Traveler* (New York: Columbia University Press, 1965).

4. Timothy Dwight, *Travels in New-England and New-York*, 4 vols. (New Haven: Timothy Dwight, 1821), 1: 411–14; 2: 250–52; John Alden, "Lovewell's Fight," *Youth's Companion*, November 1, 1849; rpt. in *Youth's Companion*, ed. Lovell Thompson (Boston: Houghton Mifflin, 1954), 883–87. On other early accounts of the Dustan (or Duston) story, see Robert Arner, "The Story of Hannah Duston: Cotton Mather to Thoreau," *American Transcendental Quarterly* 18 (1973): 19–23. Many of the episodes narrated in A *Week* are again recounted in J. W. Meader, *The Merrimack River* (Boston: B. B. Russell, 1869).

5 On Thoreau's treatment of time and history in A *Week*, see Peck, *Thoreau's Morning Work*, and Joan Burbick, *Thoreau's Alternative History: Changing Perspectives on Nature, Culture, and Language* (Philadelphia: University of Pennsylvania Press, 1987).

6. On the popularity of the White Mountains for tourists, artists, and writers, see Huth, *Nature and the American*, 79ff.; Nygren and Robertson, *Views and Visions*; and Sears, *Sacred Places*, esp. chap. 4, "The Making of an American Tourist Attraction:

The Willey House in the White Mountains." Literary sketches, engravings, and paintings of the region were virtually ubiquitous in Thoreau's day.

7. H. Daniel Peck makes a similar point in "'Further Down the Stream of Time': Memory and Perspective in Thoreau's *A Week on the Concord and Merrimack Rivers*," *Thoreau Quarterly* 16.3 and 4 (Summer/Fall 1984): 107–9 (subsequently revised for chap. 2 of *Thoreau's Morning Work*). Johnson, on the other hand, implies that Agiocochook does constitute a narrative climax, in *Thoreau's Complex Weave*, as do Stephen Adams and Donald Ross, Jr., in *Reading Mythologies: The Composition of Thoreau's Major Works* (Charlottesville: University of Virginia Press, 1988), 97–103.

8. Buell, *Literary Transcendentalism*, 221, 222. Though I dissent from Buell's view here, I am deeply indebted to his sound reading of *A Week*.

9. Alcott, *Journals*, 209–15.

10. In 1854, Higginson described *A Week* to Harriet Prescott as "the only thoroughly outdoor book I have ever seen . . . fascinating beyond compare to anyone who knows Nature, though the religion and philosophy are of the wildest" (*Letters and Journals of Thomas Wentworth Higginson*, 105). Writing to Thoreau at the same time, acknowledging receipt of a copy of *Walden*, he said, "No doubt your new book will have a larger circulation than the other, but not, I think, a more select or appreciative one" (Corr 336).

11. Froude later tempered his enthusiasm. Carlyle had difficulty finishing the book, and when he did, he wrote to Emerson that he found it "a very fantastic yet not quite worthless book" (*The Correspondence of Emerson and Carlyle*, 457). See Harding, *Days*, 252–53 for Froude's tempered opinion and other, generally unfavorable responses to complimentary copies.

12. "New Publications," *New York Evening Post*, June 8, 1849, 2. This is, to my knowledge, a previously unrecorded review. Both the "Historical Introduction" to the Princeton edition of *A Week* and Borst's *Reference Guide* identify the *New York Tribune*'s review of June 13 (discussed below) as the first.

13. "H. D. Thoreau's Book," *New York Tribune*, June 13, 1849, 1. Thoreau himself thought Greeley was the reviewer (JIII: 257), though there is a strong tradition attributing it to George Ripley. A clear and powerful argument in favor of Greeley (as well as a good survey of the critical debate over attribution) is Michael Meyer's "The Case for Greeley's *Tribune* Review of *A Week*," *ESQ* 25 (1979): 92–94.

14. Anonymous review of *A Week on the Concord and Merrimack Rivers* [unidentified newspaper, 1849?]; rpt. in *Thoreau Society Bulletin* 130 (Winter 1975): 8.

15. "A Week on the Concord and Merrimack Rivers," *The Liberator* 20.24 (June 15, 1849): 96. The obituary for Helen appeared in the *Liberator* for June 22, 99.

16. [Charles Frederick Briggs?], "Deferred Books," *Holden's Dollar Magazine* 4 (July 1849): 448.

17. Anonymous review of *A Week on the Concord and Merrimack Rivers*, *The New Hampshire Patriot and State Gazette*, n.s., 3 (July 26, 1849): 2; quoted in Harding, *Days*, 249.

18. "New Publications Received," *North American Review* 69.144 (July 1849): 273.

19. "Editor's Table," *Knickerbocker Magazine* 34.2 (August 1849): 177.

20. [Sarah Josepha Hale], Review of *A Week on the Concord and Merrimack Rivers*, *Godey's Lady's Book* 39 (September 1849): 223.

21. [Evert Duyckinck], "Thoreau's Travels" [review of A *Week*], *The Literary World* 138 (September 22, 1849): 245, 247.

22. E[vert]. A. D[uyckinck], "An Ascent of Mount Saddleback," *Literary World* 9.9 (August 30, 1851): 1–2.

23. Review of A *Week*, *Universalist Quarterly* 6 (October 1849): 422–23.

24. Review of A *Week*, *Pictorial National Library* 3 (1849): 60–61; rpt. in *Thoreau Society Bulletin* 29 (October 1949): 4.

25. Collett, "Literature of American Individuality," rpt. in *Thoreau Society Bulletin* 179 (Spring 1987): 4–5.

26. Anonymous review of A *Week*, *Westminster Review* 52 (January 1850): 309–10; rpt. in *Thoreau Society Bulletin* 59 (Spring 1957): 2.

27. Anonymous review of A *Week on the Concord and Merrimack Rivers*, *London Athenaeum*, October 27, 1849, 1086.

28. *Spectator*, October 13, 1849; quoted in Harding, *Days*, 252.

29. James Russell Lowell, Review of A *Week on the Concord and Merrimack Rivers*, *Massachusetts Quarterly Review* 3.9 (December 1849): 40–51.

29. Thomas Wentworth Higginson, "Henry David Thoreau," *Carlyle's Laugh and Other Surprises* (Boston and New York: Houghton Mifflin, 1909), 67–74.

31. Buell, *Literary Transcendentalism*, 204.

32. The book that Thoreau did *not* write here—on his excursion to the White Mountains—was, in effect, written just over a decade later by Thomas Starr King, whose *The White Hills: Their Legends, Landscape, and Poetry* (Boston: Crosby & Nichols, 1860) immediately became a classic of the genre. While the book is exhaustive in its information on the mountains, King was nevertheless most interested in their *effect* on the visitor, and so he quoted poetry abundantly, relied heavily on Emerson, and drew upon A *Week* for at least three quotations (only one of which is attributed). Emerson had recommended Starr King as a potential reviewer of A *Week* to Theodore Parker; his review would probably have been favorable (he subsequently reviewed *Walden* very favorably for the *Christian Register* [August 26, 1854, 135]). J. W. Meader's somewhat later volume, *The Merrimack River; its Sources and Tributaries, embracing a history of manufactures, and of the towns along its course; their geography, topography, and products, with a description of the Magnificient natural scenery about its upper waters* (Boston: B. B. Russell, 1869), is another alternative version of Thoreau's book: emphatically utilitarian in its orientation, and without literary pretensions, it also recounts most of the same incidents of colonial history Thoreau uses, but employs them as documenting the unambiguous triumph of white, industrial civilization. Meader also quotes Thoreau, though, drawing on his description of Plum Island (301).

33. Alcott, *Journals*, 239.

34. In A *Week* he had written of the Hindu scripture, "Tried by a New England eye . . . they are the oracles of a race already in its dotage, but held up to the sky, which is the only impartial and incorruptible ordeal, they are of a piece with its depth and serenity, and I am assured that they will have a significance as long as there is a sky to test them by" (150–51).

35. For further examples of Thoreau acting as agent for A *Week*, see Corr 377, 349, 380, 425, 431, 453, 577, 583, 611, 634.

CHAPTER 9
"SOME INTERIOR SHOOT"

1. See Clapper, "The Development of *Walden*," 93–95 on the 1852 addition of the Indian anecdote. The source for this passage was a journal entry of 1850 (J3: 130–31), but there Thoreau had not yet made the analogy to his own experience.

2. Miller, *Consciousness in Concord*, 29.

3. Both Sharon Cameron, in *Writing Nature: Henry Thoreau's Journal* (New York: Oxford University Press, 1985), and Howarth, in *The Book of Concord* (1982), argue that Thoreau regarded the *Journal* as his central literary enterprise after 1850; this judgment is echoed by the editors' introductions to J1 and J2. Peck, in *Thoreau's Morning Work* (1990), emphasizes the relationship between the *Journal* and the published work as a corrective to this tendency to isolate the *Journal*.

4. See the *Portland Transcript*, January 25, 1851; rpt. in John F. Jacques, "An Enthusiastic Newspaper Account of Thoreau's Second Lecture in Portland, Maine, January 15, 1851," *American Literature* 40 (November 1968): 385–91. See Corr 267 for the warm invitation Thoreau had received from the Portland Lyceum.

5. Thoreau did not lecture again in Plymouth until October 8, 1854, when he lectured to a small, select group (including Alcott) on "Moonlight." See Corr 337–40.

6. "New Publications," *New York Tribune*, June 19 and 22, 1852. The *Union Magazine* in which Thoreau published "Ktaadn" had been bought by the popular engraver John Sartain, who moved it to Philadelphia and added his own name to the title.

7. On the interpolation and dating of this passage's inclusion in the *Walden* manuscript, see Clapper, "The Development of *Walden*," 224–26; for the first draft of this *Walden* section see Shanley, *The Making of* Walden, 132–33; for the original journal entry, see J3: 315 (July 19, 1851). For a provocative discussion of *Walden*'s symbolism itself as based on the capitalist economic principles of exchange, see Michael T. Gilmore's chapter "*Walden* and the Curse of Trade" in *American Romanticism and the Marketplace* (Chicago: University of Chicago Press, 1985).

8. There is a striking counterpart to this passage in Thoreau's journal for November 1853 recalling his inquiries in New York about the possibility of speculating in cranberries, in addition to peddling Thoreau pencils—"Being put to it to raise the wind to pay for A Week on the Concord and Merrimack Rivers." He learned he could not sell Concord cranberries competitively, and so, he writes, "I was obliged to manufacture a thousand dollars' worth of pencils and slowly dispose of them, in order to pay an assumed debt of a hundred dollars" (JV: 512). Here indeed was the curse of trade, and the episode makes it clear how much of a burden his debt to Munroe imposed upon him. Curiously, although these unsuccessful ventures (in marketing either cranberries or pencils) involved him much more directly with the marketplace than the pastoral fantasy of trading huckleberries, they elicited no comparable outburst against the curse of trade. Whatever his resentments, Thoreau never really withdrew from either the literary or commercial marketplaces, selling both his writings and Thoreau pencils or plumbago until the end of his life.

9. See Shanley, *The Making of* Walden, 186, and Clapper, "The Development of *Walden*," 484–86, for the interpolation of this later addition. A gentler but striking-

ly similar variant of this passage would be worked into his late essay "Wild Apples" (W 5: 295–96).

10. See Clapper, "The Development of *Walden*," 857–88, on the date of this passage.

11. A copy of this contract is reproduced in Ellen Balou, *The Building of the House: Houghton Mifflin's Formative Years* (Boston: Houghton Mifflin, 1970), 150–51. See also W. S. Tryon and William Charvat, eds., *The Cost Books of Ticknor and Fields* (New York: The Bibliography Society of America, 1949), 289–90. On James T. Fields, see W[arren]. S[tetson]. Tryon, *Parnassus Corner: A Life of James T. Fields, Publisher to the Victorians* (Boston: Houghton Mifflin, 1963), and James C. Austin, *Fields of the Atlantic Monthly: Letters to an Editor, 1861–1870* (San Marino, Calif.: Huntington Library, 1953). On Ticknor & Fields, see Tebbel, *A History of Book Publishing in the United States*, 1: 394–401.

12. Tryon, *Parnassus Corner*, 170; cf. Tryon and Charvat, *Cost Books*, passim. Note the improvement in terms since their original 1849 offer for *Walden*, which proposed an edition of one thousand copies, with a 10 percent royalty (Corr 236).

13. See Corr 328; Tryon and Charvat, *Cost Books*, 289–90; Herbert Faulkner West, "Mr. Emerson Writes a Letter about Walden," *Thoreau Society Booklet* no. 9 (1954).

14. See Gary Scharnhorst, "James T. Fields and Early Notices of *Walden*," *The New England Quarterly* 55.1 (March 1982): 114–17; Joel Myerson, ed., *Critical Essays on Henry David Thoreau's* Walden (Boston: G. K. Hall, 1988); and especially Bradley P. Dean and Gary Scharnhorst, "The Contemporary Reception of *Walden*," *Studies in the American Renaissance, 1990*, ed. Joel Myerson (Boston: Twayne, 1990), 293–328.

15. All reviews and notices of *Walden* discovered to date are collected and reprinted in either Myerson, *Critical Essays on Henry David Thoreau's* Walden, or Dean and Scharnhorst, "The Contemporary Reception of *Walden*." See also Borst, *Reference Guide*.

16. Evert and George Duyckinck, eds. *Cyclopedia of American Literature* (New York: Charles Scribner, 1855), 2: 653–56.

17. George William Curtis, "Emerson," *Homes of American Authors*, 1854; rpt. in Curtis, *Literary and Social Essays* (New York: Harper & Brothers, 1894), 20–21.

18. See Hawthorne, *Letters, 1853–1856*, vol. 17 of the *Centenary Edition of the Works of Nathaniel Hawthorne*, ed. Thomas Woodson et al. (Columbus: Ohio State University Press, 1987), 261, 277–80, 471–72, 514–15.

19. Walter Harding, "The First Year's Sales of Thoreau's *Walden, Thoreau Sociey Bulletin* 117 (Fall 1971): 1–2.

20. Thomas Wentworth Higginson, "American Audiences," *Part of a Man's Life* (Boston: Houghton Mifflin, 1905), 88.

21. Bode, *The American Lyceum*, 201.

22. That day Thoreau had read his lecture "What Shall It Profit?" in Providence, Rhode Island, as part of a series of "Independent, or Reform Lectures" that also included Theodore Parker, William Lloyd Garrison, Wendell Phillips, Thomas Wentworth Higginson, and Lucy Stone, among others, so Thoreau had in fact been addressing an audience presumably more responsive to his attack on materialism than most; Thoreau was most likely invited on the basis of his "Slavery in Massachu-

setts" lecture of the previous July, which had been printed in the *Liberator*, the *Tribune*, and the *National Anti-Slavery Standard*. Nevertheless, Thoreau was probably reacting to the fact that he was now being *required* to produce a reform lecture. When invited to participate in the series he was informed that "every lecturer will choose his own Subject, but we expect *all*, whether Antislavery or what else, to be of a *reformatory Character*" (Corr 345). Not incidentally, Thoreau was promised, and presumably paid, fifteen or twenty dollars for the lecture. The other lecture of that winter which Thoreau refers to was in Philadelphia on November 21, "The Wild." William H. Furness wrote to Emerson that, from the reports he had heard, "I judge the audience was stupid & did not appreciate him." See Furness, *Records of a Life-long Friendship*, 103; also JVII: 72–76, for Thoreau's account of what seems to have been an enjoyable trip to Philadelphia and subsequently to New York.

23. See JVII: 46; IX: 245–46; and XI: 326–29, for other relevant reflections and commentary on lecturing.

24. Anna and Walter Ricketson, *Daniel Ricketson and His Friends* (Boston: Houghton Mifflin, 1902), 15.

25. See Corr 375, 379, and Harding, *Days*, 359–61.

26. See also Corr 504, 509, 514, 520. An illuminating discussion of Lowell's editorial practices, and one more sympathetic than Thoreau scholars provide, is included in Austin's *Fields of the Atlantic Monthly*, 45–50.

27. An earlier version of the following discussion was published as "The Language of Prophecy: Thoreau's 'Wild Apples,'" *New England Quarterly* 59.2 (June 1986): 212–30, and it is reprinted here with permission of the *New England Quarterly*.

28. Harding, *Days*, 436.

29. On Thoreau's use of the Genesis story of the Fall in "Wild Apples," see Kevin P. Van Anglen, "A Paradise Regained: Thoreau's *Wild Apples* and the Myth of the American Adam," *ESQ* 27 (1981): 28–37; and Robert Sattelmeyer's introduction to *Thoreau's Natural History Essays* (Salt Lake City: Peregrine Smith, 1980).

30. Bridgman, *Dark Thoreau*, 279.

31. Thoreau first read "Wild Apples" at the Concord Lyceum on February 8, 1860 (his final appearance at his home lyceum). Contemporary reports suggest it was highly successful. One auditor considered it "the best lecture of the season" and noted that "at its close there was long and continued applause." Thoreau successfully repeated the lecture the following week in Bedford (Harding, *Days*, 436).

INDEX